# SEEKING JUSTICE IN CHILD SEXUAL ABUSE

# Seeking Justice in Child Sexual Abuse

*Shifting Burdens and Sharing Responsibilities*

*edited by*

**Karen M. Staller and**
**Kathleen Coulborn Faller**

COLUMBIA UNIVERSITY PRESS  NEW YORK

Columbia University Press
Publishers Since 1893
New York   Chichester, West Sussex

Library of Congress Cataloging-in-Publication Data
Seeking justice in child sexual abuse : shifting burdens and sharing responsibilities /
edited by Karen M. Staller and Kathleen Coulborn Faller.
p. cm.
Includes bibliographical references and index.
ISBN 978-0-231-14614-2 (cloth : alk. paper) — ISBN 978-0-231-51826-0 (e-book)
1. Child sexual abuse—United States. 2. Child sexual abuse—Investigation—
United States. I. Staller, Karen M.  II. Faller, Kathleen Coulborn.
HV6570.2.S44   2009
363.25'9536—dc22                    2009024187

⊗

Columbia University Press books are printed on permanent and durable acid-free paper.
This book is printed on paper with recycled content.
Printed in the United States of America

c 10 9 8 7 6 5 4 3 2 1

References to Internet Web sites (URLs) were accurate at the time of writing. Neither the
author nor Columbia University Press is responsible for URLs that may have expired or
changed since the manuscript was prepared.

# Contents

# Note to the Reader

In keeping with the Institutional Review Board (IRB) requirements under which this research was conducted, we have assigned aliases to all locations and research subjects mentioned in this book. Nonetheless, the county, its characters, and its cases are real, and we report our findings without other modification.

# SEEKING JUSTICE IN CHILD SEXUAL ABUSE

# Child Sexual Abuse

ONE

## *Legal Burdens and Scientific Methods*

KAREN M. STALLER AND

FRANK E. VANDERVORT

Down the road, they've got a program they call,

"The Child Goes to Court" or something like that.

Wrong! I mean, if we need our kid to go to court . . .

we'll get 'em ready. . . . But it's a lot more effective

if you bore in and get a legal confession that is

presentable in court; [then] you don't have to worry

very much about preparing your kid to go to court.

—Ed Duke, Chief of Police

In his waning days as the prosecutor in St. Mary County, Mark Jameson stood one snowy morning in December 2002 before a jury and told its twelve members that in the next three days he would prove beyond a reasonable doubt that forty-eight-year old Tommy Inman had repeatedly sexually assaulted twelve-year old Takisha Johnson. Eight men and five women would hear the evidence against the defendant, much of it presented by the preteen girl, and decide Inman's fate.

Inman was charged under state law with three counts of criminal sexual conduct (CSC) in the first degree. When Jameson, in his relaxed, plainspoken manner, explained to his fellow citizens that the evidence would show that this man committed separate acts of digital and penile penetration and forcing Takisha to perform fellatio upon him, he promised one of the law's most difficult tasks: proving a criminal case of child sexual abuse (CSA) beyond a reasonable doubt.

"Beyond reasonable doubt" is a standard designed for a system that seeks to protect the innocent from being wrongly accused and convicted. If the scales must tip in favor of one side or the other, then in theory the legal system would prefer the guilty to walk free than deprive an innocent person of liberty. The power behind this presumption plays out in favor of the defendant throughout the process. The accused has the right to an attorney, the right to remain silent, the right to confront and cross-examine his accusers in a court of law, the right to a trial by a jury of his peers. Once in court, the burden rests on the prosecution to go well beyond establishing a plausible case, one supported by lower legal standards such as the preponderance of the evidence, and to convince the jury of the defendant's guilt beyond reasonable doubt.

American prosecutors possess broad discretion in determining which criminal suspects should be charged and what charges to level (*United States v. Armstrong*). When they exercise this discretion, they must take into consideration the fact that in order to get a conviction they need to meet the beyond a reasonable doubt standard of evidence. This creates a margin of error in criminal charging. Unless the prosecution is convinced of a realistic opportunity to meet the standard, it will not typically charge a defendant (Kaplan, 1965). This helps to explain why the prosecution so rarely loses a case and provides one rationale for why so many criminal cases are resolved when the defendant pleads guilty —only cases with overwhelming evidence actually result in criminal charges. There is nothing untoward about this. Indeed, the American criminal justice system is designed to achieve just this result. The margin of error seeks to ensure that innocent people are rarely charged with a crime and that individuals should not be charged unless there is substantial evidence indicating guilt.

Unique challenges presented by CSA cases are layered atop this ever-present margin of error, and over the years children have paid a price as a result. Studies suggest that vastly larger numbers of children are victimized by adults (Berliner and Elliott, 2002) than are vindicated through criminal proceedings (Jones et al., 2007; Cross et al., 2007; Walsh et al. 2007; Walsh et al. 2008; Palusci et al., 1999;

Martone, Jaudes, and Cavins, 1996; Cross, De Vos, and Whitcomb, 1994; MacMurry, 1988).

Writing in 1987, the United States Supreme Court observed, "Child abuse is one of the most difficult crimes to detect and prosecute, in large part because there often are no witnesses except the victim" (*Pennsylvania v. Ritchie*, 60). In order to prove such a case, a prosecutor must overcome a host of practical and legal problems: most cases of CSA leave no physical evidence, no injury that can be observed or detected by a medical examination (Palusci et al., 1999), and no bodily fluids that can be tested by forensic scientists.

The prosecutor must be able to convey a coherent legal narrative to the jury. Scholars have noted the significance of these legal narratives, "the resolution of any individual case in the law relies heavily on a court's adoption of a particular story, one that makes sense, is true to what the listeners know about the world, and hangs together" (Scheppele, 1989:208). The "prosecutor *must* shape his or her client's case into a coherent story" (Korobkin, 1998:10). In the case of child sexual abuse, the prosecutor must explain why children sometimes do not report their sexual victimization for months, even years; must help juries understand why, when children do report abuse, they may not tell the entire story in their initial disclosure, which can leave the uninformed juror with the impression that the child has embellished the story over time; and may need to make sense of why children sometimes recant valid disclosures of sexual abuse. They must somehow explain to average citizens what seems to be counterintuitive behavior on the part of some victims of CSA, such as why a child would run into the arms of the man who has hurt her or why a child's description of sexual victimization may contain fantastical elements.

In short, the prosecutor must construct a believable legal narrative on behalf of a child victim, however, that child may not tell the story in a way that jurors can readily understand or may not act in accordance with adult expectations about truthful storytelling, thereby casting potential doubt (Korobkin, 1998; Lempert, 1991–92).

This is only a partial listing of the difficulties that must be overcome in proving such charges beyond a reasonable doubt. Defense attorneys stand ready to use each of these difficulties to their client's benefit by sowing seeds of doubt about the child's narrative and the strength of the prosecution's case.

In the typical community response to a sexual abuse allegation, the child must make a forthright, detailed, and believable statement about the sexual abuse, which often requires the child to betray someone whom he or she loves and on whom he or she is dependent. This person may be perceived as powerful by the child, and may be able to provide a persuasive counterassertion that the child is lying, mistaken, or disturbed. Despite community intentions to minimize the number of times the child must repeat the account of sexual abuse, often children are repeatedly interviewed by a spectrum of professionals (Cross et al., 2007). This includes, when appropriate, submitting to a medical examination. If the child is convincing to professionals in the repeated interviews, and preferably if there are medical signs of sexual abuse or other evidence, the prosecutor *may* decide that there is sufficient evidence to prove the case and move forward.

Finally, the court system has its own series of burdens for the child. Usually the trial takes place after a number of procedural and other delays (Walsh et al., 2008). The child is either in a state of anticipation or prepares for the ordeal of testimony, only to have the trial postponed. Testifying involves not only direct examination, which demands yet another in-depth description of the sexual acts the child has experienced in the public or quasi-public environment of the courtroom, but also cross-examination, typically a face-to-face confrontation between the child and the defendant (*Crawford v. Washington*). A major goal of cross-examination is to discredit the child's statement, memory, or intentions. Although in recent years states have passed statutes to make courtrooms more "child friendly," often these measures are not invoked (see chapter 4). Moreover, none of these measures really do much to shift the burden of successful prosecution away from the child. Thus, the child is buffeted in a criminal-justice system designed by adults and primarily for adults. Their needs are routinely overlooked and unmet.

## CSC AND THE ALLOCATION OF LEGAL AND SOCIAL RISKS

One way to make sense of these various discussions is to consider the distribution of legal and social risks and realities that potentially exist in any case and consider their implications. In general, there are four possible outcomes. They are reflected in table 1.1.

Table 1.1  Factual/Legal Outcomes

|  |  | Factually | |
| --- | --- | --- | --- |
|  |  | *Guilty* | *Not guilty* |
| *Legally* | *Guilty plea or conviction* | Proper outcome: Found guilty | Improper outcome: False confession or wrongful conviction |
|  | *Not guilty: Not charged, dismissed, or declared not guilty after trial* | Improper outcome: Wrongful release | Proper outcome: Found not guilty |

In any given case, as a matter of fact, the suspect either committed the acts or not, which may or may not be reflected in the finding of legal guilt. Oftentimes in CSA cases, only the two parties will know the absolute truth about what happened. Our criminal-justice system attempts to sort out the innocent from the guilty throughout the legal process. In doing so, the legal system either gets it right or gets it wrong. There are two possible ways of getting it right. First, the factually guilty either confesses or is convicted of a crime actually committed. Second, the factually innocent are not charged, their cases are dismissed, or they are found not guilty. Similarly, there are also two possible wrong outcomes. The first is when an innocent person confesses to something he or she did not do (false confession), or pleads guilty or is convicted of a crime that he or she did not commit (see chapter 8). The second is when a factually guilty person is not charged or convicted of crime that was committed. The burden of proof, constitutional rights of suspects, and margin of error in charging cases all speak to the preferred status of this type of legal error. As noted, an improper outcome resulting in a wrongful finding of innocence is the preferred error in our legal system to a wrongful finding of guilt. An error in this direction, however, may carry detrimental consequences that are particularly troubling in matters of child sexual abuse from a community perspective. Since CSA is often not a single isolated act, it means that a child victim may continue to be abused. Additionally, since abusers may assault multiple victims, letting a guilty person go free may mean that other children in the community are at risk. So from a legal perspective, while we may want to minimize the risk of making this kind of error relative to the suspect to protect our individual rights, from a social perspective we may be simultaneously increasing the risk of harm to children in the community.

Errors are certainly troubling in either direction. Nonetheless, professional practitioners (such as child advocates and defense attorneys) might well line up on opposing sides when discussing which kind of error is preferable from their professional standpoint and how they would balance the relative social and legal risks. This is particularly salient when tensions arise between two different professional points of view during the handling of a single case. Obviously, *all* criminal cases are about allocating the relative risks of these mistakes and protecting, as best we can, against abuses that would lead to any kind of wrongful outcome; nonetheless, how we balance these risks on a day-to-day basis has a direct impact on the operation of justice.

## CHILD SEXUAL ABUSE: DEBATABLE PROGRESS

The St. Mary County circuit court judge who presided over the Inman trial recalled a case from his own days as the county prosecutor in the mid-1970s and used it to illustrate the difficulty in successfully prosecuting CSA cases. A ten-year-old boy spent a day with a family friend on his farm. At the end of the day, the boy's mother observed her son emerge from the farmer's truck and sensed almost immediately that something was wrong. She asked her son what was the matter. Within minutes, the boy explained that the farmer had molested him. The judge assessed the situation: "Well, I got a good case. First of all, I don't have the problem of an untimely reporting. Second, there's no problem about identification because the mother saw the man, knew the man. And third, the child's demeanor reinforced his veracity." Despite the perception of a strong case, the jury acquitted the farmer. The judge's view was that this was because until relatively recently, the public had preferred not to acknowledge that sexually motivated crimes against children happen.

Support for the judge's explanation of the jury's response to this case is provided by the academic theoretical literature on "legal storytelling." Among other things, Korobkin asserts that a critical factor linked to success at trial is the degree to which the legal narrative "reminds jurors of other stories, litigative or otherwise, that they accept as true."

Additionally, "litigative narratives—particularly the opening and closing arguments of counsel—utilize preexisting components familiar to
their constructors from stories they have read, heard, watched, or told"
(1998:13). Thus, to the extent that child sexual abuse was not characterized as a public problem in popular discourse until the late 1970s or early
1980s, the St. Mary prosecutor may have been attempting to frame his
case around a legal narrative that was not yet understood or commonly
accepted, or at least acknowledged as possible. Today, while publicly recognized, crimes of sexual violence against children are among the most
underreported and infrequently prosecuted major offenses (Berliner and
Elliott, 2002; Cross et al., 2002). Moreover, when prosecution does occur,
in a large percentage of cases defendants are allowed to plead guilty to
lesser offenses, oftentimes to charges unrelated to sex crimes (Gray, 1993).
The difficulties inherent in prosecuting CSA and the resolution of these
cases cause real problems for communities large and small.

Although some progress has been made in the prosecution of child
sexual abuse since the late 1970s this progress has not been linear. By the
early 1990s, there was grave concern in some quarters that law-enforcement
authorities and child advocates had overreacted. These defense-oriented
advocates argued that the criminal prosecution of alleged sexual victimization of children resulted in innocent persons being accused, convicted,
and sentenced to long periods of incarceration. Their arguments were
bolstered by a series of cases and appellate court decisions around the
country that called into question a number of the methods used to investigate alleged CSA. Perhaps the most prominent of these is the McMartin
preschool case from Los Angeles County, California. During the investigation, four hundred children who had attended the preschool over the
previous decade were interviewed, and investigators concluded that 369
of them had been molested. Eventually, seven defendants were charged
with 208 counts of sexual abuse upon forty-one children. A preliminary
examination was conducted over the course of eighteen months, and at
its conclusion, the seven were ordered by the court to stand trial on 135
counts. Shortly thereafter, prosecutors dropped all counts against five of
the defendants, and two stood trial. Eventually the two defendants were
either acquitted by a jury or the jury could not agree on guilt, and none of
the defendants was ever convicted of any charge (Montoya, 1993).

In *New Jersey v. Michaels* (1993), the state Supreme Court over-
turned Margaret Kelly Michaels's conviction of 115 sexual offenses that

she had been convicted of perpetrating on twenty children in the Wee Care daycare center. The court's concern about the way in which the child complainants were questioned by investigators resulted in the court's mandating pretrial "taint hearings" to ensure that the child's accounts of abuse were not contaminated by improper interviewing before they were permitted to be presented to a jury. These hearings are in practice today. As well, forensic narratives must be carefully collected in order to withstand subsequent scrutiny.

In another much debated example, the Country Walk case from Dade County, Florida, a couple was charged with molesting numerous children who attended the couple's illegal daycare center. The wife, Ileana Fuster, pled guilty to twelve criminal counts of child sexual abuse and testified against her husband, Frank Fuster. A Honduran immigrant, she was sentenced to ten years in prison, then deported from the United States upon her release. Her husband was convicted of numerous counts of sexual battery and lewd and aggravated assault on children after a jury trial and sentenced to six consecutive life terms in prison, each with a minimum sentence of twenty-five years. Although this case began in 1984 and his trial was held in 1985, litigation upholding Frank Fuster's multiple convictions and academic debate about the case continue a quarter-century later (Cheit and Mervis, 2007; *Fuster-Escalona v. Crosby*).

The tension brought about by differing views of such cases has led to a vigorous, long-standing, and multifaceted debate regarding how best to respond to alleged incidences of child sexual abuse. In the 1980s, when the intrafamilial sexual abuse of children was just emerging as a recognized public problem, prosecutors were initially reluctant to bring charges, believing that such cases were more appropriately resolved through civil child-protective proceedings in family and juvenile courts (Ginkowski, 1986). They were primarily thought to be private family affairs, and prosecutors expressed concern that intervention by the criminal courts would not be effective. Today CSA, whether within the family or not, is prosecuted more vigorously. More vigorous prosecution has, in turn, spurred a contentious debate in mental health, social services, and legal communities about various aspects of investigation, assessment, and charging decisions (Ceci and Bruck, 1995; McGough, 1995, 2002; McGough and Warren, 1994). About this debate, Jane Mildred has aptly observed that "well-known and respected scientists with impressive credentials disagree about almost every important issue related to child sexual abuse" (2003:493).

## ST. MARY COUNTY CSA INVESTIGATION PROTOCOL

When St. Mary Chief Prosecutor Mark Jameson stepped before the jury at the Inman trial in December 2002 and asserted that he would prove his case beyond a reasonable doubt, he would take on this prosecutorial risk based on the community's extraordinary commitment to prosecuting these cases. During his twenty years in the prosecutor's office, Jameson had played steward to a community-based protocol for investigating CSA cases. To some extent, the fact that Thomas Inman's case was going to trial was evidence that the protocol had failed in its primary objectives. Nonetheless, the fact that Jameson was determined to see the Inman situation to its legal conclusion was illustrative of the county's tenacious commitment to prosecuting sexual offenders.

The roots of the protocol are traceable to a handful of spontaneous experiments created in the moment to deal with some particularly vulnerable child victims. After a string of successes that surprised everyone, the protocol was reduced to formal policy, which set out the prosecutor's expectations for the community's professional practitioners who investigated CSA cases. This policy, in its totality, lifted much of the burden of persuasion from child victims and placed more demands on the community professionals—police officers, social workers, polygraph operators, and lawyers—and ultimately onto the suspected perpetrators. The protocol itself combined a series of steps, many of which are hotly debated by scholars and practitioners.

The protocol relied on six key factors (table 1.2). First was a rapid response. Child sexual abuse cases received priority and were investigated immediately. Second, law enforcement and child protective services (CPS) collaborated, with CPS doing the majority of the forensic interviewing. Third, the initial forensic interview of the child victim was captured on videotape. The county used the videotape as a permanent and authoritative account of the child's version of the facts. Other professionals who needed to hear the child's story were invited to watch the tape and were actively dissuaded from requiring the child to repeat it. This video recording preserved a single account of the child's often-emotional disclosure closer in time to the event itself and free from repeated rehearsals that can sometimes deaden the child's affect by the time a case goes to trial. Fourth, as soon as possible after a credible disclosure of sexual abuse by a child, there was an initial interview and subsequent interrogation of the suspect. At this stage, law-enforcement authorities in the community engaged in the unusual practice of showing the suspect the videotape of the child's forensic interview. The suspect was asked to confirm or deny the facts as reported by the child. This approach privileged the child's account of the events, making it more difficult for adults to simply deny the child's story outright. If the suspect claimed the child was not telling the truth, he was at pains to explain why the child would lie in such a way. In this manner the professionals pressured the suspect into co-constructing a legal narrative account of what happened that was integrated with the child's account. This is unlike the situation at trial when a child's legal narrative must stand up against an independently constructed and competing defendant's legal narrative. Furthermore, the speed with which the community reacted was designed to ensure that the suspect had not yet summoned a defense attorney. Investigators tended to get full or partial confessions. Sixth, if the suspect's explanation did not match the child's—that is, if the suspect did not confess to at least some act of child sexual abuse—he (or she) was offered an immediate polygraph. This polygraph, too, was videotaped. There is considerable additional pressure on the suspect at this point to "come clean for everybody's sake." Again, there was pressure at this stage for the suspect to co-construct a legal narrative that incorporated the child's version of the facts but in which adult professionals (and not the child) were responsible for carrying the weight of persuasion.

While the St. Mary County protocol had other formal components—medical examinations in appropriate cases, efforts to secure physical evidence such as rape kits—these six elements are the most salient. The protocol also contained informal, unwritten elements that have developed over time. These included a prohibition on plea-bargaining if the child were made to testify at a preliminary examination and a requirement that if the defendant pleaded guilty or was convicted, he would likely undergo a sex offender assessment with a local mental-health provider who specializes in these assessments. Similarly, an unwritten rule was that if the suspect/defendant passed the polygraph examination, charges were either not filed or dropped regardless of the strength of the remaining evidence.

Taken together, the aspects of this protocol—prompt response, use of videotape, interview and interrogation techniques, and polygraph—have proven an effective tool for the prosecutor's office in St. Mary County for over two decades. This county enjoyed extraordinary success in securing

## Table 1.2 St. Mary Protocol Primary Elements

1. All reports of child sexual abuse are to go initially to Child Protective Services (CPS).
2. Those that do not involve caretaker maltreatment or failure to protect are referred on to the appropriate law enforcement agency. (In most states, CPS has mandated responsibility only for child maltreatment cases, including sexual abuse, where caretakers are the abusers or caretakers fail to protect children from abusers. Cases involving non-caretaker suspects are the province of the police.)
3. As much information about the case as possible is gathered before the investigation begins. This includes determining through the Central Registry if there have been prior referrals and their disposition.
4. If the case is to be investigated by CPS, and CPS thinks the case has merit, CPS contacts the appropriate law-enforcement agency to see if it wants a joint interview with the child.
5. On cases within CPS's mandate, CPS has responsibility for interviewing the child.
6. On cases falling solely within law enforcement's jurisdiction, law enforcement may nevertheless request a CPS interviewer.
7. Whenever possible, child interviews are videotaped.
8. The child is interviewed in a place conducive to videotaping and the child's sense of safety.
9. As soon as the child's videotaped interview is complete, law enforcement conducts the initial interview with the suspect.
10. The suspect is shown the videotape of the child interview and then interrogated.
11. Even if the suspect does not confess, an attempt is made to obtain from him or her information that may corroborate facts in the child's statement.
12. If the suspect does not confess, he or she is offered a polygraph.
13. If the suspect is willing, a polygraph is offered immediately.
14. If possible, the polygraph examination is videotaped. If the suspect denies the abuse and is thought to have been deceptive, there is to be an immediate post-polygraph videotaped or audiotaped interview.
15. Law enforcement is responsible for collecting physical evidence (clothing, bed clothing, photographs and videos, sexual aids, telephone records, trace evidence, fingerprints, medical records of suspect).
16. There is a medical examination of the child, if appropriate.
17. The child is removed to a safe place if necessary.

confessions from suspects accused of sexually abusing children. Two critical consequences flowed from securing confessions early in criminal investigations. First, it resulted in high charging and conviction rates in CSA cases (compared with other jurisdictions), and second, it nearly eliminated the need for child victims to be engaged in protracted and public legal proceedings. Child-welfare advocates and scholars have long known about the trauma experienced by children who must repeatedly testify, sometimes against family members or family friends, in open court.

Yet the very efficiency and effectiveness of the response may raise some concerns (see chapter 8). While the quickness of the response and the techniques used by police interrogators and the polygraphist to secure confessions are unquestionably legal and no court would prohibit law enforcement's rapid response to a criminal act, some may be concerned when the speed with which an investigation is launched is designed for the purpose of capturing the suspect before he can consult an attorney. Similarly, while our courts have approved of police use of deceit to coax a confession from a suspect, reasonable people may feel such activity on the part of governmental actors is inappropriate. Others may believe that mere trickery is no cause for concern given the gravity of child sexual abuse. These are important and difficult normative questions about which debate will go on.

Nonetheless, compared to national norms, all three factors—high confessions, high convictions, and reducing child exposure to legal procedures—were indicators that something unusual was occurring in this community.

## QUANTITATIVE RESEARCH ON ST. MARY COUNTY

Members of our team had been studying the community from afar for some time. We had analyzed court file data from 1988 through 1998 (323 cases) to explain what factors predicted the county's success in securing confessions and convictions. These analyses had culminated in a number of published reports (Vandervort, 2006; Henry, 1997, 1999; Faller et al., 2001; Faller at al., 2006; Faller and Henry, 2000). For this book, we added additional cases (for a total of 448) and reanalyzed the data. The goal was to reflect, as best we could, the longitudinal experience of the professionals in St. Mary County from 1988 to 2000. (We could only examine a case file for research purposes and know its outcome after the case was closed. Hence, we could not include all cases from 2001 and 2002, because they were not all closed. The court-file data were not collected for research purposes. These data are merely what the prosecutor included in the case files for prosecution purposes. Like most researchers who conduct "case record reviews," we encountered some missing data; see Thoennes and Tjaden, 1990.) These analyses demonstrated the efficacy of this protocol and consistency in its efficacy over time. Some of our most significant findings:

- *Charging decisions.* Criminal charges were filed in 69 percent of all CSA cases referred to the prosecutor's office between 1992 and 1998, according to statistics kept by Mark Jameson. (His predecessor did not keep such statistics.) Of those not charged, the primary reason was that the suspect had passed a polygraph examination.
- *Videotaping.* The child's disclosure was videotaped in 71.3 percent of the cases (318 cases). When CPS was involved, 84 percent of the cases were videotaped. That dropped to 58 percent when only law enforcement was involved. The average age of children who were videotaped was 11.3 years (with those not videotaped on average 12.4 years).
- *Polygraph.* The suspect was offered a polygraph in 62.5 percent of the cases (245 cases). Of those 177 actually received a polygraph (72 percent). Of those who received a polygraph 65 percent were videotaped (115 cases). The polygraph examiner deemed 58.2 percent of the suspects who received polygraphs deceptive (105 cases). In the remaining cases, the polygraph operator found no deception in 15.3 percent (27 cases); and was unable to form an opinion in 4.5 percent (8 cases). An additional 21.5 percent of the suspects (38 cases) confessed during the polygraph itself.
- *Confessions.* Altogether, 64.4 percent of the suspects (270 cases) confessed to some act of sexual abuse during the investigation. The researchers could determine the extent to which the suspect's confession corroborated or did not corroborate the child's disclosure in 95.6 percent of the cases (256 cases). Of these, in 139 cases the child's report was fully corroborated and in another 119 cases the suspect's confession partially corroborated the child's report. In cases in which a confession was obtained, 38.9 percent (104 cases) occurred in the initial interrogation and viewing of the child's videotape.
- *Pleas and convictions.* In 72 percent of the cases (316 cases), the suspect pleaded guilty to a sexual offense. In 73.7 percent of cases (224

cases), the child's disclosure was videotaped, and there was a guilty plea. When there was no videotape, defendants pleaded guilty in 74.6 percent of the cases (75 cases).

• *Court appearances and sentencing.* Children testified thirty-three times. Of these, thirteen times were at preliminary examination, twelve times at trial; only four children testified at both. (The court file did not indicate at what hearing the child testified in three cases.) Eighteen CSA cases went to trial over thirteen years. The defendant was found guilty in seven of the sixteen cases for which there is a trial outcome. In the 342 cases where the sentence was in the court file, 124 received a prison sentence; 128 received some jail time with or without probation; and nine received only probation.

While these findings continued to confirm that the county was interesting, they told us very little about why it was so successful. It appeared that a more personal and nuanced understanding of the community and its processes was necessary to gain that kind of insight. We came to ask a different set of questions: Why was this community so successful in dealing with CSA prosecutions? What would professional practitioners in the community say about the protocol and its workings? In their view, who or what made it work so effectively? Could it be used elsewhere? What did the protocol look like in action? Was there a darker side to such a policy? What were its political or social costs?

Scholz and Tietje posit, "The more complex and contextualized the objects of research, the more valuable the case study approach is regarded to be" (2002:3–4). Our interests were certainly moving us toward seeking answers to complex and contextual questions. We decided to address these questions using a case-method ethnographic approach.

## QUALITATIVE CASE STUDY METHOD

David Thatcher noted that "case study is one of the major research strategies in contemporary social science" and has been employed by sociologists and political scientists as well as in professional fields like social work, education, and business" (2006:1,631). A number of prominent scholars have written books on this approach to inquiry, among them Yin (2003a, 2003b), Stake (1995), Scholz and Tietje (2002), and Gillham

(2000). Furthermore, a number of researchers have utilized the method with great success to study atypical events (such as Diane Vaughan's much acclaimed work on the Challenger space shuttle disaster; see Vaughan, 1996) and everyday practices (Yin, 2004; Stake, 1991) alike.

Case study is uniquely suited for answering certain kinds of questions. Scholz and Tietje note, "Most of the time, the case study approach is chosen in research fields where the biographic, authentic, and historic dynamics and perspectives of real social or natural systems are considered" (2002:4). St. Mary seemed ripe for a case study approach because we wanted to know why it had been so successful handling CSA cases over time, who or what was responsible for this success, and how the various institutional systems (including criminal justice and child protective services) worked together in a natural setting.

The benefits of case study have been identified as threefold. First, case studies are generally explanatory in nature and deal with causal relationships. They seek to answer *how and why* questions. So the focus is not on whether something works but on *how* and *why* it works the way it does. Thus, case studies attempt to unpack and answer questions about *processes*. Case studies examine human behavior in complex, real-world contexts.

Second, case studies are credited with capturing the worldview of the participants and thus provide an interpretative framework for understanding common practices and actions. Indeed, we found the interplay between individual actors and their beliefs in conjunction with policy (both formal and informal) in St. Mary County to be critical. The goal was to understand processes from the perspective of those involved. Unlike more "objectivist" forms of inquiry, case study is interested in "subjectivity" or "phenomenological meaning" (Gillham, 2000:7). This is significant not only as a matter of general interest, but also because of its practical implications. Understanding community practices requires knowing something about how individual agents make sense of their world and take action based on these belief systems.

Third, Thatcher has made a compelling argument that case studies make another, greatly underappreciated, contribution to "normative theory—theories about the ideals we should pursue and the obligations we should accept" (2006:1,631). He argues that normative case studies contribute to understanding important public values. We believe our study findings in St. Mary County and our arguments that the entire community endorsed the notion of "shifting the burden" and "sharing the responsibilities" sits squarely in this line of important research documenting how public values are enacted by and in community contexts. We believe that "normalized justice" in St. Mary County is generating entirely different rates of CSA prosecutions and convictions than in other counties in the United States.

In addition to these three major advantages of case-method design, and in light of the current evidence-based practice movements occurring in a number of areas of professional study including social work, there is a final potential benefit of this method. We are increasingly discovering how difficult it is to move effective interventions and treatments "into the field," in part because real-world phenomena require considering complicated intersections between individual actors, policy and program guidelines, and cultural and environmental settings in a given social and historical context. A case study, such as that in St. Mary, can begin to reveal some of the significant factors at play in the field that may be inhibiting the movement of "best practices" developed by academics in "laboratories" into real world practice. Thus, while the academic literature produced by legal, social-work, and other social-science scholars, may take firm positions relative to the merits or lack thereof of some procedural practices employed in the community (such as videotaping forensic interviews with children or the scientific merit of polygraph tests). If the practitioner operates from a belief system that is at odds with the scientific literature, it is highly unlikely that he or she will integrate this knowledge into daily practice. Examining how a community "enacts" justice by unpacking the specific values and practices of the community actors involved in seeking justice helps illuminate the limitations of existing empirical literature. This schism is worthy of study.

In our work, we started off by defining the empirical unit of investigation as the "protocol," that is the written policy created in the prosecutor's office for investigating CSA cases in the county. This quickly proved to be problematic, in part, because while all community professionals were very aware of how day-to-day practices played out, many were unfamiliar with the actual written protocol. (This supports our contention that features of the protocol were simply incorporated into normative practice.) So it became clear that studying the policy per se was too narrow a focus. We necessarily expanded our attention to include both the informal and formal practices for handling CSA cases in the community—both present practice and that recalled about the recent past. The net result was conceptualizing the project as an embedded case study, in which the various interdisciplinary perspectives and practices could be woven together to understand the general operation of justice (in matters of CSA) in the community as a whole.

Case-based and community-based research is sometimes criticized for lacking scientific rigor or dismissed as being "only one" example and therefore not generalizable to larger populations, or too "subjective." These critiques tend to miss the very point of case-method research. The truth is that generalizable research projects are "ill-suited to the complexity, embedded character, and specificity of real-life phenomena" which are the subject matter of case study (Gillham, 2000:6). Furthermore, the "criteria of objectivity may not be applied in holistic case studies. Holistic case studies are a highly subjective affair and include the personal value system of the case study team" (Scholz and Tietje, 2002:21). The very point is to get to these subjectivities and understand how they are linked to specific outcomes.

## ST. MARY AS A CASE FOR STUDY

We posit four reasons why St. Mary was an appropriate subject for study. First, while St. Mary is like other jurisdictions in some respects, we argue it is unique (and hence worthy of attention) because it has been unusually successful in convicting offenders in CSA cases despite the fact the community is relatively resource-poor. In our earlier quantitative studies cited above, there were indications that something set this community apart. We compared the statistical findings to other studies of the criminal prosecution process (Cross et al., 2003). There are also national data sets of crimes against persons and property, but these statistics are not reported in sufficient detail to allow direct comparisons of the success of St. Mary County to national statistics. The exception, however, is a study of all the CSA cases over approximately the same time frame as our quantitative data in Rhode Island (Cheit and Goldschmidt, 1997). Statistical comparisons using the ratio of successful criminal prosecutions for sexual abuse to the population indicate that there were 4.2 times as many successful prosecutions in St. Mary County as in Rhode Island. We contend that St. Mary's conviction rate is significantly higher than other known jurisdictions such as to justify studying how the county obtains them. Indeed, this contention is borne out by three articles published in *Child Abuse & Neglect* in 2007, which derive from a study of children's advocacy centers (Cross et al., 2007; Jones et al., 2007; Walsh et al., 2007).

Second, St. Mary's protocol flourishes in a resource-poor county. Most other programs that have received national attention have required substantial additional resources, funded either by the federal government (for example, Santa Clara County, California; Giarretto, 1980) or substantial community contributions (for example, the National Children's Advocacy Center; Carnes and LeDuc, 1998), or both. Furthermore, most nationally prominent programs are in fairly affluent communities. The fact that St. Mary has not required extraordinary financial resources makes that possibility of adaptation more likely and makes it a compelling case for investigation.

Third, to the extent that St. Mary is like many other resource-poor jurisdictions, it is important to examine its everyday practices. In many disciplines studying everyday practices has gained prominence, and social scientists have recognized that there is much to be learned from doing so. The fact that other communities may be doing variations on elements of the protocol (such as videotaping forensic interviews or conducting joint law enforcement/CPS investigations) does not negate the importance of studying the processes in detail in a single community. In fact, the findings presented should allow other jurisdictions to determine where their own community practices are similar to, and different from, those presented here.

Fourth, we contend that what is critically significant in St. Mary County is its integrated and holistic approach to CSA that cuts across professional disciplines and utilizes a variety of approaches in conjunction with each other. The protocol is more than a single innovation; it incorporates a number of practices and strategies both formal and informal. While the individual steps may not be entirely new, investigating the integrated, systematic, holistic, interdisciplinary treatment is.

St. Mary County offers one model of intervention. While we do not hold it out as an *exclusive* model for other communities to replicate in detail, we do suggest that by unpacking the values embedded in St. Mary's approach, we begin to expose the operation of justice in an applied case example. Other communities are invited to consider these values-in-action and to ask how they might inform, reorder, or conflict with the way values organize their own community practices when delivering justice. In short, this study can serve to inform other communities faced with a similar series of value-based decisions when they implement and integrate their child welfare and criminal justice systems and attempt to develop systematic models for supporting sexually abused children.

## THE RESEARCH TEAM AND DATA COLLECTION

Our trips down and back to St. Mary to watch Mark Jameson try his last case as chief prosecutor during the three-day Inman trial marked our first journey into the community for observational data. Four out of the six members of the research team attended. Of the four of us who made those pilgrimages to witness all or part of the trial, three were familiar with the community only from our previous studies of court files. For us, the community held some mystery as we ventured into it, to look around, for the first time. The fourth member, however, was serving as an expert witness at the trial for Chief Prosecutor Jameson. This pivotal player was both research team member and community member. In the parlance of qualitative research, he was an insider and our primary gatekeeper for this research; he was also actively engaged as part of our research team.

Our colleague and Jameson's expert witness was Jim Henry. Henry had first arrived in St. Mary County as a CPS worker in 1980. Henry, along with his law-enforcement buddies Ed Williams and Ed Duke and polygraph operator Rick Rivers, had been present since the earliest days of the protocol (see chapters 2 and 3). Together with the prosecutor, this group of men functioned as an interdisciplinary team. They breathed life into the protocol, but perhaps more important, the protocol took shape around their personalities, and expertise and its values were institution-alized and transmitted to others in the process. Of this core group, Rick Rivers is still there two decades later, occasionally running polygraphs on suspects for the prosecutor's office in CSA cases. Williams has since retired, but he remains an active member of the community. Duke has been promoted to chief of police. In 1990, Henry left the community in body but not in mind or spirit. He routinely returns in order to testify in criminal trials involving CSA, always as an expert witness for the pros-ecution. After leaving St. Mary County, Henry continued his career in CPS as a supervisor before returning to school to earn a doctorate in social science with a concentration in social work. It was at this point that he began to turn to St. Mary County as a site for his research. He joined the faculty at Western Michigan University in 1997.

Although Henry's roles have changed over time, his curiosity about what he experienced in St. Mary County and his desire to examine systematically what had gone on and disseminate that information to broader audiences have been unwavering. It was through him that the rest of our research team, one by one until we were six, became engaged in serious study of the county, its policies, its practices, and its people.

Henry first approached Kathleen Faller, a professor at the University of Michigan School of Social Work, in 1998 about using court-file data for study. Faller, a member of the faculty since 1977, has specialized in CSA. Around that initial nucleus grew an eclectic and energetic group: Bill Birdsall, economist, former priest, and associate professor emeritus of social work; Frank Vandervort, a clinical professor of law, practicing attorney, and child advocate; Karen Staller, an assistant professor of social work and retired attorney; and Elana Buch, a student in the University of Michigan's Joint Doctoral Program in Social Work and Anthropology.

The group that constituted the research team was interdisciplinary and diverse. We ranged in rank and experience from doctoral student to emeritus professor (and all ranks in between); our degrees number four PhDs, two JDs, a divinity degree, and three master's degrees. Our disciplines represent social work, law, economics, religion, and anthropology. Our experiences spanned forensic social work, public interest law, program evaluation, policy analysis, qualitative research, and statistical modeling. We were associated with two different universities. In short, the research team that sought to study the county has a wide range of credentials—academic, professional, and practical—as well as a variety of professional sensibilities and viewpoints. Scholz and Tietje have argued that "because problems do not usually end at disciplinary borders, case studies often require an interdisciplinary approach and teamwork" (2002:5). Our research team appeared uniquely qualified for the task.

We worked for over a year collecting empirical evidence for this study. It included observations of two trials, hearings, and other court proceedings, extensive formal interviews, videotaped recordings of both child interviews and polygraph sessions, informal "hanging out" at various local restaurants, taking photographs of the environment, collecting documents that included written protocols, annual reports, manuals, newspaper articles, trial transcripts, letters of commendation, and other community artifacts, and recording fieldnotes of each of our excursions into the community.

Our initial foray into the community did not go unnoticed. The arrival of four outsiders to watch the Inman trial was sufficiently unusual that it caught the eye of a local journalist who covered the court beat. While asking who we were, he admitted to being bored by the same old testimony by expert witness Jim Henry in the same old sexual abuse cases. He lamented the fact that there had not been a murder in the county in several years. Given his boredom and eagerness to find something new to write about, we should not have been surprised that the local newspaper carried an article entitled "Experts Keep Eye on County" on our second day in the field.

Over time our presence was less strange, at least to those with whom we became most familiar and built relationships. One measure of our growing familiarity with the research site is recorded in the evolution of notes on the "soup place," a regular lunchtime destination of a number of court personnel, including one helpful judge and his buddies. We came to know the soup, the regular crowd, including the judge, and the owner, Bill, and they came to know us. This is demonstrated in some of the field notes on our trips:

> Soup today was good. Though it's hot and muggy, the menu is still Chili and soup of the day. Today it was Italian Wedding Soup, which was delicious. Two of the Judge's lunch crowd were there; no judge though.　　　(Buch)

> We were a bit early for our interview, so we went . . . around the corner to have a cup of soup and hear the gossip. There was a "Support Bush, Support Our Troops" sign in the front yard of the shop.　　　(Buch)

> Nell and I had soup at Bill's behind the court annex. Owner's name is Bill. Hellos all round.　　　(Birdsall)

> Got to town at 11:45 in good time to have soup with the good old boys at Bill's. The two guys who are the Judge's buddies . . . greeted "The Professor" and I joined them.　　　(Birdsall)

In addition to demonstrating our growing familiarity with the community locals, these fieldnotes point to the significance of having a multidisciplinary research team, sitting in different relationships to each other and the community to collect data. They reflect the relatively different "eye" that Birdsall, an emeritus professor, and Buch, an anthropology and social work doctoral student, brought to the research project. This is critical, since the information recorded in fieldnotes became empirical evidence for our case study. Relying on one or the other alone would have decreased the richness of the overall material. Buch noted tastes, flavors, mugginess, and environmental context. Birdsall recorded his developing interpersonal relationship with the "soup place" inhabitants through his references to the "good old boys," "Bill," and "The Professor." Buch would unlikely be welcomed in the same manner as "The Professor" at the soup place, and Birdsall was unlikely to register details such as the taste of the soup in his notes. There are two important implications. The first is that there is an interactive effect between and among research team member and community players that influences the very empirical evidence from which study reports will later be constructed. Second, different kinds of recorded observations—interpersonal and environmental—made available a rich mix for reconstructing the scene and the community. While Birdsall's notes helped us consider the relationships among the various players, Buch's illuminated the context in which to situate those actors. Our sense of the scene, and interpretations about the community, would be different had the soup choices included lemongrass or miso and the sign planted in the front lawn had read "Kerry for President" or "Another Family for Peace."

In addition to observations recorded in fieldnotes, formal interviews were conducted with twenty-seven judges, prosecutors, defense attorneys, law enforcement agents (including state troopers, sheriffs, and city police officers of several ranks), CPS workers, polygraph operators, therapists, and community advocates (see table 1.3). We used Jim Henry as an insider to gain access to many of these people, but we also used a snowball sampling strategy, asking each of those we interviewed whom else we should seek out and then followed up on those suggestions. With the exception of one active defense attorney who declined our request for interviews, everyone we asked consented. We are confident that we talked to all the major players in community at least once.

Table 1.3  Key Players in St. Mary County

Prosecutors and Judges

George Richter, Prosecutor/Judge
Charles Davis, Prosecutor
Mark Jameson, Prosecutor/Judge
John Hunter, Prosecutor
Paul Fassbinder, Judge
Jane Jacobson, Prosecutor

Defense Attorneys

Richard Nowak
Sam Huff
Brian Muller

Law Enforcement Officers and Polygraphists

Ed Williams, State Police
Ed Duke, Police Chief
Shawn Duffy, Detective
James Ford, Police Officer
Jeff Penn, Detective
Rick Rivers, Polygraphist
Jason Touhy, Polygraphist

Social Workers and Victim Advocates

Jack Moor, Child Services Manager and CPS Supervisor
Carol Bragg, CPS Supervisor
Donna Wagner, CPS Supervisor
Cecilia Berg, CPS Worker
Jim Henry, CPS Worker
Cindy Carbone, CPS Worker
Laura Cook, Victim Advocate
Susan Connor, Victim Therapist
Mark Reggio, Offender Evaluator

Community Advocates

Chris Kovac, Videographer
Cindy Fassbinder, Community Educator
Mary Fitzgerald, Community Coordinator

In general, one to three members of our research team conducted each interview. Our intention was not to overwhelm the person being interviewed, but rather to bring multiple lenses to the interview observations and questioning. The interviews were semistructured, with general domains specified in advance. The participant was offered an opportunity to review the interview protocol beforehand if they choose to do so. Some of them did and others did not. We shared this interview protocol in advance because we felt that reflection on the questions would only enhance and enrich the empirical evidence we collected.

All of the interviews were tape recorded and transcribed. There were several iterations of the interview transcripts. First, a skilled transcriptionist produced a complete transcript of the audiotape. We sent these transcripts back to the interviewees and encouraged them to make any corrections or deletions to the record that they wanted. The point was to give them final say over the "evidence" from which we were to work. Remarkably, given the busy schedules of the professionals we interviewed, almost all of them read and returned the transcripts. Some made minor editorial or spelling corrections, filled in missing dates, and the like. Only one deleted a small section of sensitive information that the informant felt was best left out of our evidence pool. We honored this request, and we had made it clear to all of the people we talked to that they would have the opportunity to revisit their own words before we used them as study evidence.

## INTERPRETATIONS, FINDINGS, AND PHILOSOPHICAL DIFFERENCES

We spent the next several years analyzing the data, integrating it with our previous study findings, and writing up the entire project. We worked as a team throughout the project. We have met, once or twice a month, over these years for two hours at a time to collaborate in all stages of the project. Analysis started with debriefing after each interview and foray into the community. The team discussed and considered the implications of each of these experiences. As the interviews were conducted, transcribed, and sent to and returned from the participants, we discussed them one by one as they became available to us. This allowed us to begin to understand what each individual was saying about his or her experiences of case handling in the community. We began to piece together timelines of events and people's careers that helped provide a structure for understanding the historical context and evolution of ideas about the protocol. In addition, from these discussions began to emerge some themes about how individual community members approached their jobs, the cases, or the issue of CSA. For example, many had individual but deeply held personal philosophies on what constituted truth, justice, fairness, and other ideas that ultimately helped explain how and why they acted in their professional capacities the way they did.

After considering the individual viewpoints, we began clustering them by roles in the system; examining the prosecutors together, the defense attorneys together, the police officers together; and the like. In doing so, we started to frame an understanding of the disciplinary perspective on CSA cases in the community. Only after making sense of the individual stories and perspectives provided to us by the participants, then crafting them together as an institutional group, could we begin to synthesize the information and piece together some sort of community narrative. Metaphorically, this project is not unlike considering an orchestra in which individual musicians make up the various sections—such as the strings or woodwinds—and these sections then contribute individually and collectively to the orchestra's whole performance. The difficulty at this stage was maintaining a delicate balance when it came to using individual perspectives to understand the operation of community practices as a whole. We have tried, in the chapters that follow to balance those concerns. It was only at this final stage of synthesis that our research team began to understand the community's collective commitment to justice.

As a team we had both to honor and to guard against Jim Henry's insider status. Once employed as a caseworker in the community, he continues to serve as a consultant for the prosecutor's office after almost two decades. Henry never conducted any interviews by himself; instead, one or more other team members, who usually took the lead during the interview, accompanied him. In a few cases, most notably when talking to his fellow "sex busters," his personal relationship with the interview subject led to empirical evidence that had the flavor of reminisces among old friends, where other research team members stepped in with questions primarily to clarify ideas. Our sense is that this actually enriched the data and reflected shared understandings of a common history. We acknowledge that this team of insiders influenced our final understanding of what happened in the community, although we have tried to challenge their dominant viewpoint and amplify the voices of differing accounts.

In addition, other members of the research team formally interviewed Henry, treating him as a research subject, recording his responses and using the empirical evidence as with all other participants. Nonetheless, Henry also fully participated at the analysis and interpretive stages of this project. Certainly he has influenced the final reporting of this study; however, his interpretations did not go unchallenged in team meetings. Thus, we have used excerpts from Henry's formal interview as well as his first-person account in this book. We have tried to keep his roles as "study participant" and as "researcher" separate. Research-team members using different evidence or interpreting the evidence on hand differently often challenged Henry. Sometimes our insights surprised him; nonetheless, they have been worked into the text. These differences, like everything else in this book, were either negotiated until agreement was reached, or the disagreements are made transparent in the text. We believe that the diversity of viewpoints and the varying degrees of knowledge about the community enhanced the rigor and strengthened the findings we report.

## PHILOSOPHICAL DIFFERENCES AND THEIR SIGNIFICANCE

There were inevitable moments of tension among team members, but we believe these squabbles ultimately make the work stronger and frankly speak to larger structural issues. These differences expose important disciplinary or professional sensibilities and priorities. For example, the attorneys on the team tended to express concerns about suspects' rights, while child advocates worried primarily about child safety.

One memorable example of these differences came when attorney Frank Vandervort used the word "manipulative" to describe a polygraph operator's tactics in seeking a confession in one case. Jim Henry and Kathleen Faller, first and foremost child advocates, strenuously objected to this interpretation. They favored characterizing it as "persuasive" rather than manipulative. This is no small matter. With each word selected, we send a message to the reader about how we understand and judge what we saw. At the heart of this particular interpretive dispute are important differences in disciplinary sensibilities. Attorneys, particularly defense attorneys, and child victim advocates have different levels of sympathy for the suspect's position.

This dispute was not settled in the first instance and flared up again as we began to finalize chapters of this manuscript for publication. Evidence is drawn from a flurry of emails between team members exchanged under a subject heading reading, "My two cents on the poly chapter." It started with attorney Frank Vandervort raising two concerns about a draft of the "polygraph chapter." In it, he accused Faller of being "too easy on the polygraphists when it comes to the question of whether they use coercive techniques when questioning the subject and as evidenced in their behavior before, during, and after the polygraph." Vandervort pointed to a number of "psychologically coercive" tactics. He noted that the practices are lawful but argued that we should "grapple with the normative question—is this behavior acceptable, desirable, to be encouraged? Do the ends justify the means? Perhaps. Perhaps not." Faller responded by pointing to the evidence and argued that it was important to "watch some of the polygraphs before concluding they are more coercive than community professionals describe them," and she noted that, "those descriptions are in the chapter." Vandervort's response is worth considering both for its specific rebuttal and because it carries with it larger messages for thinking about the material in this book:

> I think we would lose credibility if we don't recognize forthrightly that the police use manipulative and psychologically coercive techniques when questioning suspects. The evidence that they do is clear—even overwhelming—both generally and in our study. . . .
>
> If a social worker used the sorts of techniques in questioning a teenaged victim of sexual abuse that the police routinely use in questioning teenage suspects, they would be tortured on the stand and the case thrown out with the suggestion that the social worker led the kid into making a false allegation. But the police not only get away with this sort of questioning, but are encouraged by the law to engage in it. I think we should be straightforward in recognizing this inconsistency.

In jest, Faller ultimately teased she was going to "ramp up the discourse" by characterizing the confrontation as one between "those on the side of the angels and those on the dark side." Henry weighed in by proposing that we include a section about our "philosophical differences on 'manipulation.'"

We do so here, and we have tried to be transparent about these differences and others throughout the text, although we admit we have primarily taken a child-friendly lens to the material. In our text, the word "manipulation" has remained, but not without comment about its contentious nature. We hope by making these disputes present in the text we bring a richer and more transparent approach to our interpretation of the material.

However, we also feel strongly that readers recognize that these philosophically based practitioner differences do not merely reflect methodological disputes to be ironed out for presenting the work in this book. These differences exist and play out in real-world contexts and practice as well. As noted by Elana Buch, in one of her emails in response to this discussion:

> Personally, I'm not sure we need to settle our philosophical differences regarding these important issues as much as we need to share them with the reader. Part of what is interesting to me is that the differences in our group are reflected in our interviews, suggesting that these issues are perhaps similarly problematic for many U.S. communities grappling with the consequences of child sexual abuse. These tensions are themselves an important finding.

This has serious implications for understanding the findings presented in this book and considering their application to other communities. These philosophical differences of opinion are deeply engrained in professional education, training, and practice. They reflect ideological positions conveyed from the earliest days of professional socialization into a discipline and are perpetuated through the institutionalization of professional practice. These philosophical differences—in whatever form they may arise—cannot be ignored if communities are interested in working toward some sort of integrated approach to justice in CSA cases. However, other communities will need to make their own decisions about how to resolve these tensions.

## WRITING UP THE STUDY

We had several false starts in writing up this study—or perhaps they are better understood as preliminary analyses that ultimately led us to this final product. We had choices to make about how to organize the material and how to report what we were finding. Like every other aspect of this project, this too was negotiated. We circulated drafts of chapters in their different forms, and everyone has influenced the final outcome of each. Authorship is assigned to the primary writers of each chapter and was agreed upon as a team; however, the influence of all team members on the final overall product should be recognized. Nonetheless, because every chapter was primarily penned by a different research team member, each retains a distinct voice that reflects the disciplinary training and professional sensibilities of its writer. For example, Faller's chapters reflect a more formal social-science format, Buch's chapter on narratives reflects her anthropology training, and Vandervort's defense chapter indicates his legal background. We have left these different voices in place, in part, as an important reminder of the interdisciplinary nature of this project that did not attempt to smooth over difference but rather paused to take note of them.

For their parts, the study participants were sent a copy of the book prospectus and annotated table of contents. They were invited to ask questions or request chapters if they so desired. In addition, Rick Rivers and Ed Williams received a copy of chapter 3 and were invited to comment.

As we analyzed the data, arguing over its organization, interpretation, and presentation, we came to realize that we had several separate but interrelated stories to tell. One was about the protocol as a written policy and as a form of professional practice. As written policy, the protocol articulated a series of innovative approaches to investigating CSA cases. However, with time the specific written policy became less significant than the values that were at its heart. These values were institutionalized through iterative, ongoing, community-based practice as professionals tackled individual cases. It is this incorporation of the policy's basic value structure, in particular its child-centered focus, which came to animate the entire operation of justice in the St. Mary community. So we discovered that as either a written policy or a professional practice, the protocol was conceived and implemented by committed individual law-enforcement officers, CPS workers, and prosecutors. This led us to a fundamental question: "Is it the people or the protocol that are making the community so successful?" This question is, of course, inextricably intertwined with another crucial question: "Could this approach to investigating and prosecuting cases of child sexual abuse be replicated in other jurisdictions?"

In the first part (chapters 2–3), we provide a profile of the extraordinarily dedicated professionals who conceived, refined, and applied the protocol. We turn to the written protocol as a policy and its implementation as a practice tool in the second part (chapters 4–9). In the third part (chapters 10–11), we examine the overall practice in St. Mary County and provide study conclusions. In addition, throughout the text we measure what we were learning in the community against what we knew from the academic and social-science literature. Scholz and Tietje once again provide some guidance: "Case study work has to be conceived of as a collective activity, both within the study team and between science and society. This promotes a kind of cooperative learning and collective rationality" (2002:24). Certainly our study was a collective activity within the study team, but in this final product we hope that it also serves as a connective link between "science" and "society."

We discovered that, unlike most jurisdictions in which the burden of proving CSA cases rests directly on child victims, St. Mary County has shifted it onto the shoulders of professional practitioners, including prosecutors, police officers, polygraph operators, CPS workers, and mental-health specialists. Once shifted, the burden is also shared among all the community professionals who act in their own professional capacity, of course, but must also act within the parameters of the community's established norms for handling cases. While other jurisdictions have sought ways to accommodate children—for example, by allowing them to testify outside the eyeshot of the defendant or by developing a forensic interview protocol (involving structured interviews designed to withstand adult scrutiny in court)—these accommodations tinker only at the margins in an otherwise unmodified legal process. St. Mary County took a more radical and comprehensive approach to the problem. The community found a way to achieve justice by renegotiating the relative power of the players within the process in ways that enhance the protection of children while protecting the defendants' constitutional rights. It does so by maximizing procedural advantages for child victims.

What St. Mary County practices have done, in essence, is to shift that margin of error in favor of the child victims of sexual predation. In this one county, children have a more level playing field in the criminal-justice system because the adults in the community have assumed responsibility and developed a system that seeks to prevent that abuse, to respond in a quick and coordinated fashion when sexual abuse is alleged, and to protect the child from further abuse and from the trauma that sometimes results when the communal systems set up to protect children actually result in harm to them. The protocol also protects the rights of the suspect, although it gives him or her no more protection than is insisted upon by the law and takes pains to ensure that innocent people are not charged or convicted. It also focuses its sentencing authority on meting out retribution in proportion to the crimes found to have occurred, as well as on providing treatment to act as a tertiary form of prevention (Faller et al., 2006).

We do not mean to give an inaccurate impression that St. Mary County is alone in its understanding of the importance of shifting the burden from children to professionals when, in fact, professionals across the country are committed to taking steps toward the goal of reducing trauma to children. However, we do believe that St. Mary County has acted dramatically on this concern and thus conceptualized a holistic approach to CSA cases that begins at initial disclosure and is consistent through final prosecution. In short, this county has moved beyond individual professionals taking steps within their disciplinary silos and has instead embraced and acted on the public value of reallocated burdens.

What follows is the story of how this one small community has responded to the needs of its sexually abused children by making these cases a priority. This is a story about a community agreeing on priorities, sticking to them, and acting on them. It is a tale about a set of particularly charismatic people who forged a policy, as well as dedicated professionals who kept it alive for decades. There are lessons here for other communities: lessons about what kind of trade-offs must be made, what kind of buy-ins must be achieved, what kind of charismatic characters are more likely to make it work, and what kind of energy is required to keep all the pieces at play in place.

Although we had started the entire project with a very basic overall research question —Why was this community so successful in its dealing with child sexual abuse?— in the years since our initial foray into the community, the interplay between questions and answers got much more complicated. We now seek to answer this question: How is power reallocated within the community of professionals in ways that enhance protection of children, secure convictions of offenders, and facilitate the treatment of both victim and offender in a timely manner? We address this question, in all its complexity, on the following pages.

This book explores our findings by closely examining the policy, practices, and players in this small and anomalous community to illuminate how it shifted much of the burden of criminal cases off the shoulders of its smallest and most vulnerable victims and shared it among adults. It also looks at some of the community's failures. In doing so, this case study raises critical issues about justice and fairness. What is just? How is justice best served? For whom? This case study should serve as a metric for other communities and for other professional practitioners in evaluating their own stance toward the questions of what is just and how their personal and professional values put that notion of justice into practice.

People, Personalities, and
Protocol Development

**PART 1**

Prosecutors and a Protocol　　TWO

*Switching Doors and Staying in Place*

KAREN M. STALLER

"So, you're cleaning out twenty years of junk,
huh?" asked one of our research team members
as he glanced around the half-packed office
of Chief Prosecutor Mark Jameson.
"Yes, well, files that I've kept around and
personal things," said Jameson. "When I took
over as chief assistant in 1982, I moved in here.
When I took over as prosecutor in 1992, I didn't
want to move all my stuff, so I had them take the
doors off the hinges and just switch the two doors.
'Cause [the other one] said prosecutor on the door."
—Mark Jameson, Chief Prosecutor

St. Mary County was originally settled by French missionaries who
made their home among the native Nottowa-Seepes Indian tribes. The
legacy of this marriage of Native American and French immigrants is
evident in the names of the small towns, rivers, and landmarks that dot
the county, which was formally organized in 1829. Two years later, in
1831, Prochainville was settled. Since its founding it has been the county

seat, and just eleven years after that, its first courthouse was erected there. To this day, its name bears the spelling of its French heritage, but the pronunciation was long ago alternated to make it more comfortable for the American tongue.

Prochainville, itself, is not much more than a seven-by-six block geographic area. You can drive from one side to the other in less than three minutes, depending on how long you paused at the stop signs that dot the main drag. Driving into town along this main street from the east, you pass the social services office on your right, then the jail and the sheriff's office in rapid succession on your left, followed by one edge of the county fairgrounds. Three blocks later, in the exact center of town, is the county courthouse, in which the county prosecutors and judges spend their working hours. The old courthouse sits back from the main street surrounded by a well-manicured lawn hosting a World War II memorial, a plaque designating the courthouse a historic landmark, and a festive little bandstand (see figure 2.1). Along with the grounds and the parking lot, this court complex takes up one entire block of this tiny little town. There is no doubt that the courthouse is both the town's central focus and its crowning jewel.

The courthouse complex really consists of two connecting buildings. The old courthouse is an elegant and newly refurbished redbrick building with a cornerstone that was set in 1899 (replacing the first courthouse, built in 1842). The clock tower, which is perched atop the building, is by far the highest point on the horizon. It is a building of timeless charm, both inside and outside. The "new" courthouse (built around 1975) is far less architecturally appealing. It is a square, squat compact building with a functional focus (see figure 2.2). It is where the working business of the court takes place on a daily basis. Its design is typical of the period, and some of the drab, well-worn furniture of the decade is still in evidence in the courtrooms.

Inside, the new courthouse is decorated with eclectic objects of readily apparent significance. There is a framed collection of police badge insignia from all the departments within the jurisdiction. Down the hall from the prosecutor's office is the "Freedom Shrine," a wall of reproductions of a diverse mix of American documents. Across the hallway is a large picture frame containing the photographs of the forty-six members of the County Bar Association. All of them are white, and only four of them are women.

Figure 2.1   St. Mary County's old courthouse.

Court officers, security guards, and the metal detector, familiar to most U.S. courthouses, are located at the juncture between the old and the new buildings. Visitors must pass through security to get to the "new" building, with its working courtrooms (family, district, and circuit) as well as to the judges' chambers and prosecutors' offices. But visitors can wander the old building freely and, if they do so, will stumble

Figure 2.2  St. Mary County's new courthouse.

upon one display after another of historic relevance, including a free-standing antique safe, a large walk-in safe, a large gilt-framed historic map of St. Mary County, and a display case with a book entitled *The History of the Courthouse*. In the old courthouse, the courtroom had recently been restored to its initial style, and the original fixtures—which had been carefully packed away and placed in storage during the dormant period—were reinstalled (see figure 2.3). Oddly out of place amid all the majesty of the inlaid polished marble floors, sweeping staircase, and rich wood paneling sits on display an old battered and stained machine, with a placard reading, "County's First Computer." Although it is hard to know if it was placed there tongue-in-cheek, continuity and a respect for history are evident at every turn.

If one were to trace imaginary concentric rings around the courthouse and into the community, the outermost ring would contain the Lutheran church, the Horseman's Association, the Lion's Club Park, and the wastewater treatment plant. Orbiting a bit closer would be the public schools with their athletic fields, a mobile-home park, the village cemetery, and the Fairview Medical Center. Closer still is a Catholic church,

Figure 2.3  St. Mary County's old courtroom.

a Methodist church, the 1867 Carriage House Coffee Shop (cheerfully painted a deep red), and a quaint residential neighborhood with an uneven appearance—some houses in disrepair, others lovely and well kept, sitting side by side. Ever-present as a distant backdrop is the old courthouse clock tower, which dominates the otherwise low, ragged skyline of Prochainville's residential neighborhoods.

Directly across the street from the courthouse is the Baptist church, as is a building containing the Land Resource Center, the Drain Commissioner, Veterans' Services, and the Department of Corrections. Along another edge of the courthouse block, and again across the street, is the only local bar (which serves a choice of Budweiser or Miller beer) and whose bartenders regularly pour drafts for an unlikely mix of court personnel—clerks, judges, prosecutors, defense attorneys, and police officers. Also on that block are the Historical Society, a hardware store, and the United Way office. Wedged in between the United Way and the hardware store is the storefront office of Brian Muller. Muller is one of the regulars in a cadre of defense attorneys who routinely make appearances in the courthouse.

Across the street from the courthouse annex is a lovely old peeling Victorian house. A stranger might pause to consider its architecture but certainly would not know, without an insider's guidance, that through its back entrance is a restaurant that survives on the daily routine of its patrons—officers of the court and locals. It draws a regular and routine lunch crowd, offering up two homemade soups a day (see chapter 1). Planted in the front yard is a "Support Bush, Support Our Troops" sign.

Perhaps the most interesting leg of the tour around the courthouse block, however, is to its west. Situated between a brightly painted free-standing wooden structure advertised as the Hair Depot and the U.S. Post Office (which flies a black and white POW/MIA flag directly under the national flag) is the town library. The building is constructed of tidy white clapboard; two neatly manicured evergreens bracket the front door, along with another American flag—the second on this side of the block—that flutters proudly when there is a breeze.

The library is a cozy, two-room affair. One contains an extensive collection of books on the history of the state dating to the 1800s, as well as a computer linked to the Internet. Before the courthouse computer system was upgraded, attorneys regularly crossed the street to the library to check their email. The second room in the library is for children: a large two-story fortlike structure named the "Quiet Cottage" with a ladder and carpeted upper tier. A sign notes, "Reserved for our young readers and their books," and a carefully hand-painted vine of ivy snakes its way decoratively around the structure. Pint-sized round tables and matching child-sized chairs are scattered around the room. A stained-glass image of a young boy stretched out on his stomach reading a book hangs in the window next to a bookshelf (which has a top shelf crowded with stuffed animals). There is a thriving, crystal-clear aquarium well stocked with goldfish and leafy green aquatic plants on a lower bookcase quietly gurgling.

In short, as is evident from even the briefest tour of the surroundings, Prochainville is a small patriotic American town that values its history, its veterans, its religion, and its youngest citizens. In particular, it is a community that tends to its children as is evident from the neatly kept little library that allocates half its space to their comfort and reading pleasure. More important for our story, however, is that just across the street in the "new" county courthouse, Chief Prosecutor Mark Jameson and his immediate predecessors have paid particular attention to the safety and protection of the county's children for over three decades.

## INTRODUCING CHIEF PROSECUTOR MARK JAMESON

It was the second week of December 2002 when three members of the research team first entered the new courthouse in search of Mark Jameson, the then-chief prosecutor of St. Mary County and a lifelong resident. Jameson was cleaning out his office of the last twenty years in anticipation of a move necessitated by his recent election as district-court judge. During his previous promotion from chief assistant prosecutor to chief prosecutor, Jameson had merely asked the courthouse maintenance crew to unhinge the office doors with their stenciled job titles and switch them rather than going to the time and trouble of actually moving. But this latest promotion required relocating to the second floor where the courtrooms and judges' chambers were situated (see figure 2.4). It was a move that was being both celebrated and mourned by the prosecutorial staff on the first floor. A large banner reading "Congratulations Judge Mark" was draped outside the office along one wall of the communal space housing the small but busy group of lawyers and staff who constituted the county's prosecutorial team. In addition to the banner, there were holiday decorations unapologetically celebrating Christmas scattered around the assorted workstations.

Jameson's office had mostly been packed up, but there were some working files and personal artifacts still around. A photograph showed Jameson, hair parted squarely in the middle, conservatively dressed in a white shirt and blue suit with a white carnation tucked into his lapel, his arm draped around an attractive young woman (soon to be his wife) wearing a shiny taffeta turquoise gown with short puffy sleeves. A second photograph showed Jameson, with his hair still parted in the middle and looking of much the same vintage, but this time surrounded by his still attractive but matured wife and a crop of three teenaged boys standing on the outer steps of what appears to be a courthouse with an American flag prominently in view in the background. Jameson's boyish good looks defy aging, making it difficult to believe that one of those sons was now attending an Ivy League college.

Figure 2.4 St. Mary County's new courtroom.

Still hanging on Jameson's wall was a framed certificate of admission to the state bar, which bore the signature of the current circuit court judge and soon-to-be colleague, George Richter, whose office was also upstairs. On Jameson's desk—set there in preparation for our arrival—were two sheets of paper. One listed the names of thirty-four people convicted of felony sex offenses in 2002. The other had the names of twelve pending cases.

At this moment of transition, Jameson had willingly, even eagerly, seized on our request to participate in this study. As he said, it was "a good time to talk about this and look back on where we've been." With its respect for history and tradition, looking back and talking about the past is something this community does by nature. It is a community of stability and continuity. Perhaps because of that, it is a community that has produced a fine crop of oral historians, willing to reflect on what they have been doing, and where they see things going. They are universally proud of what they have done.

## SWITCHING DOORS AND THE PROSECUTORIAL CAST

The prosecutor's doors may have been removed from their hinges and switched from time to time, but the stock of players has—for the most part—remained remarkably stable for decades (see table 2.1). Before serving as chief prosecutor, Jameson had been chief assistant to then-chief prosecutor Charles Davis. Another lawyer, John Hunter, joined Jameson in December 1986. When Davis left in 1991, Jameson easily slid into the chief prosecutor's position, while Hunter moved up into Jameson's vacated position. When Jameson moved into the judgeship, Hunter became chief prosecutor. Davis himself had arrived in 1977 as legal intern to the then-chief prosecutor, George Richter—the same George Richter who was now circuit court judge and had signed Jameson's state bar certificate. If all that seems confusing, its real significance may be that there had been an interlocking and stable succession and progression of players moving in orderly succession from legal intern to assistant prosecutor to chief prosecutor to judge for decades. In fact, John Hunter finished his term as chief prosecutor at the end of December 2008. As this book moved to publication, a new prosecutor took over in January 2009. This shift in leadership marked the first time in three and a half decades that the position was filled by someone who did not have a longitudinal history with the office and thus served as an appropriate closing point for this study.

When Judge Richter was still chief prosecutor, he had lived directly across the street from the courthouse. He remembered a hard-working young man named Charles Davis, who commuted fifty-three miles each way to get to his legal internship in Prochainville. "I'd get up at seven o'clock and look out the window and his car was already there. He didn't take a lunch and he worked until six o'clock at night. And he'd go drive back to Canton, cook his dinner, go to bed, and then get up early and stop at McDonalds for breakfast." Richter was so impressed with his law-student intern that he recalled, "At the end of the summer, when I went to the prosecutors' convention, I put him in charge of the office." When Davis finished his summer stint and returned to finish law school in the fall, Richter phoned him monthly in the hopes of wooing him back to St. Mary County, and, as Richter reported victoriously, "I got him." Davis returned after graduation and quickly moved up into the chief prosecutor position in 1981 when Richter was appointed circuit court judge.

Table 2.1 St. Mary County's Prosecutors, Chief Prosecutors, and Judges, 1969–Present

---

George Richter

Assistant Prosecutor, 1969–1971
Chief Prosecutor, 1971–1981
Judge, Circuit Court, 1982–

---

Charles Davis

Legal Intern, 1977–1978
Assistant Prosecutor, 1978–1981
Chief Prosecutor, 1982–1989
Left community

---

Mark Jameson

Assistant Prosecutor, 1982–1991
Chief Prosecutor, 1992–2002
Judge, District Court, 2003–

---

John Hunter

Prosecutor, 1986–1991
Assistant Prosecutor, 1992–2002
Chief Prosecutor, 2003–2008

---

Davis left the county in 1991 to become a federal prosecutor in a much larger city, but not before leaving an indelible mark on the prosecutor's office—and not before spending an influential decade as Jameson's boss and shaping him from legal intern to chief prosecutor. "He was," Judge Richter reflected on Davis, "just one of a kind."

This core foursome of men of law—Richter, Davis, Jameson, and Hunter, with their interweaving role exchanges—had managed the justice system and set its priorities in the community for the thirty-five years before our arrival. Foremost on this list of office priorities was protecting children in the community and prosecuting child sexual abuse (CSA) offenders. These concerns were ones first raised by Richter, who was frustrated by the problem but did not have a solution. Charles Davis tackled CSA with innovative and experimental techniques that were ultimately crystallized in written policy (and referred to as simply "the protocol"). Jameson diligently maintained and institutionalized this protocol, and its features lived on with Hunter. What will happen after Hunter's retirement remains to be seen.

"So the protocol that Charles made," Jameson started his account of the protocol's history on a day when our research team was there, "was geared toward getting legally admissible confessions." He handed us the "original" protocol, a seven-page, typewritten document, entitled "Child Sexual Abuse: Protocol for Investigation of Criminal Sexual Conduct (Child Victim)." The current version, which he also had handy, had been expanded dramatically to sixteen pages, with seven separated attachments. This expansion is attributable in part to the enactment of a state statute in 1998 that required counties to adopt joint investigation protocols for a variety of cases, including child sexual abuse, and in part to the simultaneous adoption of a statewide forensic interviewing protocol. Interestingly, however, St. Mary was approximately fifteen years ahead of the statewide curve in attending to these elements. Somewhere and somehow, this original policy took on a life of its own.

## THE LEGEND OF CHARLES DAVIS

Charles Davis hit the St. Mary's County prosecutor's office like a lightening bolt. Chief Prosecutor George Richter, a man with a strong belief in going after the best, had been persistent in his pleas that Davis return after graduating from law school. "One of the things that I learned early on," reported Richter, "is I want to hire the brightest people I can hire. If they're brighter than I am, so be it." Davis was extremely bright and well seasoned. No starry-eyed rookie of life, he had already served a stint in Vietnam before attending law school. As one veteran police officer said of Davis, he "was a grunt in Vietnam in the Marine Corps, and, boy, you could tell it. I mean, you can tell a Marine but you can't tell 'em very goddamned much. That's Davis." Working as much alongside as under Chief Prosecutor Richter, Davis was no pushover; later, as chief prosecutor himself, he would run the office like the Marine Corps—efficiently, effectively, and with full command of the word "leadership."

Davis's intelligence, drive, energy, and passion ignited the small office, changing its tempo and temperament. The new duo of Richter and Davis was productive. Richter remembered the dramatic increase in trials and its spillover effect on everyone around them, including a shorthand reporter named Franklin. Franklin was used to being in court about 30 percent of his time, which left him plenty of other daylight hours to transcribe hearings and trial transcripts for extra income, but Franklin complained that with the new team of Richter-Davis he was in court 90 percent of the time. Richter sympathized; poor Franklin got "two years behind in his transcripts. He didn't have time to work on them, and his requests for transcripts increased enormously. . . . I think we tried twenty-seven cases one year." In part, Richter attributed this to Davis's aggressive and inflexible negotiating strategy. "His plea-bargaining was unreasonable. He would put a cut-off date well in advance of the trail date. The defendants weren't ready yet to bite the bullet." Unlike many young prosecutors who are willing to work toward settling a case with a defense attorney right up until seconds before a scheduled trial, Davis refused that kind of flexibility. When Davis told a defendant it was time to deal, the defense team either dealt or lost the opportunity permanently. The regulars quickly learned that Davis was not kidding.

In 1981, when Richter moved into his judgeship, Davis easily took over as chief prosecutor and shaped the office in his own image. He was a man of vision and considerable energy. He believed in taking risks, trying things, and hearing people out if it would promote the public good. More than anything, he believed in breaking down institutional barriers that got in the way of promoting justice. He was not hesitant to take on the task of shifting well-engrained institutional attitudes and perspectives, even if that meant converting people one by one, until everyone understood that the community shared problems and needed to assume the burden of solving them collectively. He was both leader and dictator, expecting the constituent parts of the community to work together like well-greased machinery. He listened when he needed to, but he did not tarry with the incompetent.

Of course, all that drive did not come without a price. A portrait of respect and a bit of intimidation that he instilled emerged in a collage of voices of people who worked for him and with him, including judges, lawyers, police officers, and social workers:

- "He ran the office like a Marine Corps. He was a Marine. He just was no-nonsense." (Judge Richter)
- "Charles Davis could . . . I mean, shit, I've seen him come across the desk at [a police officer] one day. Just because he said something about the Marine Corps. Holy shit! That's just the personality he had." (Police Officer Duke)

- "He would just knock on the door and say, 'I'm here and this is how it's going to be and I don't care what you think.'" (CPS Supervisor Wagner)
- "He excelled and demanded excellence of everyone who worked for him. He was a perfectionist and he was free with criticism and he took it very emotionally any time that a jury found against his position and very emotionally any time a jury decided against any of us that tried cases for him. But he never yelled at us." (Prosecutor Hunter)

The difference between "yelling" and being "free with criticism" was a subtlety that may have been lost on some of those on the receiving end of Davis's energetic scrutiny. After all, according to one of our other informants, the prosecutor who uttered those words about being "free with criticism" had "quit twice and Charles fired him once or something like that" in the space of a matter of years. The chemistry between the two was combustible, but the resulting fallout was always short-lived.

Nonetheless, given the expectations Davis placed on others, it was inevitable that how his intensity was interpreted said something about the self-confidence level of those who came before him and where they sat relative to Davis's authoritative reach. Certainly Davis's intensity was most often attributed to his passionate commitment to excellence and his insistence that this meant that everyone perform to his demanding standards of professionalism. Jim Henry, who was a young child protective services (CPS) worker when he met Davis and clearly admires him, recalled vividly his first encounter with the prosecutor, which included some one-way yelling at the baffled beginner:

> I remember when I first met Charles. I came in and there was a termination [of parental rights] hearing and I was brand new. 1980. And I'd come into his office and I sat down and he gets up and he slams the door and he starts yelling. I hadn't even met him yet.
>
> He says, "Don't you know I keep awake at nights thinking about these cases? Where are the reports?"
>
> That was just the intensity of Charles.

Whether slamming doors or vaulting office furniture, Davis was a man who had trouble sitting still. Henry reflected on negotiating case strategies with Davis, "Charles demanded, I mean, *demanded* continually excellence from everybody and didn't mind getting in your face. I can remember many cases of us arguing back and forth. And he'd walk around the room. He has that energy. I mean, that was Charles from the get-go. 'How come you didn't do this?' or 'how come you did that?' Or whatever. It was always like that with him."

Of course, of critical significance here is the fact that Davis felt no hesitation in holding a CPS social worker from the state system to his standards. If reports from those foster-care cases were important to Davis's own business, then not only had those report better be on his desk, but their content also had better reflect impeccable work. No matter that the worker in question was hired, housed, and supervised in an entirely different institutional system and formally was not under Davis's direct supervisory reach.

In spite of the collective memories offered by a universally admiring bunch of foot soldiers, in a recent exchange between old colleagues, Charles Davis himself didn't recall any disagreements during his tenure as chief prosecutor.

> CHARLES DAVIS: I don't remember arguing about anything.
> JIM HENRY: Oh, yeah! Right, yeah! I can remember you screaming at me.
> CHARLES DAVIS: I can't remember that.
> JIM HENRY: Yeah, you can't remember that, eh? Man, I remember it well. And it wasn't good.

"Perhaps," suggested Henry later, "he has mellowed over time." Alternatively, perhaps Davis's memory tarnished at a different rate from those on the receiving end of his case-handling advice. Or perhaps Charles Davis did not come out on the losing side of disagreements often enough to bother remembering them. Whatever the case, the collective memory of those around Davis overwhelmingly supports the conclusion that he was a force to be reckoned with, and a fiery figure at that.

At least this is true of the collective memory of the men. Women, on the other hand, do not report any of this tension. Mostly they remember his intelligence and determination. One recalls, "Davis was a truly 'left-brain' guy whose cognitive processing resembled a well-programmed computer—amazing!" Henry's supervisor Donna Wagner, a woman with considerable experience in the field, reported, "I thought he was cute . . . his intelligence and his energy were—whoa! That just blew me away." She continued, "I respected him," but acknowledged, "I suppose there are other sides to these kinds of personalities that make things happen, maybe you don't want to live with day after day. I don't know, but I thought about it many times, 'What happened there in St. Mary County that things worked like they did?'" There is no disputing that Charles Davis was at least part of the answer to that question.

In spite of all the frenzied fury, Davis exhibited an extraordinary commitment to galvanizing the community and breaking down institutional boundaries that got in the way of serving justice or promoting community well-being. This included, but was not limited to, addressing the existing squabbling among law-enforcement agencies that were supposed to be functioning collectively under his leadership. Richter recalled his own days as prosecutor: "There was a lot of rivalry and jealousy and bitterness on the part of these police departments toward each other. It was a real problem. I guess my perception was that it was outside of my control and there wasn't very much that I could do about it." In those days, if a defendant moved from one jurisdiction to the next, cases were simply closed. "You know," reflected Judge Richter, "we were just trading criminals." But Davis changed all that. "[Now] law enforcement looks at it if there's a problem in [one community]; [the next community over] has a problem."

The effort was consistent with Davis's vision of shared community well-being and responsibility. It was also reflective of his persistence in building relationships and breaking down barriers. "When Charles Davis became prosecutor," continued Richter, "he went after them and he would hold meetings and training seminars and gradually that sense of rivalry left." Like the framed collection of police department insignia that hung outside the prosecutor's office door, the message was one about importance of unity in pursuing justice.

Davis also learned a thing or two from his former boss, George Richter. One of the lessons was about the importance of cases involving children. Said Davis of his mentor, "From very early on, George Richter impressed this on me . . . and I came to realize it, you know, the abuse and neglect cases are probably one of the most important cases in the office. More important a lot of times than the criminal cases. So we see both sides. And so we recognize the importance of not only getting a criminal prosecution but making sure the child is protected." Davis understood that he had a special responsibility to children. He saw his

PEOPLE, PERSONALITIES, AND PROTOCOL DEVELOPMENT | 50

duty as both protector and prosecutor thereby spanning the missions of CPS and criminal justice. CPS supervisor Donna Wagner remembered of Davis, "He would ride his bike out to a kid just to show him that I'm plain old Joe. He would go to the foster home to see the child. He would meet the child in a park instead of his office. You know, those things matter to kids." This blended mission—protecting children and prosecuting offenders—began to take hold, and it shaped Davis's view of his personal and professional responsibilities. It was a view that he imparted to others.

Judge Richter acknowledged that during his tenure in the prosecutor's office, he had "a very difficult time getting convictions in criminal sexual conduct cases." So while abused and neglected kids were protected in probate court, the prosecutor's office had little success in securing criminal convictions. Richter bitterly remembered losing a criminal trial, which he thought would be a slam-dunk, involving the sexual abuse of a little boy by a neighbor (see chapter 1). Later, when Richter spotted the foreman of the jury of the case on the golf course, he cornered him and asked what had happened. The answer appalled Richter. It amounted to "the ostrich syndrome in operation. If we stick our head in the hole in the ground, we can deny that this stuff happens." This tendency to denial infuriated Richter. It meant that offenders got away with molesting children without penalty. Richter passed on his sense that this was intolerable and unjust to his protégé Charles Davis. It was a problem that needed to be addressed, and Davis knew that it would take the whole community to do it.

## CHRIS KOVAC: BARBER AND VIDEOGRAPHER

There is some confusion over the source of the original idea for videotaping victims, which—in Charles Davis's hands—would become one of the cornerstone elements of the protocol. "I think he watched a show on television about confessions in California and said 'let's try that,'" reported Mark Jameson. Davis vehemently denied that scenario. "I can't remember the source. And I'm positive it wasn't TV. It was either something I read or something I heard at one of our prosecutor's conferences. One thing I'm clear. I didn't hear it on TV. It came from a *credible* source."

It seems unlikely the idea would originate with a local barber, although it is a local barber who is given much credit for getting the ball rolling initially. This barber did own a piece of video equipment in the earliest and bulkiest days of the technology's development, and in 1982 the prosecutor's office did not. Reported Mark Jameson matter-of-factly, "He helped start this; his name is Chris Kovac and he is a barber by profession. But he was a videographer and he bought a bunch of video equipment in the early '80s."

Chris Kovac, a U.S. Army veteran who had attended barber school in Detroit, married and settled in a place called Victory Falls, only to discover that the prime suspect in an ugly murder—which had left a young child wandering around in a pool of her mother's blood in a public parking lot—lived two doors down the street from him. It was too close for comfort for the soon-to-be-father, so in search of a "kinder and gentler" area of the country to raise a child, Kovac moved his pregnant wife into an apartment building owned by his grandfather in St. Mary County. It seemed just the kind of place to bring up children safely. It was also a fine spot to set up a barbershop, which he proceeded to do. He quickly built a regular clientele that included local law-enforcement officers, lawyers, and judges.

Long before video cameras were commonplace, Kovac purchased one of the earliest models and enjoyed his newfound hobby of videography. In the early 1980s, he decided to try to apply his talents to practical projects and began recording for the "civil service side of the law." This included the depositions of doctors or other expensive experts in personal injury lawsuits. Ultimately, his big break as an applied videographer came, as fate would have it, when the body of "a gal who had been missing" was discovered just off a highway leading into St. Mary County. Kovac immediately saw the advantage of taking his technology out of the office and on the road. He contacted his police-officer friends and "asked them if the prosecutor would mind [me] videotaping the scene." It was, in Kovac's mind, "an excellent way of bringing the scene to the jury" as opposed to "bringing the jury out to the scene" in the case of an eventual trial.

Chief Prosecutor Charles Davis permitted the videotaping after the crime lab had been through the area. Kovac set to work with all the intensity of a Hollywood movie director. "It was my suggestion that we have a police detective walk away from the camera so that the jury could actually see the distance from the road that the body was found." So Kovac "had the detective walk out to the location, turn around, and then come back." The barber-director reflected, "It gave perspective to that scene." The crime scene video—in addition to another one Kovac had recorded for the prosecutor's office, capturing the testimony of an expensive Chicago-based expert witness—were both shown at the murder trial. "The end result," he happily concluded, "was a conviction."

In hindsight, what seems significant about this piece of crime scene footage is that Kovac intuitively recognized and began demonstrating to the prosecutor's office that the video camera was not just some fancy, enhanced audio-recording machine. Furthermore, the newly emerging technology was more tool than toy. It added an entirely new dimension to making records and capturing information. For one thing, it breathed life into the narration. You could see and hear who was speaking. Second, it froze a moment in time and captured its feel, its tone, and its tenor. After all, you could tell jury members that a body was found sixteen feet from the road, or you could visually take them in tow and walk them along the isolated path with the camera running in real time, underbrush crunching underfoot. Third, videos could add an emotional element to the scene. Videos enhanced the drama in prosecutorial storytelling. Fourth, a videotape was perpetually replayable, so that a captured moment could be aired to any number of audiences months or even years later, in any setting, and would summon up the look and feel of the moment it was recorded, undiminished by the passage of time. In short, you could transport others back to another point in time and space without just describing it to them. Finally, videos could be shown to multiple audiences in order to create a shared experience that would otherwise have to be replicated in a way that distorted or diminished the essence of the experience. Videotaping, according to Kovac, is a good way of "capturing a true moment in time."

It was sometime after the crime-scene trial, Kovac says, that he suggested to Charles Davis that they videotape child victims in criminal sexual conduct (CSC) cases. Which way the ideas flowed—from Davis to Kovac or vice versa—is mostly irrelevant; what is relevant is that the prosecutor's office began contracting with Kovac to be "on standby" and to do all official videotaping for the prosecutor's office. It is truly remarkable but also characteristic that this particular prosecutor was willing to capitalize on any resource that presented itself—including the unlikely services of a local barber with a passion for experimenting with the latest video technology—if it could help him win cases. Seeking justice was a joint community venture, and in this resource-poor community, Davis was not about to squander any assets at his disposal. If a local barber could be useful in prosecuting cases, a local barber was welcomed to the team.

## CINDY CARBONE'S PIVOTAL INTERVIEW

There are some minor controversies over the source of the idea to video-tape a CSC case, but one thing is universally agreed upon—the first CSC interview captured on videotape in St. Mary County was a heartbreaker. Cindy Carbone, an experienced CPS worker in the community at the time, conducted the interview. Carbone's death makes it impossible for us to ask her to help resolve the historical debate over whose idea it was to lug that clunky video equipment over to the local Intermediate School District building and capture the interview on tape. However, everyone associated with the case remembers it. It was unforgettable.

In particular, Carbone's younger colleague—the long-haired, self-identified hippie, Jim Henry—remembered "seeing that video. The girl was extremely limited." The girl was not a child by any chronological measure of age; in fact, she was in her early twenties. However, Rick Rivers, a polygraph operator who was also called in to work on the case, described the young woman as "probably age-wise maybe [like] a five-year-old." Everyone associated with the case knew that this limitation in her mental capacity was a fatal impediment to successful criminal prosecution of the offender. Rivers and Henry remembered the significance of this limitation decades later. She was, they agreed, "no witness." In short, it was clear to all the professionals involved that this young woman could not possibly successfully carry the weight of the case in a criminal prosecution if her testimony was required in court. Nonetheless, it was impossible not to be emotionally moved by the videotape. The young woman had been shown drawings of anatomically correct adults and children (Groth and Stevenson, 1990). Rivers recalled, "When she went through the interview process, she was showed drawings. And she would take a pin—and she got very emotional—and started poking on the part of the body. And it showed on videotape what he had done."

It was the combination of the emotional intensity, the graphic detail, and the undeniable information being conveyed by this extremely vulnerable young woman that that made the video so painful and so persuasive, that it startled even seasoned professionals. "It was because the girl was so limited, the tape was so convincing," insisted Henry.

The videotape also galvanized the prosecutorial team into action. Just removing this child from her home was not enough. Besides, the prosecutor's office had already been confronted the defendant once before. The girl's father, the alleged offender, had abused one of his other daughters previously. He had just finished serving time for it. In the first case, the child recanted her story. "Her father took a plea of nine months. I was just infuriated," steamed Rivers. "This guy got nine months for what he did to his daughter. So he gets out and then he abuses his retarded daughter."

Because "this girl could never be a witness," Chief Prosecutor Charles Davis had summoned Rick Rivers to aid the police officers in the case. Unless Davis's team could elicit, between police interrogation by a seasoned officer and a polygraph test administered by Rivers, some sort of confession or admission from the father, there would be no criminal case. In the view of the professionals, there would be no justice. The father would get away with what he had done with impunity. Worst of all, they all knew, he would just keep on doing it to this young woman or to others.

Rick Rivers recalled the events of the day. Immediately after Carbone's interview, everyone saw the tape, and the police set out to find the suspect. They found him and invited him back to the prosecutor's office. Rivers was waiting to talk to him for a second time about sexually abusing yet another of his daughters. Rivers reported the suspect walked in and greeted him like an old friend. His self-confidence and arrogance infuriated Rivers.

Rivers set to work, using both his anger and his dogged determination to get the father to accept responsibility for his behavior, "I just had so much distain for the guy; I didn't like him. . . . He would roll in his religious issues about how honest he was and how he believed in God. I was just incensed with him because he was such a liar" (see chapter 6). Rivers was patient. He sat and listened. He continued to listen respectfully as the man "quoted scripture and the law." Finally Rivers felt he had established a "fairly good rapport" with the man. "I knew there was an emotional investment in this." It was at that juncture that he showed the father the videotape of his mentally retarded daughter angrily jabbing pins into the body of an anatomically correct drawing of a naked woman. Rivers appealed to the suspect's religious side. "He lost it and confessed," reported Rivers triumphantly.

## HITTING THE JACKPOT

Recalled social worker Jim Henry, Carbone "had done the first video-taped interview, and Davis liked it so much. Davis was very excited about doing some more." Davis gambled again, and he discovered that the pay-off was enormous.

*Bing, bing.* Another CPS worker, Kate Edison, did the second video recording. It was a particularly repulsive case. It, too, involved a suspect who had been in prison before. He came back to the community and started abusing young boys. According to Jameson, his acts involved a dog and "real strange stuff." Henry agreed: "The boys told a horrific tale of this guy doing innumerable sexual things to them." The videotaped narrative captured the boys telling everything, "the dog, the implements" and everything that the boys had alleged. The subsequent sequence of events mirrored those that had occurred in Carbone's case. "Again [the police] brought the guy in," said Henry. "Didn't think the guy would con-fess, showed him the videotape, they went to work and he confessed." Those were the first two CSC videos, and both experiments had led to unexpected confessions.

*Bing, bing, bing.* Since the prosecutor's office was now two for two in CSC case confessions when videotaped interviews of the child were shown to the suspect, Davis decided more deliberately, "Let's try it again. So a call came in on a CSC case—a little girl." Recalled Henry, "She was about seven years old. Mom's boyfriend had penetrated her digitally and there was some oral sex involved." In this small community, where pretty much everyone knows everyone else, Mom's boyfriend turned out to be an old grade-school classmate of Jameson's. "I had gone to elementary school with. He was a strange kid and he came from a poor family, and he moved away. I hadn't seen him since third grade."

The prosecutor's office didn't own its own mobile video camera. Davis reasoned that there was no point in spending limited resources on equip-ment that Kovac already had. So Henry remembered going out into the field. "I went out and did an audiotape interview of the child. Very brief. Enough to get a statement that this guy did some things and we brought the child in that same afternoon." Chris Kovac was called in. He set up his video camera in the prosecutor's library area back at the courthouse, and by 2:00 in the afternoon, Henry was interviewing the girl again.

It was déjà vu all over again. Jameson reports what was quickly becoming a standard sequence of events: "Same thing, we bring Chris Kovac over, we call him up on notice, we get the guy, and we video the kids, show him the tape, he confesses." So concludes Henry, "*Bing, bing, bing* . . . we had three confessions back to back. That really solidified

Charles's position that we gotta do this." The videotaped interview of a child victim and immediately confronting the suspect with the videotape was earning its way into a permanent place in community practice.

The confessions impressed Davis. But more, all the professionals working on these cases were coming to realize what Kovac had intuitively understood—that there was something powerful about these videotapes that had far greater impact than an audiotape or written statement. Says Henry, "I think they weren't pieces of paper, but they were a real story. You know when Cindy [Carbone] did that very first one and you see this kid who can hardly talk. And then you see Kate [Edison] and you know these two boys who were very poor and disheveled talking about what they did with this guy and the dog. And this little seven-year-old girl who's a cutie. That just reinforced, 'Hey, what could be more important than this?'"

These videos apparently packed an emotional punch that was hard for any audience—including the suspect—to resist. So a practical sequence of events that included videotaping children, showing the videotapes to the suspects, and offering the suspects immediate polygraphs, resulted in CSC cases beginning to take on a rhythm that was working for the prosecutors, the police officers, the polygraph operator, and the CPS workers. In addition, the speed with which the process was executed was critical to its success. The interviews with suspects occurred, more often than not, on the same day as the child's disclosure. In addition, although the suspect was often not officially in legal custody at the time of questioning, the practice was to offer him his Miranda warning at the outset, providing warning to the suspect that went beyond what was constitutionally required.

Kovac remained under contract and on call for about two and a half years until he "kind of developed burnout. And on the last instance of running the camera and watching this interview, it bothered me so much that I just said to Charles Davis, 'I can't do this anymore. This is emotionally affecting me. . . . So what I'd like to do is leave this equipment with you.'" By that time, the practice of using the video recorder was firmly in place, even if a formal protocol was yet to be written down. While Kovac bowed out of his role in the process, he did so only after convincing a small group of community professionals of the value and power of videography in capturing children's emotional disclosures and its effectiveness in shifting some of the relative burdens in sexual abuse cases from children to adults.

While the community's trial-and-error and experimental approach of discovering the power of the video recording was an unmitigated success, there were also experiments that did not go as well and were discarded along the way. The most notorious of these involved three or four early experiments with planting a concealed microphone on either a child or parent and attempting to get evidence directly from the suspect on audiotape. While children were carefully selected for this experiment and suspects thoughtfully targeted, this method required that the prosecutor's office secure a search warrant. Although the prosecutor won a conviction in the first of these cases, the practice was quickly abandoned. It was, according to Henry, "a bureaucratic nightmare" to obtain the search warrant. Second, and more important in Henry's view, this particular technique "wasn't good for kids." So in the end, the practice was abandoned because, "it was just too much for the kids."

## THE BIGGER PICTURE AND COMMUNITY INVOLVEMENT

It is little wonder the local barber had reached a saturation point of hearing the troubling tales of children in his community. More and more cases were coming into the prosecutor's office. "This came on just like a tsunami," says Davis, "All of a sudden, bang. I thought it was going to go away. You know that this was an aberration." In fact, child sexual abuse did not come from nowhere, nor was it an aberration. As Judge Richter noted, it had "been going on for millions of years," or, as a veteran police officer noted, "We know that CSC had been going on for hundreds of years. Okay? This is nothing new." But, he continued, "all of a sudden [it] became like the top of everybody's interest." Indeed, Davis acknowledged, "The real explosion in child sexual abuse in St. Mary County was sort of contemporaneous throughout the country sometime in the early '80s, I believe." Child sexual abuse, as social problem, had emerged on the national, state, and local policy agendas. In 1974, the Congress enacted federal legislation known as the Child Abuse Prevention and Treatment Act (CAPTA), which President Richard Nixon signed into law on January 31, 1974. This legislation provided federal funding to support state efforts in the prevention, assessment, investigation, and treatment of child abuse. Among other things, it required that states have in place mandated reporting systems for cases of suspected child abuse and neglect. As states struggled to comply, the impact of these efforts began to be fully felt by the early 1980s. Even more significantly, the act was amended in 1981 to include, for the first time, sexual abuse on the list of forms of maltreatment necessitating reporting. The "explosion" in sexual abuse cases that Charles Davis described thus corresponded with the shifting federal requirements. States were confronted with dramatically increasing numbers of reported sexual abuse cases with few procedures or guidelines in place for dealing with them.

In St. Mary County, the issue was being attacked head-on while the state continued to flounder. At the local community level, social worker Donna Wagner reported, "We had two initiatives. One was an educational piece. The other was trying to successfully prosecute without chewing up kids in the meantime. And that was going to be tough. The educational piece really went out first." So the community began to focus on a two-pronged strategy.

While the men of law enforcement were out rounding up suspects and getting them to confess, a group of women, for the most part, were taking on the roles of organizing and educating the community. In fact, one busy up-and-coming lawyer declined an offer to get involved with community efforts but recommended his wife, Cindy Fassbinder, for the job. Fassbinder readily took on the task, and, together with Donna Wagner and a handful of others, organized a group in the early 1980s called the Child Abuse and Neglect Counsel, better known as CAN Counsel. Both women agree that a dedicated core group worked hard to make things happen in those early days. It was "a unique time when there were some very energetic individuals," said Wagner. One reflected, "That core group of people who started the CAN Counsel saw a need and were really compelled to do something about child sexual abuse. I think they were just exceptionally committed people."

The group decided to tackle the issue of child sexual abuse as its first major project and was quickly confronted by its own ignorance about the topic. According to Wagner, "None of us really knew a lot about it. But we knew we wanted to do something about it. We thought, 'Well, we have the intelligence, we've got the energy and we had the relationships' that we felt we could really do something. We really believed we could make a difference. One of the first things we started [with] was, 'Well, how big of a problem is it in St. Mary County?'"

It turned out the answer to that question both astonished and horrified the group. After doing some preliminary investigating and comparing county statistics with those of the state, said Wagner, "we were shocked to see that we had so many incidents of sexual abuse. I said, 'Holy cow, if the community knew this, the community would want to do something about it; and it's important to be doing something about it.'" The group made sure the information was published in the local newspapers as part of its efforts at informing and educating the public.

The response was predictable. According to Wagner, people started to ask, "So what are you going to do about it?" The CAN Counsel went back to work designing an experimental prevention program. It explored how other communities were handling prevention education in the school system and found a program it liked across the state called Speak Up and Say No. CAN Counsel started to design a similar program for children in the St. Mary community. The original design targeted kindergarteners and third-graders. One social worker, Susan Connor, who was among the earliest organizers, remembered receiving "nasty phone calls from so-called religious conservatives who didn't want their children subjected to such sexually suggestive materials." In spite of some resistance, a Catholic school in the area was first to sign up for the experimental program, while public school acceptance lagged behind. So the group went where it was welcomed, starting with the Catholic schools in the area. In the mid-1980s, the first presenter, Susan Connor, entered a handful of classrooms to talk to children about "good touches" and "bad touches." The program continued to grow over the next two or three years until virtually all the community schools, public and private, participated.

The consequence of offering these educational programs was predictable. It created new awareness and, with it, new business for everyone involved in any aspect of CSA cases. According to Wagner, "So while the kids were being educated, they started to talk. We found that there were even more problems in the community than those statistics led us to believe. Now we were really excited that we had found something that really needed our attention." Furthermore, it was not just the children who were being educated, but teachers "recognized children's comments in years to come that caused them to make referrals. So it was sort of like a little breeding ground for referrals. I said, 'Yikes!' Now you're going to reap the rewards of all these educational presentations. That's the result of educating the public." It all started with "getting the community excited about the fact that you've got a problem and that little education program," Wagner noted, "was just spinning us along."

Susan Connor remembered, "Our local agencies were truly overwhelmed in the mid-1980s with abuse reporting and allegations, and many of the men (they were all men in those years) struggled to comprehend both the reality and the emotional trauma of sexual abuse. Very little specialized training was available for law enforcement people at that time." Donna Wagner agreed that the next step was training, "We got more referrals. While the CAN Council was making cross-agency relationships that had to happen in order for successful prosecutions to happen, they were also recognizing the need for all of us to be better trained about how to interview children. That was going to be the toughest part, because that's where it all starts" (see chapter 4).

While the CAN Counsel was busy educating children about safety, an intersecting group of professionals, organized by Chief Prosecutor Charles Davis, had put together a panel of speakers who traveled around the school district to speak with "staffs of each school district about sexual abuse reporting, court procedures, etc. Everything you ever wanted to know about child sexual abuse and didn't know to ask." It was as important to convey the message that reporting child sexual abuse was not just a serious matter; it was also a legal requirement. State law mandated reporting for professionals such as teachers, social workers, doctors, and nurses who came into contact with children.

Once again, the prosecutor's office, with Chief Prosecutor Charles Davis at the helm, was willing to put some bite into the educational process where necessary. It was a crime for mandated reporters to fail to report suspected child abuse or neglect. Jameson recalled that early on, after a counselor failed to report, "he got charged with a crime. It's a misdemeanor to fail to report under the child protection law. So we charged him. We got everybody's attention and the resolution of that was, we did a training [in the local community] on the Child Protection Law (CPL) and then we dismissed the charges." So the point was not punishment; it was about getting the community properly educated and complying with the state mandate.

In short, the first of the two community initiatives—education—was being delivered on several fronts. Children, teachers, parents, school administrators, all members of the community were hearing the messages about child sexual abuse in an educational blitz that included the participation of community members, prosecutors, and CPS workers. That left the second part of the two-prong initiative left to deal with, "prosecuting without chewing kids up," as Donna Wagner characterized it.

## "PROSECUTING WITHOUT CHEWING KIDS UP": FROM PRACTICE TO WRITTEN PROTOCOL

Susan Connor remembered Chief Prosecutor Charles Davis bringing a group together in his conference room around 1984 "to make suggestions/decisions involving court protocol [and] establishing a uniform videotaping procedure for the children." It was a multidisciplinary group that included the Department of Social Services staff, community leaders, police officers, a state trooper, court officials, and attorneys. Judge Richter understood the advantages of this community coordination. "I think people see the advantages of cooperation and of working together . . . it makes the whole system better when everybody has a stake in it." Chief Prosecutor Davis remembered being part of a process that necessarily included all the community stakeholders, "We developed a protocol, and one of the things that we did with this protocol was to get the input of every person, all these multiple disciplines, because they all had something to contribute. And if the end result is the truth, which is what I always felt that our justice system should be seeking, [we] needed to refine this to make it a way of seeking the truth." The prosecutor's office had already experienced the "*bing, bing, bing*" effect in its success with videotaping kids and getting confessions. It was just a matter of formalizing the informal networks, getting everyone to buy in to the procedure, and writing down the rules.

For Davis, the process was one of crafting together from multiple sources. "You pick up on somebody's ideas, you steal from other people what works, you write them down and then you change it." Although Davis did not remember with certainty whether his original motivation for the protocol was avoiding multiple child interviews or inducing confessions, he does remember capitalizing on a process that was already partially in place, "Hey, this is working. Let's do it all the time. Let's have a protocol." Not surprisingly, it is Charles Davis who most eloquently summarized the real genius and beauty of the protocol:

In a lot of jurisdictions, there are institutional clashes. You know, cops don't like prosecutors. Prosecutors don't like cops. And you add Protective Services. So you've got three institutions that don't necessarily like each other. [The goal is] getting all three proponents to work together and understand that they have the same mission. First you're going to get success from the cops, who say, "We've got confessions." There's nothing that they like better than confessions. And second, Protective Services, you've got to get the kid protected and out of the home. And the prosecutors, "Hey, listen. We got a plea out of this case." So once they see it works and it's going to make their job easier and they're going to achieve their goal.

In its essence, the protocol seemed practically and conceptually perfect: Cops got *confessions*, CPS workers got *safe children*, and prosecutors got *pleas and convictions*. The protocol elegantly wove together the primary concerns of three major constituencies so that everyone who played by the rules came out a winner. One agency or institution need not compromise its primary goal in the service of another. It was a harmonious solution to the complicated problem.

Perhaps one of the most remarkable things about this story is how Davis was willing to capitalize on whatever resources were available to him without worrying about turf wars or egos. Ideas and innovations could come from a barber, a hippie social worker, concerned teachers, former marines, whoever might offer some insights and contribute to solutions. Equipment such as Kovac's video camera could be borrowed even if the prosecutor's office did not have the resources to make its own purchases. The services of polygraph operators or videographers could be contracted on an as-needed basis. In a world where lack of resources is often offered as an excuse, Davis simply used everything available to him and made it work with what he had.

According to Davis, a protocol is just about "writing down what you do." Ultimately, that is what the prosecutor's office did under Davis's guidance, and it has continued to amend that written policy ever since. The original protocol that Davis wrote was a short seven-page affair, but it contained the core concepts that had emerged from early successful practical experiments with CSA cases. The protocol started with a statement about the mutual responsibility of law-enforcement agencies and CPS in notifying one another in cases of suspected child abuse and neglect, including sexual abuse. While the protocol instructed police

officers on the importance of obtaining information beforehand, it recommended that CPS workers conduct interviews with children. Furthermore, the protocol captured Davis's willingness to defer to and trust CPS
expertise in interviewing children even if the case was not one in which
it had any jurisdiction. For example, if the suspect were not one of the
child's caretakers, the case would not find its way onto the CPS caseload.
Nonetheless, in such situations, the protocol noted that "a CPS worker
might be willing to offer assistance and conduct an interview." Although
the protocol acknowledged the probability that some of these interviews
would be conducted by police officers, this apparent willingness to invite
experts from another system as an integral part of the police investigation is indicative of the county's early understanding of the significance
of professional cooperation and boundary crossing in order to successfully prosecute CSC cases. Resources, including professional expertise,
were shared across usually jealously protected disciplinary boundaries.
This vision, seeing resources as part of a community whole rather than
within a disciplinary or institutional silo, permitted otherwise limited
community assets to be leveraged.

Probably because the video technology was so new at the time,
when the first protocol was committed to paper, extensive passages were
devoted to the "equipment" including what to use, how it should be used,
what should be captured in the camera's frame, as well as warnings about
protecting the audio track of the video recording by attending to the relative volume of children's voices versus those of adults and taking care to
avoid the unwelcome intrusion of competing noise from buzzing fluores-
cent lights. Some of these aspects are now covered in statutory provisions
on videotaping.

Interestingly, original protocol users were warned, "in no circumstances, should a message be conveyed, either explicitly or implicitly, that
the child will not have to repeat the story" during preliminary explanations of the procedure to children and their parents. Nonetheless, in
practice the goal of sparing children the burden of repeating the story to
multiple audiences would become one of the driving forces behind the
prosecutor office's implementation of the protocol. Charles Davis's legal
game of hardball with defendants regarding plea offers and deadlines,
learned as a legal intern, took on a new dimension in CSA cases. St. Mary
prosecutors began to remove plea offers from the negotiation table for
any defendant in a CSC case who insisted a child testify at a preliminary

hearing. This practice was never formalized in the written protocol, but nonetheless was commonly understood by all the regular courtroom players in St. Mary County. So while protocol users cannot promise that the child will never have to repeat his or her story, as a practical matter, the prosecutor's actions tended to support that goal.

Perhaps the most significant features of the early protocol specified law enforcement's responsibilities relating to interviewing and arresting a suspect, showing him (or her) the videotape, and offering a polygraph. Under the policy, investigating police officers were required to "view the videotaped sessions simultaneously or shortly thereafter" and make a decision about whether an immediate arrest was appropriate. The protocol noted, "Even if an arrest warrant is not immediately obtained, the suspect should be interviewed immediately. Frequently, although you may have probable cause for arrest, you may wish to attempt to have the defendant come in voluntarily. (Do not call him up and ask him to come in. Go out and meet with him personally.)" The protocol notes the relative sequencing of events:

> After the victim has been interviewed on videotape, the alleged perpetrator must be thoroughly interrogated. The interview of the defendant, along with the interview of the victim, is absolutely the most critical component of a CSC case. All legal methods should be employed to obtain an accurate, trustworthy, valid confession. Experience has shown that a person who commits sexual abuse is likely to confess, at least to make some partial admissions, after viewing the video taped statement of the victim. Thus this videotape must be shown to the defendant. Read the suspect Miranda rights before showing the videotape.
>
> A comprehensive statement should be taken from the suspect even if he does not confess. The interviewer should attempt to get the defendant to acknowledge many of the facts supplied by the victim, despite the fact that the perpetrator may not acknowledge guilt. For example, one type of defense is that the perpetrator had never been alone with the child; thus, if this is admitted (or not denied), part of the battle has been won. Sometimes a non-denial has significant evidentiary value at trial.

Although this attempt at getting confessions was an element of police investigations for any type of crime, the protocol placed a special emphasis on the importance of either full or partial confessions in cases in which children were victims. Every element of the crime or every fact to which the suspect confessed represented one fewer element or fact that a child had the burden of explaining. For every partial confession a bit of the burden of proving the case shifted off the shoulders of the child and onto those of the adult prosecutors. Asserting early pressure on the suspect around these details was an integral and important step in shifting the relative balance of power in the ultimate prosecution of CSA cases.

The longest section of the original protocol, and the final tool in the arsenal for pressuring the suspect to confess, was the polygraph policy:

> The polygraph examination is a valuable tool in this type of investigation. If a suspect is interviewed by an officer and no confession is obtained a polygraph examination should immediately be offered to the defendant. If a defendant has requested an attorney or informed the officer that he does not wish to talk anymore, questions about the case should cease. However, if a suspect is willing, a polygraph examination should be set up immediately. . . .
>
> The polygraph examination itself should be video or audio taped if possible. A post-polygraph interview should be conducted by the polygraph operator if the defendant is cooperative. Obviously this interview should also be preserved on video or audiotape. Many valid confessions are obtained at this stage of the investigation. A skilled polygraph interviewer may often induce a suspect to confess or may [sic] incriminating admissions.

The protocol takes care to protect the suspect's rights. If the defendant was in custody, the polygraph must be conducted before the District Court's arraignment and the polygraph exam must not cause "undue delay" in the defendant's arraignment. Furthermore, "if the defendant is confirmed as truthful and [sic] his or her denial of sexual misconduct," then officers are advised "to reevaluate the case." While this is written in conditional language and leaves it to the officer's discretion whether to continue with the investigation, in practice officers began to put complete trust in the findings of one of its regular polygraph operators, Rick Rivers (see chapter 6). This came to take on critical significance in the general practices of St. Mary County and had implications for shifting the relative power structure in enacting justice in this community. So much faith was placed in the polygraph operator that defense attorneys in the community were willing to allow their clients to undergo a polygraph with him as a preemptive strike (see chapter 8).

## REDEFINING SUCCESS: INTEGRATING DISCIPLINARY VALUES

Although the currently mellow and reflective Charles Davis insisted, "I don't think there was a whole lot of resistance from the police department" in implementing the protocol, veteran members of the policing community remembered it differently. Noted one such officer, "The initial transition to this protocol was, I won't say bloody because it never came to blows but there was a lot of resistance. A lot of resistance." With ten years of public service already under his belt, the last thing this officer felt he needed was "some starry-eyed attorney that's gonna make the world revolve in the other direction because of some bullshit protocol that he made up. But I will tell you, you know Charles Davis, he is stubborn. I was gonna use the word strong-willed but he is stubborn. And once you set down and kind of talk through this thing man to man, it became abundantly clear that we both actually had the same goal in mind."

Apparently that is what Chief Prosecutor Charles Davis did, person-to-person and one-by-one, until he had a team of converts willing to promote and implement his innovative protocol for prosecuting CSC cases.

Law-enforcement officers began to see the protocol as an overview or map that made their jobs easier and performance better. Said one, "The guidelines . . . were for us to make us winners to make us succeed. That's why the guidelines work and we were believers in them. It wasn't to cause us hardships." Said another, "The protocol made everything a lot simpler. You knew, you do #1 and then you do 1a, 1b, 1c, and then you move onto 2." If they followed the protocol, "There should be no hang-ups getting it admitted as evidence." That had advantages for everyone. From the officers' perspective, one said, "I mean there's not a cop in the world that wants to go to court and get his ass kicked around by a defense attorney. So isn't the solution to that [to] be prepared, do your job the right way? And all they [defense attorneys] can do is moan and groan and piss over at the Beacon Club because they got their ass kicked by some stupid cop that followed the protocol and got [an] admissible statement from the victim and got an admissible confession and all kinds of admissible evidence."

There was no doubt that all the players in the community began to think as a team. Says Officer Williams, "it all started to fold together," and "a comfort level between agencies that was instrumental" developed. Officer Duke noted, "You lose the blinders. You don't concentrate so much on the perpetrator anymore. And you get a total picture." He argued that the protocol "changed the way we did CSC investigations. We were all able to become kinder, gentler police officers." CPS worker Donna Wagner noted that Davis and "I talked frequently. . . . We were responsive to each other. The same thing with the state police. If they called, everything stopped and we talked to them because we knew they wouldn't call"—unless it was important.

From the community perspective resistance dissipated as each constituent group came to realize that its own needs were being met. However, even more remarkable was the fact that as the individuals realized that their own professional practice needs were being addressed, they began to arrive at a blended mission. Police officers began to see that they could not worry only about dealing with the bad guy; they also had special responsibilities to the child. "This protocol really changes you. I mean, I'm still concerned about what's going to happen to this guy, but . . . I have other concerns that point in the direction of my victim—their support group, be it grandma, grandpa, mom, older brothers and sisters, that type of thing." They came to see videotaping children as a great investigatory tool for gaining confessions, which were necessary because children otherwise had to tell their story in court, usually without the benefit of additional physical evidence, and were at risk of being overpowered by the testimonial evidence of adults. Officers came to understand their mission in CSC cases involving children as special. "They're unique. The outcome is so critical that we get that confession. . . . This is an innocent child. This is pretty important. I take it very seriously. This isn't like 'Who stole my bicycle?'" Cops recognized that when they did their jobs right, "this case actually turned out to be relatively easy for the prosecutor to prosecute."

CPS workers began to realize that their work involved not only protecting children but also helping prosecutors to secure a convictable case. Among other things, this had the added benefit of reducing the risk that the offender would be able to abuse other children. CPS worker Jim Henry began to ask, "How can we best preserve and protect this child as well as prosecute this guy?" Answering that question required a broader vision of his responsibility working on these cases. "How can I get this so that it satisfies that criminal piece? It was that tension." So he came to understand that his mission of protecting children should not limit his focus. It had to include being thoughtful about what Chief Prosecutor Charles Davis needed in order to successfully prosecute his cases as well (see chapter 4).

The prosecutor's office began to redefine the very meaning of "success" institutionally. For many prosecutors' offices across the nation, success and failure are measured by wins and losses. Many prosecutors will not even pursue CSA cases because they are so hard to win (see chapter 1). But listen to Jameson—who would work under Chief Prosecutor Charles Davis for a decade and then inherit the protocol and "tweak it" for its next decade of service—respond to our question about how *he* defined success:

> Resolving the case without the child having to testify. No, I can resolve a case by dismissing it, so that isn't it. Resolving the case with a conviction—with a satisfying conviction. There is a balance. Mom may want the guy strung up with the maximum allowable sentence, but they don't want the child to testify. So you've got to try and balance what can we accept as an acceptable sentence, but yet not have the child have to testify. . . . You try to balance between assignment of responsibility and protection of the victim.

So this is how one small, rural community, under the leadership of a forceful and charismatic prosecutor, came together and negotiated a new and shared understanding of success that ended up giving pride of place to the needs of its youngest citizens. In doing so, it did not ask any practitioner to compromise his or her professional values, but it did seek to integrate these philosophical and practice orientations in a way that kept professionals focusing on serving the community as a whole.

At the end of our first day of community-based observation and our initial interview with Jameson, he escorted us out of his office. In a small anterior waiting room, a teenaged girl and her mother were sitting patiently. Jameson greeted them warmly. Jameson's last official act in office as prosecutor would be a trial, *People v. Inman*. As befitted the final exit of this particular prosecutor, it was a "CSC 1" involving a child victim, to be tried in Judge Richter's courtroom. The girl, sitting in the waiting room with her mother, was a reluctant witness in Jameson's final trial as chief prosecutor. We will tell that story later in this book.

# Sex Busters | **THREE**

JIM HENRY

And [the police chief] says, "Williams, who is

that guy?" Well, Jimmy looked like he does right

now, and [the chief] says, "Who's that guy?" I said,

"well, it's Jim." He says, "Well, how come he's not

in handcuffs then?" He was serious; he thought I

was bringing in some longhaired guy that I'd just

arrested for drugs or something. "Well you better

put him in handcuffs." I said, "Oh no, he works for

social services. He's a child services investigator."

—Officer Ed Williams on Jim Henry

My ten years as a child protective services (CPS) worker in St. Mary County changed me. Gone is my naive belief that life is fair. Gone is my denial that children can easily overcome sexual-abuse trauma with help from professionals. I know now that my denial was self-protective. I did not want to acknowledge and feel the pain of maltreated children. I was afraid of my own pain. What slowly replaced my denial was an awareness of a deep grief that still lingers to this day. My career in child welfare has been shaped by this grief. Even now, when I train others, testify, and write to advocate for reform in the child-welfare system, grief is an ever-present companion.

Years of child-welfare experience, reading and participating in empirical research, and constant reflection have convinced me that practices that place children at the center of system interventions are a necessity if children are to be both protected and healed. Yet, changing existing child-welfare practices demands that professionals be committed, innovative, self-reflective, and willing to challenge and—when necessary—to change themselves. These qualities are rare, since the primary goal of most child-welfare professionals is to survive the multiple challenges of high caseloads, bureaucracy, intense pain that comes from working with traumatized children and their families, and the fear of making a wrong decision that could bring irreparable harm to a child. Such pressures often harden child-welfare professionals. They become complacent, assuming that because they are the "good guys" saving children, whatever they do is for their good. Such false beliefs ultimately put children at risk and prevent professional self-reflection and growth.

My first job, as a CPS worker in St. Mary County, fortunately exposed me to a group of committed, innovative people far different from the norm. My experiences with these people have shaped my child-welfare career of twenty-eight years. I learned what can happen when a group of community professionals prioritize the needs of sexually abused children. I have been inspired by that knowledge and championed that cause ever since. My experiences at St. Mary ignited my passion to serve maltreated children that still drives my work today. However, my introduction to one of the key players, who left an indelible mark on me, was far from welcoming. I received a wake-up call that I recall as vividly as if it happened yesterday.

The thunderous door slam still reverberates in my ears. It marked my first experience with Chief Prosecutor Charles Davis. Not a "Hi" or "Hello, my name is Charles," but rather the sound of his crashing office door as my welcome and introduction. It was followed by a harsh bark, "Why was your report late? This is a parental termination case. This is important!" They were his first words to me, and they were delivered with much agitation. My heart jumped into my throat as he continued by questioning my competency and my commitment on my very first case—ever. Me, an idealistic young social worker, standing helpless in this stranger's office, being attacked by this tough ex-marine, now the prosecuting attorney. I mustered only a few words in self-defense: "I had no idea you were waiting for my report. No one told me." But Charles heard none of my responses. I left his office that day with a message branded into my brain. "If you want to help children, be prepared. Don't just say you care for kids. Words mean nothing. Anyone can say they care about maltreated children. What you do is what counts." I deeply respect Charles Davis for that message. He embodied it in his work. I have tried to embody it in mine.

Charles's driven leadership directed the development of St. Mary's unique sexual-abuse-system response long before other professionals in the state had taken up the issue. He was willing to think and act outside the narrow box of past legal and social-work practices. He would argue, cajole, and yell at me —depending on whether the moment called for force or reason—in order to convince me that he was right. Simultaneously, he had an amazing ability to listen to my view and, if it made sense, a willingness to change his own. Charles and I came to appreciate our differences while simultaneously joining in the goal to protect children, not only from their abusers but also from further harm by the systems designated to protect them. Our stories together reflect how those goals were actually met.

Charles's response to my phone messages about a new sexual abuse case was predictable. I can just see him in my mind's eye, perusing his handwritten messages and discovering one from me. In a fury, he would read the note, sigh deeply, yell, "Oh shit," and immediately pick up the phone and call me. Once connected, he would skip the polite formalities and normal conventions such as "Hello" or "How are you?" and demand an investigatory update. "Have you interviewed the child? Did you videotape the interview? Where is the alleged offender? Is the mother cooperative? How soon can you be here with the police?" One endless set of questions with no pauses until he was ready for my answers. I learned not to take the irritation or anger in his voice personally. I came to recognize that Charles's grief for sexually abused children manifested as anger. He reacted strongly when child sexual abuse occurred in the county he loved and grew up in. He was appalled at the victim's loss of childhood innocence. His anger galvanized him into action, and he would not stop until the child's safety and community justice were secured.

In contrast to Charles, my grief manifested through sadness. A lump still swells in my throat today, more than twenty years later, when I sit and hear a sexually abused child's story. It took me a long time to learn to feel the pain. I have come to believe that the willingness to enter into the pain of a child's story provides a safe meeting place for children to tell their story. Being present for their stories lets children know they are being heard on multiple levels. Sexually abused children need someone who is not afraid of their fear, guilt, and shame, to sit with them. Rarely is someone willing to do so.

So as Charles's anger and my sadness met, it pushed both of us to another level of grief, but it simultaneously fueled our commitment to protect children. On one cold, dreary winter day I called him about a referral on a twelve-year-old girl who had disclosed to a family friend a long history of being fondled and penetrated by her stepfather. I knew, even before I called Charles, that the facts of the case would precipitate his fiery investigative fervor. Hearing the facts, Charles reacted. He wanted to know if the other members of the "Sex Busters" were working with me on this case. He believed that the facts of the case were so serious and complex that he wanted only the Sex Busters to investigate. His voice and words made it clear that there were to be "no mistakes." I told him that indeed the other Sex Busters were on it. His voice softened.

## ENTER THE SEX BUSTERS

The Sex Busters were State Police Officer Ed Williams, the investigating trooper; Rick Rivers, the polygraph operator; and I, the CPS worker. Interestingly, no one seems to remember who actually first called us that. The name was pirated from the cover of *Time Magazine* and an article highlighting the federal government's crackdown on pornography (Stengel, 1986). The three of us had successfully investigated so many sexual-abuse cases that the name seemed fitting. To this day, we each have a Sex Buster plaque that was given to each of us when we departed. My plaque now hangs in my office reminding me of friendship, commitment, and the sexually abused children with whom we worked.

Ed Williams, a veteran state trooper with his crew cut, wide body, broad smile, endearing laugh, and gift of gab, could put anyone at ease, even the most hardened offender. He wore his state police badge with great pride. He viewed himself as a sentinel for the American way of law and order. To me, he epitomized the small-town cop that everyone knew and respected. He was a country boy from start to finish. His position as state police public-service officer placed him in the schools, conducting child sexual abuse (CSA) investigations and doing public-relations work such as running a booth at the county fair. The job was the perfect fit for his likeable personality. He was president of the local Little League. Everywhere we went people smiled and greeted him like a longtime friend. Even those whom he had previously arrested seemed to respect and appreciate him. For all of Ed's influence and power in the county, he was not self-promoting. After three years working with Ed, I learned that he had received the State Medal of Honor—not because he told me, but because I was snooping around his office one day. As I scanned the pictures on the wall, I came upon a photograph of him receiving the honor and an accompanying newspaper clip. I read with amazement that a mentally ill man had shot him in the chest at close range during a crisis call in St. Mary County. When asked, Ed downplayed the event, spending most of the time explaining how thankful he was for wearing his bullet-proof vest. His humbleness reminded me again of his commitment to service, not the seeking of personal gain.

Rick Rivers, a man cut from the same uniform as Charles Davis, was a short, stocky ex-marine who had served in Vietnam. His war experiences, which he rarely spoke of, haunted him, but they drove him to search for truth, his own and others' (see chapter 6). Armed with his polygraph machine, he entered each investigation with vitality fueled by his "hunt for truth." Despite his observable toughness, he had an ability to make even the most perverted offenders feel comfortable and heard. He combined a genuine respect for a person's humanity with believing that everyone must be accountable for his or her actions. He had an unparalleled record in the community for obtaining confessions. I attribute this to his willingness to communicate respect to the alleged offender, verbalizing and appreciating their shame, no matter how heinous the sexual offense. He conveyed to the offender the importance of regaining self-respect by telling the truth.

Then there is me, Jim. Others describe me as a rebellious ex-hippie, still sporting blue jeans, sandals, long hair, and Fu Manchu mustache. Of course, such an outward appearance was purposeful. It reflected my opposition to the "system." In contrast to Charles and Rick, who had served in the Vietnam War, I had been a conscientious objector. I viewed the court system as flawed, riddled with inequality, and driven by the American myth that justice is served. However, I was willing to participate in the very system I disdained in order to protect and advocate for children. Others, especially cops, in conservative St. Mary County, where two-thirds of the citizenry are registered Republicans, were initially very suspicious of me. I took it as a challenge to disarm even the most right-wing conservative with my smile, warm disposition, and ability to relate to children. Ed told me one day after we had worked together closely for a year that initially he had distrusted me because of my hair and attire. How that all changed as we became trusted colleagues and good friends!

Back to the case. On a freezing cold day during the Christmas holidays, the Sex Busters met in Charles's office before contacting the child to strategize on how to approach this new investigation, which we would find would extend over two months and consume a great deal of physical and emotional energy. The unfolding drama would become one of the most personally and professionally challenging cases that the Sex Busters ever encountered. As usual Charles, as prosecutor, directed the meeting, emphasizing the necessity of following the sexual-abuse protocol's key components: responding immediately, videotaping my interview of the child, interrogating the alleged offender (done by Ed and Rick) immediately following my interview, offering the suspect an immediate polygraph with Rick if he denied the allegation, and consulting during the entire process with Charles Davis.

The child, Kathy, age twelve, had just left a friend's home and was heading back to her mother and stepfather's home, according to the caller, who reported digital penetration and fondling. Keeping with the protocol, Ed and I went to the home of the mother and her husband in hopes that mother would grant permission for me to interview Kathy at the courthouse. Such an effort to get the child to come to the courthouse was unique to St. Mary County; in other jurisdictions across the state, the child would have likely been interviewed in her own home. To preserve the interview of Kathy on videotape, she needed to be interviewed outside the home. School was not an option, since the children were on Christmas vacation. To interview Kathy at home, where the sexual abuse was allegedly occurred, would likely have resulted in her denial of abuse. CSA is a secret act. Disclosure would be extremely unlikely because Kathy lacked safety and feared her stepfather.

The investigation commenced on the same morning as our meeting with Davis. My tentative knock on the large green duplex door reflected my anxiety. I knew, as a CPS worker, that the response on the other side of the door was unpredictable. An irate parent or a young child scared and alone could answer. Yet, having Ed, in his bright blue trooper uniform, alongside calmed my anxiety. My experience told me that people on the other side of the door were much more likely to be compliant with an armed police officer than a social worker.

A tall, middle-aged woman slowly opened the door just enough to stick her head around and ask in a gruff voice what we wanted. I explained that I was from CPS and wanted to talk with her about a concern that had come to our attention regarding Kathy. She allowed us in to her tidy but sparsely decorated living room, calling to her husband, who apparently was in the back of the house. A large television set stood out. The mother had a dazed look on her face, as if she had just woken from a deep sleep. Quickly her look changed to suspicion and defensiveness, questioning why we were there. I introduced Ed and myself, asking her and her husband if they would accompany us, with Kathy, to the courthouse for an interview. I was careful not to reveal the specific nature of the complaint, hoping that they would cooperate. If she refused, our options were limited. I could not force her to bring the child for an interview. Obtaining a court order would result in a delay that would provide ample time for mother and husband to talk with Kathy about the allegations. Their talking to and/or threatening her before the interview would have made it ever more likely that Kathy would not disclose. I breathed a sigh of relief when she agreed to follow us to the courthouse. I could feel my heart pounding as we approached the courthouse, knowing that the next two hours were potentially going to alter the course of this twelve-year-old girl's life.

Kathy's mother consented to an interview of her daughter. I took Kathy to an upstairs room, while her mother and stepfather waited in the lobby. Rick Rivers had set the video camera up in a conference room. Kathy cautiously responded to my initial benign questions, giving one-word answers. I became keenly aware of my own nervousness; Kathy was going to be difficult to interview. I explained the video camera in my usual way: "The camera is here so that you don't have to keep telling your story over and over. There are other people in the next room who will be watching." My experience explaining the camera honestly with children had almost always been positive, responses I later documented in research (Henry, 1999). No child had reacted negatively, although professionals from other counties thought having a camera in the room would make it more difficult for children to disclose. I wanted children to know as much as possible during and after the interview to minimize any potential feelings of being tricked or deceived to gain their disclosure. The more I could eliminate system surprises and secrecy the greater likelihood that they could experience safety and trust with me.

I used the interviewing techniques I had developed, inasmuch as there were no state protocols for child interviewing at the time. I wanted to help Kathy relax her defenses in hopes of her disclosing. From my years of experience, I believe that interviewing is both a science and an art. It demands the interviewer's full attention to the child. Getting children to feel safe enough to confide their secret of sexual abuse to a stranger is an enormous challenge. The child's disclosure is a sacred act of blind trust, for children do not know what will happen once their secret is out. As the interviewer, my responsibility is to ask questions to help them tell their stories, to listen, and to embrace the intense emotion often attached to their memories and words.

When Kathy appeared comfortable, I began to probe gently into her relationship with her mother and stepfather. Kathy was reticent to reveal anything. She skillfully deflected my questions. Yet, when I asked questions about her stepfather, I noticed that Kathy's breathing rate increased and her swallowing became more like gulping. I sensed that Kathy had something too painful to tell. Knowing that this was my only opportunity to interview Kathy, I was unwilling to give up. If Kathy could not tell me now, then I knew future disclosures would be highly improbable because she would undoubtedly be on the receiving end of threats by her stepfather.

After about forty minutes, we took a bathroom break. I consulted with Ed and Rick—who had been watching on closed-circuit television—about what I should do next. We all thought Kathy was not going to disclose, but her nonverbal cues and defensiveness made us believe that something had happened to her. I decided that the mother should be brought into the interview, hoping that her presence would encourage Kathy to disclose. This was an unusual and desperate strategy because the mother's position was unknown. In an attempt to gain the mother's support, I explained the allegations before I brought her into the room with Kathy. She communicated shock and vowed to support any disclosure. However, five minutes into the interview, Kathy's mother verbally discounted the allegations against her husband. She communicated a clear message to Kathy that she was not to say anything, explaining that her "husband would never do anything like that. Any touching he did was not meant in a sexual way."

I felt anger exploding within me as my body tightened and my face grew red. The mother had betrayed her daughter. Somehow I managed to swallow my emotions because I did not want to alienate Kathy. I quickly ended the interview by removing Kathy from the room.

Her mother's betrayal further convinced me that Kathy had been sexually abused. Yet there was no real evidence to support my belief. I did not want to let Kathy go home, but I could not prevent this because she had not disclosed. My only chance was to phone the adult friend who had made the initial complaint, hoping that she would be willing to talk directly with Kathy about what Kathy disclosed. To call the referral source during the interview was an unorthodox act. I took a huge risk because so many variables had to align for this phone call to result in disclosure. The referral person would have to be home, she would have to be willing to talk with Kathy, she would have to be supportive of Kathy telling me about the sexual abuse, and Kathy would have to trust the referral source. But, I figured this was my only chance. Fortunately, the friend was home and agreed to talk with Kathy.

The gamble paid off. Within minutes of being on the phone, Kathy burst into tears, sobbing, "I am afraid. I am afraid." I allowed Kathy to remain on the phone, sobbing and talking, for a few minutes. After she finished the phone call and she calmed down, we returned to the camera room; her mother had been escorted out by Ed and Rick. Kathy quickly returned to sobbing and crying to my questions. Clearly Kathy was in significant distress, but she had still not disclosed any sexual abuse. Kathy interrupted my questioning with a tearfully statement that sounded like a request, "My mom will be mad at me! I don't want to go home if I tell." After reassurance I would do all I could to keep her safe and still in tears, Kathy disclosed three separate incidents of sexual fondling. None of these incidents involved penetration. With the disclosure documented on videotape, it was time for the other two Sex Busters to move into their respective roles with the stepfather while I petitioned the juvenile court for Kathy's removal from home.

Having watched the entire child interview, including the mother's responses, Ed and Rick were convinced that the stepfather had sexually abused Kathy. Ed and Rick brought the stepfather to another conference room area and began the interrogation. Ed played the "good cop," emotionally supporting and connecting with the stepfather, while Rick challenged his story. After two hours of interrogation, the stepfather confessed to all three incidents of fondling plus another one that Kathy had not even disclosed. I was amazed at their remarkable skills that produced this confession.

A juvenile court hearing that same day placed Kathy in foster care. Kathy cried, being extremely relieved that she was not going home. She admitted that she was afraid what her mother would do to her now because she had told. A Sex Busters meeting with Charles Davis resulted in a warrant for her stepfather's arrest. That night over a cold beer—actually more like six—the Sex Busters rehashed the day's events, attempting to come to terms with our own emotions. Most painful for me was the mother's betrayal. I had never witnessed such an overt attempt by a mother to silence a daughter's disclosure of sexual abuse. This mother was willing to sacrifice her own daughter's safety to protect her husband. Several weeks would pass before we discovered how deep this betrayal actually was.

A few days after the interview with Kathy while visiting her in the foster home, she subtly hinted her sister might also have been sexually abused. Despite no specific sexual abuse allegations, I had strong suspicions. Ed and I headed north 150 miles a few days later to a residential treatment home for troubled teens where Kathy's seventeen-year-old sister resided. I took a copy of Kathy's videotaped disclosure with me. The sister watched the videotape with Ed and me. Initially, she was stoic and emotionally distant, but as the videotape progressed, she broke into tears. She disclosed in almost incoherent sobbing that her stepfather had impregnated her four times between the ages of eleven and seventeen. She revealed that, as painful as it was to watch Kathy's interview, Kathy's courage inspired her to tell her story as well.

The Sex Busters investigation did not end with the sister's disclosure. During the next two weeks, I kept thinking about the mother's betrayal of Kathy. Her betrayal had been so calculated. Because of that and a visit I had paid to the stepfather in jail, I wondered if the mother had sexually abused Kathy as well. I consulted with Charles and the Sex Busters; we decided that I should interview Kathy again, this time to probe about her mother's potential involvement. A part of me did not want to intrude on Kathy's adjustment to foster care. Kathy had been quite emotional, yet was developing a relationship with the foster mother. I had never interviewed an older child whose mother may have sexually abused her. I knew this would be extremely sensitive and likely evoke significant emotions, including guilt and shame, in Kathy. Yet, not to ask if indeed she had been abused by her mother, would mean the secret would not be told any time soon, if ever.

I decided to videotape the second interview. If there was a disclosure about the mother, I wanted it on tape to avoid Kathy's having to retell the story. I was nervous as I sat down in the courthouse office with Kathy. I once again explained the purpose of the video camera. She was surprised that I had the camera, assuring me that she had told me everything she remembered about what her stepfather had done. At that point I told her I did not want to talk about her stepfather, but about her mother. A deadening silence descended on the room. Kathy's eyes avoided contact with mine; she stared at the floor.

Tiny tears formed on the corners of both her eyes. The silence continued. I sat quietly, not knowing what to say next. Pain seemed to fill the room, especially the lump in my throat. After what felt like an endless moment, I acknowledged verbally what I was seeing and feeling. I noted her tears and admitted to my own sadness. She nodded, and the trickle of teardrops turned into sobbing. I waited until her sobbing subsided and then with a hushed voice asked her to tell me about what had happened with her mother. I was not prepared for her story of her mother's sexual abuse of both her and her sister, of how Kathy's mother taught her and her sister to perform oral sex. After describing this, Kathy said that her mother would make her do sexual things with her stepfather. Pictures were taken. The sobbing returned and signaled the end of the interview. Kathy could talk no more about what happened with her mother.

Within a few hours, the Sex Busters confronted Kathy's mother with Kathy's statements of sexual abuse. Kathy's mother initially denied the allegations. However, she did agree to an immediate polygraph. After the administration of the polygraph, her mother admitted to teaching and coercing Kathy and her sister to have oral sex. She denied the group sex with Kathy and her husband, but admitted that one time she did have Kathy touch her vagina.

That night the Sex Busters once again gathered for cold beers. However, this time silence dominated more than conversation. Each of us sat there ruminating on the day's events, attempting to make sense of mother's sexual violations of Kathy. No explanations assuaged the grief in any of us. The lump in my throat was bigger than ever now. Swallowing was hard, even though the beer tasted great. Ed just sat there shaking his head. Rick broke the silence, raising his voice in anger, disgusted with the mother. Nothing relieved the pain that night except the beer and the silent communion among friends.

Reflecting back on those days, I am amazed that despite enormous personal differences that we bound together for the well-being of children. Personal and professional agendas were transcended to create a systemic response to sexually abused children. Charles Davis and the Sex Busters were all remarkably strong personalities. Yet, no one marked off his territory and engaged in turf wars. With our concerted effort came phenomenal success in the protection of children and the prosecution of the offenders. Charles Davis and the Sex Busters were famous throughout the county. Community professionals viewed the three of us as a well-oiled CSA-busting machine. As irreverent as the name Sex Busters may sound, it became a badge of honor.

Charles Davis was a visionary and taskmaster who set no limits when it came to protecting children. His belief that his protocol would protect the physical safety and emotional well-being of children was presumptuous, yet inspiring. His introduction of videotaping into the protocol at the time he did was controversial, yet brilliant. CPS and law-enforcement officers struggled at first, knowing that their interview styles were now subject to review and criticism because of the videotaping. I remember the first videotaped interview I ever conducted. I was scared to death. Here I was with this sexually abused child trying to balance her need for support and my need to gain information while simultaneously knowing that I was going to be subject to future critique, especially by Charles. In reviewing that first videotape, I discovered it captured my promise of an ice cream cone to the girl when we were done. Although I was aghast by my statement suggesting bribery, the alleged offender confessed within hours of watching his stepdaughter's videotape. I became an instant believer in the power of the tape.

Growth and change demand risk. I was willing to expose my novice interview skills on tape if I knew the chances of a confession would increase and the probability of the child testifying would decrease. Ed and Rick convinced me that videotaped interviews with children were powerful tools in obtaining confessions from offenders. I also knew that the victims' mothers were much more likely to believe their children if they witnessed their emotions on the videotape firsthand. I knew that the healing process would be accelerated for the child and family if the mother believed and the offender confessed.

When Charles decided to enter the unexplored territory of developing a child sexual abuse protocol back in the mid-1980s, before the formation of the Sex Busters, there were no best-practice guidelines across the country to adopt. A few ideas circulated nationally, but no research existed to demonstrate the efficacy of any particular protocol. However, Charles forged ahead, undaunted by critics and skeptics, believing that a novel and potential risky protocol, constructed from ideas gleaned from jurisdictions across the country, and his own ideas, could be successful. Charles's courage and willingness to risk controversy and criticism for innovation in child sexual abuse was foundational to the protocol. It became the task of the Sex Busters to implement the protocol, making it a reality, and to convince others through our successes that Charles's vision produced better outcomes for children, their families, and the community.

The Sex Busters' investigative success required our trust in each other's expertise. I interviewed the child; Ed interrogated the suspect; Rick ran the polygraph. On occasions when CPS was not involved, Ed would sometimes call me to conduct the interview anyway, especially if the child was young. There was no ego involved over what were his cases and what were mine; it was about whose expertise was needed. Unfortunately, times changed soon after the Sex Busters went their separate ways, and professional and territorial boundaries dictated who was responsible for the case. A well-delineated protocol, constructed by new local CPS administrators, outlined which agency was responsible—CPS or the police—and consequently threw out the transcendent team concept that had guided the Sex Busters' success. However, by then, the Sex Busters had trained select police detectives in interviewing children, which minimized the need for a CPS interview. This training effort was spearheaded by the prosecutor's office, which recognized the need to institutionalize the protocol and interviewing process, independent of the personalities.

At the time, we believed, though without empirical evidence, that professionals could minimize trauma in sexually abused children through implementation of a child-centered protocol. The protocol and those employing it believed that the burden should not be on children to prove that their disclosures were truthful, but on the professionals who investigated and intervened. Too often professionals blame the poor quality of children's disclosures for failed investigations and prosecutions, when in reality negative case outcomes were often the result of professionals' failing at some part of the task of investigating these crimes.

The Sex Busters melding took remarkably little time. Initial suspicions arising from personal and professional differences were acknowledged and subsequently discarded. Each investigation reinforced the importance of serving children in a more synchronized supportive manner. The painful challenges brought on by the children's stories cemented our efforts and our commitment. We depended on one another as we struggled with the complexity of the cases and the grief that often accompanied our experiences together.

Each of us exhibited a unique emotion that mirrored a stage of grief. Charles and Rick's was anger, Ed's bargaining, and mine sadness. So many times a cold beer after an investigation served as a healing elixir for wounded hearts, tired bodies, and weary minds. Venting about the day's events, laughing about the craziness of the day's experiences, and sharing the personal emotions about the children's pain became a ritual that sustained us. Such times became therapeutic, as we acknowledged and expressed our feelings and lamented about children's stories. Drinking at the well became a metaphor for internal replenishment so that the next investigation and next day would receive the same commitment and vitality as the last. Unbeknown to others in the community, the name Sex Busters did not mean professional success for us, but rather a brotherhood of commitment, passion, and personal meaning.

The Sex Busters became a transprofessional entity whose commitment to children surpassed individual allegiances to our home agencies. Each of us exceeded and at times transgressed agency policies to benefit the children we served. Numbers of hours worked, schedules, and other constraints were not barriers to our investigations. When referrals were received, all was dropped. Quitting time was determined by a finished investigation, not the hour on the clock. Calls to our wives informing them of our late arrival home became common.

The administrative support from our respective agencies was critical to the success of the Sex Busters. This was especially true for Ed and me. The commander of the State Police post allowed Ed enormous freedom to prioritize CSA cases within his duties. He did not micromanage Ed's time, despite the notoriety Ed was gaining in the county as a sexual-abuse investigator. My boss was committed to the development of the protocol and permitted me to be available to the prosecutor, even when the case did not mandate CPS involvement. He relieved some agency pressure on me by occasionally extending paperwork deadlines. He did

I left St. Mary to become a CPS supervisor in a more populated adjacent county. I sought the position, hoping to apply my experience, expertise, and energy to produce better outcomes for children. I had the naive idealism that I could champion a new investigatory protocol for CSA modeled after St. Mary County. I was confident that the essential elements from the St. Mary County protocol could be exported into a much larger, complicated, and formal system. I was wrong! Despite my efforts, energy, and advocacy, I was not able to transform that system. There were some successes, the most significant being videotaping of sexually abused children (after four years) at the local child advocacy center under certain circumstances dictated by the prosecutor. But, after seven years of effort, the investigatory system basically remained the same: fragmented, adult focused, poorly coordinated, and slow to react. I learned many lessons including the necessity of having likeminded individuals within each profession involved in the investigatory process. Without allies, continuous roadblocks, the by-products of system distrust and inertia, appeared. The investigatory process was extremely slow, cumbersome, and frankly not the county's primary focus. The turf wars I experienced outside St. Mary's significantly increased my appreciation of my Sex Busters' experiences.

Despite my physical departure, I never really left St. Mary County. Memories of the Sex Busters were fueled by disappointments in the larger county. Daily, I would catch myself longing for the camaraderie of the past. After six months at my new job and mounting frustration, I received a call from the then-current chief prosecutor requesting that I testify as an expert witness in a sexual abuse case. I immediately said, "Yes." My eagerness was really about my desire to return and recapture the past, not the specific case in question. I needed a physical reminder of past successes to erase mounting present disappointments. My initial expert witness experiences, along with my frustration as a supervisor, fueled my desire to obtain a PhD. I returned to the St. Mary County courthouse, greeted by familiar faces, appreciation, and expert status that I did not have in my current supervisory position. Testifying as an expert in child sexual abuse thrust me into a new, valuable role and allowed me to reconnect to the people that had kindled my professional passion for protecting child victims. In my new role, I was testifying in court explaining the dynamics of sexually abused children to a jury to help them understand why children rarely immediately disclose. The Sex Busters were gone, but I could support St. Mary's ongoing commitment to sexually abused children, which renewed my belief that professionals could be successful in protecting victims and prosecuting offenders.

I did not particularly like being a supervisor. As a supervisor, I missed the contact with the children. I was a malcontent in the office. I often accompanied workers under the guise of assisting them, but deep down I knew it was about my needs. I started my PhD program shortly after I became a supervisor in hopes of starting another career where I could intervene with maltreated children more directly. Seven years later I became a professor. During seven years as a supervisor and seventeen years in protective services, the children and the system had changed me, but I had no regrets for the years I had spent there.

I entered academia with a dream of starting a trauma assessment center for maltreated children. I was convinced, and still am convinced, that if we are to meet the needs of maltreated children, we must have a comprehensive understanding of their needs. After two years of garnering university and community support, I received a local foundation grant for $20,000. My next adventure helping children began.

Reminiscent of my Sex Buster days, I found committed and passionate experts who wanted to make a difference for maltreated children. We quickly formed a transdisciplinary assessment team that included social work, medicine, occupational therapy, and speech pathology. Eight years later, the team, with the help of more than two hundred student interns from the various disciplines, has assessed more than 1,700 maltreated children. We utilize a comprehensive neurodevelopmental approach with the goals of identifying the impact of trauma and prenatal alcohol exposure on children's neurodevelopment and behavior. Each week I am honored to listen to children tell their life stories. We teach student interns to embrace these children's stories and the pain that accompanies them. The professional and personal lessons learned from my St. Mary days guide my interactions with the children, student interns, and other professionals today. The lumps that I first felt in St. Mary County still form in my throat when I hear the children's experiences.

Our trauma center has received two large federal grants that support trauma-informed child-welfare training, trauma-informed school programming at the elementary and Head Start levels, and comprehensive trauma assessment. Through grant activity with the National Child Traumatic Stress Network, I have participated in the development of a national trauma-informed curriculum for child welfare workers and resource parents. Our trauma-center staff members have been teaching all new child-welfare workers about child trauma in our state for the past four years. During the four years of a grant, we have trained more than seven thousand people at the local, state, and national levels in trauma-informed care for maltreated children.

Along with my duties as director of the trauma-assessment center, I continued my role in St. Mary County as a CSA expert. Appreciation of my expertise by the prosecutor's office, the circuit court judge, and CPS has reinforced my desire to maintain relationships with many people in St. Mary. Ed Williams is now the county fair director, a position of high esteem in the county, which fits his gregarious style and generous personality. As often as I can, I make a point to visit him at the fairground, which is just down the street from the courthouse. Rick Rivers is still conducting polygraphs but is rarely summoned anymore in St. Mary. It is unclear why, but the changing of the old guard has occurred.

## CONCLUSION

My first professional experiences in St. Mary County shaped my entire career. I learned what can happen when committed professionals are creative and actually collaborate to design and develop a child-responsive system that takes the burden of proof off sexually abused children. A few professionals can start a chain reaction that can have far-reaching implications for an entire community. Skeptics not only are quieted but also often jump on the bandwagon when they see success. Twenty years later, this realization still spurs my advocacy for system change. I have not succumbed to burnout and skepticism, despite unending challenges, because I have seen how systems can change when professionals think and act outside their traditional roles.

Along with my professional development in St. Mary County came enormous personal growth. I realized that professionals who work with child sexual abuse cannot avoid pain. I discovered that in order to be with children in their pain, I had to recognize and be with my own. Still today, I am aware of my grief when hearing another child's story. This embracing of pain began in St. Mary County. There, I learned that my grief was inseparable from my professional duties and that sitting with likeminded professionals soothed the pain, bringing healing to my grief.

Protocol as Process | **PART 2**

Investigation of Child Sexual Abuse

# FOUR

*Interviewing Victims and*
*Interrogating Suspects*

KATHLEEN COULBORN FALLER

And the key to that interview is, first of all you

need somebody in there who knows how to talk to

victims, but you need to record that interview. So

that forever and ever, especially when you get the

perpetrator in there, you've got this videotape to

show him so that there is no misunderstanding of

what little Susie or little Jimmy said.

—Ed Duke, Chief of Police

Investigation of child sexual abuse (CSA) involves at least two separate and distinct elements: the child interview and the suspect interrogation. In St. Mary County, the child interview was intended to be the beginning and the end of the child's participation in the investigation. Once the child was interviewed, professionals used the videotape recording of the child's disclosure to move the case forward. Thus, the videotape aids the police officer and forms the basis for the suspect's interrogation.

In many communities and cases, child protective services (CPS) workers interview possible victims, while law-enforcement officers interrogate suspects. But the highest-quality investigations are collaborative and synthesize sources and pieces of information into an organic whole. Our findings in St. Mary County suggest that first-rate CSA investigations require planning; cooperative undertakings; selective professional boundary breaching, including engaging in activities that go beyond those rigidly defined by the job; and thinking about families and cases holistically.

In this chapter we discuss how St. Mary County professionals initially discovered and institutionalized a process that resulted in quality investigations. This discussion is followed by an illustrative case from which lessons about the investigative endeavor are drawn. Then we document how the professionals in St. Mary County describe collaborative investigations and the protocol in the 1980s and early 1990s and after 2002, when we conducted our research. Comparing differences in protocol implementation over time raises some general concerns about CPS and law enforcement working hand in glove. We discuss these issues and make observations about their relevance to St. Mary County.

## IN THE BEGINNING: LEARNING TO CRAFT CHILD INTERVIEWS

In the early 1980s, when St. Mary County decided to do something about sexual abuse, other child-welfare professionals were still preoccupied with serious physical abuse and the conundrum of child neglect and were not yet routinely dealing with sexual abuse. As a consequence, there was little guidance about community case management of CSA, and almost no guidance about how to actually conduct a child sexual abuse investigation (Sgroi, 1982).

In St. Mary County, the written protocol developed from a series of lucky guesses. The community tried strategies that proved successful— videotaping the child interview, showing the videotape to the nonoffending parent to elicit that parent's support, showing the videotape to the suspect in an effort to elicit a confession, and using the polygraph as the next strategy to elicit a confession (see chapter 2). Davis spoke of how the county overcame the traditional tension between CPS, law enforcement, and the prosecutor's office: "it worked in St. Mary County . . . probably because of the personalities [the Sex Busters and himself] and probably because [the community] was smaller" (see chapter 3). CPS Supervisor Donna Wagner pointed to at least five additional factors that made investigations work. They included conducting high-quality child interviews; making a concerted effort to learn from those interviews and creating a collaborative environment for doing so; spending limited resources wisely and efficiently; having support from administrative superiors who committed to a common goal; and maintaining good and trusting relationships (both within the CPS team and with other parties, including the prosecutor's office and police).

### Child Protective Services Review of Videotapes

One of the real challenges of the work was actually interviewing abused children in a way that was sensitive to the child but also elicited a persuasive account. Because there were no guidelines for these interviews, professionals in St. Mary County used their own common sense and one another's expertise. They engaged in a process of peer review: CPS, law enforcement, and the prosecutor examined their fledgling child interviews via their videotapes and together learned from them.

Jim Henry commented on this process of video review and critiquing, expressing thanks for the support he received from his superior, the director of social services, who reportedly said, "'We're all going to watch these video tapes. When we do 'em, we're going to watch 'em and train,' . . . which was enormously helpful. So . . . you watch yourself on video and you say, 'Why did I do that?'"

Being critiqued was sometimes a painful experience. As Donna Wagner noted, "it exposes your mistakes, that's for darn sure. It keeps you kind of humble. And you've got to be willing to be humble." She, too, noted the importance of supervisors' creating a supportive environment where learning could take place. "At our staff meetings we would try to be secure enough to put on the table what happened in your case, so that we could all learn from it," she said, adding that it was particularly important to be tolerant of learning "without scaring people away." She insisted that her workers "be personally strong enough to withstand that exposure. And then the critique that it comes from." One of Wagner's most eager students was Jim Henry, who described the following experience of being the subject to peer review as a "classic":

I had done an interview of . . . this girl. . . . Mom and the guy had threatened to kill her . . . and this was a very difficult interview because she didn't want to talk. . . . And it's so interesting on that tape is that I have my hand on her leg like this [shows us], and I'm leaning over and I say to her at one point I said, "Would it be helpful for you if I put my hand on the arm of the chair to make you feel better?" Totally oblivious to the fact that I had my hand on her leg.

## Lessons Learned

In the field of CSA interviewing, interviewers can often be so intent on gathering information that they are unaware of their body language. Henry's cluelessness during the interview is an extreme example. More common are interviewers who by facial expression or body posture reveal their belief or disbelief in the child's words. For example, interviewers may nod when they hear what they want to hear. Supervisor Donna Wagner viewed bringing these idiosyncrasies to the attention of her workers as essential, although she recognized that the worker would be "on pins and needles because they know people are watching [the video] and ten people are going to see it later." These tapes were an essential step on the road to improvement. She said, "That should be part of the training. To know that they're going to be critiqued: how they shift their leg, how they toss their hair, what eye contact they had, and every little thing and there's a better way maybe then to do it. And we're here to learn that the interview I do tomorrow is better than today's. But it won't be unless I'm able to look at today's."

Wagner and Henry described how, in the early days, they also learned to be aware of questioning techniques from reviewing their videos. Wagner saw the video as both "the epitome of exposure" and the ultimate learning opportunity. County professionals quickly discovered that they asked too many close-ended questions, ones requiring a "yes" or "no" response. Using the videos, they trained themselves to ask more open-ended questions, giving children the opportunity to provide information rather than merely to affirm or disconfirm information provided by the interviewer.

These challenges for interviewers of children who have been sexually abused are fairly universal and are the topic of research and practice advice today (see, for example, Lamb, Orbach, and Hershkowitz, 2007). For example, an open-ended probe would be, "Tell me about Mr. Jones [the suspect]," which invites a narrative, as opposed to, "Did Mr. Jones touch your peepee?" which is a close-ended probe (Yes/No). Children's responses to open-ended probes and questions are not only more accurate (see Orbach and Lamb, 1999), but they are more defensible in court (Myers, 1998). Open-ended probes are also more likely to elicit a narrative account of what happened (Faller, 2007). In St. Mary County, which privileges the child's version of what happened, it is extra-important to obtain a narrative account (see chapter 7).

As Henry put it, "And watching how each of us would do that in terms of too leading versus open-ended versus you moved too soon." The "you moved too soon" issue referred to the pacing the interview—choosing the appropriate moment to ask about abuse, tolerating silences, waiting until the child has had an opportunity to respond to a question, and not interrupting the child's narrative or response. Again, pacing of questions is another issue that persists today for interviewers.

Although what Henry described certainly makes a great deal of sense, it took another fifteen years before professionals in the child sexual abuse field began to institute peer review of videotaped interviews (see Davies and Faller, 2004; Faller, 2005). Getting and giving feedback on interview techniques as a method to improve interviews is now considered best practice.

## Law Enforcement Review of Videotapes

CPS workers were not the only ones learning lessons from reviewing their videotapes. Other participants in the protocol learned from one another and from their mistakes. Ed Williams appears to have been the first police officer to take the plunge and start doing child interviews. Ed Duke, who was police chief and now is retired, did not want to be outdone and pirated questions from Williams. Officer Duke also reported on his thinking process, recalling that he said to himself, "'I'd like to get better at this, but I just haven't had that much experience.' You watch a couple of those videotapes and you'll get a lot of experience." Officer Duke described how viewing videos and interviews helped him learn: "I've actually been in the room when the video is going on in another room watching the monitor because, by God, if it works for Ed Williams, it might just work for me. I mean, hell, I'm gonna cheat. I'm gonna take some notes and I'll remember to ask that question. That was a damn good question! You know, that type of thing."

The craft of interviewing children involves both asking "good," open-ended questions and covering the bases so that all the abuse details are obtained. Interviewers must learn the "who," "what," "where," "when," and "how" of the child's victimization. Having a catalogue of good questions, perhaps first on paper but ideally in your head, helps make an interviewer skilled.

Thus, the St. Mary County professionals who took on the role of child interviewer were learners as well as collaborators. They were also risk-takers, wanting new skills and being willing to be subjected to the scrutiny of their peers. These were transformational experiences for them.

## Prosecutor Review of Videotapes

In the early days, the final level of scrutiny was by the prosecutor, Charles Davis, who would view the videotape and pass judgment. Henry described the process:

> Charles Davis was . . . the ultimate critiquer. . . . He would watch those [videotapes] and he would say to you, "What the hell are you doing?" Charles was saying, "You know I got to get a criminal case here." And so . . . he would say to me, "Jim, that was a good interview. Jim, that was a bad interview." And, "You know you shouldn't have done this. You shouldn't have done that." So it was not only just watching but having Davis's feedback as somebody who certainly communicated [that he was] a man of integrity, to say, "I want a clean case."

Davis set the community standard and taught others how to deliver a "clean case," such that the child interview would support a successful criminal case. A priority goal of the investigation was to conduct interviews and interrogations that would lead to a criminal conviction. But that does not mean that the goals of child safety and child well-being were second in priority. There appeared to have been a community consensus around all three goals, even though each profession had its individual primary objectives. Under Davis's strong leadership there was collective ownership of the endeavor. Wagner spoke wistfully about the lack of "turf issues" in those days. It was all about building relationships and maintaining them. She and Davis spoke frequently, and both immediately answered each other's calls. Their responsiveness included being willing to understand the needs of others. Both at the supervisor level, such as between Davis and Wagner, and at the front-line level, such as between Henry and the other Sex Busters, it created an integrated and holistic approach to CSA cases in St. Mary County. But what did it look like in action?

## A CASE IN POINT

A good investigation is much more than a good interview. Jim Henry and St. Mary Chief Prosecutor Mark Jameson separately described a case that demonstrates the characteristics of high-quality investigations: case planning, collaboration, and boundary crossing and blurring that ultimately resulted in a successful outcome.

The case started with a twelve-year old girl, Kathy, described by Jameson as "a big girl," and her stepfather, Ethan Osborne. Jameson told the research team that Kathy was vague in her disclosure when Henry interviewed her, describing her father's grabbing her "butt" and "pinching her boobs." Henry said, "She told me this much," showing a smidgen of space between his thumb and index finger. State trooper Ed Williams and polygraphist Rick Rivers interrogated Ethan and he confessed to something slightly different, "grabbing her crotch when she was walking by." So Henry said, "Ed let him go home, and said (playing it kind of friendly), 'Well, we'll contact you in a couple of days.'" Kathy was placed in a foster home.

However, when police did a criminal records check, they discovered that Ethan was no neophyte child abuser. He had a manslaughter conviction in another state for killing his two-year-old child. Henry described him as a "hardened criminal," while Jameson told us that this crime made him a "habitual offender."

At that point, they were ready to arrest Ethan, but he and his wife could not be found, even though their apartment was right across the street from the courthouse. Henry said, "Well, they lived probably about a mile from [the CPS office]. Maybe not even that far. So I would go by all the time just 'cause I knew they were hanging out there. So I went there one day . . . in the afternoon and I'll never forget it. I knocked on the door and—and they said, 'Come in.' Well, I came in and he's got a knife to the wife's throat, and said, 'You guys aren't going to get me.' And so you know I'm like, 'Oh, man! What is this?'"

At the time, Henry had a student intern with him. He was in a quandary about what to do, but he said, "I didn't think he would do anything, because you know they had a relationship." Henry sent the student to contact the police, but he stayed behind until nearly twenty police officers showed up, probably the totality of law enforcement for St. Mary County. Henry said, "Well, there's all these cops, you know, and you hear him [Ethan] screaming, 'I'm going to kill her! I'm going to kill her!'"

Since the Osbornes' apartment was right across the street from the courthouse, Jameson and a former FBI hostage expert, Barry, who lived in St. Mary, arrived and took charge. Henry stayed for the next three hours until the conclusion of the case. "I'm in the room, this guy's [Ethan] in the room, and the cops. I walk in and out 'cause Barry's . . . talking him down. . . . Finally he [Ethan] said, 'I've taken some drugs.' So he's getting you know he's groggy supposedly, and Ethan was an actor. So we said, 'Well, we'll call an ambulance.'" Two police officers showed up disguised as Emergency Medical Services personnel. Henry said, "So they go in and they're going to check him for blood pressure. So as soon as they checked him for blood pressure, then, they cuffed him." Jameson remembered the case a little differently. He said the cops gave Ethan some water, which had sleeping pills in it. In any case, the police officers, in EMS disguise, "got the guy out of there and got him arrested and locked his ass up," according to Jameson.

But the complexity and collaboration on the case continued. Ethan repeatedly telephoned CPS worker Henry and Trooper Williams from jail. According to Henry, he begged them to visit. "He says, 'Come on over here [to the jail]. I want to talk to you guys.'" Henry wondered why Ethan was reaching out to them because he and Williams were the ones who "locked his ass up."

Finally, Henry decided to go over to the jail and talk to Ethan. Henry reported Ethan had instructed, "'Bring Mandy [Ethan's wife] with you.' So I bring Mandy over there. I'm sitting over there talking to him and he's talking to me." Mandy was crying. Henry ended the session without any clear idea of the session's purpose.

Puzzled by this encounter with Ethan and Mandy, Henry pondered the case over the weekend. "Finally, it comes to me that, you know, he's trying to tell me that Mandy was also involved. All right? The mother! So the first thing that Monday morning I go in and interview Kathy, and you know so it's very sad. . . . Kathy tells all about Mom sticking things inside of her and the threesome, and Ethan taking a picture." In Jameson's recollection, those "things" were cigars and hangers.

Henry immediately conveyed this information to Williams, who secured a warrant to search the apartment for the photographs. Henry and Williams conducted the search together. They found suggestive but not pornographic pictures of Kathy. Henry recounted, "We arrested Mandy right away, and of course Rick Rivers is available immediately [to polygraph her] because we all planned this."

In chapter 3, Henry describes how he and Officer Williams went to a residential treatment center in an adjacent state where Kathy's seventeen-year-old sister was living and showed her the video of Kathy's interview. Kathy's sister told them, "You know, Ethan is the father of all my babies." The older sister had had four pregnancies. She had kept the last baby. The baby was born out of state. After learning these facts, prosecutor Jameson urged the authorities in that state to file criminal charges against Ethan, but they declined.

The St. Mary case had a successful criminal court outcome, although Jameson and Henry differed in telling about the process somewhat. In either case, the indisputable facts are that Ethan was sentenced to twenty-eight years in prison, and Mandy to eight. This was an uncommon outcome, for female perpetrators are uncommon; only five were identified in the St. Mary court file data, while in other studies, female perpetrators range from 1 to 5 percent (Faller, 1995; Freeman and Sandler, 2008). Many cases involving female offenders, like this one, also involve a male offender.

In summarizing the successful outcome of this grimly serious case, Jameson said, "What made it work was the experience of Jim Henry, the experience of Rick Rivers, the polygraph operator, the experience of Ed Williams, the state police officer who was working it, and the experience of our office to stay on it all the way through prosecution and sentencing."

But all was not perfect on this case. Kathy's knee was the one Henry had unwittingly put his hand on in the now-classic video recording. He learned about the effect of this touching three years later, when Kathy no longer had a place on his caseload. Consistent with his boundary-stretching practices, Henry went and interviewed her and asked her why she was so reluctant to disclose Ethan's abuse at the outset. Kathy told him that his hand on her knee reminded her of how Ethan would approach her when he intended to sexually abuse her.

## Lessons Learned from Kathy's Case

This case example is instructive in many ways. Throughout the investigation, the professionals planned collaboratively and communicate constantly. Although they each engaged in role-specific tasks, they were flexible and willing to cross professional boundaries, sometimes going well beyond their roles. Jameson attributed case success to their "experience," but it was more than experience. There was fluidity in their understanding about how to work these cases.

At the beginning, note that all three of the Sex Busters were working in close collaboration—the CPS worker interviewing the child, the state police officer and the polygraph operator interrogating the suspect. Likewise, Williams did a criminal history check, but he went one step farther by communicating the findings to Henry. The police had the responsibility to arrest Ethan, but Henry took it upon himself to regularly to check Ethan's apartment. The child had been removed and was in a safe place, so there was no continuing child-protection issue. Henry's job was over until future legal proceedings were held. Looking for the suspect should be a police responsibility.

Most CPS workers would have rapidly retreated as soon as they encountered an agitated Ethan with a knife to his wife's throat. From a safe distance, they would have called the police. Henry's commitment to the case and belief in role blending led him to stay. Relying on his clinical skills and previous knowledge of the Osbornes, he believed that neither he nor Mandy was in imminent danger and that the case was best served by awaiting the arrival of the police.

Close collaboration again was seen in calling Jameson, the prosecutor to come to the scene. Of course, the fact the prosecutor's office was right across the street from the suspect's apartment helped. Following his appearance, consistent with the role of the prosecutor in the protocol and, indeed, in most communities, Jameson took over. Most CPS workers would not have stayed for three hours of hostage negotiations. Yet, Henry had a relationship with these parents and their child. He had an interest in the overall case handling and the connection of the various parts of the case. The fact that Henry stayed during the hostage negotiations may have been one of the reasons Ethan reached out to him when he was in jail. Henry responded to Ethan's persistent pleas to pay him a visit in jail and bring his wife—again an example of going beyond job boundaries.

Both the visit and collecting Ethan's wife suggest an extended commitment to understanding this family and its dynamics. Henry remained preoccupied with the case over the weekend—an illustration of the priority placed upon sexual abuse cases. This preoccupation resulted in a breakthrough in his understanding of the Friday session and an immediate response on Monday morning. He interviewed Kathy again, another example of boundary stretching because Kathy was safe, but he worried that he missed information relevant to the criminal investigation.

Henry and Williams together conducted a search for pornographic pictures of Kathy, based on a warrant obtained by Williams. While normally a social worker would not have been present for the execution of a search warrant, both the front-line police officer and the social worker (and presumably their supervisors) saw this as a joint activity. Collaborative action was again seen in confronting Mandy about her involvement in Kathy's abuse. Rick Rivers was waiting in the wings to polygraph Mandy after Henry interviewed her. Finally, Henry and Williams took an out-of-state trek to the residential treatment center to see Kathy's sister, an example of collaboration, boundary stretching, and commitment. When Henry and Williams learned that Kathy's sister had been abused, too, Prosecutor Jameson reached out to another jurisdiction in the hope that it would pursue additional criminal charges.

## THEN AND NOW

Kathy's case illustrates how much more goes into a successful investigation of a sexual-abuse case than interviewing a child and interrogating a suspect. However, most of the professionals we interviewed in St. Mary County agreed that the level of collaboration and priority had not persisted for the entire twenty years that the protocol had been in place. Describing present practice, Shawn Duffy, a police officer involved in investigations, stated, "Child Protective Services has their role, I have my role, and then the prosecutors have their role to conclude the job. We all work together but we're not all there at the same time."

Wagner provided a contrasting description of early practice. CPS supervisor in the beginning and foster-care supervisor at the time of her interview, the twenty-two-year child-welfare veteran said, "We lived and breathed this stuff [sexual abuse investigations]. If a call came in, everything

[else] sat, and you went." She said this was true for all of the professionals, not just CPS worker but also police officer, polygraphist, and prosecutor. She illustrated by saying that if Charles Davis, the prosecutor who crafted the protocol, wanted an investigation, "breakfast stopped."

No longer directly involved in the investigation of criminal sexual conduct (CSC) cases, she worried, "I'm not so sure where we're at today." Assistant Prosecutor Jane Jacobson, who carried out sex crimes prosecutions for a time, described the Sex Busters as "a well-oiled machine" but said, "the machine sort of started falling apart."

Similarly, Chief Prosecutor Mark Jameson described professional response as he was about to leave the prosecutor's office and become a judge: "Someone comes in with a CSC investigation on a small child and they'll run out the back door." He caught himself, qualifying this assertion, saying, "That isn't true across the board. We've got some very good CSC cops in the county," naming several. He added, "But some people who really cared about what they were doing and made it all work [moved on]." In the beginning, this melding of CPS and law-enforcement roles worked well because of the compatibility of personalities and the fact that both Jim Henry and Ed Williams "had a heart for kids," as did Charles Davis and Rick Rivers.

## INSTITUTIONAL SUPPORT

Prioritizing successful outcomes in CSA cases was more than just the commitment of frontline professionals. There was community and institutional support for close collaboration among CPS, law enforcement, and the prosecutor's office. In St. Mary County, this collaboration preceded by fifteen years mandated collaboration, which is now codified in the Child Protection Law. Henry put it this way: "Moor, the agency director, was very much in favor of it, saw it as a great possibility. At that point, the informal network between Moor and Charles Davis, Donna Wagner, as administrators was positive. And the boundary of 'this is CPS or not CPS' was not there. The sexual abuse [cases] needed to be done. Moor was very open to saying, 'We'll do it.'"

Wagner believed that her job included facilitating this boundary-spanning for the front-line workers under her supervision. So while Wagner understood her responsibility to train good CPS interviewers, she also believed that she should "free them up enough from our bureaucratic obligations so that they could be available to do those interviews in a timely fashion. And we bent the rules a little here and there to see that that happened." She provided, as example, the delayed report. 'Henry, where is that report?" She mimicked in a frantic voice, "Oh, I gotta go do an interview.' 'Oh, all right; get me the report later when you get back.' You know, you've sort of made allowances because it was your priority, too." In the end, if there was a price to pay, supervisors were willing to pay it. Said Wagner, "If there was heat to take for it, you just kind of took that heat."

Veteran police officer Ed Duke sums up the St. Mary County experience: "The reason why it was successful here is a combination of a stubborn prosecutor and some department heads that bought into the program." But Ed Williams, who was then a community-services officer and had more freedom to collaborate, had the ability to dedicate himself to sexual abuse for a different reason. He believed "the post commander and my sergeants had no control over me because I'd come in in the morning and then I'd be gone with Henry or Rivers working CSCs day in and day out, weekends, nights, evenings." Although the community protocol remained, institutional commitment was perhaps not as strong as it was in the beginning. The success rate in criminal cases remained high, but there may be different factors that account for it; for example, the confession rate remained at 64 percent of those charged, and the number of cases that went to trial was consistently 4 percent. The proportion of suspects offered a polygraph remained at higher than 60 percent, and the proportion of pleas to a sex crime was consistently about 70 percent. As Jameson, the second prosecutor, observed when comparing the beginning to 2002: "And so those people, my predecessor, Charles Davis, Jim Henry, those early cops, made it all work, and so now it just sort of perpetuates itself."

## WORKING TOGETHER WITH SEPARATE MANDATES, MISSIONS, AND METHODS

Our interviews with the professionals in St. Mary County suggested that great successes characterized the beginnings. A number of participants in our study find the current role differentiation frustrating, but blended boundaries and role sharing have their limitations. Child protection and law enforcement have different mandates and missions and typically employ different methods.

## Mandates

In terms of mandated jurisdiction, CPS is only responsible for cases in which caretakers pose a threat to their children, in sexual abuse, cases in which the caretaker is the alleged offender or has failed to protect the child from sexual abuse and thereby is neglectful. Research on identified cases indicates they are about evenly split between intrafamilial sexual abuse, which is within the CPS mandate, and extrafamilial sexual abuse, which usually is not (Faller, 1994).

In contrast, law enforcement has a mandate to investigate all crimes, regardless of the suspect-victim relationship. Although there are criminal statutes that cover all types of child maltreatment in the state, sexual abuse and life-threatening physical abuse take precedence for police over neglect and emotional maltreatment. CPS, on the other hand, is supposed to investigate all types of child maltreatment by caretakers. In most communities, child neglect and minor physical abuse comprise about 70 percent of their caseload, and sexual abuse only about 10 percent (National Child Abuse and Neglect Data System, 2004). These differences in CPS and police mandates suggest the need for community negotiation about when to partner and when to uncouple.

## Missions

Moreover, CPS and law enforcement have different missions. The mission of child protective services is to ensure child safety and well-being. The mission of law enforcement is crime investigation. CPS workers are out to save children; police officers are out to catch criminals. As Officer Shawn Duffy put it, "I think Protective Services concentrating on the child to make sure the child's safe. My role is to make sure the bad guy tells me and the bad guy's put someplace where he can't do this anymore."

In addition, the amount of evidence these agencies need to achieve their missions differs substantially. When Jim Henry was a CPS worker, the amount of evidence required to substantiate a child protection case was "some credible evidence." One could roughly quantify this standard as a 25 percent probability that child abuse or neglect had taken place.

The amount of evidence necessary for the family court to gain temporary jurisdiction over a child in a child protection proceeding is a "preponderance of the legally admissible evidence," sometimes referred to as 51 percent of the evidence (*United States v. Rosa*, 1542).

To terminate a parent's rights in a civil child-protective proceeding, the court must find a legal basis to do so by "clear and convincing evidence," or 75 percent of the evidence (*State v. Hodge*, 376). In contrast, a criminal case must be proven by legally admissible evidence that demonstrates the defendant's guilt "beyond a reasonable doubt," or 95–99 percent probability that the person charged committed the crime (*People v. Johnson*, 980). In the case of children who qualify as Native Americans under the Indian Child Welfare Act, the standards of proof are higher—clear and convincing evidence to take temporary jurisdiction, and beyond a reasonable doubt to terminate parental rights.

The different proof levels for different legal actions are displayed in table 4.1.

The reader may wonder rightfully what scale professionals use to determine whether their evidence meets the necessary standard. The answer is that the weighing of evidence takes place in the minds of the people making the decisions—initially CPS workers and police officers, and later judges and juries. Thus, the weighing of the evidence is, to a substantial degree, subjective.

Moreover, court requirements for victims who are witnesses vary depending upon whether the case is child-protective or criminal. In a child-protection case there are statutory provisions that may make child testimony unnecessary (Child Welfare Information Gateway, 2008). In

Table 4.1 Different levels of evidence required for CPS actions and criminal prosecution

| Standard of Proof | Percentage | Action |
| --- | --- | --- |
| Some credible evidence | 25 | Open a CPS case |
| Preponderance of the evidence | 51 | Take temporary jurisdiction of a child |
| Clear and convincing evidence | 75 | Terminate parental rights |
| Beyond a reasonable doubt | 95–99 | Prove a criminal case |

contrast, if a criminal case goes to trial, the child almost always must take the witness stand.

Consequently, in a given case, CPS might be successful in carrying out its protective mission while law enforcement is unsuccessful in its prosecutorial mission. Indeed, the child-protection statutes in many states require a separate decision regarding safety when law enforcement recommends not charging the suspect (National Center for the Prosecution of Child Abuse, 1997).

Because of the different missions, different standards of proof required, and differences regarding the necessity of child testimony, joint CPS–law enforcement investigations are not easily effected. In their book on collaboration, Donna Pence, a sex-crimes investigator, and Charles Wilson, a child-welfare administrator, review the research on these collaborations and find that successful efforts are uncommon. They characterize the alliance between CPS and law enforcement in CSA cases as an uneasy one (Pence and Wilson, 1994).

## Methods

Complicating the sexual abuse investigation process further, the methods used for its two major components, the child interview and the suspect interrogation, are essentially diametrically opposed. Both investigative endeavors seek to uncover the truth, but by very different strategies.

### Child Interviewing

The child interviewer is admonished to approach the child interview with multiple hypotheses (for example, that the child was sexually abused, or that the child was not). A child-friendly place, such as a special interview room, is recommended for the interview (Jones et al., 2007; National Children's Alliance, n.d.). The interviewer should begin by trying to make the child comfortable and building rapport. The interviewer gives the child space and follows the child's pace. Touching the child is usually not advised.

The interviewer is supposed to scrupulously avoid leading, pressuring, or coercing the child (Faller, 2007; Poole and Lamb, 1998). Information should be obtained from the child, not supplied by the interviewer with a request to confirm or disconfirm (Faller, 2007). The interviewer employs questions that are as open-ended as possible and attempts to elicit a narrative account from the child about what, if anything, happened. For example, the interviewer might begin with probes such as, "Tell me why you came to talk to me" or, "Tell me everything about what happened from the beginning to the end" (Sternberg et al., 2000). The interviewer waits for the child to stop talking before using additional open-ended probes, such as "Anything else?" "What happened next?" (Faller, 2007).

Children are usually reluctant to disclose sexual abuse, but the interviewer is advised to avoid leading questions and not to manipulate the child, for example, by offering incentives for disclosure or citing dire consequences for failure to disclose.

Ironically, interviewers are often unaware they are manipulating. In his interview, Henry described a second enlightening peer-review experience. An early videotaped interview was of a seven-year-old girl. He told her, "Well, you know, when we get done, we'll get some ice cream." Prosecutor Charles Davis spotted this manipulation and used this interview clip widely in training to illustrate unintended cajoling, or as Henry characterizes Davis's admonition, "Don't ever say 'get ice cream.'"

Despite the temptation, interviewers are advised to avoid vilifying the suspect to children. As Officer Jeff Penn noted, "You can't make him out to be that pervert in prison and we're going to keep him there. Although that's the way I feel."

Most child interviews are of short duration, on average about an hour (DeVoe and Faller, 1999). Limited-length interviews are responsive to the child's short attention span and the need to avoid "interview fatigue," which refers to a hypothesis that when child interviews are long, children may affirm incorrect acts and facts just to get the interview over with or because they are no longer able to attend to the questions (Faller, 2007). It is interesting that a parallel process has been noted in false confessions by suspects, which are associated with protracted interrogations (Kassin, 2006).

The series of strategies just described reflect the fact that children are more suggestible than adults and a concern that interviewers may elicit false allegations by pressuring the child or asking leading questions.

## Suspect Interrogation

In contrast, interviewing and interrogating criminal suspects has the goal of eliciting a confession or, at the least, admissions that are legally damning

(Kassin, 2006; Layton, n.d.; Leo, 1996). Pioneers in developing and defin-ing police interrogation techniques were Inbau and Reid. According to the Reid technique (Inbau et al., 2001), there is a brief preinterrogation interview that determines the suspect's guilt (Kassin, 2006). The inter-rogation then proceeds on the presumption that the suspect did what he or she is accused of doing, and the goal of the interrogation is to get the suspect to "give it up" (Leo, 1996). This view of suspect interrogation is reflected in Ed Duke's comment: "You know, and the way [to] corroborate [the child's statement] is when you get done sucking on the perpetrator's nose, his head's all caved in and he's told you exactly the same thing that little Susie told you."

In St. Mary County, the belief by police and other professionals that the suspect did the crime is not an unreasonable one, given that the child has already disclosed. Moreover, existing research has found false accusa-tions of sexual abuse by children are uncommon (Faller, 1984, 1988; Jones and McGraw, 1987; Oates et al., 2000; Trocme and Bala, 2005). Nonethe-less, holding this hypothesis when entering into the interrogation process is very different from the multiple hypothesis process advised when ini-tiating the child interview.

Other interrogation practices include deceiving the suspect by indicating that police have information they do not, in fact, possess, such as fingerprints or DNA evidence (Kassin, 2006; Kassin et al., 2007). In St. Mary County, police used the child's videotaped disclo-sures to confront the suspect (see chapter 5), but former Chief Pros-ecutor Charles Davis believed that many suspects thought that these child interview videotapes were admissible in court. State law has since been changed and now permits limited use of videos in court, but at the time they were inadmissible. It was a misconception that neither law-enforcement officers nor the prosecutor's office felt compelled to clear up.

The interrogation venue should be sparse, and the suspect should be positioned so that he or she feels disadvantaged (Inbau et al., 2001). In addition, the interrogation process may involve deliberate invasion of the suspect's physical space (Layton, n.d.). This may be done to trigger discomfort or to feign intimacy (Leo, 1996). Touching the suspect is a strategy that is recommended as a way of getting the suspect's attention and demonstrating camaraderie (Inbau et al.; Layton, n.d.). Usually the pace of the interview is determined by the interrogator, not the suspect

(Layton, n.d.). Interrogations frequently last several hours (Kassin, 2006). If the suspect attempts to protest innocence, then he or she is interrupted (Inbau et al., 2001; Layton, n.d.). Leading questions are employed extensively, and brief affirmative responses from the suspect are sufficient, although narrative accounts of the perpetration are also welcome (Kassin, 2006).

Manipulation of the suspect is the stuff of good interrogations (Kassin, et al., 2007; Inbau et al., 2001). Although Mirandizing the suspect is required when suspects are in custody, in a survey of 631 police investigators, Kassin and colleagues (2007) describe a series of maneuvers employed to circumvent the effect of the Miranda warnings. These include interviewing suspects when they are not in custody, gaining an implicit waiver (reading the rights but not requiring suspects to affirm they waive), and minimizing the importance of the Miranda protections.

In St. Mary County, officers Mirandized suspects even though they were not in custody. However, Officer Ed Duke made this comment about reading a suspect Miranda rights:

> I don't want anybody to think that I would ever intentionally violate somebody's constitutional rights, but if you read a Miranda, I mean you know as an investigator whether you're going to lock their ass up when they show up. . . . So you better read a Miranda. And my whole take on Miranda is: it's their rights and they're not mine. So I'll read a Miranda the first thing. Get that shit out of the way. "Now we're going to watch a 45-minute videotape [of the child's disclosure]." And you know what? They have all those constitutional rights that I've made sure to remind them of and protect 'em, and they don't remember a goddamned one of 'em. So you move right on to the interrogation mode.

For Duke, the purpose of reading the suspect his rights was to assure that the legal case was protected. Indeed, in 80 percent of cases, suspects waive their Miranda rights (Kassin et al., 2007; Leo and White, 1999). Duke read the rights before the suspect viewed the child-interview videotape so that rights would be remote and the child's disclosure foremost in the suspect's mind when the actual interrogation began.

Duke then went on to cite a case where this strategy evidently was very successful against a man he called a "nasty, nasty, nasty" CSC suspect:

And when he gets done watching the videotape with myself and Rick Rivers, he jumps up out of his chair and I thought, "Ooh shit, I'm gonna really get to smack this son-of-a-bitch in the mouth," 'cause I didn't care much for him. He jumps up and he says, "I got one goddamned thing to tell you guys. Everything them boys says is true." Oh, my God, oh my God! I couldn't believe him. Shit, guys don't say stuff like that. I mean this was just some nasty shit."

Duke expressed his surprise in the suspect's animated confession. He added: "You know, I always tried to make sure that I protected their rights as much as they needed to be protected."

Use of psychologically coercive and manipulative methods during the course of interrogation is expected (see Inbau et al., 2001) and has been found to be legal (*Minnesota v. Murphy*; *Miranda v. Arizona*). Although physically harmful methods to induce a confession were found to be a violation of the suspect's constitutional right in the 1930s (*Brown v. Mississippi*), interrogators may attempt to appeal to the suspect's concern for the child or other aspects of his or her better nature as a strategy to elicit a confession. A common theme in the interviews with law-enforcement professionals in St. Mary County was one of being a kinder, gentler interrogator. Rick Rivers emphasized the importance of forming a relationship with the suspect:

There has to be some level of connection. It may be small and it may be major, depending on the individual. But you have to invest something into that interview process as far as getting to the truth, no matter where it's at. And it's—and not to judge. I mean it's—it's easy to judge because then you can divorce yourself from the act itself and you don't have to have anything emotionally connected to it. That's the easy process. Anybody can walk in and say, "You're a liar. You're a no good S.O.B." and walk out. Well, he won't talk.

Ed Williams said the following about sex offenders:

I wasn't happy with 'em, but the other issue is that I knew I had a job to do and the job was to do what I could to get them to tell what they did because it would help everybody. And that would help that child who has already been victimized. So there was sometimes you can just swallow and smile and try not to be two-faced about it, but just turn to 'em and say, "Hey, I'm your best friend and you better be talking to me. I mean we need to get this out. I need to help you. Do you think you need help?" "Yeah." "Okay." Well, then you're in the door. You know, there was a lot of same peer group people [other police officers] who didn't understand how I could smile after I got this guy to confess to fifteen-years-to-life felony. But then I did [laughs]. After he was already cuffed and stuffed we might say, why then you celebrate and say, "Okay. That was good. That was good."

Usually interrogators are "two-faced about it." They rarely form an alliance with a sex offender because they genuinely empathize with the suspect, but rather for the utilitarian purpose of obtaining a confession or getting at the truth. Given the nature of their sex crimes, the lack of genuine empathy is to be expected. Ed Williams's comments reflected the tensions among being nice to someone who has done something "nasty," as Ed Duke would say, manipulating someone into admitting a crime with a sentence of fifteen years to life, and the disdain of colleagues because he is nice to sex offenders.

## Challenges in Interviewing Children

The typical police officer receives much more training in interrogating suspects than in interviewing children about possible abuse. St. Mary County officers were no different. Shawn Duffy, a police officer for more than fifteen years with more than two hundred child interviews under his belt, said about his training in interviewing children: "No, I've never been formally trained and I've been to the Reid Interrogation School, you know, but never been formally trained in interviewing children. Never." Moreover, many police officers are reluctant child interviewers. Ed Duke made the following observation: "I have guys here that don't feel comfortable talking about sex with their wife. So . . . that's gonna be a real hard sell to get 'em to sit on the floor and talk to somebody that they don't know about sex."

The voices of the law-enforcement professionals we interviewed in St. Mary County reflected the struggle and degree of discomfort with the child interview. Ed Williams articulated these feelings in describing how it felt to have to do child interviews: "Cause I felt uncomfortable at that time. Now later, as we had to, as we couldn't get a social services person available immediately and or the parent would bring the child to the [state police] post, at that time, then I started doing a few [child interviews]. But it was out of necessity." This discomfort was reflected as well in Ed Duke's description of himself conducting a child interview: "I did a three-year-old victim one time. And it's like, 'Oh shit, this ain't fun.' I mean I'm struggling. I'm fat, dumb and happy and sitting on the floor with this little girl trying to get her to tell me what mommy's boyfriend did to her, okay?"

Finally, because child victims are typically reluctant to talk, they can be very frustrating to deal with, increasing the temptation to resort to manipulation and psychological coercion. This is a special risk for law-enforcement officers, who are trained in interrogation techniques that rely upon manipulation and various forms of coercion, but other professionals may also experience the frustration and desire to compel children to talk.

## ST. MARY COUNTY SOLUTIONS

The lack of congruence between the law-enforcement role and training and child interviewing was reflected in policies that ceded the child interview to CPS, as was found early on in St. Mary County. Although that policy changed as expertise grew in St. Mary County, it also changed because Moor left and the new director decided CPS was not going to do law enforcement's work. Pressure of other types of cases and ever-present budget constraints also likely influenced a shift away from sexual abuse as a priority. Interviews with CPS investigators and law enforcement in 2002 indicated variable response to accommodate the case and the law enforcement jurisdiction. Cecilia Berg, a CPS worker who followed in Henry's footsteps, described the collaborative process:

> We would determine what the venue would be so we knew which police department to notify, make them aware of what was going on, and then they would have an officer available to meet with us at the school or hospital or wherever we were going to be doing the interview. They generally seem to prefer one of us to take the initiative in the questions. I'm sure a lot of that has to do with the intimidation of an officer being present. They will generally kind of sit back quietly off to the side and many times even come without their uniform on. But it's nice to have them there; not only the fact that

they're hearing firsthand what's being said, but if there are questions that we miss getting or getting complete enough answers that they need, that they are able to then either tell us or ask the questions themselves.

Berg described a good solution to the dilemma of police discomfort with interviewing children and their need to know. She also raised another rationale for CPS to conduct the child interview; children may be more frightened of a police officer than a CPS worker.

But evidently this was not the only way investigative roles were divided in St. Mary County in 2002. Carol Bragg, the CPS supervisor and Cecilia's immediate boss, saw joint investigations somewhat differently and described more variation. Bragg said:

> Local law-enforcement agencies do get that attitude. They see us as a resource for them and . . . they're not necessarily a resource for us. . . . Usually with State Police, it's usually together more often times than not. Sheriff's Department, it often times they want to defer to us and they'll say, "Just send us your videotape now." So things aren't the way they used to be. It used to be always together and now it's not always together. It just kind of depends on a case-by-case basis. Sometimes . . . if we have 'em in here . . . with the forensic interviewing protocol, you're not supposed to have all these extra people in there, so they may look at it from the observation room. So it's more and more CPS doing it and local communities local officers disengaging it and saying, "Give us your videotape; we'll review it and then we'll send it on to the prosecutor." They, historically, of course, want to do the perpetrator interviews. They're much more comfortable with that area.

Bragg's statement reflected the reemergence of Charles Davis's observation that these institutions "don't necessarily like each other and work well together." In addition, both Bragg and Berg described practices for situations in which CPS has a mandate to be involved in the investigation; that is situations in which the offender is within the family. These practices do not address cases involving unrelated offenders. Their responses suggested that boundary stretching and priority on sexual abuse, regardless of who the offender was, were no longer part of the CPS response.

This change in response was captured in one of the first things Carol Bragg said in her interview: "As to actually using the protocol, I don't." What she probably meant was that she did not perceive the CPS role as embedded in the larger community commitment to justice in child sexual abuse cases. Probably she viewed herself and her workers as answerable to her superiors in CPS rather than to the St. Mary County community through the prosecutor's office. The CPS manual, which is the manual for the entire state, drove her practice. Although CPS cooperates with law enforcement on cases within the CPS mandate, they apparently no longer go out of their way to conduct child interviews on cases outside their mandate.

## CONCLUSION

Core to shifting the burden of proving sexual abuse from the child to the community is institutional support and frontline collaboration. Commitment to the addressing sexual abuse and flexibility of roles were key factors in St. Mary County's development of a "well-oiled machine" for investigating child sexual abuse allegations. This unique collaboration could not have happened were it not for the community consensus that children come first, the support of supervisors, like Wagner, and agency administrators, like Moor, and the determined leadership of the prosecutor's office.

But, as the discussion of the differences in mission, mandate, and method of child protective services and law enforcement illuminates, this alliance is of necessity an uneasy one (Pence and Wilson, 1994) and must be periodically renegotiated. When the protocol was first developed in St. Mary County, these differences between child protection and law enforcement were overridden by the commitment and the charisma of the key players. The more traditional division of labor reported by professionals as we completed our data gathering in 2002 appeared to be an accommodation to the differences in mission, mandate, and method of the investigators. An important factor in this settling into more traditional roles was the development of state and federal policies related to child sexual abuse that did not exist when the "Sex Busters" first developed their "well-oiled machine."

Finally, our data gathering ended with the end of an era in St. Mary during which many assistant prosecutors became chief prosecutors, and then some transitioned to be judges. A twenty-eight-year-old prosecutor was recently elected, with roots in the community but no history in CSA prosecution in the community. How he will handle those cases is unknown.

# FIVE

# Professional Practitioners' Views on Videotaping

## Capturing and Conveying a Child's Story

KAREN M. STALLER AND

FRANK E. VANDERVORT

I mean, you've gotta have balls the size of coconuts

to go against some of these kids, because you can

see the wings on their back.

—Ed Duke, Police Chief

When St. Mary County first experimented with capturing children's interviews on videotape, it stumbled on two primary advantages, although Prosecutor Charles Davis was uncertain about the driving force behind the initiative—"the idea to avoid multiple interviews, [or] to induce confessions." Among other things, the county discovered that if young accusers confronted adult suspects through the medium of videotape, the suspects seemed to confess. At the same time, these children would not have to be subjected to multiple interviews. These two factors, preserving the child's story and encouraging confession by suspects, are central to the mission of shifting the burden of proving the case from the child onto the professionals.

Although these core factors continue to be foremost on the minds of the professionals in the community, what is truly remarkable about the decision to videotape the initial interview with a child is the breadth of arguments that are now made in its favor and the diversity of sources from which they come. Professionals from all walks of the child-welfare and criminal-justice systems can find the good in videotaping. Furthermore, the benefits they identify span every stage of the process from initial assessment to trial. Videotaping child interviews seems to have garnered almost universal community support in St. Mary County. In part, this may be because the constituent players in the process do not take an isolationist view of videotaping, but rather see it as part of an overall investigative process. As such, it can be used to facilitate and accomplish their individual professional goals. In contrast, much of the scholarly literature on the pros and cons of videotaping children is limited to one stage of a larger legal process, the investigative phase before charges are filed, and the possible consequences that videotaping at this stage may have on a subsequent trial. What has not been fully considered in the literature is how use of videotaping may work in concert with other investigative methods (see Stern, 1992; Veith, 1999; Vandervort, 2006).

## IS VIDEOTAPING BEST PRACTICE?

Professionals have recognized the importance of accurately documenting forensic interviews with children who may have been sexually abused (Faller, 2007; APSAC, 1990, 1997). Practitioners and researchers alike have experimented with, studied, and debated the most effective means of documentation. Three methods of documentation have been examined: note taking (contemporaneous and noncontemporaneous), audiotaping, and videotaping.

### Note Taking and Audio Recording

Note taking has been the most widely used method for documenting forensic interviews (Faller, 2007). Researchers have studied its efficacy. Lamb and his colleagues compared "verbatim contemporaneous" notes taken by Israeli Youth Investigators, a group of forensic interviewers, of twenty interviews with children suspected of having been sexually abused with transcripts of audio recordings of these same interviews (2000).

They found that "the Investigators' notes misrepresented both the information elicited from the young interviewees and the way the information was elicited" (Lamb et al., 2000:704). Despite their best efforts, the interviewers' "verbatim" notes failed to capture many important details, including both information central to the child's disclosure and information about the prompts used by interviewers. They found that audio recording was far superior at capturing the content of forensic interviews with children. Similarly, Berliner and Lieb (2001) compared methods of documenting forensic interviews of children in sexual abuse cases in Washington State. Like Lamb and his colleagues, Berliner and Lieb found electronic recording to be much more detailed and accurate than interviewers' efforts at verbatim note taking. Research, then, strongly supports some form of electronic recording of forensic interviews (Faller, 2007). The question is what type of electronic recording is better, audiotape or videotape. Lamb's research team concluded that while audiotaping was far superior to note taking, videotaping was better still because "even audio recordings . . . may ignore some nonverbal gestures and cues, rendering video recordings superior" (Lamb et al., 2000:705). However resolved the debate may be in the research community, it still continues to rage in the practice community.

## The Debate Over Videotaping

At about the time professionals in St. Mary County began to videotape their forensic interviews with children in the mid-1980s, others around the county were also finding value in what was at the time a new technology becoming more readily available (Faller, 2007; Dziech and Schudson, 1989). In the mid-1980s, some saw videotaping as the answer to the conundrum of investigating and prosecuting cases of child sexual abuse (CSA) (Cares, 1986; Colby and Colby, 1987; Faller 2007). Videotaping was advocated by those who believed it could reduce the number of interviews the child needed to endure, could ameliorate negative impacts of the legal system on children, for instance, by permitting the child's videotape to be admitted into evidence rather than the child's live testimony, and would lead to higher rates of confession by suspects (Faller, 2007; Dziech and Schudson, 1989). Some prosecutors were early advocates of videotaping as an effective means of insulating children from our adversarial legal system (Cares, 1986). By the late 1980s, however, a number of problems posed by videotaping began to emerge (Faller, 2007). Defense attorneys began to use the videotape effectively to challenge the child's account of sexual abuse and, more importantly, the form of interviewer questions. They asserted that interviewers improperly influenced children, using leading and suggestive questions or promising to reward them for their disclosures. Thus, videotaping proved to be a double-edged sword. Some jurisdictions that previously utilized the technology abandoned the practice; others declined to adopt it (Faller, 2007). Here we will describe the arguments pro and con of defense advocates, prosecutor advocates, and child advocates.

## Defense Arguments

Concern about how children were questioned by investigators precipitated a call by important academics that investigative interviews with children be routinely videotaped (Ceci and Bruck, 1995; Lamb et al., 2000; McGough, 1995; McGough, 2002). Videotaping, they argued, preserved important evidence and protected criminal defendants' rights by providing a verbatim record of the interview, including any undue influence exerted by law-enforcement or child protective services (CPS) personnel (McGough, 2002, 1995).

In general, defense-oriented advocates have called for the routine use of videotape as a means of ensuring fairness. They argue that the due process clause of the Fourteenth Amendment to the Constitution, which is meant to ensure the "fundamental fairness" of legal proceedings, requires that the state preserve evidence of a crime that is in the possession of law enforcement. Relying on the U.S. Supreme Court's ruling in *Brady v. Maryland* (1963), Lucy McGough, of the Louisiana State University Law School, has argued that law-enforcement officers and prosecutors have a legal duty to preserve for defense examination and use evidence that they have gathered in the criminal investigation of suspected child sexual abuse. McGough acknowledged, however, that the Supreme Court in *Idaho v. Wright* refused to read into the due process clause a requirement that forensic interviews with children be preserved on videotape (McGough 2002). Despite this, McGough pointed out, the highest courts of some states have urged that investigative interviews of children be videotaped. She cited, as examples, *State v. Townsend*, a 1994 Florida case in which the court briefly addressed the issue of videotaping, and Justice

Huntly's 1989 concurring opinion in *State v. Giles*, a companion case to *State v. Wright*, which was ultimately appealed to the U.S. Supreme Court as *Idaho v. Wright* (McGough, 2002).

## Prosecution Arguments

Unlike the prosecutors we studied, many around the country have expressed opposition to videotaping investigative interviews with children or have been slow to sign on to the use of videotaping as the most effective form of documenting interviews (Myers, 1998; Stern, 1992; Veith, 1900). Some have categorically dismissed the use of videotaping as unnecessary, even counterproductive (Stern, 1992; Veith, 1999). They argued that recording interviews placed disproportionate emphasis on relatively minor points in a child's statement about abuse, and that the videotape itself received disproportionate attention at trial while other, more important, evidence (for instance, medical) might be undervalued or disregarded entirely (Stern, 1992). These prosecutors were also concerned that defense attorneys would exaggerate interviewer errors, again shifting attention away from important evidence provided by the child. They assert that videotaping the interview with the child does not improve interview quality and that attention should be focused on interviewer skill building (Veith, 1999). Additionally, those opposed to videotaping emphasized that it was impossible to videotape every child disclosure about sexual abuse, that children would be intimidated by the recording equipment, thereby inhibiting disclosure, and that equipment problems rendered videotaping ineffective (Stern, 1992). Legal professionals, some argue, are ill prepared to assess properly a forensic interview (Veith, 1999). Furthermore, judges and lawyers were insufficiently trained in the complexities of child development and the social-science research on interviewing children or the expert witness testimony that may accompany the child's videotape (Veith, 1999). Finally, these individuals express concern that the child's videotape could be misused to the detriment of the child-witness (Faller, 2003, 2007).

Thus, many prosecutors and prosecutorial organizations have opposed mandates to preserve forensic interviews via videotape. For instance, Lamb and his colleagues observed that the American Prosecutors Research Institute "actively discourages the electronic recording of investigative interviews, and agencies in only a small number of jurisdictions within the United States require forensic interviews to be electronically recorded" (Lamb et al., 2000:705). Because of their opposition, the legislative reforms that prosecutors and others initially sought stopped. McGough, a proponent of videotaping, has observed that "prosecutors constitute a powerful force, and their reluctance or outright opposition may help to explain why videotapes are so infrequently made and why statutory reform has slowed to a standstill" (McGough 2002:188). Yet, over time, numerous prosecutors' offices, law-enforcement agencies, and child advocacy centers have instituted policies of routinely videotaping interviews with children during sexual abuse investigations (see California Attorney General, 1994; Cross et al., 2007).

## Child Advocates

Many child advocates have argued for videotaping (Avery, 1983; Faller, 2007; Henry, 1999; Henry, 1997), advancing several other rationales: it captures the child's statements about his or her experience of abuse and reduces the need for repetitive interviewing, which is traumatic for the child; it preserves evidence of the child's emotional state when disclosing abuse, which can then be used at trial; it insulates children from the rigors and trauma of participation in the legal process; and it can lead to improved interviewing techniques and reduce suggestive or coercive questioning.

Child advocates have also asserted that the use of videotaping has reduced the incidence of recantation by children; has assisted a non-offending parent in acknowledging that his or her child has been sexually abused and helped that parent to be more supportive; and could be used to prepare the child to testify at trial—which can take place as much as a year after the investigation—by refreshing the child's recollection of what investigators were told.

Other arguments advanced in support of videotaping are that it increases the number of confessions by defendants; that it captures the child's account of his or her abuse while it is still fresh in the child's memory, before it erodes or is influenced; that interviewers who videotape will be able to focus their entire attention on the child because they will not need to take notes; and that videotapes can be used in pre-trial decision making. They also point out that where videotaping of children's investigative interviews has been utilized, it enjoys the support of the professionals involved. Their research has specifically disputed the prosecution-oriented advocates' argument that videotaping equipment will inhibit children from disclosing abuse (Henry, 1999; Berliner and Lieb, 2001).

## THE ACADEMIC DEBATE RESOLVED, WITH PROVISOS

The weight of academic and researchers' opinion has evolved strongly in favor of videotaping forensic interviews (Faller, 2007; Berliner and Lieb, 2001; McGough, 2002; Ceci and Bruck, 1995; McGough, 1995; California Attorney General, 1994; Perry and McAuliff, 1993). As John E. B. Meyers, a legal scholar and perhaps the nation's leading expert on evidentiary issues in CSA cases, has said, "Probably the best way you can encourage competent practice in interviewing is to videotape. You can have peer review; you can uncover and expose incompetent interviewing when it has occurred. There is just no better way to do it" (Vandervort, 2004). Similarly, Michael Lamb, a leading researcher in the field, and his research colleagues have called videotaping the most efficacious means of capturing and preserving child interviews (Lamb et al., 2000).

While academic researchers endorse efficacy of videotaping forensic interviews and many jurisdictions now utilize videotaping (California Attorney General, 1994; Stephenson, 1992), many prosecutors still oppose its use (see Cross et al., 2007). Thus, despite strong research evidence and legal opinion about the benefits of videotaping forensic interviews, there is still an active debate among practitioners about whether videotaping should be used. This debate has its limits.

Because the debate about videotaping has taken place largely related to criminal proceedings, the viewpoint of the broader community is missing (Vandervort, 2006). "The purpose of a criminal court," the Supreme Court has observed, is "to vindicate the public interest in the enforcement of the criminal law while at the same time safeguarding the rights of the individual defendant" (*Standefer v. United States*, 25). When the criminal-justice system makes a mistake, either by convicting the innocent or by permitting the guilty to escape judgment, there is a price for the community. When the crime under consideration is child sexual abuse, that price is indeed high. The failure to detect sexual abuse leaves that child at risk of continued victimization. The consequences of being sexually abused can be enormous for both the individual victim and for the community. Among these is an increased need for mental-health services, increased substance abuse, sexual-behavior problems, and victims becoming perpetrators (Berliner, 2002). Also largely missing from the current debate about videotaping is any consideration of other investigative techniques that may be used in conjunction with videotaping. Absent from the literature, for instance, is any discussion of how videotaping of children's interviews should relate to the interrogation of the suspect or its role in leveraging guilty pleas.

The question that has been debated is, "Should investigative interviews with children be videotaped?" But videotaping is not the panacea that will solve all criminal-justice challenges with responses to sexual-abuse allegations (Stern, 1992). Reframing the question is critical to placing the issue of videotaping in proper context. The better question is, "When used with other investigative techniques, does videotaping serve the public's interest in accurate criminal-justice decision making by enhancing the truth-seeking function of investigation and prosecution?" In short, too much of the debate about videotaping has taken place in a vacuum, away from other important investigatory considerations (Vandervort, 2006).

By limiting the debate, the discourse is missing lessons that can be learned from understanding videotaping in a larger investigative process, in which its uses are numerous. It is our contention that pausing to hear the lessons reported by professionals in St. Mary County is a way of enriching the overall debate because it considers videotaping in the context of an integrated, working, community-based protocol.

In the next section, we look at the uses of videotape and the arguments made on its behalf by the entire community of professionals. Specifically, we look at use of the videotape to determine the nature and character of the case; to avoid multiple interviews of the child; to convince doubting nonoffending relatives; and to convince defense attorneys to advise clients to accept pleas. We examine community theories about the link between videotaping and confessions (particularly the use of the videotape in interrogations of suspects); its use to pressure defendants to waive preliminary examination; and its use in preparing the child witness for court and for impeachment at trial. Finally, we provide an overall summary of the lessons offered by St. Mary County regarding the use of videotapes.

## VIDEOTAPING CHILDREN AND ITS USE IN ST. MARY'S OVERALL PROCESS

Charles Davis posed a hypothetical of the problem for the prosecutor's office if a CPS worker's interview of a child is not videotaped. "Let's say social worker Jim, for example, did an interview and it wasn't taped. We'd want to know," said Davis, "how's this kid going to come across? Should we take the case criminally? Or just leave it to Protective Services? Then there was: is this kid going to be persuasive? You get a better sense of how the kid's going to come across by actually seeing the kid being interviewed. It's better than Jim saying 'Well yeah, I interviewed Helen. She seems pretty [good]. . . .' 'Well, we [the prosecutors] are going to have to put her on the witness stand, so I'd better talk to her too.' Multiple interviews. Again, police agencies might want to [interview also]."

Explicitly and implicitly embedded in this hypothetical are a number of questions that could be addressed by the videotape, had it been available. Among them are these:

- What is the nature of the case (criminal or not)?
- Are there sufficient allegations to bring criminal charges?
- If so, what level of crime should be charged?
- How strong is the case?
- Is the child a good witness?
- Is the child persuasive?
- Can professionals in one domain rely on the assessments of professionals in another? (Can a social worker do an interview *for* law enforcement?)
- What does the prosecutor need to see and hear directly in order to move forward?
- What does the police officer need to see and hear directly?

By taping the child's interview, a lot of questions begin to be addressed about the *content* of what is covered in the interview and about the *character* of the *case* and the *victim*.

## DECIDING ABOUT THE CASES

Unlike larger jurisdictions where geography, personnel, and philosophy separate family court from criminal courts, no such divide exists in St. Mary County. Both the family court and the criminal court are housed in the same building, share facilities and some staff. Furthermore, the St. Mary County prosecutor's office, unlike many jurisdictions of similar size, takes an active interest in family-court matters. One prosecutor in the office is assigned almost exclusively to family-court cases, and this prosecutor provides a direct link between what is happening in family court and the chief prosecutor. Therefore, the chief prosecutor is directly responsible for supervising decisions that get made on handling children's cases that may be moving through both systems simultaneously. This interest and knowledge about the totality of the legal proceedings facing a single family is unusual.

The first of the decisions to sort out is whether to "leave it to child protective services." As noted in chapter 4, child-protection cases must involve abuse by a family member or caretaker who lives within the same household as the child. Where a person legally responsible for the child has not protected the child from sexual abuse, he or she may be considered neglectful. The ultimate objectives of the child protection laws are the safety of the child and the preservation (where possible) of the family. Children can be removed from their homes and placed in foster care, although very few sexually abused children are removed in St. Mary County; data from 1988 to 2002 show that only forty-one children were removed from home, about 9.2 percent of the total cases (Henry and Faller, 2000). The family court supervises these cases, in which termination of parental rights is the ultimate sanction.

In contrast, criminal cases are entirely different creatures. A criminal proceeding is intended to assign guilt for violation of the law and to punish that individual. In these matters prison time is the ultimate sanction for a defendant who either pleads guilty or is found guilty, but lesser penalties such as jail time or probation as well as orders to participate in treatment may be involved (see chapter 9). Although there is an attempt to coordinate civil and criminal court cases, criminal matters will proceed independently from whatever is happening in family court. Furthermore, criminal cases can involve any offender and are not restricted to those involving a family member or caretaker.

Under state law, a defendant may be charged with one of four degrees of criminal sexual conduct (CSC). First and third degree involve penetrating offenses, while second and fourth degree involve the touching of the child's private parts for the purpose of sexual gratification. Children may not disclose the abuse immediately. Court file data from St. Mary County indicate a mean delay of two years between the onset of sexual abuse and disclosure (Faller and Henry, 2000). When children do tell, the evidence of abuse usually consists only of their story. There is rarely physical evidence, either because of the delayed disclosure or because the abuse is not the kind to result in physical injury (Muram, 1989). An additional complication is that some children recant their abuse accusations. Retractions may occur because of pressure from family or the offender or when the child experiences the consequences of reporting abuse (Malloy, Lyon, and Quas, 2007; Sas and Cunningham, 1995; Sorenson and Snow, 1990), such as removal from the home or the jailing of a parent.

In St. Mary County, the child's videotape, along with whatever other evidence has been gathered, is used to determine in which court or courts to proceed. However, assessing the basic facts to make this determination is only the first step. If the prosecutor's office decides to proceed with a criminal case, it must next determine what level CSC case to charge. This decision will turn on the factual assessment of how the child's allegations line up with the statute and the strength and persuasiveness of the evidence. Among other things, this will partly be determined by how good the child will be as a potential witness. Can she or he testify? Is she or he credible? Is she or he persuasive? The answers to these questions have a direct bearing on case-handling strategies.

The prosecutor's office finds the videotape useful at all these decision points: determining which court, determining what level CSC, determining the strength of the case. The prosecutor's office uses the videotape for all these determinations. As prosecutor John Hunter explained regarding the videotape, "I'll frequently charge a case without looking at it." He adds, "I won't refuse to charge a case without looking at it. . . . So it's useful in evaluating a case." This comment really speaks to the power of the videotape to persuade a prosecutor to move a case forward, even if the facts are not as strong as the prosecutor would like.

## AVOIDING MULTIPLE INTERVIEWS

Although the professionals in St. Mary County uniformly agree that avoiding additional trauma to the child by reducing the number of interviews is critically important, many professionals must have access to the child to do their jobs well. While there is currently some evidence to suggest that the multiple-interview problem has been addressed by the field (Cross et al., 2007; Malloy, Lyon, and Quas, 2006), at the time St. Mary was developing and implementing its protocol, the problem of multiple interviews was common in the United States. This problem takes on three primary forms: the multiple-player problem, the changing cast of characters problem, and the expanding audiences in increasingly public forums problem. By making the videotape readily available to the community of professionals who need access to it, St. Mary County has all but eliminated the need for children to be repeatedly questioned.

First, there is a long list of professionals who must hear the child's story. This includes police officers investigating the case, the prosecutor charging the case, defense attorneys defending the case, the CPS workers making plans for keeping the child safe and keeping the family together, and medical professionals examining the child. In addition, the child's lawyer in the child-protection proceeding, foster-care workers who work with the family, and the child's therapist need to know about the abuse. Each of these professionals must "hear" the story and to some extent assess the credibility of the child in order to decide how to proceed. In many jurisdictions, a child victim will be passed along to these professionals, who are strangers, to repeat the facts. This is frequently confusing and traumatizing to children. Police Officer Ed Williams reports,

> You know, there was a time [when] the child had been interviewed by social services and they wouldn't tape it or at least they wouldn't videotape it. And then the law enforcement would have to interview and then maybe the assistant prosecutor or the prosecutor and so you could figure out what the child was saying or how they were going to act when they got on the stand. And all of a sudden we're hurting these kids because they had to go over this three and four and five times. Every time by a stranger. By this videotaping on the original thing, that child most of the time never had to tell any stranger again—only the therapists or the people that were trying to help them.

Interestingly, he draws a line between the professionals whose mission it is to "help" a specific child and those who are working a public "case" in which the child is merely a necessary component of the process but not the object of intervention. Thus, the point is to limit not only the number of investigative (or forensic) interviews but also the number of retellings that are associated with trial or hearing preparation and performance.

Second, in many jurisdictions, large and small, there is high turnover of child welfare and other staff (General Accounting Office, 2003; American Public Human Services Association, 2001; Flower, McDonald, and Sumski, 2005). Thus, during the life span of a CSC case, the child may have to talk to several professionals in each system. She may have to speak to her new caseworker in CPS, a new police officer investigating the case, a new prosecutor assigned to try the case. Some researchers have suggested the problem of multiple, *different* interviewers may be as damaging, or more so than multiple interviews per se (Cross et al., 2007). Police Chief Ed Duke used the problem of shifting prosecutors to illustrate the point: "I take my blue sheet to Prosecutor B and he authorizes. Come prelim time, Prosecutor C now has the case. And I don't know why that happens, but it does happen. Prosecutor C only needs to watch the videotape, and he or she knows what your victim is gonna say." So now, in Duke's scenario, the child does not have to repeat his or her story to both Prosecutor B and Prosecutor C, but rather the burden shifts to Prosecutor C to do his or her homework by viewing the videotape.

Third, there is the problem of asking a child to report his or her story in front of an expanding audience of strangers in increasingly public forums. While the child may simply have to tell about abuse privately to a social worker or a police officer at the outset of the investigation, as the case moves forward there is the need to testify at preliminary exam in front of a judge, defense attorney, defendant (probably the most traumatizing), prosecutor, court personnel, and whomever else might be wandering about the courtroom. Down the line is the possibility of being called upon to testify at a trial that expands the audience and the public nature of the proceeding to include a jury and other courtroom spectators. This process of public telling may need to be reenacted in the family court, although there are more protections for child witnesses in family court than in criminal proceedings. Using the videotape as a tool to elicit confessions, admissions, or encourage accepting plea bargains early in the case results in reducing or eliminating the need for public testimonies.

In essence, videotaping can solve, simply by sharing the tape, all these problems without further traumatizing the child. Moreover, during the time span of our study of St. Mary County, state law was changed to permit the use of videotaped statements of the child made during an interview in various legal proceedings. These statutes permit the admission of the child's recorded statements in the preliminary hearing of a criminal case as well as in the preliminary and dispositional phases of a child-protection proceeding. Thus, the only point in the legal process at which the tape cannot be used in lieu of the child's live testimony is at trial.

## CONVINCING DOUBTING RELATIVES

One difficulty often faced by children who make allegations of sexual abuse against a member of her family is the disbelief of the nonoffending parent or caretaker (Staller and Nelson-Gardell, 2005). This is problematic for children who are left without a support system at home. Furthermore, disbelief can (not unreasonably) contribute to children recanting their allegations (Myers 1998; Sorenson and Snow, 1991). An added benefit of the videotape is that these doubting parents are sometimes persuaded. Said former Chief Prosecutor Davis, "We realized one advantage of that was quite often . . . the woman . . . was very reluctant to believe the child. . . . And we found that there were occasions when we showed that [the video] to the other spouse and it was very persuasive. . . . Helen's not making this up. It's pretty clear. So that was an added benefit."

## CONVINCING DEFENSE ATTORNEYS: PLEA BARGAINING

Like the other professionals, the defense attorney must assess the merits of the case, including the child's veracity and persuasiveness, in order to provide counsel to his or her clients. In particular, the defense attorney must help the client understand the benefits and risks of a bench or jury trial rather than accept a plea bargain offered by the prosecutor early in the case.

For the defense attorney, the videotape turns out to be as good an assessment tool as it has been for the prosecutors. In addition to the basic facts, the defense attorney can also evaluate the child's potential ability to sway a jury. The videotape allows the defense attorney to see the victim without the victim's ever having to set foot in court. Of course, this is beneficial to the child, but it also permits the defense attorney to provide better and more insightful counsel to his or her client.

If the defense attorney refuses to watch the videotape or is not persuaded by what it contains, as former Chief Prosecutor Charles Davis puts it, he may inform his client, "Hey, you're going to go in there and you're going to walk." Of course, the consequences of this kind of counsel are, "you're not going to get a plea out of the guy." For Duke, walking away from a plea after seeing the videotape can be foolhardy. He posed the following scenario where the defense attorney has done some preliminary work checking out his client: "Defense attorney comes in [and says], 'Now wait a minute. You know, I've had my client evaluated, and there's no way this happened.' So you sit down. They watch the videotape, okay? Because they don't have a right to talk to your victim at that point in time. They watch the videotape. Now this is where they start rolling the dice. Is it worth the chance to go against what they've got going for 'em? Cause it is a big roll of the dice. I mean, you've gotta have balls the size of coconuts to go against some of these kids because you can see the wings on their back."

Adds Davis, "A lot of these cases deal with client control. Some attorneys either aren't willing to or don't have client control. But if you can convince the defense attorney; that's what plea-bargaining is all about; it's convincing the defense attorney." For the St. Mary prosecutor, if the suspect has not already confessed to the allegations, then showing the defense attorney the videotape is the next step in moving the case toward a plea. Davis continues, "If you get a defense attorney who says, 'Hey, listen, I saw that [videotape] and this kid is good,' then you are going to increase the probability that the defense attorney will lean on the defendant to accept the plea."

## THEORIES ON THE LINK BETWEEN VIDEOTAPES AND CONFESSIONS

Some commentators have argued that videotaping forensic interviews with children will increase rates of confession, although the precise mechanism of this process has not been discussed (California Attorney General, 1994; Dziech and Schudson, 1989). Others are more skeptical, asserting that a statistically significant increase in guilty pleas has not been proven to be associated with videotaping forensic interviews (McGough, 2002). There is no doubt that law-enforcement officers in St. Mary County believe that the child's videotape helps secure confessions. Charles Davis argues that the "key benefit" of the system was that "at the very early stages we showed that [the video] to the offender. That coupled with the subsequent polygraph induced a lot of confessions." Ed Williams insists that it became evident early on that the videotape was a "tremendous tool for eliciting confessions from defendants." However, this blanket assertion of the link between showing the suspect the videotape and confessions leaves open the question of *why* it leads people to confess. The law-enforcement and CPS communities in St. Mary County offer many hypotheses as to what this connection might be.

First, there is a strong and pervasive belief that offenders—particularly those who have a familial relationship to the child, when confronted with the child's videotape, cannot deny the pain they caused. They feel guilty and confess. *Seeing* the child is a much more moving experience than either reading a transcript or having a police officer recite the basic facts. CPS supervisor Donna Wagner points to a specific case involving a father and his teenaged daughter: "When she was interviewed on the videotape, it was so obvious in her body language and her tone of her voice and the pauses, what she had really experienced. You would have missed that in a typed transcript, or a synopsis of what she said really happened on what date, what time, where. You would have missed that. And that's what pulled at that father's conscience and allowed him to tell his story. So, for me, that videotaping was wonderful. I mean, it was really helpful." Charles Davis refers to this as the "sympathy factor," saying, "They see the kid going through this, and it's a little bit different than being confronted with, 'Well, Helen said such and such.'"

Among other things, these professionals believe that suspects are forced out of their comfort zone of denial when confronted with the child on videotape. "I think the perpetrators when they felt like it really hasn't affected the kids or it hasn't impacted on kids, they can kind of be in that denial phase," says social worker Carol Bragg. "I think one of the major things is they can get into this mode, this denial kind of thing, 'I'm not hurting anybody; they want to do it; it's not hurting them.' And then when you see the videotape, I mean, this is a child's face. You see tears, you see fright. You hear those things. They hear those things, and then they can't ignore them any longer. Oftentimes a perp can love a child and still do it, and so I think the combination that they truly love their victim and the fact that they're hit square in the face, you know, gosh this has had a bad impact. This has hurt them."

Donna Wagner pointed to this moment of conversion in a case she worked on in which the offender rationalized his behavior by arguing he was actually *helping* his daughters learn about sex, until directly faced with their pain and embarrassment:

There was a father that was doing sexual education—that's what he called it—with his two daughters. The daughter revealed to a teacher and she was probably twelve or thirteen years old—and she had an older sister who was tight-mouthed, but the younger sister's interview on videotape came through very well. So when the police first talked to Dad, it was, you know, "It's my responsibility as a father to educate my daughters about what sex is, and what their sexual organs are, and how they work, and what sex feels like," you know, whatever. He was pretty self-righteous about his obligations as a father, and when the offender saw the videotape and the girl cried and how embarrassed she was . . . how violated she felt, that man had compassion for his daughter's pain. It was the pain . . . the tears, and the [fear] that she expressed on the tape that . . . allowed him to reveal what [had] actually been going on with the other daughter also. So somehow the child's suffering allowed him to tell the story.

Ed Williams goes one step farther, suggesting that offenders confess because after seeing the videotape they understand not only what they have put the child through but also what will be required of the child in the future if they continue to deny what happened. "I believed they confessed when they see . . . because they knew they didn't want the child to do that in front of strangers."

Another argument linking the videotape to confessions is a belief that videotape essentially buttresses the child's position in two ways. First, it forces adults to focus on the child's story; it requires adults to stop and pay full attention. If the child has the time, space, and attention to tell his or her story, the suspect must listen and essentially address the child's version of the facts. Second, in doing so, it seems to amplify the child's otherwise muted voice. John Hunter refers to the first of these as "ignoring" the child and the second as "drowning" her out. He says, "The offender frequently has a relationship either with that child or with other children and has learned over years that essentially a child can be drowned out and ignored by the defendant talking over the child. And he can't do that when he watches the videotape. He is forced to accept the fact that people might well believe what that child says, and [is] much more likely to confess after watching the videotape of the child."

Both drowning out and ignoring the child can happen because of the adult's privileged power status. Most often adults win during a back-and-forth volley of accusations. However, the videotape makes the adult confront not only the content of the allegations but also the child's emotional response. Jeff Penn, a police officer, talked about this phenomenon. "Before it was just a matter of 'I'm an adult and she's a child.' I say 'No' and she says 'Yes.' And you go back and forth. You need something in this type of case. The interviews of the child and the interviews of the adult are unique and enlightening in our cases. And in this type of investigation, there's very often very little physical evidence."

## THEORIES RELATING TO POLICE INTERVIEWING AND INTERROGATION

A cluster of arguments suggests that the link between the videotape and confession really is the result of the additional opportunities it affords police officers during their interviews and interrogations of the suspect. They can use the videotape as an investigative tool in a variety of ways. The most obvious, if not the most creative, is that the videotape can provide factual information about the case that both the police officers and the polygraph operator can use. However, veteran officers in St. Mary County use the videotape in other ways.

First, some watch the suspect *watching* the videotape. Veteran officers insist that reading the suspect's body language when confronted by the child's story helps them assess the case itself. In addition, it helps them to decide on a strategy for further interrogation that is tailored to that particular suspect. Ed Williams explains this procedure:

Then play a portion [of the videotape]. Maybe not all, but just a few minutes of it. With that and from the training from the state police . . . the defendant would normally use certain techniques and body language without saying anything could tell you what happened or didn't. And more than once, the first few I remember when the child would say something and they would nod in the affirmative. Now they didn't confess. But just the way they nodded, the way they opened their stance or their sitting position or covered their mouth. Do things that we had been learning in interview techniques that meant specific things that meant denial or whatever. With that information you could then interview the suspect and use the right angle.

For this police officer, the video offers an opportunity to observe the suspect's behavior in ways that become useful in forming his subsequent interrogation strategy.

In addition to using the videotape as a tool for watching suspect behavior, police officers can use it as a counterpoint to the suspect's own version of the facts. This takes several different forms. One is to ask the suspect directly if the child is lying. Officers believe that suspects, particularly those who have a familial relationship with the child, are reluctant to label their child a "liar." Says Penn, "You can start off with, 'Is what she's telling me a lie?' They're reluctant to call their child a liar. If the answer to that question is equivocal, rather than a blanket denial, it opens up the door for asking the suspect to separate out which *parts* of the child's story are truthful and which parts are not." Penn continues, "I don't know how many times I've heard this: 'Well, I wouldn't say that she's a liar.' You know you've got 'em when they won't give you, 'Absolutely! I don't know where that's coming from. That's a lie.' It [the video] is a great investigative tool is what it is."

The inability of the suspect to deny completely the accusations of the child increases the likelihood that the suspect will start confirming or admitting parts of that story, thereby corroborating elements of what the child has said. The strategy, according to another officer, is to talk to suspects long enough without showing the videotape until they "start to get aggravated." At that point the officer will suggest something like, "Hey, you know, if it's not true, let's watch the videotape and then you tell me what you don't like. You tell me what you don't agree with. Why is she lying about this? If she's lying about this, why isn't she lying about that? What is she lying about?" According to the professionals in the community, this strategy of obtaining admissions to parts of the child's story—if not full-fledged confessions—is enhanced by the instinctual desire of most suspects to escape responsibility. "First, most people confess in order to minimize their conduct," reports Charles Davis, "Helen's talking about this happened on ten different occasions. He says, 'Well, you know, there was one night. I had too many beers and it happened once.'" Now the suspect in Davis's hypothetical case has admitted that something happened, but he disputes the extent of the sexual abuse.

The videotape is a lot more persuasive than just repeating the basic facts to the suspect, according to Duke. "But it gives a whole new meaning to sitting there verbalizing with somebody about things that somebody told you as opposed to, 'Sit back. Relax. Pay attention. We're going to watch this videotape.' And I've had the perpetrator say, 'You gotta turn that off. You gotta turn it off. You gotta believe me, Mr. Duke, it wasn't my fault.'" This is music to the ears of a police officer. Says Duke, "I love to hear that shit, 'It wasn't my fault.'" Once the suspect retreats from outright denial to claiming that the fault was not his, then the police officer has him. While this might not lead to a full confession in which the suspect agrees entirely with the child's version of the story, it certainly leads to enough admissions that the prosecutor's office can charge the defendant and increases the odds that the defendant will accept a plea bargain.

One strategy used by Officer Shawn Duffy is to essentially suggest alternative versions of the child's story in order to help the suspect down the path of minimizing his behavior, thereby admitting to some of the accusations. "Why would she say that if it wasn't true? She could have made up a whole bunch of stuff that made it sound like a lot worse than what it was. Maybe you did it accidentally. Maybe you didn't know. Were you drinking at the time or something like that? And that's where the videotape comes in handy. 'Oh, oh, yeah. I remember, I could have done that.' And then they'll sit there. The longer I get them to sit in that chair, the better off I am."

Yet another strategy employed by the police is using the videotape to narrow the suspect's escape routes out of his version of the story. Here the officer offers the suspect an opportunity to tell his version of what happened before showing the tape. "So they come in with an air of confidence and we'll start talking to them about their relationship with the child." Reports Officer Penn, "'Hey, hi, Joe Shmuck, how are you getting along with Sally?' 'Oh, great.' 'Well, what kinds of things do you do?' 'Well, I take her here and I take her there.' What he doesn't know is you're cornering him [from] later saying, 'Hey, she never did like me and she's out to frame me.'" Particularly in cases where the child is younger, Penn says, suspects invariably report having a great relationship with the child. "I'm a super father and she's a great daughter and loves me." The next step of the process is to confront the father with the videotape of his own child: "It's very productive in getting you into the next stage, the interrogation portion of it, you know where this loving great child who has this wonderful relationship is breaking down on tape or is telling about what he's done." So a skillful officer can use questioning the suspect first in a way that leads the suspect into a version of the story or description of events that is difficult to back out of once he has seen the videotape.

## THE PRESSURE TO WAIVE PRELIMINARY EXAMINATION

The purpose of the preliminary exam is for a judge to determine if there is sufficient evidence to hold the defendant for trial on the charges. This exam is held before a district-court judge. The prosecutor's office must establish that there is probable cause to believe that the charged crime was committed and that the defendant committed it. If the prosecutor fails to demonstrate with sufficient evidence that the charged crime was committed, charges may be reduced or dropped. For example, if the prosecutor has charged criminal sexual conduct in the first degree, a penetrating offense with a victim under age thirteen, the court may find the evidence presented only supports a charge of criminal sexual conduct in the second degree—a touching offense rather than a penetrating offense. If the prosecution meets its burden, the defendant is bound over to the circuit court to be tried. Historically in this state, the child was required to testify at the preliminary hearing stage in a CSC case. More recently, the law was amended to permit the prosecution to introduce the child's videotaped statement in lieu of the child's live testimony, but it is not yet clear how often this provision will be utilized. For defense attorneys in jurisdictions that do not videotape, the preliminary exam is frequently the first opportunity he or she has to evaluate the child's performance as a witness. However, the prosecutor's office in St. Mary County takes the position that the videotaped record of the child is an adequate substitution for testimony at preliminary exam and strongly discourages the defendant from hauling the child into court. In fact, the office expects the defense to use the video in lieu of preliminary exam and to waive the defendant's right to a preliminary examination altogether. Chief Prosecutor Jameson invites the defense attorneys to preview the tape. "If you want to know what the kid said, come watch the videotape and I believe the child will testify consistently with that and they'll be bound over." According to Chief Prosecutor John Hunter, "Since one of the defense's uses of the preliminary examination is discovery, viewing the videotape is as valuable as having the child testify for the defense. So it's a substitute at preliminary examination." The St. Mary County prosecutor's office drives a very hard bargain at this stage of the process. It is reflected in the reporting of three generations of prosecutors:

• "This particular office has a policy that if the defendant takes a case to preliminary examination in the District Court and makes the victim testify, then they either don't get a plea deal or it's more stringent than it would have been then if they had waived the exam." (Judge Richter)

• "And you say, 'Listen, you know, you put that kid through preliminary examination and that changes the ball game.'" (Former Chief Prosecutor Davis)

• "We have a policy that if you make the child testify at preliminary examination, there is no plea offer." (Chief Prosecutor Jameson)

• "One of the kind of little landmines that prosecutors plant in here is—and, by God, mark this down in red ink on your little daily planner—'If you make my victim go to prelim, all pleas or possibility of pleas is out the window.' There is not a defense attorney with a clear conscious that's going to subject their client to all those possibilities, that exposure, so to speak, by making the victim come in and testify at a prelim." (Police Chief Duke)

It is a sizable incentive to the defendant to either accept a plea early or at the very least to waive the preliminary examination. The regular defense attorneys in the county are well aware of the stringent position of the prosecutor and the consequences of ignoring it. The net result is that "a very high percentage of the defendants waive the preliminary examination," as Jameson explains.

## PREPARING WITNESSES FOR COURT APPEARANCES

The videotape has a life well into the CSC case, possibly including trial and, if necessary, sentencing. The prosecutors offer at least five reasons for using the videotape as tool for preparing a child witness for trial or for a preliminary examination, if the defendant has not waived it: (1) It offers a place to start, (2) It minimizes embarrassment, (3) It refreshes the child's recollection, (4) It reduces inconsistencies in the child's testimony, and (5) It permits the child to verify the truth before being put on show in the courtroom.

On the first point, Jameson mentioned the upcoming Inman trial: "My little girl is coming in Monday and the first thing I'm going to do is we're going to sit down and watch the videotape together so she doesn't have to retell me everything. . . . We use the videotape because it's a place to start, so I don't have to start from ground zero with a child and say, alright, tell me what happened."

On the second point, the prosecutors believe that watching the videotape with the child is a way to reduce trauma by minimizing embarrassment. Says Prosecutor Jameson about his child victim, "She and I have watched the videotape. She knows I know what she said. . . . She knows I already know what happened and she knows she told me." In this case the child does not have to shoulder the burden of starting from scratch in recalling and reporting the events to the lawyer, thereby reducing embarrassment.

On the third point, all the prosecutors agree that watching the videotape with the child is way to refresh his or her recollection. "So then I don't have to sit here and question her. She can see herself on the videotape again and it preps her for trial and it refreshes her recollection because it's sooner in time," says Charles Davis. This is critical, in part, because many months may have passed between the initial interview and trial. Davis talks about that passage of time: "Let's say on January 3 there's an interview of the child. . . . Let's say the trial doesn't happen until like November. Okay. And then when you prep witnesses for a trial you talk to them and say, 'What did you say?' 'Helen, do you remember when you talked to Jim, the social worker? Well, we're going to have a trial and I'm going to be asking the questions, let me do this. Let me show you the tape.'"

On the fourth point, refreshing the child's recollection by showing her the videotape has the added benefit of reducing, although certainly not eliminating, inconsistencies in the child's version of the story. Jameson explains that "it makes it more likely that her testimony will be consistent." John Hunter points out, "I think you could show videotape to a child a dozen times before a hearing and I will guarantee you that they will give some testimony in direct conflict of what's on that videotape. It's just part of the process. But it's still a lot closer than they otherwise would have been."

On the fifth and last point, Charles Davis used the videotape as a reference point for verifying the facts, in part, by offering the child the opportunity to correct any statements that seem incorrect. Davis used to tell his victims, "So can you tell me if that's what you now remember or if you forgot something. Or you may have said something wrong then." He provides a further example: "It's a better refresher and recollection than if I say, 'Isn't it true you told Jim the social worker that it was your birthday?' Because she may say, 'Well, I never said that.' She says, 'Oh, yeah. You know I said it was my birthday but I remember I got a bicycle and I never got a bicycle on my birthday. I got a bicycle on Christmas.' So actually it's even good for trial preparation to show the videotape as opposed to sitting down with the witness [and asking her to recall the facts]." This allows the prosecutor to address inconsistencies with the child or to prepare arguments explaining them before trial.

## THEORIES ABOUT USING THE VIDEO FOR IMPEACHMENT AT TRIAL

There are two ways that the videotape can be used for impeaching witnesses. First, it can impeach a child witness if his or her statements at trial differ from what was said on the videotape. Second, the defense can cross-examine the person who conducted the interview by calling into question the interviewer's questioning techniques.

Although the risk of impeachment is probably the most important vulnerability for those who oppose videotaping, those arguments hold little sway over the lawyers—both prosecutors and defense attorneys—who practice in St. Mary County. Defense attorneys do not use the videotape for impeachment purposes very often. There are several reasons given. The first is a now-familiar one: If you are a defense attorney, you do not want the jury to see the emotions of the child captured on tape. Says Prosecutor Hunter, "A defense attorney would be a fool to allow the jury to see that heartbreak of the first disclosure. . . . In my opinion, the jury is very likely to say, 'Well, I don't believe what the child testified to, but I sure believe in that videotape that he's guilty.'" Hunter notes that the defense may be better off with an emotionless child on the witness stand, which can occur with repetition, as a result of treatment, or as time passes: "So they really aren't played very much for that reason. The jury can see the emotional process of letting go of this trauma to them when you see the videotape. A lot of times, by the time you rehearse [a child witness] it flattens out the affect. You've created a little automaton. But that emotional difficulty that that child has revealing this incident during that videotape is just very gripping on the jury." A seasoned defense attorney, Sam Huff, agrees: "The videotape oftentimes makes it more solid for the prosecution than it would [otherwise] be."

Jameson argues that even if the videotape is shown because of inconsistencies, it is only fair to the defendant, and the prosecution must simply deal with the consequences as a matter of justice. "My attitude has always been that it is what it is. If the kid said it happened on Tuesday in Mom's bed on the tape and in court she said it happened on Saturday on the couch. Well, it's inconsistent. Now, granted, if you don't videotape, nobody knows it's inconsistent, but shouldn't you be fair to the defendant also? If it is inconsistent, well, let's deal with it."

Charles Davis offers yet another strategic approach to inconsistent statements: "There's a very strong argument that it can be used for rehabilitation purposes and especially putting inconsistencies in context." So if the videotape is used to impeach a child, the prosecution can argue that enough of the surrounding tape should be shown the jury to put the inconsistent statement in context. This allows the jury to get a better feel for the significance of the inconsistency, if any. From the defense attorney's point of view, however, it allows the jury to see more video footage of the vulnerable child, perhaps more than would serve the defense's initial interest.

"Just because the child tells it differently this time doesn't mean that the defense attorney really wants to show that videotape," observes Hunter. Defense attorneys do not see attempts at impeaching children with an inconsistent statement as a particularly useful strategy for two reasons. First, most inconsistencies are too minor to be of use (perhaps because the child has reviewed the videotape in preparation for trial). "The degree of variance," says defense attorney Sam Huff, "is oftentimes so minor that it's insignificant." While such nitpicking might be damaging when dealing with adult witnesses, impeaching a child on such trivial matters rarely wins over a jury. "I mean, it's usually close enough that the kid's going to get the benefit of the doubt," Huff asserts. He adds, "In all the years that I've been doing it, I never had a situation where the girl says on the videotape, 'Well, he did it this way,' and we get over here and it's totally different or something else." Jameson agrees: "We have never really gotten bitten by it. It's like we never lost a case because a child said something different on the videotape."

Of course, a defense attorney can also choose to show the videotape in order to attack the questioning techniques employed by the professional who conducted the interview; however, the defense must still weigh the risk of showing the jury what the child looks like during the process. Donna Wagner points to that strategy of defense attorneys in discrediting the interviewer's techniques but still finds value in videotaping. "You know," she mimicked a defense attorney, "see her tone of voice; she's trying to suggest the answer to the question. Did you see when she touched that child? She basically told the kid what to say. They [defense attorneys] try to use the videotapes against us. In the long run, I think they're worth doing."

## OVERALL LESSONS FROM THE COMMUNITY

What are the overall lessons that St. Mary County provided about the benefits of videotaping children as part of the protocol? Among them are that doing so:

• Can amplify a child's voice so that it is not drowned out by offending adults, which is of particular importance in cases that involve young children and/or little physical evidence;

• Can help convince otherwise doubtful family members of the veracity of the child's allegations, which may strengthen the child's support system;

- Reduces the number of times a child must tell his/her story to strangers, which may reduce trauma, help avoid embarrassment, and decrease the likelihood of recantations;
- Creates a common record that can be shared among professionals so that each has access to the same information;
- Can be utilized by professionals to aid prosecutors in deciding whether to charge the case criminally, assess the credibility of the child as witness and the persuasiveness of the child as witness, evaluate the facts of the case, and aid defense attorneys in deciding whether to move forward with their client's case or urging the client to accept a plea bargain;
- Can be used by police officers as an investigation tool to gain facts for use in suspect interview and/or interrogation, examine how the suspect reacts to the tape; confront the suspect with the vulnerability of the child; and question the suspect about the veracity of the child's version of the facts increasing the likelihood of admissions.
- Can freeze in time the emotional reactions exhibited by the child, his or her age at telling, and perhaps preserve the immediacy of the event;
- Reduces or eliminates the need for the child to testify;
- Helps refresh the child's recollection of what he/she said in the past;
- May reduce inconsistencies; and
- Allows the child to correct the record as necessary before the case goes to trial.

## CONCLUSIONS

The national debate about the efficacy of videotaping has diminished. Most academicians and researchers support videotaping of forensic interviews of children; some prosecutors and prosecutorial advocates remain holdouts. However, we assert that it is an error to view videotaping in a vacuum apart from other investigative and case management practices. The efficacy of videotaping needs to be examined in context.

St. Mary County resolved the videotaping issue in the 1980s and articulates a comprehensive and diverse yet very thoughtful set of reasons for videotaping, none of which has been empirically tested. Nonetheless, these reasons constituted the belief system upon which the community actors based their actions, which in turn had concrete implications for children, suspects, and professionals. It is worth wondering about some of the assumptions that undergird these ideas. For example, there is an assumption about the child's disclosure that seems to suggest that it is possible to get all pertinent facts, captured at one time, in one interview, and on one videotape. It also assumes that the child will provide a single coherent and persuasive account and that the interview will be good enough. What happens if that is not true? There is an assumption that most offenders feel guilty about what they have done. What does that suggest about the kind of offenders St. Mary assumes it has? These assumptions are worthy of further empirical exploration and verification.

# Polygraph Magic | **SIX**

KATHLEEN COULBORN FALLER

I don't know anybody . . . that could set in a room

and listen to Rick Rivers (the Polygraph Magician)

for two hours without confessing to something.

Okay? You just flat-assed are going to confess.

—Ed Duke, Chief of Police

In St. Mary County, the polygraph of the suspect was a critical part of the protocol. If, during the police interview, the suspect denied sexual abuse disclosed by the child, he or she was offered a polygraph. This component of the protocol built upon state statute, which entitles every individual accused of a sex crime the opportunity to demand a polygraph examination. (Although the suspect has a right to demand a polygraph if accused of a sex crime, the U.S. Supreme Court has held that law enforcement cannot compel a suspect to take a polygraph because of the Fifth Amendment right against self-incrimination; see *Schmerber v. California*.) However, in the hands of St. Mary professionals, offering the suspect a polygraph was another instance of the community's creative approach to legal requirements, and it played a central role in shifting the burden of proving the case from children to community professionals.

If the suspect passed the polygraph, the prosecutor's office either did not file charges or dropped them if charges had already been filed. For this reason, the polygraph became a pivotal moment in the life of a child sexual abuse (CSA) case in the county. Many in the field of sexual abuse would worry about the centrality of the polygraph in decision making because the polygraph itself is suspect, in terms of its ability to differentiate truth-tellers from liars. Moreover, because of the polygraph's fallibility, it is not admissible in most court proceedings (Cross and Saxe, 2002; Faller, 1997). However, like so much else about St. Mary's protocol, it was impossible to isolate this step in the process and debate its relative merits without fully understanding how it fit with the community's overall approach. Although the official function of the polygraph was to determine the suspect's truthfulness, it appeared to be a tool to support the child's account, to level the playing field between child and adult, and to shift the relative balance of power in the criminal-justice process by moving the confrontation between competing versions of the event and the "truth-finding" (or fact-finding) moment of the case out of the courtroom and into the interrogation room. This confrontation happened between an adult professional polygraphist and the suspect, not between child and defendant at trial. Thus, the child and his or her story retained power in the process that otherwise would have been greatly diminished as cases moved formally into trial.

It was also impossible to separate out the success of the protocol as policy from an assessment of individual operators administering the polygraph tests for this community. A persistent theme was not only that sexual abuse cases turned on the polygraph results but also, to be more precise, that they turned on the opinion of one man, whom we dubbed the "polygraph magician," Rick Rivers. Although there were two polygraphists in St. Mary County, Rivers held a special place in the development of the protocol and the centrality of the use of the polygraph.

Rick Rivers was one of the original Sex Busters (see chapter 3). His professional growth, like that of other young community professionals, coincided with the development of the protocol and its institutionalization. However, in many ways, his personal philosophy about the polygraph as a tool, his theories about sex offenses and offenders, and his commitment to protecting children were also an integral and indistinguishable part of the entire process. They were almost certainly core features of its success. In no small way, the community protocol became entrenched and accepted by other professionals because of Rick Rivers, because of both his personal integrity and his professional philosophy.

Praise for him came from every professional circle in the community, including child protective services (CPS) workers, law-enforcement agents, and prosecutors. Pioneering child welfare supervisor Donna

Wagner, a close collaborator with the Sex Busters, said of him, "I have an immense amount of respect for him. Obviously loves what he does. And he is just so good at it. I've seen some videotaped interviews of his work and my mouth just hangs open because he's just great at interviewing!" Perhaps most remarkable, however, was the fact that the community defense attorneys also endorsed Rivers's work. Without their willingness, or at least their acceptance, of this particular step in the process and their faith in this particular man, it is unlikely that the protocol would have been as successful as it has been.

In this chapter we introduce the two polygraphists; explore the particular aspects of Rivers's philosophy; explain the general polygraph process, St. Mary's protocol, and the procedures St. Mary uses to augment the polygraph; describe advantages to the child of that polygraph practice; and consider the heated debates about polygraphs more generally.

## INTRODUCING THE POLYGRAPHISTS

Rick Rivers looked like a plainclothes detective, well-dressed and spiffy, cop-style, with hair trimmed and perfectly shined shoes and knotted tie. In the period we focused on, Rivers did most of the suspect polygraphs in CSA cases. Jason Touhy, the county's other polygraphist, looked like a sheriff, in cowboy boots and a fine leather jacket, emblazoned with the shield of the Sheepshead Sheriff's Department. Touhy had spent many years conducting polygraphs on sex abuse suspects in an adjoining county and did some sex offender polygraphs in St. Mary. However, Touhy immediately and repeatedly deferred to the unique expertise of Rick Rivers in sexual abuse cases in our discussions with him. "Rick Rivers does most of the sexual assault polygraphs here," reported Touhy, "Rick kind of specializes in that." Although Touhy was willing to do criminal sexual conduct (CSC) polygraphs for the county, he would just as soon not. "If you need them done," he told prosecutor Mark Jameson, "absolutely, I'll be happy to do them, but if Rick wants to do them that would be fine too." More often than not Rivers did the polygraphs. While Rivers continued to thrive on child sexual abuse cases, Touhy admitted that he was burned out.

Although Rivers and Touhy attended the same polygraph school in the same year, 1976, and cited the same polygraph experts, Inbau and Reid (1977) and Warren Holmes (1995), as sources of their knowledge,

Rivers had developed a complicated and relatively complete personal philosophy on the art and science of polygraph testing, particularly as it related to CSA cases. Touhy offered a comparative view on the process. Touhy pointed out that different kinds of crimes and criminals required different kinds of polygraph techniques. A burglar, he observed, "he's the type of guy that's going to brag about that crime." On the other hand, a sex offender, "a person that's actually been involved in a sexual assault, has probably not told anybody." It is secreted between offender and victim. Therefore, the approach to a "reserved" and "quieter" sex offense suspect requires an entirely different set of techniques from those used against a burglar's bravado.

Both men became interested in the polygraph as police officers. In Touhy's case, a neighboring local sheriff's department sent him to school, and he spent the next ten years doing nothing but polygraph exams. He reported that when he started in the mid-1970s, "there was no polygraph law per se, so one of the first things investigators would do was ask you to test the victim, and obviously that's changed. Thank goodness!" (In the same statute that gave the accused the right to demand a polygraph, victims of sex crimes were protected from law enforcement's request that victims take one. However, if a victim requests a polygraph, he or she may have one administered.)

Rivers, who already had a bachelor's degree in criminal justice, tired of being a police officer, describing it as "shift work." He decided to attend polygraph school, paying for it under the GI Bill. His work in St. Mary County started almost immediately after graduation. "I started in 1977 after I went to polygraph school in '76. When I hired in, they didn't have any polygraph available, and the new sheriff coming in decided that he thought that it would be a good tool to utilize. So once I did my internship and was licensed, I started doing polygraph testing for them."

It turned out that the county commissioners were not nearly as keen on this innovation as the local sheriff. "I'll tell you how bad it was," laughed Rivers. "I had to buy my own instrument. Okay? An old three-pin Deceptograph polygraph instrument. And it got to a point where I didn't feel comfortable with that because we needed more. I bought the next instrument—which was an electronic. It was a Stoelting Ultrascribe polygraph instrument. The county was really—for lack of a better word—they had no interest. I think in the financial aspect. They didn't see the need for upgrading." Rivers's early willingness to buy his own equipment was paralleled by barber Chris Kovac's willingness to haul his heavy video equipment to any venue where it might be needed to tape a child interview. Nonetheless, with the advent of the Sex Busters and the development of the county's CSA protocol, Rick Rivers found an institutional home for his work and achieved local-legend status.

## THE POLYGRAPH MAGICIAN

Rivers clearly loved his job and his role, a love that had not diminished in twenty years. "I think the one thing in this field with sexual abuse—the more you learn, the more you don't know," he said. It was this quest for learning more about child sexual abuse and offenders that motivated his work, much as in the case of all the pioneers in St. Mary County.

There are several interrelating aspects of Rivers's philosophy that are worth pondering. They include focusing on the act and not the actor, the relational aspect of the polygraph interviews; the dynamics of child sexual abuse and getting to the "why"; and the nature of truth and innocence in the process. Finally, however, he disclosed that, in part, his love of his work was motivated by "the thrill of the hunt."

### The Act, Not the Actor

Rivers, a self-identified God-fearing Irishman, an ex-Marine and Vietnam veteran, acknowledged struggling with anger long after the war ended and attributed his redemption to his much beloved wife. His Vietnam experience—he described the "carnage" inflicted on his unit, suffering 10 percent casualties in only four days—was seemingly inexplicably reopened with U.S. involvement in the Persian Gulf. For Rivers, partly with his wife's help, he turned his gaze inward and he "started spending more time with understanding where my vulnerability was and how I felt about everything." He associated his improvement as a professional with this inward exploration of his own personal history, his past, and came to accept that "everybody's fallible, everybody has weaknesses, or whatever you want to call vice."

Tied to this understanding that good people can do bad things, in certain contexts, developed a deeply rooted sense that to do his best work with polygraphs he needed to be nonjudgmental. Admittedly when he started his work with child sex offenders, "my first reaction was disdain." However, "Once I started understanding where my feelings were and my vulnerabilities," he reported, "the more I could see their vulnerabilities." It was this turning inward and greater self-awareness that allowed him to better understand CSC suspects.

"It's the act," he declared, "It's not the person. It's the act they've committed." For Rivers it is possible to revile the "act they've committed" without condemning or judging the person who committed it. To do otherwise, in his view, was bad professional practice. "It's easy to judge because then you can divorce yourself from the act itself," he explained, in that way "you don't have to emotionally connect with it or even come to understand it." Rivers dismissed that kind of response as "easy." "Anyone can walk in and say 'you're a liar. You're a no good S.O.B.' and walk out [saying] 'Well, he won't talk.'" However, since this "easy" approach gets you nowhere, Rivers focused on the behavior in context. He used this wedge, separating act from actor, as a key aspect of his interview strategy. In Rivers's view, it is easier for a suspect to admit to a bad act if he is not being personally judged.

## Relationships and Vulnerability

Although interviewers of every stripe will discuss the need for rapport building, it may be even more critical than usual in cases involving sex offenders, in part because of the secret nature of the crime. Rivers believed that the polygraph operator must start by making himself vulnerable. He used this relational framework: "I mean, it's that investment. If you don't invest something, you're not going to get anything back." Said Rivers, "If you don't invest part of yourself into that process, the person sitting on the other side is going to tell right off that you're disinterested."

Rivers believed that if he used himself to form an alliance with an offender, it ultimately led to the offender's being honest. He claimed that his success rested in "the way in which I approach each individual" and that there must "be some level of connection." It wasn't the polygraph per se.

## Dynamics of Child Sexual Abuse and Getting to the "Why?"

As one of the Sex Busters, Rivers had to "work closely with a lot of PS [protective services] workers, like Jim Henry, and others . . . to really get more involved in the whole aspect of how we were handling sexual abuse cases." These others included Chief Prosecutor Charles Davis, since polygraphs were conducted in the Prosecutor's Office. In addition, Rivers was one of the earliest members of the American Professional Society on the Abuse of Children (APSAC) in the State. It may be that from these contacts Rivers came to fully appreciate both his role in the process and about what Rivers called "the dynamics of child sexual abuse. "Rivers observed, "Some people say, 'well it's about sex.' It's not; none of it's about sex."

Rivers defined his quest as to getting to the "why?" Although others in the community and even our research team measured Rivers's success by confession rates, the goal of his interviews and interrogations was not confessions. Instead, it was understanding the "why" of the suspect's behavior. As he said, "To understand, to talk with them. Why? What was going on? What was going on when this first started?" Because he thought concurrent events in the offender's life play an instrumental role, he carefully collected information about these dynamics during the polygraph pretest. He added, "I found that the more I understood about some of the activity that . . . the possible offender was involved in and understanding . . . some of the dynamics behind it, then if I understood them, the more I understood about the offender, the better able I would be to at least identify with some of the emotions and feelings that put them into the environment to commit the act. It was a step-by-step process. There's a lot of trial and error."

So Rivers recognized he was on a quest for private, personal information that required a relational approach. If he could understand the why, he could empathize and begin to drive a wedge between actor and action, using knowledge of the circumstances that led to the behavior. By focusing on the why—what were the circumstances, situations, explanations, and justification— Rivers believed he got to the truth.

## Truth and Lies and the Protection of the Innocent

Rivers asserted, "I was taught a long time ago when I went to polygraph school that the issue with polygraph is protection of the innocent." This may seem surprising, given the general public's characterization of a polygraph as a "lie detector" test designed to catch liars. However, this assumption that he was working for the innocent led Rivers to insist that he approached each case without an opinion, despite what information other professionals may have gathered before him. Rivers said he tried not to prejudge: "I try to start with a clean slate from scratch and systematically go through the interview process."

While other professionals were likely to note Rivers's ability in obtaining confessions, Rivers himself dismissed this focus and reframed the issue by asking, "What about the percentage of people who passed, that you cleared? They can get on with their lives. I mean that is more of a test than the ones you catch." The polygraph, he reiterated, is primarily to find the "truthful people." The goal is to unravel the story so thoroughly that any layers of falsehood are stripped away and until you are left with the truth, whatever that truth might be.

For the purposes of the St. Mary protocol and its reputation in the community, there were some very important consequences of Rivers's assumptions. They may help to explain the community professionals' faith in this man. Rivers did not see himself as operating primarily as an arm of law enforcement. In this regard, Rivers completely rejected the notion that he was a "hired gun" for the prosecution. Rivers was adamant about the independence of his professional judgment. In his words, "If you tell me that guy lied—that guy's a sex offender, and he walks in there and he's passed a polygraph test and I don't think he did it, if you think I'm going to interrogate, you are crazy. I'm not. There's no way. There's no way. If I don't feel that person did it, there's no way I'm going to say that person did it, even if you have the hounds outside the door. That's not going to happen." In this way, and operating from the assumption he was protecting the innocent with the polygraph, in theory, Rivers functioned more like a jury and judge than a law-enforcement agent, assessing the suspect's story and passing judgment on its truthfulness.

## The Endorphin High

But Rivers also understood that his investment reflected some of his personal issues. He reflected on the "endorphin high" of the chase, saying, "I guess it goes to the stimulus of the hunt and the success of the hunt. . . . He [a colleague] says because of my own issues with Vietnam, I say what's interesting is . . . the endorphins that are released. I mean, you can never get a high; you can never get to that point again ever. With me that's what I'm looking for. I don't know. I—I don't think so. Maybe I am. I'm not sure. But I get that energy surge of that everyday process. I think that maybe I'm just an endorphin junkie. I'm not sure [laughs]. I think that's part of it. I really think it is."

So Rivers had a personal stake in getting to the why and the truth. He reflected, "And over time what the nice thing is . . . is that I continue to grow from the process. And they still fascinate me, offenders still fascinate me."

## THE POLYGRAPH PROCESS

Even for professionals who work with sexual abuse cases and hear about polygraph results, the actual process of conducting a polygraph exam is largely a mystery. The training Rivers and Touhy have received guides them to divide the polygraph session into three parts—pretest, test, and posttest.

At the beginning of the polygraph session, both Rivers and Touhy took great care to assure that the person understood both why the polygraph was being conducted and his or her rights. The suspect was reminded explicitly of the charges or other reasons for administering polygraph. For example, in one of the polygraphs conducted by Touhy, the suspect had confessed earlier to Rivers, without even being polygraphed, and then recanted. The suspect requested a polygraph to prove his innocence.

Touhy, in a nonconfrontational manner, chronicled the events leading to the polygraph. Rights articulated include that the person's participation is completely voluntary, that he or she does not have to answer questions, that he or she has the right to stop the polygraph exam at any time, and that he or she may stop the polygraph and consult a lawyer. The suspect is then asked to sign a statement acknowledging these rights and that he or she is waiving them. Over and above these admonitions, the subject is Mirandized, even if not in custody. St. Mary County demonstrates more than the required attention to suspects' rights in that its officers Mirandize suspects routinely before a police interrogation. Police are not required by law to Mirandize until after arrest. As is well known, Miranda rights include the right to remain silent, the right to an attorney, and the right to discontinue questioning at any time (*Miranda v. Arizona*).

## The Pretest

The first part of the polygraph session consists of gathering information about the subject (as polygraphists call the interviewee) and building rapport. This part is reminiscent of a mental-health assessment, but its functions are broader and somewhat more devious. Although this phase has the goal of getting to know the subject, the pretest is used also to gather information that later can be employed in interrogation, if the subject is determined to be deceptive.

Here is a sampling of the type of information the polygraphist attempts to elicit. There are questions about family background, for example: one- or two-parent family, happy or unhappy childhood, did well or poorly in school, number of siblings. There is also attention to adult family relationships—marriages, divorces, children, and current connectedness with family.

There are health and mental-health questions. Does the subject have any physical symptoms, medical problems, or past hospitalizations? Is he on any medications (some can affect polygraph charts) and is there a pattern of substance use (which also might affect polygraph charts)? In addition, there are questions such as, "Who is the person you most respect in your life? Who is the person whom you least respect?" and, "Who are two people you trust?" Subjects are asked to describe their best experience as an adult and worst experience as an adult and a child. These queries may elicit accounts of child abuse or neglect. Information about criminal history as a juvenile and adult and military experience is also gathered. This line of inquiry may be followed by a question about whether the subject ever has told a serious lie.

Within the context of initial data gathering, however, the polygraphist may be quite flexible, having liberty to gather information based upon case-specific knowledge or what is happening in the interview. Illustrative is a case involving a thirty-six-year-old man with a drinking problem who was accused of sexually abusing an eight-year-old girl who, with her parents and brother, had moved into a room in his house, reportedly without his knowledge. The man stated that he had four criminal convictions as an adult, two involving substance abuse. Rivers learned that the suspect is supposed to be attending substance-abuse treatment twice weekly, last had a drink two days earlier, and is drinking regularly, thereby violating his probation, and he then began an investigation into the suspect's substance abuse around the sexual-abuse incident.

## The Test

The second part is the test itself. The subject has electrodes stuck on his or her fingers, a blood pressure cuff placed on the arm, and two bands around the chest. The subject's heart rate, breathing rate, and galvanic skin response (whether the fingers sweat) are measured and recorded on charts as the subject is asked questions pertaining to the sexual acts of which he or she is accused (Kokish, 2003). There are no surprise questions; after being hooked up to the machine, the subject has an opportunity to listen to the questions at least once before being asked to answer them.

## The Posttest

If the polygraphist determines that the subject has been deceptive, the posttest involves an interrogation. The goal in this part of the polygraph session is to elicit a confession. Here are some strategies employed in the interrogation process: The polygraphist might emphasize the importance of telling the truth for both the subject and the child—owning up, taking responsibility. The child's disclosure may be repeated and the child's videotaped interview referred to. The polygraphist may emphasize the child's believability and lack of motivation to lie.

An opposing series of strategies may also be used, centering on minimization of the sexual abuse. The polygraphist may suggest that there was no sexual intent in the subject's acts. For example, in one polygraph interview with a suspect who was drunk when he molested, Touhy offered that it was an alcohol problem, not a sexual problem. Similarly, the polygraphist may point out that other offenders have committed worse sexual acts or propose that the child is somehow to blame. Illustrative is what Rivers said in one polygraph examination, suggesting that the child may have initiated sexual contact; he then posited that if the child was the initiator, the child was probably sexually abused by someone else. This suggestion gave the suspect a way both of minimizing his abuse because the child started it and of positively comparing himself to a hypothetical earlier offender, who was worse because he was first. These strategies reflect the training both polygraphists received at the Reid School (Inbau et al., 2001).

Alternatively, confrontational strategies may be employed. The polygraphist may point out inconsistencies in the subject's statements, may suggest the ludicrousness of the subject's explanations for the allegations, or may assert that the polygraph charts do not lie. The same inconsistencies or ludicrous explanations may have been accepted by the polygraphist, who may have merely said "Okay" in the pretest during rapport building.

Some of these strategies may seem manipulative, even psychologically coercive, but they are standard fare in a police interrogation (Leo, 1996; *W. M. v. State*) and are legal (*Frazier v. Cupp*). Moreover, as we noted, Rivers said that there is no subsequent interrogation if the subject was not deemed deceptive during the polygraph charting.

## THE ST. MARY PROTOCOL AND THE POLYGRAPH

We learned from our visits to the county, interviews with the polygraphists, and watching videotapes of polygraph examinations that the polygraph process was much more than a three-part session. It incorporated drama and was coupled with other strategies.

There was a special chair. The actual chair in which a St. Mary County subject would sit is not conducive to relaxation (see figure 6.1). The polygraph chair appeared to be one typically used in medical laboratories to elevate patients' arms for drawing blood. This chair was convenient for the polygraphist, when the actual test was being administered, and inconvenient for the subject, who had to sit with arms half-raised or slumped in the chair for the two or more hours that he or she was not hooked up to the machine.

In addition, the polygraphist would exit the room intermittently, leaving the subject anticipating what would happen next. As Touhy put it, "There are built-in breaks for psychological reasons on the individual. In other words, you may get to a certain point on the pretest and you want to take a break to let that soak in and reinforce itself in the subject."

During part two, when a subject was hooked to the machine, he was admonished to close his eyes and not to move. The polygraphist might adjust the electrodes or manipulate the blood-pressure cuff, which required physical contact.

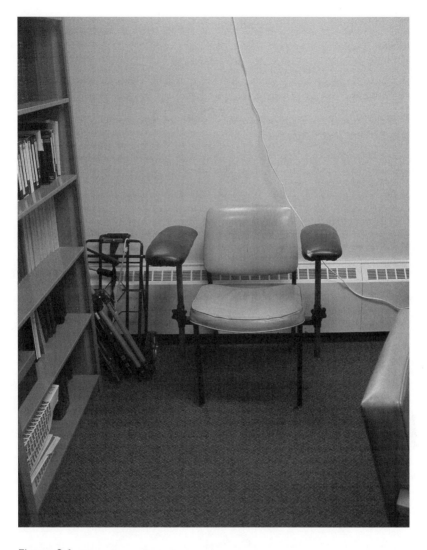

Figure 6.1 The polygraph chair.

During the test, the subject would listen, eyes closed, to the deadpan voice of the polygraph examiner asking questions and the buzz of the needles on paper recording his emotional reactions to the questions. The actual "running of the charts" might be done several times. Usually, the first time they were run, the subject would be told to listen to the questions with eyes closed and body perfectly still, but not to respond verbally.

The polygraphist would explain that the machine would be reading the subject's physiological reactions to the questions, the purported actual data for determining honesty or deceptiveness. The polygraph operator might then adjust the machine, informing the subject that he was adjusting it to the subject's specific bodily responses. The polygraphist might repeat running of the charts, suggesting there was something amiss with the subject's prior answers.

A final strategy was that the interrogation might be protracted. The polygraphist creatively employed a range of strategies calculated to get the subject to "give it up," to tell the truth, to "be a man" and own up to his transgressions. The total length of a polygraph session is usually two to three hours, sometimes longer, certainly a great deal longer than a child forensic interview.

St. Mary polygraphists employed additional procedures to enhance the polygraph's impact. These included using the child's video, requiring the investigating officer to attend, observe, and consult during the polygraph administration, videotaping the polygraph session, itself, and speed in polygraph administration.

## The Child's Videotape

The polygraphist used the child's videotape in preparation for the polygraph session. In addition, often the polygraphist showed the suspect the child-interview videotape in order to directly confront the suspect with the child's words. Rick Rivers said, "And I would sit there and allow them to watch the tape and . . . view what they were watching and see what their reaction was."

Rivers described a case involving a repeat offender and his retarded daughter. The child had little language, so she used anatomical drawings to convey what her father had done, taking a pin and pricking the relevant parts. Rivers said the father was "over helping the church or some youth group," and the police brought him in late at night. The father started by quoting scripture. Rivers showed him the videotape. Rivers said, "I didn't do the polygraph on him; so I sat him in the room." "I say, 'You're religious and I'm religious. And I believe in God.' I say, 'Do you believe in predestination?' And he says, 'Oh, yes.' . . . I say, 'That's why God probably put you in this room with me. Because He wants you to tell the truth.' And he lost it and confessed." The confession was crucial to holding the father accountable because the child would not have been able to testify. Rivers added, "We wouldn't have had a case."

## The Role of the Investigator

In many communities, the polygraph occurs in a vacuum. The polygraphist constructs the questions using only the police report. This document can be very sparse. As discussed later in this chapter, polygraph results are more accurate the more specific the questions are (Kokish, 2003; Saxe, Dougherty, and Cross, 1987). In St. Mary County, the investigating officer must attend the polygraph, watching the polygraph from an adjacent room on a monitor. Periodically, the polygraph examiner would exit the session to confer with the investigator about, for example, the questions to use or about case facts.

Touhy found this requirement extremely helpful. "Another example of that during CSC polygraphs . . . it's mandatory that the investigator be present while the exam is being conducted and would in fact be watched and monitored in another room. . . . As an examiner, I'd leave the room and take a short break like between the pretest and the testing phase, and the investigator would pick up on things that were said during the pretest that weren't said or were different than what were during the investigation. So in the CSC case it was mandatory that the investigator be there, which was . . . a great idea."

## Videotaping the Polygraph

Finally, of note is the fact from the earliest days of the protocol, Prosecutor Charles Davis made the decision to videotape all polygraph interviews. This included the pretest, the polygraph charting, and the posttest interrogation. This videotaping was no cutting-edge media production. The camera was a regular camcorder (figure 6.2) that sat on a bookcase in the prosecutor's modest conference room, facing the "polygraph chair."

The decision to videotape originally made Rivers wary. "Davis decided, 'Well, we're going to videotape the polygraphs.' I went, 'Oh, Lord.' You know, it's like the emperor with no clothes [laughs]." But he quickly came around. Rivers pointed to problems with videotaping on a case in another jurisdiction involving state police: "They had those issues with the state police in the city with five hours of interview or something.

Figure 6.2  Researcher Birdsall points to the video recorder used in polygraph interviews.

And the police just stopped [videotaping polygraph examinations]. There's no more videotaping." The case involved a man whose car plunged into the river. He and his wife escaped, but their four children drowned. He was interrogated and polygraphed by police over many hours about the drownings and eventually confessed to murder. Videotapes made of the interrogation and polygraph process were used to support a finding that his confession to murdering his children was involuntary. Although his confession was excluded from his trial, he was nevertheless convicted of his children's murder. Rivers said, "I'm of the opinion, well, if you're against videotaping, what are you trying to hide?" And I said, 'What am I trying to hide?' Absolutely nothing.'"

## SPEED, CHILDREN, AND THE PROTOCOL'S POWER

From the outset, one of the most important aspects of the protocol was teamwork, and with that came an understanding that speed worked to the child's advantage. While Touhy reported that "back then" he used to get cases "within twenty-four hours," he admitted, "Now it's probably within a few days."

Rivers insisted that originally "we did 'em as quickly as possible." He described the process. "I was on call basically twenty-four hours a day. . . . If Jim or one of the other workers or one of the other officers did an initial investigation, and depending on what the information was, if the child was in the home, the risk factor of the child being in the home, they wanted to get it done right away. As soon as possible. I mean, there were times that, you know, 9:00 at night you get a call, 'We got one. Where do we want him to take it [the polygraph]?' He says, 'We have him right here right now, and he's willing to do it now.' You drive down and do it."

Rivers and Touhy had profoundly different views about the significance of timing, and this difference of opinion went directly to the heart of the differences between the protocol in the hands of its original creators and the professionals in 2002. Touhy saw the delay of several days before conducting the polygraph as useful. "I don't believe it's advantageous to test him as soon as possible. I think as time goes on, he becomes a better subject for a polygraph exam because his stress level builds."

Rivers could not have disagreed more. In Rivers's eyes, speed served two critical functions. The first was getting to the truth. The second was protecting children. An implicit assumption embedded in his theory about speed of administering the polygraph was that innocent people will not be harmed. In fact, they benefit from being cleared that much faster. However, the likelihood of getting to the truth from the guilty would be enhanced. Said Rivers, "If you wait till the next day . . . if they get an attorney, you've lost every opportunity to interview or interrogate the guy. So that was the risk. We did them as quickly as possible hopefully to get to the truth."

Embedded in Rivers's assumption was that the first thing a defense attorney would do was advise his client not to talk, thereby delaying the questions about what happened until later in the process. While this delay strategy might appear manipulative, it is not a defense attorney's job to "get at the truth" but rather "defend" his or her client in a system that delays the truth finding until trial and, once there, imposes a very high standard of proof beyond reasonable doubt on the prosecution. Talking to the suspect before he or she invokes this right to an attorney and not to talk changes the power dynamic and, as a practical matter, eases the burden. In this way, the speed by which professionals operated created a tactical advantage for the child.

In addition to securing an attorney, a time lag before administering a polygraph also allows the suspect to "set up his support system," said Rivers. He saw the consequences of the delay as having a further effect on the child: "What happens is the pressure of that kid recanting is substantial." Finally, Rivers added, "I think for the most part, the protection of that child is probably the most important part of that process. And to other children who could have been abused if this guy gets away with it. Because once they get away with it, I mean, it's an open door."

Coupled with its role of getting at the truth is its role in the larger context of the protocol: child protection and preventing the child from having to testify. Rivers emphasized the importance of victim safety repeatedly. He clearly was distressed by the practice in other counties of taking to court only criminal cases that are certain wins. Speaking of those counties, Rivers said, "But the message you give to these kids is they say something happened and you won't prosecute because they're not 'good witnesses'; they will never tell you again. . . . Our responsibility is to these kids no matter what," he said, pounding the table for emphasis, "and I think that's one thing that's different in St. Mary County."

All told, benefits to the child from administering the polygraph quickly are substantial. For the immediate case at hand, the playing field is temporarily leveled between child victim and adult suspect. First, the child is physically protected from a possible offender. Second, the suspect cannot discredit or threaten the child, which would diminish the power of her accusations. Third, the suspect must deal directly and immediately with an adult professional (Rivers) about the truthfulness of his story relative to the child's. Fourth, the child need not confront the suspect directly nor tell the story again; the suspect views the child's videotape. Fifth, the suspect will not have time to invoke the full spectrum of criminal-procedural advantages available to him. Sixth, as a practical matter, this makes meeting the burden of proof in the case easier. Seventh, in addition to serving the needs of the specific case, if the suspect is an offender, other children and possible victims in the community will be protected. Finally, it sends a clear message to other would-be perpetrators and other victims about the seriousness of the crime.

## DEFENSE ATTORNEYS, VIDEOTAPING, AND
## SUPPRESSION HEARINGS

If all this seems unfair to the suspect, even manipulative as some research team members claim, it is critical to understand how the community, particularly defense attorneys and criminal defendants, have come to see the polygraph in general and Rick Rivers in particular.

Not surprisingly, Rivers himself set a standard in this regard. "My real litmus test is once they've made admissions, do these people come back and try to say that they were treated unfairly? Very few. I don't think we've ever, I can't think of the last time that we had a suppression hearing."

The record around suppression hearings—which challenge the voluntariness of a confession—is remarkable. Fellow Sex Buster Jim Henry was astounded by it. "Everybody's talked about the trust in Rick Rivers. He never lost a suppression hearing in all of those years. He *never* lost a suppression hearing." The significance is that Rivers's confessions were simply not seen as involuntary. Rivers elicited confessions, but he did not coerce anyone.

Furthermore, defense attorneys did not view Rivers as a "hired gun" for the prosecution. In fact, Rivers was more than willing to administer polygraphs at the request of the defense. One defense attorney readily acknowledged that he "will go ahead and allow a polygraph to be conducted by the prosecutor" because both sides, defense and prosecution, use Rivers to conduct them. Huff, a defense attorney who handled most of the CSA cases, appeared to have great respect for Rick Rivers, or at least an appreciation of other people's respect for him (see chapter 8). When Huff had a client accused of a sex offense, he got his client to take a private polygraph with Rivers. If a client passed a Rivers-administered polygraph, that was the end of the case.

The transparency of the process, as reflected in videotaping the entirety of the polygraph session, from the outset certainly facilitated the acceptance of the polygraph. Court file data indicate that more than 80 percent of the polygraphs were videotaped. Although we do not know the reason the remaining polygraphs were not videotaped, the suspect has the right to decline to have the process videotaped, as well as to decline the polygraph, itself.

Defense attorneys were always invited to review the videotape. Said Rivers, "They had to see what this guy said. Did I put words in their mouth? Did I tell them what to say?" Rivers believed that his reputation was solid among defense attorneys because they knew "what you see is what you got." They knew he did not "have an agenda walking in. A lot of them trust me; they trust that I'm going to do a professional job and I'm not there as an advocate . . . of the prosecutor or law enforcement. I think that's fairly clear."

Said Richard Nowack, yet another regular defense attorney, who also evidently respected Rivers, "Rick Rivers is good, too. When he confronts people after they've shown up to be not truthful in the lie detector, Rick's been able to do some good confessions and admissions that way. And I don't think he's coercive." Nowack made a differentiation between being coercive and persuasive. "I have never seen him being other than persuasive." Accusations of being persuasive are not going to win a defendant or his defense attorney a suppression hearing.

## THE PROFESSIONAL POLYGRAPH DEBATE

The polygraph use in St. Mary County seems barely touched by the empirical and professional controversy about polygraph accuracy. Historically, polygraphs have been used in two primary venues: to screen people for employment situations (see DeClue, 2003; National Research Council, 2002) and to screen individuals accused of crimes to determine if they may have committed them (Abrams and Abrams, 1993; Kokish, 2003; Raskin and Honts, 2002). Polygraph evidence is inadmissible in court, except in very limited circumstances because of concerns about its accuracy. Courts have consistently held that the polygraph evidence is inadmissible at trial because it lacks validity and reliability as a measure of whether someone is telling the truth. However, polygraph evidence may come in at points in the legal process other than actual trial and when the issue is not guilt or innocence of the accused.

In the 1980s, when the federal government was considering expanding polygraph use for employment screening purposes, the U.S. Office of Technology Administration undertook a comprehensive review of the research on the polygraph (Saxe, Dougherty, and Cross, 1987). The researchers produced a report advising against the expansion of polygraph use, because rates of false positives (a person testing as lying when they were not) and false negatives (a person testing as truthful when they were lying) were unacceptably high. The polygraph, in the field studies the researchers examined, performed at slightly better than chance (50–50) rates. Results were improved when the person believed in the polygraph and the questions were narrowly focused. Comparable conclusions were drawn in a more recent review of the polygraph research (National Research Council, 2002).

Nevertheless, criticisms and dismissal of the polygraph are hotly disputed by polygraph proponents (see Abrams and Abrams, 1993; Raskin, 1988; Raskin and Honts, 2002; Williams, 1995). Often polygraphists themselves, they cite their own set of field studies and claim selection bias in studies examined by the skeptics (Abrams and Abrams, 1993). In their own appraisal, they may cite accuracy rates as high as 90 percent (Cross and Saxe, 2002; Faller, 1997; Kokish, 2003; Williams, 1995).

Challenges to the polygraph boil down to its *validity* and *reliability*. *Validity* refers to the issue of whether responses recorded by the polygraph reflect that someone is actually lying or telling the truth. *Reliability* is defined as whether subjects' responses are consistent from one administration of the polygraph to the next and whether polygraphists score polygraph charts similarly.

With regard to validity, the polygraph measures autonomic nervous system responses to questions—usually heart rate, breathing rate, and galvanic skin response. Proponents of the polygraph believe that increases in autonomic arousal signal deception (see Abrams and Abrams, 1993), but skeptics point out there is no empirical proof that this is so (Cross and Saxe, 1992; 2002). In fact, skeptics say, autonomic arousal could derive from merely being asked a question about sexually abusing a child, causing a false positive (Ben-Shakar, 2002; Cross and Saxe, 2002; Fiedler, Schmidt, and Stahl, 2002). Moreover, some of the same autonomic nervous system reactions occur when people become frightened, excited, or sexually aroused and are not specific to lying (Cross and Saxe, 2002; Faller, 1997).

Furthermore, there are specific challenges to the most common polygraph strategy, the "control question technique," used to obtain a baseline for arousal responses. Control questions are about fairly universal transgressions, and arousal responses to them are contrasted with responses to "relevant questions" about the crime (Raskin et al., 1988). Typical examples of control questions for other crimes are whether subjects ever cheated on their income tax or took something from a store without paying for it. The assumption is that innocent subjects will exhibit greater arousal to control questions, and guilty subjects will exhibit greater arousal to relevant questions. Unfortunately, this is an unproven theory (see Ben-Shakar, 2002). Polygraph opponents also point out the difficulty of developing a control question for sexual abuse, a query about a universal, but minor sex crime, to use to measure baseline responses (Cross and Saxe, 1992, 2002; Murphy and Murphy, 1997).

There are two types of *reliability* that have been questioned with the polygraph. One is interrater reliability—that is, whether two polygraphists score a set of charts the same, as deceptive, not deceptive, or inconclusive. In laboratory studies, the person who gave the polygraph scores the charts more accurately than someone who scores results based only on the charts (Raskin and Honts, 2002). The second is test-retest reliability, or whether the subject produces the same charts with repeated polygraph administrations. Arguably, individuals become desensitized to the process of being hooked up to the polygraph machine and to being asked questions about sexual abuse, and their arousal to the procedure and the questions diminish over repeated sessions. Indeed, in some polygraph studies, lack of interrater and test-retest reliability have been demonstrated (Cross and Saxe, 2002; Faller, 1997).

Practitioners have also objected to the use of the polygraph with sex offenders. They point out that because of personality traits commonly found in sex offenders (lack of empathy, an ability to rationalize their behavior, and habitual lying), sex offenders are not good candidates for the polygraph (see Faller, 1997). Since often sex offenders feel little or no guilt, they may not experience autonomic nervous system arousal to the polygraph questions.

Many victim supporters report tragic experiences with individual cases in which the child made a coherent, detailed disclosure, but the suspect passed the polygraph. These circumstances are especially tragic when the suspect is the child's parent, because not only does the child suffer injustice, but the offender also continues unsupervised access to the child (Faller, 1997).

Despite questions about the *validity* and *reliability* of the polygraph, there is ample evidence of its *utility* or *manipulative effect* (National Research Council, 2002). Its manipulative effect, however, has been demonstrated in already identified sex offenders, as opposed to those accused. These are sex offenders who are either in treatment or on parole. With these populations, the polygraph is used in conjunction with other measures, such as regular monitoring, an in-depth interview, and plethysmography (a procedure that measures erectile response to questions about sexual acts or to sexual material, using a strain gauge that goes around the penis) (Faller, 1996). Cross and Saxe (2002), in their review of research on the manipulative effect of the polygraph on admitted sex offenders, have noted that using the polygraph versus just an interview increases the admissions to sexually abusive behaviors. These include admitting to a greater number of offenses, more victims, more types of offenses, more high-risk sexual behaviors, greater force and intrusiveness in sexual acts, a larger age range and both genders of victims, and the use of pornography. Kokish (2003) reports comparable positive effects of the use of polygraphy with admitted sex offenders.

Because of the polygraph's utility in monitoring and making sex offenders come clean, many sex-offense experts now support polygraph use and incorporate it into their intervention programs in conjunction with other detection and monitoring measures (see ATSA, 1997; Kokish, 2003; Leberg, 1997). So the controversy is more complicated than proponents, who have a professional and financial interest in demonstrating the efficacy of the polygraph, versus the skeptics, who are concerned about its scientific validity and reliability. Good researchers and disinterested practitioners now support its use with confessed offenders.

In their article "Polygraph Testing and Sexual Abuse: The Lure of the Magic Lasso," Cross and Saxe (2002) begin with a bit of polygraph history. They note that the precursor of the current polygraph, the "systolic blood pressure test," was invented by William Marston, a Harvard-trained psychologist. Interestingly, Marston was also the inventor of the comic-book character Wonder Woman. The character, derived from Greek and Roman mythology, was presented a gift of the Lasso of Truth by the Olympian gods. Wonder Woman's Magic Lasso compelled those caught in it to tell the truth. Cross and Saxe's position is that the polygraph can have a notable manipulative effect on believers, but, unlike the Magic Lasso, it is not a lie detector, despite its allure.

## THE COMMUNITY COMPACT

As previously noted, St. Mary County gave inordinate responsibility to the polygraphists to get the truth from the offender and to relieve the child of the burden and the trauma of testifying in court. Central to this shift of responsibility was the assumption that the polygraph works, that it *is* a Magic Lasso. So if the suspect passed the polygraph, the case was not charged, or, if already charged, it was dismissed—even if there was physical evidence and a compelling disclosure by the child. Conversely, if the suspect was determined to be deceptive, he was interrogated by the polygraphist, often for two or more hours. Research that uses DNA evidence to establish "ground truth" has shown that protracted interrogation is a characteristic of false confession cases (see Kassin, 2006).

Jim Henry talked about the community's trust in Rivers and the machine. A suspect would take the polygraph, and the other professionals would say, "'Rick, what do you think?' And just as [Prosecutor] John Hunter said, 'Hey, they passed the poly.' You know, bingo, you know it was that trust . . . in Rick. So right or wrong, that was the evidence that we had . . . and everybody knew that. You know everybody had this [trust in] Rick Rivers and even the defense attorneys. . . . And they knew that we trusted him [Rivers] and if he [the suspect] passed, then, you know, we couldn't do anything with him."

The St. Mary's court file data support Hunter's assertion. One hundred and four suspects confessed before they could be offered a polygraph, presumably during their initial police interview. Of the 177 suspects who were offered and took the polygraph, thirty-eight confessed during the polygraph process, and twenty-seven (15.3 percent) were determined "not deceptive." In twenty-four of the twenty-seven not deceptive cases, charges were not filed or were dropped. (Being determined "not deceptive" does not necessarily mean the suspect did not commit and admit to a crime. Of the three whose cases were not dismissed, one had already completed terms of deferred prosecution, one received five months' probation and a $210 fine, and one received probation.)

Everyone in the community knows that this unwritten agreement means that some offenders escape the criminal-justice system and some children do not experience justice, but that is what it takes for the majority of children to be protected and for all professionals, even to an extent the defense bar, to cooperate on sexual abuse cases.

The research and our interviews would suggest that the process of polygraphy is fundamentally an art rather than a science. Polygraphists do not rely entirely on the machine. They employ their perceptual and persuasive skills. And St. Mary County had a consummate artist to rely upon in the person of Rick Rivers.

As we ended out data collection, the county was relying upon Jason Touhy to conduct most of its polygraphs. Rick Rivers had contracts with the Department of Corrections to polygraph convicted offenders before they were released from prison on parole to assure that they have addressed all their offenses. This shift, along with the retirement of Prosecutor Hunter and election of a new prosecutor, may signal an end of an era.

## CONCLUSION

The pivotal role of the polygraph was a hallmark of how sexual abuse cases were handled in St. Mary County. Its emergence and centrality to the investigative process in large part was a function of community trust in Rick Rivers. The machine is simply a tool. Criticisms of the polygraph's validity and reliability that characterize the larger professional debate about the polygraph are well founded. Every community that evaluates the role of the polygraph in its decision making about allegations of sexual abuse, the honesty of the sex offender, and the potential for recidivism needs to be mindful not only of this debate but also its nuances.

But like other parts of the St. Mary protocol, the polygraph should not be evaluated in isolation. Its use is embedded in other formal and informal aspects of the protocol, such as assuring that the polygraphist watches the child's videotaped interview, having the investigative officer present to observe and assist in the polygraph administration, and videotaping the polygraph process in its entirety. The first two measures assure that relevant and specific questions are employed during the polygraph administration, which improves its validity. The last guarantees that a complete and accurate record of the polygraph process is available to prosecutor and defense alike. These formal and informal components are arguably much more important than the "smoke and mirrors" components of the polygraph process.

# SEVEN

# Shifting the Narrative Burden Throughout Investigations and Prosecutions of Child Sexual Abuse

ELANA D. BUCH

Basically, when you've got somebody

that confesses, they don't go to trial.

—Chief Prosecutor Charles Davis

This chapter focuses on the ways that children are relatively disempowered narrators in U.S. legal settings and how the St. Mary County professionals increased the legal power of children's disclosure narratives while simultaneously decreasing the frequency with which children were actually required to narrate abuse experiences. In legal settings, adults are widely believed to be more accurate and believable narrators than children (see Ceci and Bruck, 1995). Standard child sexual abuse (CSA) cases generally rely upon children's abuse narratives to prosecute adult defendants and therefore are very difficult to prove. Available legal scholarship on the narrative dimensions of law focuses primarily on various aspects of narrative performance during trials (Amsterdam and Hertz, 1992; Bennett and Feldman, 1981; Brooks, 1996; Gerwitz, 1996; Mertz, 1994; Philips, 1984; Tiersma, 1999). Our study of the St. Mary County CSA protocol suggests that a great deal of the criminal-justice system depends upon narrative practices that occur long before a case goes to trial. The protocol and those who implemented it systematically intervened to shift the narrative burden of criminal sexual conduct (CSC) cases from children to adults both before and during trials.

The linguistic and ideological terrain of the U.S. legal system places specific demands on witnesses (a kind of narrator) in order for their stories to be recognized as true descriptions of past events (Keane, 1997; Ochs and Capps, 1996; Povinelli, 2002). These narrative demands can be particularly problematic in the prosecution of child sexual abuse. The term "narrative" is often used synonymously with "story," and in the case of personal narratives it has been defined as "one method of recapitulating past experience by matching a verbal sequence of clauses to the sequence of events which (it is inferred) actually occurred" (Labov, 2008). In personal narratives told verbally, the person telling the story, or narrator, can add layers of meaning through nonverbal communication and can also moderate how he tells his story in hopes of achieving the desired response in the audience. Those narrators who act as witnesses in legal settings need to tell their stories in a manner that convinces their audiences (attorneys, judges, juries, and so on) that the story they tell is a factually accurate representation of past events.

Children are sometimes thought to be unreliable narrators of their personal experiences owing to their active imaginations and impressionable minds. Beyond these general concerns about children's narrative abilities, the processes through which children disclose experience of sexual abuse commonly include delays in reporting, denials, incremental disclosure, and sometimes recantations (Summit, 1983), which can make it difficult for legal actors (such as judges and juries) to recognize them as true. Furthermore, courtroom settings can be particularly intimidating for children, which can inhibit their ability to provide convincing testimony about their experiences (see Dziech and Schudson, 1989). For these reasons, children are generally seen as highly problematic legal narrators about their experiences of sexual abuse (see Ceci and Bruck 1995).

The U.S. legal system makes a series of narrative demands on investigators, judges, lawyers, victims, suspects, and witnesses in order to pursue justice. Those empowered to decide if a crime was committed (police and prosecutors) and if the accused party is guilty (judges and jurors) generally lack first hand knowledge of the event(s) in question. Therefore, these decision makers must learn about the event through physical and verbal evidence. Yet disparate pieces of evidence remain incoherent and incomplete unless they are ordered and woven into a recognizable and credible narrative of a particular crime. Such a narrative is expected to be chronologically ordered and coherent, and to provide concrete details answering the basic "who, what, where, when, why and how" questions about the criminal event(s) being prosecuted. Decision makers also need to decide if they believe various witnesses' narratives are true, which includes evaluations of whether the narrating witnesses' words seem to match her physical and emotional demeanor. In criminal cases more generally, the responsibility to produce a recognizable and coherent narrative of a criminal event (here termed the "narrative burden") falls on attorneys who are themselves limited by witnesses' narratives of the event. Because of the typical lack of physical evidence or other witnesses, CSA prosecutions place an unusually heavy narrative burden on child victims.

In the United States, before any kind of crime can be charged, a crime must be reported (a kind of narrative), which police detectives (and in the case of child abuse, child protective services) then investigate by gathering available physical evidence and witnesses' verbal statements (another kind of narrative). Then the prosecuting attorney evaluates the available evidence to decide if he thinks the allegations are true and if the evidence meets the legal standards for a punishable offense. To decide if the report is true, the prosecutor must evaluate if the reporting witnesses are credible, which might also include considerations of any incentives witnesses might have for reporting the crime (Philips, 1993). The prosecutor has to take into account whether the available witnesses will be perceived as reliable narrators while testifying at trial, and determine if witnesses' various narrative perspectives can be made to constitute a coherent overarching narrative of the crime in question. If the prosecutor chooses to file criminal charges, the suspect is entitled to a preliminary examination, during which a judge determines if the alleged crime occurred within the court's jurisdiction and if the available evidence, including key witnesses' narrative testimony, establishes probable cause. Before trial, both prosecutors and defense attorneys may rehearse their witnesses' testimonies beforehand so that those witnesses can grow accustomed to telling their narratives in the form of answers to legal questioning. At the trial, defending and prosecuting attorneys then need to order and synthesize the available physical evidence and testimony in a way that accesses culturally recognizable narrative tropes regarding the type of crime at hand and minimizes evidence that contradicts or confuses their preferred narrative of the event in question (Brooks, 1996; Gerwitz, 1996; Korobkin, 1998). Prosecutors and defense attorneys then communicate these overarching case narratives to judges and juries in their opening and closing statements.

In CSA prosecutions, decisions regarding the credibility of witnesses are likely to be predicated upon assumptions members of the community share about the relative narrative capabilities of adults and children (James, 2007; Keane, 1999; Ochs and Capps, 1996). We do not have sufficient evidence to evaluate what assumptions the general population of St. Mary County had about adult and child narrators. However, among the professionals we spoke with, children's verbal narratives were thought to be prone to inconsistency and incompleteness and to lack legally necessary details. Nevertheless, these professionals also tended to find children's narratives of sexual abuse compelling, and thus seemed to distinguish between the special demands the legal system places on narratives and narrators and their personal criteria for evaluating children's narratives. Assumptions about the shortcomings of children's narratives in legal settings are similarly evident in broader academic and legal writing about children's narrative abilities, where it has been argued that children's narratives are vulnerable to imaginative elaboration and adult manipulation (Ceci and Bruck, 1993, 1995). However, at least in St. Mary County, children were also believed to be relatively unskilled at manipulating the physical and emotional signs of emotional distress, whence the belief of these professionals that the truth of children's experiences could be read from their bodies, if not from their verbal narratives. While adults were believed to have more consistent memories and a better control of historical fact, adults were also believed to have somewhat greater control over how they present themselves to the world (Goffman, 1959). Thus, adults were thought to be better able to produce false bodily signs to match deceptive verbal narratives. Polygraph tests are supposed to make visible those bodily signs of deception (such as heart rate) that cannot be perceived by the naked eye and thus are considered less susceptible to adults' ability to manipulate their bodies to disguise deception.

Our analysis suggests that one of the principal ways St. Mary County was able to achieve high rates for charging (69 percent) and convicting (76.3 percent of those charged) CSC suspects (Faller et al., 2001, updated) was that the county's protocol for prosecuting CSA cases shifted the narrative burden of these cases from child witnesses to a range of adults, including the suspect, child protective services (CPS) workers, police investigators, prosecutors, and even expert witnesses at trial. The protocol accomplished this shift in several stages that gave precedence to and built upon children's abuse disclosures. In doing so,

## CHILDREN'S DISCLOSURES AS PROBLEMATIC
## LEGAL NARRATIVES

As already noted, CSA cases pose unique challenges for investigators and prosecutors because additional witnesses and physical evidence are rarely available to support child victims' narratives of their abuse. One of the most significant obstacles to successfully prosecuting child sexual abuse is that it appears that many children do not disclose their abuse (Lyon, 2002b). While it is difficult to measure the rates at which sexually abused children do not disclose their abuse, studies of adults who describe a history of sexual abuse as children document failure to disclose during childhood. These studies include large general population surveys and smaller samples and ask respondents whether they told about their sexual abuse during childhood. Nondisclosure rates for women range from 33 percent to 92 percent (Bagley and Ramsey, 1986; Finkelhor et al., 1990; Lyons et al., 2002; Palmer et al., 1999; Russell, 1986; Russell and Bolen, 2000; Smith et al., 2000; Ullman, 2003). For men, nondisclosure rates range from 42 percent to 88 percent (Finkelhor, 1979; Finkelhor et al., 1990; Johnson and Schrier, 1985).

More recently, London and colleagues (2005) reviewed eleven surveys of adults, who were asked about sexual abuse during childhood, using a range of methodologies. The majority of adult victims did not report their sexual abuse during childhood. When one study of eighteen-year-olds, employing a very broad definition of sexual abuse, is excluded (Fergusson, Horwood, and Lynskey, 1997), the disclosure rate is 31 percent. Four studies in this review documented the rates of official report (to law enforcement or CPS), which averaged 13 percent.

Although the findings suggest that nondisclosure of sexual abuse was characteristic of about two-thirds of victims, and only a small minority of cases came to the attention of professionals, the findings derive from reports of sexual abuse from generations past. Arguably with recent increases in public and professional attention to the problem of child sexual abuse, children more readily report. In addition, St. Mary County is exceptional for its concern about child sexual abuse, which likely positively affects disclosure rates.

There are also a modest, but growing number of studies in which sexual abuse is highly likely to have occurred because there is an independent indicator of sexual abuse, such as compelling medical evidence or an audio or video record of the abuse. These studies reveal a high frequency of disclosure failures, partial disclosures, and disclosure as a process rather than an event, at least for some children (Bidrose and Goodman, 2000; Faller, 1988b; Lawson and Chaffin, 1992; Lyon, 2007; Sorensen and Snow, 1991; Terry, 1991). Illustrative of medical evidence studies is a review by Lyon (2007). He examined twenty-one studies of children with gonorrhea ($n = 579$). The medical field has definitively determined that gonorrhea in children cannot come from bedsheets or toilet seats, but rather is transmitted by sexual contact. Of the children in Lyon's aggregated sample, 42 percent of children old enough to provide a narrative (over three years old) disclosed when they came to the attention of professionals, providing compelling support for concerns about nondisclosing children.

Two recent studies illustrate children's disclosure failures even when there is audio or visual evidence of sexual abuse. Bidrose and Goodman relied on audiotapes and photographs from a case in New Zealand involving four female victims and eight male offenders (2000). The review of the tapes and photographs supported 318 sexual and related acts involving these girls, but only 194 acts (61 percent) were described by one or more of the victims. In Sweden, Sjoberg and Lindblad (2002) examined videotapes made by a single offender of his sexual abuse of ten victims, nine boys and one girl, over an eight-year period. The researchers compared the abuse on the videotapes to disclosures during the victims' police interviews. No child disclosed sexual abuse before the police interview, and five denied the abuse when interviewed by the police. No child disclosed a sexually abusive act that was not on videotape. Altogether the children who did report sexual abuse to the police revealed 102 incidents of sexual abuse, but there was a marked pattern of minimization of the victimization.

These two studies add to the evidence that many children fail to disclose or do not disclose all of their sexual abuse when questioned by professionals. In our court file data from St. Mary County, only 8.3 percent of the children are recorded as having denied sexual abuse when initially asked. However, almost all of these cases involve children who disclosed in a forensic interview. This means that an adult was already aware of and had alerted authorities to the possibility that the child had been sexually abused. Thus, these findings do not reflect the full extent of disclosure failures in the county.

It is relatively common that disclosure of sexual abuse does not occur as a discrete narrative event in the context of a forensic interview, but rather occurs in therapy. Forensic-interviewing best practices suggest that interviewers treat initial interviews with child victims as though disclosure will occur as discrete events in which children describe their abuse in response to open-ended questions. However, approximately 40 percent of children do not disclose during a forensic interview, in which case disclosure may become a much lengthier process requiring a clinical rather than forensic orientation (Faller, 2007; Lamb and Sternberg, 1999). Predictors of disclosure during a forensic interview include prior disclosure, the victim's not having close relationship with the offender, and the victim's having a supportive caretaker (Faller, 2007; Malloy, Lyon, and Quas, 2007). Clinical interviews incorporate greater attention to rapport building, support, and pacing and may incorporate the use of leading questions or supportive media (such as dolls) depending on the child's needs. Child disclosures occurring in the context of clinical process rather than during the discrete event of a forensic interview can be problematic as legal narratives because they are more susceptible to defense accusations that the clinician implanted "false memories" in the child's mind, or at least "contaminated" the child's account. Forensic interviewers must thus balance between legal considerations regarding the context and content of child's disclosure narratives and psychological considerations for the child's well-being and recovery. Clearly, a large number of sexually abused children are unable or unwilling to tell disclosure narratives at all, and many who do disclose only do so in legally problematic (clinical) contexts and thus become problematic narrators of their abuse experiences.

St. Mary County CPS workers, court officials, police officers, and prosecuting attorneys shared the belief that even when children were able to disclose their experiences of abuse within a forensic interview, children's limited narrative abilities could create significant challenges to the successful investigation and prosecution of child sexual abuse. Their beliefs were consistent with research findings that show that children's process of disclosing sexual abuse does not always correspond well with the legal system's need for chronological, consistent narratives. Best practices in child interviewing include asking open-ended questions and obtaining a narrative from the child. However, for many, and perhaps most children, disclosure of sexual abuse is not simply an "outcry" (a spontaneous report to a trusted person) followed by an interview by protective services and/or police, who use open-ended probes, to which children respond providing a coherent, detailed account. The child's typical reaction to the experience of sexual abuse is to maintain secrecy, to be co-opted by the offender, perhaps eventually to disclose, and sometimes to recant after the child experiences the familial and system response to the sexual abuse disclosure (Lyon, 2002; Olafson, 2002; Olafson, Corwin, and Summit, 1993).

This series of responses to the unwelcome and unanticipated boundary violation that sexual abuse represents was first described in the literature by Roland Summit, a psychiatrist and pioneering practitioner and thinker in the sexual abuse field. Summit called these responses the child sexual abuse accommodation syndrome (Summit, 1983). This literature also indicates that, for many children, disclosure is a process that may involve initial denial and later recantation (Olafson, 2002; Sorensen and Snow, 1991). These findings fit with victim therapist Connor's practice experience in St. Mary County, as she told us "children were terrified of 'telling' and the possible consequences from their families. No one could eliminate that fear for those children." CPS workers in St. Mary County also told many stories in which a child victim had given an explicit, detailed disclosure of sexual abuse, but later, fearful of the consequences, recanted his or her stories. The legal difficulties posed by cases in which a child has recanted were vividly illustrated by a trial that our research team observed involving a child victim who had disclosed and recanted several times over several years of abuse by her stepfather. In legal contexts, children's normal practice of denying and/or recanting sexual abuse disclosures can be used by the suspect's defense attorneys to create doubt about the veracity of the child's narrative, and it can thereby limit the usefulness of a child's narrative as legal evidence.

The credibility of a child's disclosure of sexual abuse as a legal narrative often plays a significant role in determining whether or not a CSA allegation is charged and prosecuted as a criminal offense. In deciding whether to charge a case, the St. Mary County prosecutor must evaluate not only the quality of the child victim's disclosure, but also the child's potential as a witness, even though relatively few CSC cases actually make it to trial. In St. Mary County there were only eighteen CSC trials over a fourteen-year period. In making this decision, every prosecutor must consider this:

Jurors must decide that something did or didn't happen based on the credibility of the live speaker's performed narrative tested against similar but conflicting narratives. Credibility depends on the apparent truthfulness of the speaker, which may have more to do with acting ability, articulateness, and personality traits than with honesty. It also depends on the believability of the narrative itself, and here "literary" qualities like consistency, coherence, and persuasive rendering of detail often carry the day. (Korobkin, 1998)

The professionals we interviewed in St. Mary County often described children as emotionally powerful but legally inadequate narrators of their experiences because children do not always understand that their experiences constitute a violation; because they sometimes forget or are inconsistent about specific details regarding abuse; because they are easily influenced by family members and worry about the consequences of telling their stories; and because their ability to talk about abuse varies greatly depending on the context in which they are asked to share their stories. Moreover, all the professionals we interviewed in St. Mary County shared the belief that both the legal case and the victim's mental health were seriously damaged when a child had to retell his or her narrative of sexual abuse in multiple contexts and to multiple listeners. CSA experts share this belief (Cross et al., 2007).

The professionals we interviewed in St. Mary County told a number of stories about the challenges to successful prosecution created when children were able to describe their experiences of sexual abuse but did not narrate these experiences in a legally convincing manner. Police Officer Shawn Duffy told us that children did not always describe their sexual experiences with adults as a kind of violation. Duffy suggested, "Adult victims know they're a victim, I think you treat them differently because you know that they are victims of a crime. They know that they've been violated in some way. I think that's just the difference. Adult victims know they've been violated. . . . Kids don't know that." Duffy argues that children were treated differently than adults because they are less likely than adults to use the language of victimization and violation that investigators expect in sexual abuse narratives. On the other hand, Henry argued that in his experience, sexually abused children often did identify themselves as victims and experienced sexual abuse as a violation. Clearly, law enforcement professionals' expectations of sexual abuse narratives did not always match with the way children actually narrated their abuse.

In addition, sometimes children were able to frame their experiences of sexual abuse as violations but were unable to provide the kinds of specific details called for in courtroom testimony. For example, in a CSC trial that we observed in St. Mary County, the twelve-year-old victim was able to give a detailed description of landmarks leading to the scene of her sexual assault. However she could not identify the location using unique features such as street names, and defense attorneys were able to raise questions about whether the scene of the crime was actually within St. Mary County (see chapter 10). Furthermore, the kinds of details children were required to provide to tell legally credible narratives changed over time in St. Mary County. For example, child therapist and social worker Susan Connor explained that at the time the protocol was developed, children's descriptions of their sexual abuse were often sufficient to convince CPS workers and prosecutors that the child's story was true, although "today it is possible to make up a halfway credible story because all the info is available all over the media, in books, and on the Internet. In the 1980s, the stories were new and the details shocking. If a child had that kind of detailed information, we figured they had experienced it, and we wanted them removed from that horrible, dangerous situation." Thus, in the 1980s, county professionals' belief that children did not have substantial knowledge of sex acts unless they had personally experienced them enhanced the narrative credibility of any child who could provide sexually explicit details. By the time we interviewed Connor two decades later, sexually explicit information was widely available in public media, making these kinds of details insufficient to convince professionals that children were telling legally credible narratives of sexual abuse.

Sexually explicit details may have been sufficient for CPS to remove the child in the early years of the protocol's development, but they sometimes provided insufficient evidence of abuse in the courtroom. Chief Prosecutor Charles Davis explained that the narrative credibility of child victims also depended on the child's ability to provide a variety of specific contextual details about her experiences of abuse: "Let's say you have a little girl, a five-year-old girl . . . who was sexually abused and her first interview she said that it happened 'on my birthday when I was four years old.' And you get to trial and she recalls that it happened on Christmas. And she was wrong and so she can be impeached by her prior inconsistent statement as to when it happened."

Davis explained that at trial, prosecuting attorneys could sometimes remedy these inconsistencies by further probing children's memories. For example, the reason that the child thought that the sexual abuse occurred on her birthday was that she associated the abuse with having received a bicycle as a gift, but upon further questioning she recalled that the bicycle was actually a Christmas gift. In determining whether to charge CSC cases, prosecutors must rely on their judgment and experience to decide whether the contextual details provided in child victims' narratives are consistent and detailed enough to be used as credible evidence in the courtroom. St. Mary County's unique investigation protocol was apt to elicit confessions from suspects, which frequently rendered children's testimony unnecessary.

As other chapters of this book have shown, the protocol prescribed forensic interviewing techniques that attempted to mitigate concerns about children's narrative credibility by helping children narrate their abuse in a detailed, consistent manner so as to better meet the legal system's demands. Particularly by allowing CPS workers with substantial training and experience interviewing children to conduct CSC interviews with victims whether or not CPS was officially investigating the case, St. Mary County focused on adult's responsibility for improving children's narrative credibility. Informally, the protocol and peer review also focused on improving the forensic interviewing skills of both police officers and CPS officers. This training was intended to insure that children's initial disclosures of abuse provided the kinds of narrative details and consistency required by the legal system. As CPS supervisor Donna Wagner told us, "If you don't have a good interview, if you're with a very vulnerable child that's probably been traumatized and not going to have an easy time telling the story, if you don't get a good interview, you're dead in the water. So we knew that that's where it would start. We also knew that that was probably where our least experienced people were going to be."

Wagner, like many other professionals in St. Mary County, recognized that the legal system requires traumatized children to narrate their experiences of sexual abuse in particular, legally credible ways, even in the earliest phases of abuse investigations. Without legally credible narratives from children, as she phrased it, "you're dead in the water." Yet even as Wagner spoke about how critical these narratives are, she placed the burden of eliciting these narratives on adults who must "get a good interview" rather than on vulnerable children who are "not going to have an easy time telling their story."

Those adults who regularly conducted child forensic interviews talked at length about the moral and emotional weight of their responsibility simultaneously to provide children with emotional support and help them narrate their experiences of sexual abuse in a legally credible manner. For example, Henry told us that his goal when interviewing child victims is "to get a story as objectively as possible with as minimal trauma as possible to the child. And that to me is the essence. I know as an interviewer that I've got to get an objective story. If I don't, I'm messing the kid up. At the same time, how can I create a supportive environment for that kid?"

Henry, so clearly focused on his responsibilities as an interviewer, suggested that it is within his ability to elicit or "get" a legally credible story from child victims, and he assumed that he was personally to blame for the negative consequences to the child if he was unable to elicit such a narrative. Note that Henry was simultaneously concerned with both the legal and emotional repercussions of the child's narration. Even at this early phase in the investigation, the narrative burden of proving child sexual abuse was shifted at least partially from the child victim to an adult professional.

Once the child has told his or her story, Henry argues that the interviewer becomes a steward or protector of the story, responsible for protecting both the integrity of the child's narrative and the child's well-being. Part of accomplishing this, Henry later argued, is ensuring that the legal system and those prosecuting the abuser take the child's story seriously and convict the abuser.

## CONFESSIONS AND THE EXERCISE OF NARRATIVE POWER

Individual aspects of the protocol address particular concerns related to children's narrative ability in legal settings and may improve charging and conviction rates. However, professionals in St. Mary County argued that the protocol was far more valuable because it comprehensively shifted the narrative burden from adults to children throughout the investigation of CSC cases and thereby minimized the likelihood that a CSA victim would have to retell his or her story in a courtroom in the first place.

The videotaped records of children's interviews and disclosures powerfully captured both child victims' verbal narratives and their affective states and were an important method of increasing the authority of children's narratives (Corwin, 1995). Though children's abuse disclosures are often fragmentary, police investigators in St. Mary County were able to use the basic facts and events described in children's disclosures to establish a general outline of the abuse events and the context in which they occurred. Police investigators and polygraph operators then pushed suspects to respond directly to and fill in the narrative framework established by children's disclosures.

Children's developmental limitations and incomplete language socialization sometimes meant that they did not know how to narrate their experiences of sexual abuse in legally convincing ways. However, professionals in St. Mary County told us that the adult suspects they encountered generally understood how to construct stories to deny the child's allegations. Adult's storytelling proficiency was one of the principal justifications given by law enforcement officials for the protocol's mandate to interview suspects as soon as possible after a child had been interviewed. Shawn Duffy told us, "The suspect needs to get in here too, because once the victim's in here and the suspect has knowledge, he's going to start thinking, 'Okay. What do I need to do?' And the longer he's thinking of stories that he can make up, the harder it's going to be for me to sit down and get him to tell me what he did because he's going to have all this defense and all these stories."

With professionals videotaping their interviews of children as soon as sexual abuse was reported, suspects did not have time to construct their own version of the abuse event and instead had to respond to the specific narrative scaffolding established by children's disclosures. Videotaped interviews also made suspects confront children's physical displays of trauma and distress. The visible signs of the child's trauma, as depicted on the videotape, were often seen as indexing at least the emotional, if not the factual, truth of the child's story to both prosecutors and suspects. Thus, even when a child's verbal narrative did not provide sufficient detail about the abuse event to prosecute the crime, the videotape could still help convince adults—both perpetrators and prosecutors—that the abuse occurred. Donna Wagner explained that sometimes law enforcement and suspects relied more upon the bodily and nonverbal aspects of a child's narration than the child's verbal disclosures to decipher the truth: "Just because you don't get a kid to reveal, doesn't mean it wasn't . . . worth doing. But then when the young gal, when she was interviewed on the videotape, it was so obvious in her body language and her tone of her voice and the pauses, what she had really experienced. . . . And that's what pulled at that father's conscience and allowed him to tell his story."

Numerous professionals in St. Mary County similarly argued that the visible, bodily signs of a sexually abused child's distress captured by videotapes directly caused suspects to confess. Investigators and prosecutors in St. Mary County provided us with two complementary interpretations about how being confronted with the child's videotaped narrative of sexual abuse caused suspects to confess: that suspects attempted to reassert their narrative authority by providing a minimizing account of the events outlined by the child's narrative, and that suspects' emotional attachments to children trumped their assertions of narrative authority. Prosecutor John Hunter told us that the videotape was particularly important in establishing children's narrative credibility to adult suspects who were accustomed to assuming that their stories would always have more authority than a child's story: "The offender frequently has a relationship either with that child or with other children and has learned over years that essentially, a child can be drowned out and ignored by the defender talking over the child. And he can't do that when he watches the videotape. And he is forced to accept the fact that people might well believe what that child says, and is much more likely to confess after watching the videotape of the child."

Hunter argued that by visually documenting a child's emotional state during disclosures, the videotape helps convince suspects that the children's narratives may in fact be highly persuasive as legal evidence. In doing so, the videotape diminishes the adult suspects' assumptions about their relative power as legal narrators and thereby convinces them to provide their own narrative versions (confessions and admissions) of the events in question that at least minimally correspond with children's narratives.

The process of diminishing suspects' assumptions about their greater power as legal narrators does not necessarily occur automatically once suspects have watched a videotape. Rather police investigators and polygraph operators in St. Mary County told us that after showing suspects the videotape, they used a variety of interview strategies to coax confessions out of them. These investigators generally used the videotapes to establish the basic storyline of the abuse event or events in question and then encouraged suspects to contest only specific details children's stories. In responding to the details of the child's disclosure, suspects frequently and inadvertently accepted the general outline of the children's narratives, thereby implicitly admitting to committing some level of sexual abuse. For example, police investigator Shawn Duffy told us that his usual strategy when interviewing a CSC suspect who consistently denies the abuse was to

> talk to 'em as long as I can, and if they start to get aggravated, I say, "Hey, you know, if it's not true, let's watch the videotape and then you tell me what you don't like. You tell me what you don't agree with. Um, why is she lying about this? If she's lying about this, why isn't she lying about that? Or maybe her story's different. You tell me what you don't like about that. What is she lying about?" Unfortunately for them, they will watch it and then I'll say, if it wasn't something real bad, I'll just say, "Well, he touched me on you know in between my legs on the outside of my clothes." You know, "Why would she say that if it wasn't true? She could have made up a whole bunch of stuff that made it sound like a lot worse than what it was? You know maybe you did it accidentally. Maybe you didn't know. Were you drinking at the time or something like that?" You know, "Well, I could've."

Jeff Penn, another police investigator, told us that he strategically examined suspects' relationships with child victims as a way of rhetorically cornering suspects into verifying the general outlines of children's narratives. Penn told us that before watching the videotape, suspects would often claim that they had strong, loving relationships with the child and did not understand why they were being questioned. Penn said that he would respond to these suspects thus:

> We'll have 'em watch that tape. And it's very productive in getting you into the next stage, the interrogation portion of it, you know, where this loving, great child who has this wonderful relationship is breaking down on tape or is telling about what he's done and so forth. You go right into that . . . you can start off with, "Is what she is telling me a lie?" And they're very reluctant to call their child a liar. I don't know how many times I've heard this: "Well, I wouldn't say that." You know when you've got them when they won't give you, "Absolutely. I don't know where that's coming from. That's a lie."

Penn was thus able to parlay the suspect's characterization of his strong, loving relationship with the child, combined with the videotape of the child's narrative, into a situation in which the suspect must admit that the children's narrative is at least partially true. The interrogation strategy described by Duffy and Penn involved a kind of linguistic bait and switch playing upon widely shared ideologies about what kinds of speakers are believable narrators of their own experiences. While encouraging the adult suspect to exercise his assumed power as a more credible narrator than the child, this investigative strategy nevertheless privileged the children's general narrative over the adult's specific denials. In both interrogation examples, the interrogators privileged the child's narrative by asking the rhetorical question, "Why would she say that if it wasn't true?" By using the child's overall version of events to establish the framework of what occurred, this strategy altered the assumed and usual dynamics of narrative and linguistic power in legal settings.

Chief Prosecutor Charles Davis argued that the videotape generally convinced suspects that it was in their best interest to provide their own minimizing versions of the abuse account because suspects recognized the persuasiveness of children's narratives. When suspects realized that they would only be believed if they could explain and respond to the visible and highly believable bodily and affective signs of the child's trauma, they were motivated to provide a plausible narrative about what caused the child to be so disturbed. Davis argued that while suspects frequently diminished the extent of the abuse in their responses to children's videotaped narratives, they were nonetheless cornered into admitting to some degree of criminal sexual conduct:

> The offender sees, "Oh, this is pretty damaging." And I think at some extent, there was a sympathy factor. They see the kid going through this, and it's a little bit different than being confronted with, "Well, Heather said such and such." The other reason is . . . the chance for the offender to minimize. He says, "Heather's talking about, well, this happened on, you know, ten different occasions." He says, "Well, you know there was one night. You know. . . . I had too many beers and it did happen once."

Davis, along with a number of investigators and prosecutors in St. Mary County argued that viewing children's emotional distress simultaneously prompted both emotional and strategic reactions in adult suspects, both of which worked to increase the likelihood of at least a partial confession. A number of other professionals in St. Mary County argued that the emotional effects of trauma, so poignantly conveyed through the videotapes of children's disclosures, was a critical factor in motivating suspects to respond with their own version of these stories.

While police investigators and polygraph operators tended to be far less protective of suspects' confessions than CPS workers were of children's disclosures, investigative professionals spoke of feeling a similar sense of responsibility for the narratives they elicit. Many of these investigators told us that their sense of narrative responsibility stemmed from their commitment to helping victims. For example, Ed Williams told us that he would act sympathetically toward suspects and try to befriend them as a strategy to make them more comfortable sharing their stories. Williams told us that he was often conflicted about acting so friendly with suspects because although he "wasn't happy with them . . . the other issue is that I knew I had a job to do and the job was to do what I could to get them to tell what they did because it would help everybody. And that would help that child who has already been victimized." According to Williams and many of the other police investigators we interviewed for this study, it was their duty to use any legal strategy necessary, including various forms of psychological and emotional manipulation, to "get" confessions or admissions from suspects. Officer Ed Duke similarly argued that the protocol's procedures helped police gather evidence (particularly victim's videotaped abuse disclosures) in such a manner that they "actually controlled what happened" and thus were able to get suspects to respond to abuse allegations in a manner that frequently led to confessions. Much like Williams, Duke spoke about his dedication to "getting" suspects to provide legally admissible narratives,

> You bore in and you get a legal confession from that guy that's presentable in court and now you don't have to worry very much about preparing your [victim] to go to court. You know, it's these things, without a doubt, I can't think of anything that is more traumatic to kids than to have something like this done to them. And if I've got to spend an extra hour to with dad to get him to tell me about this, I'll spend a couple extra hours. It's worth it.

While police officers and polygraph operators regularly justified using their ability to emotionally manipulate suspects to get confessions as necessary to protect child victims, several of these professionals expressed a significant amount of concern for the suspect's well-being and suggested that they did not take the power to get confessions lightly. Williams told us that,

> The only problem I ever had is when I'm trying to elicit this confession and this guy's all of a sudden spilling what he knows and then in the back of my mind, I'm thinking, "this guy's just telling me what he's telling me I'm going to put him away for fifteen years to life. I wonder if he realizes that. 'Cause you know what, I do." And I don't know. Man, this is terrible, look at the power, look at what I just put on this person.

Like the forensic interviewers who elicited children's disclosures, these professionals believed that the power to elicit painful and damaging narratives made them responsible for the suspects' well-being, which sometimes conflicted with their role as law-enforcement officers. The county's emphases on treatment as well as incarceration for sexual offenders may have helped police investigators manage these conflicted feelings.

Taken together, the protocol's procedures and the interrogation tactics used by St. Mary County professionals were highly successful at getting suspects to confess to CSA crimes. Eliciting confessions is perhaps the most comprehensive and successful way to shift the narrative burden of proving CSC cases from children to adults because the adult suspect's confession can largely substitute for the child's disclosure throughout the remainder of the prosecution. Even though suspects are likely to make only partial confessions, confessions are considered highly credible legal evidence of guilt so long as they can be shown to have been made voluntarily (Brooks, 2000; Kamisar, 1980; Kassin, 1997; Pearse et al., 1998; Wrightsman and Kassin, 1993). In St. Mary County, when police investigators and polygraph operators elicit a confession from a suspect, they try to encourage the suspect to provide as many narrative details as possible regarding the sexual abuse, which helps establish the veracity and the voluntariness of the confession itself while minimizing the need for the child victim to provide such details. Polygraph operator Rivers told us,

> Once you've initiated the acknowledgment of what they're saying, then what I usually attempt to do is try to get back as far as what was going on at the

time and why they did what they did. How they felt. If they can acknowledge . . . what they were doing in connection with that act itself, there's no
way that that confession is going to be called a false confession. . . . We're
explaining what they're feeling and how they're feeling it, when it took place.
Then what do they have as a defense mechanism to come back on saying,
"This wasn't true"?

Strategies such as the one described by Rivers thus bolstered the legal
credibility of the suspect's narrative and simultaneously decreased the
need for child victims to narrate their abuse experiences in a legally credible manner. Police officers and polygraph operators told us that many
suspects only admitted to a small part of the abuse they were accused
of. However, even when a suspect only confessed to part of the abuse
the child disclosed, prosecutors were likely to negotiate a plea-bargain
with the defense and thereby eliminate other narrative burdens on the
child, particularly the burden of giving courtroom testimony. The high
rate of confessions and subsequent plea-bargains made through the use
of the protocol is perhaps the most definitive way that St. Mary County
shifted the narrative burden from CSA victims to adults. As Davis told us
after being asked to identify what he considered a successful case, "I can
think of a lot . . . of pleas, and . . . basically when you've got somebody
that confesses, they don't go to trial." While confessions are the goal of
police investigations in lots of counties and for lots of crimes, St. Mary
County professionals, using the systemic procedures prescribed by the
protocol, played upon shared assumptions about narrative authority to
shift the narrative burden from sexually abused children to both themselves and their suspects.

## BARGAINING TO SHIFT THE NARRATIVE BURDEN BEFORE TRIAL

Though eliciting confessions from suspects was the preferred and most
decisive method of shifting the narrative burden from children to adults
in CSC cases, the St. Mary County prosecutor's office also used its power
to negotiate plea bargains to minimize further the narrative demands
placed on child victims. Obviously, flexible plea-bargaining had strategic value to the prosecutor's office because CSC cases are so difficult
to win at trial. However, Prosecutor Hunter explained that his office's

plea-bargaining policies were a matter of victim protection as well as legal strategy: "We have very rarely absolutely insisted on a conviction as charged because we really prefer not to run the risk of loss of a case or traumatize the victim on a case. These cases are better for everybody if they're resolved." The focus on convicting CSC offenders without going to trial was seen as a way of protecting both child victims and the case itself from the narrative risks inherent in legal trials. Prosecutors in St. Mary County used their ability to negotiate plea bargains with defendants to alter narrative burden on children in two ways: first, to prevent children from having to testify at preliminary hearings and at trials, and second, to encourage adults to declare their guilt formally and publicly.

Professionals in St. Mary County uniformly believed that children were traumatized by repeated, legally oriented narrations (as opposed to therapeutic narrations in clinical settings), and thus strove to avoid requiring the child to narrate her experiences at every possible stage in the legal process. While videotaping children's disclosures minimized the number of times children told their stories to investigators and prosecutors, St. Mary County prosecutors went one step further to minimize the narrative burden born by children: they created incentives for defendants to waive their right to have the child testify at the preliminary exam. Whether or not a suspect confesses, when a defendant is charged with a crime, he is entitled to a preliminary hearing in which a judge reviews the evidence against him in order to determine that there is sufficient evidence for a trial. The legal principle of *corpus delicti* means that even when a suspect confesses, the prosecution is required to provide additional corroborating evidence to ensure that the suspect is not falsely confessing to a crime that never occurred. In CSA prosecutions, this stage of the legal process often creates an additional narrative burden on child victims because their disclosures are so frequently the only corroborating evidence of sexual abuse. Typically, these children have already had to repeatedly narrate their traumatic experience of abuse to CPS investigators, police officers and prosecuting attorneys prior to the preliminary exam. Prosecutors in St. Mary County told us that they tried to encourage suspects to waive their right to have child victims testify during preliminary exams for both pragmatic legal reasons and to protect the child from the further trauma of testifying in the courtroom. As pragmatic legal strategy, it made sense for prosecutors to try to avoid having child victims testify at preliminary exams because children were sometimes intimidated by formal courtroom settings and became unreliable legal narrators of their abuse. For example, Charles Davis told us that he once prosecuted a CSC case that was dismissed even though the defendant had confessed to the abuse because the child was unable to testify at the preliminary exam. In an attempt to mitigate the narrative demands on children at this stage of CSA prosecutions, Judge Richter told us, "This particular office has a policy that if the defendant takes a case to preliminary examination in the District Court and makes the victim testify then they either don't get a plea deal or it's more stringent than it would have been then if they had waived the exam."

The focus on negotiating a plea often led prosecutors to accept partial admissions and convictions for lesser charges than might be justified by the children's disclosures. These bargains were considered frustrating, if pragmatic, compromises made because prosecutors generally believed that it was more important to minimize the narrative burden on the child than to convict defendants of the highest degree of criminal sexual conduct possible. Within the plea-bargaining process, the prosecutor's office emphasized the importance of defendants' shouldering the narrative burden of the case by offering incentives to defendants who pleaded guilty rather than no contest. Members of the St. Mary County legal community, including the defense bar, were widely aware of the prosecutor's policy of reserving bargains that included mandatory treatment (either instead of or supplementary to decreased jail or prison time) for those defendants who admitted their guilt. As Jameson told us, "For one thing, you got to plead guilty and admit that you did it. No-contest pleas don't get into the treatment program. You've got to get up and say, I did it. I put my finger right on her or I did whatever, you know, what makes you guilty."

Prosecutors explained that guilty pleas and confessions were important because they validated the child's narrative and because they helped convince reluctant adults in the victim's life (such as nonabusing mothers who had been dating the abuser) that the child was telling the truth about having been sexual abused. In this way, prosecutors in St. Mary County were attentive to, and tried to minimize, even those narrative burdens shouldered by CSA victims that extended beyond the legal system itself. Prosecutors and judges in St. Mary County also believed that only those defendants willing to shoulder the narrative burden of child sexual abuse through confessions and guilty pleas were amenable to treatment. Many of these professionals, in fact, spoke of confession as the first step of treatment itself; as Judge Richter told us, "Most of the cases are settled by plea. It is very, very important to the defendants' recovery . . . that they take responsibility." Jameson similarly observed that confession "impresses the judge, when you come in right from the get go and accept responsibility. Say, okay I did it, I'm sorry, I'm not going to make the child testify. I'll do whatever you want me to do in terms of treatment. I'll take my punishment." Here, Jameson suggests, the judge explicitly ties the defendant's willingness to substitute his narrative confession of the abuse event or events for the children's testimony as an important part of seeking justice in sexual abuse cases.

## NARRATIVE RISKS AND REMEDIES DURING THE CSA TRIAL

Throughout the investigation and prosecution of CSA cases professionals in St. Mary County worked to shift the narrative burdens of these cases from child victims to adult investigators and suspects. Ideally, the various procedures of the protocol accomplished this shift by procuring confessions and thereby avoided the narrative demands trials make on children. As Davis told us, "usually when you have the protocol, you don't go to trial . . . because the idea is to get a confession. And the most difficult cases are the cases where you go to trial without a confession. And those are the cases that are just embedded in my memory." Why were the CSA cases that went to trial the ones that were seared in the memories of so many of the St. Mary County professionals that we interviewed? It is at trials that children's narrative vulnerabilities became both most obvious and most problematic to the prosecution of CSA cases. Yet, even when the protocol had failed to produce a confession and failed to eliminate the need for a child to testify, professionals in St. Mary County continued to focus on minimizing or shifting the narrative burdens placed on the child through out trial preparations and the trial itself.

Children's limitations as legal narrators are most apparent in courtroom settings, where their narratives are evaluated as legal evidence rather than as psychological truths. Both prosecuting attorneys and the therapists responsible for preparing children to testify at trial suggested that children's ability to successfully tell their stories at trials depended greatly on the courtroom context and timing. Therapist Connor told us,

Therapeutically speaking, there was almost always a window of opportunity for the testimony—a time during the treatment process when the child was best prepared emotionally and cognitively to tell the story one more time and do it well. A child/teen needs a certain level of calm, controlled anger to have the strength and motivation to talk about such yucky stuff in front of adults—and the perpetrator. . . . Unfortunately, the timing was not always good. Some cases dragged on for months, even years, and the child and family would be finished with counseling and ready to look forward, not backward.

On the other hand, Jim Henry told us that sometimes children found the courtroom setting so frightening that even those who had previously told coherent, detailed narratives were intimidated and made poor witnesses at trial. In one poignant case, Henry told us of a child who was on the witness stand and found herself unable to finish her testimony after the defense attorney blocked her view of Henry, whose calming presence was critical to her ability to tell her story:

> I interviewed the kid. The kid told me a good, detailed story. Mark [Jameson] says, "We're going to get this guy even though she's five." At the prelim I'm up there in front with Mark. The kid's right there and we all know in court, you can't do anything but smile. She keeps looking at me and tells the story. This guy, the neighbor did this, forty-year-old man doing stuff. Putting his finger in her vagina. Sam Huff watched the whole thing. The first thing Sam does is get between me and her. The kid never said a word. The case [was] dismissed.

There was little that prosecutors or therapists believed they could do to change the slow pace at which CSA cases are tried, or to alter courtroom dynamics that children find threatening. However, they employed a number of strategies to minimize both the risks to children's narrative credibility and the trauma that these professionals associated with children testifying in CSC trials. Before trial, a prosecutor watched the child's videotaped disclosure with the child to help her recall the narrative she had already told. Prosecutors argued that this practice increased the consistency of children's testimony while preserving the affective power of their narratives. Prosecutor John Hunter told us that if child witnesses were asked to tell their stories too many times before the trial, the affective dimension of their narrative flattens, and then "you've created a little automaton." While prosecuting attorneys used the videotape to help the child prepare to narrate his experience of abuse at trial, the victim advocate in St. Mary County tried to get the child acclimated to the courtroom setting so that she would be familiar with both the place and the process. These practices were seen as minimizing the trauma children experienced from testifying, increasing children's comfort on the witness stand and thereby the likelihood that these children would be able to credibly narrate their experiences of abuse during trials.

Despite the professionals' efforts to shift the narrative burden before trial, many of those children who did testify at trial were not able to tell coherent, legally credible narratives about their experiences of sexual abuse. In other cases, defense attorneys attempted to erode the jury's confidence in the credibility of the child's disclosure by highlighting narrative discrepancies and reversals that occurred within the disclosure process. Yet even in these most challenging cases, the prosecutors in St. Mary County continued to try to shift some of the narrative burden onto adults' shoulders by calling an expert witness to help jurors understand some of the common psychological reactions of abused children and how these reactions influence the narratives they tell about their abuse. By helping jurors to interpret the frequently fragmentary, sometimes contradictory, ways that sexually abused children often narrate their experiences, the expert witness—who was none other than our own Jim Henry in his post–Sex Busters incarnation as a professor of social work at a nearby university—shifted a portion of the narrative burden of providing evidence in child sexual abuse onto his own shoulders. As an expert witness, Henry was unable to comment on a specific child's testimony, but by discussing a hypothetical case, he instead provides the jurors with psychological findings intended to help them understand how and why children are often legally problematic narrators of sexual abuse. For example, in the Inman trial, where the child's disclosure of sexual abuse was challenged by the defense because the child had not immediately disclosed the abuse to her mother, and because the child later disclosed in stages, Henry reported research findings suggesting that delayed and partial disclosures are both common features in children's process of disclosing abuse:

The research on child abuse and specifically, child sexual abuse about disclosure is that oftentimes when children are first confronted with did something happen or a question is asked, that they deny that it's happened because getting back to what I said earlier, they're afraid of the response, and so what their first inclination is to protect themselves and to say no, it didn't happen, and so it's a common phenomenon for children to initially recant or not recant, but to deny what has happened.

As Henry's testimony continued, the prosecutor proceeded to ask if the various disclosure stages of the hypothetical child were common among sexually abused children. For each stage of the disclosure, Henry told the courtroom audience about relevant research data, about sexually abused children's common disclosure process, and about key factors determining if a child is able to disclose, all supporting the idea that this hypothetical child's disclosure process was typical and therefore implying that the hypothetical child's initial denials and reversals should not necessarily be seen as negating the truthfulness of the child's later disclosure of her sexual abuse. By providing the court and the jury with a more nuanced understanding about the complex psychological processes affecting sexually abused children's ability to narrate their abuse, Henry worked to change the criteria the jury used to evaluate the credibility of their disclosures and courtroom testimonies. In doing so, Henry shifts some of the burden of constructing a credible legal narrative away from the child and onto himself.

## SUCCESSES AND LIMITS OF SHIFTING THE NARRATIVE BURDEN

Child sexual abuse cases are notoriously difficult to prosecute because so many of them rely primarily upon the ability of child victims to narrate convincingly their experiences of abuse in order to investigate, charge, and convict child sexual abusers. Serving the twin goals of protecting children from additional traumas and convicting sexual offenders, the investigatory protocol and practices developed in St. Mary County systematically minimized and shifted the narrative burden of sexual abuse cases from children to adults at every possible juncture. While children's disclosures remained essential to initiate and investigate CSA cases, county professionals believed that it was their responsibility to create interview environments that safely facilitated children disclosing their experience of abuse in legally credible ways; coax suspects to provide their own confession narratives that corroborate children's abuse narratives and therefore minimize additional legal demands on children's narratives; offer incentives for waiving preliminary exams to decrease the number of times children are required to repeat their narratives in public settings; and explain common processes of children's narrative disclosures of abuse to juries in order to diminish courtroom attempts to discredit these narratives. Embedded in these procedures were two interconnected assumptions shared by St. Mary County professionals: that within the legal system children are both disempowered and deficient narrators of their experiences of sexual abuse, and that the experience of narrating abuse within legal settings was therefore highly traumatic for children. Rather than directly challenge these assumptions about children's narrative deficiencies and the inability of the legal system to recognize children's narratives as true, the protocol primarily works to minimize the effects of these assumptions on the prosecution of CSA cases. Thus, the protocol implemented a vision of normalized justice that valued shifting the narrative burden to adults but did not fundamentally alter the distribution of linguistic power between children and adults in legal settings. As a coordinated set of policies and practices, the protocol consistently recognized and tried to improve the status of children as inadequate narrators of their own experiences in legal settings, even as it reproduced cultural assumptions to that effect. When the protocol worked well and suspects confessed to the abuse, the responsibility to construct legally credible narratives in CSA cases was systematically shifted from child victims to the adults charged with investigating and prosecuting these cases, and ultimately to the adult perpetrators.

## LESSONS FOR PRACTICE

• Child sexual abuse investigations and prosecutions typically rely on children's narratives to provide evidence of the crime.

• Children are disempowered legal narrators.

• The narrative burden of proving child sexual abuse can be shifted from children to adults throughout the investigation and prosecution of CSA cases.

• Shifting the narrative burden from children to adults protects children from the trauma of testifying in courtroom settings and from additional sexual abuse. Practices that shift the narrative burden to adults also improve the legal credibility of critical evidence in CSA investigations and prosecutions.

Shouldering the Shifted Burden    **EIGHT**

*The Defense Attorneys*

FRANK E. VANDERVORT

There's no law that says the cops and prosecutors

can't lie. And, of course, they do, every day. . . .

They never want to get us involved because if

we got involved, they can't do the protocol.

—Sam Huff

Sam Huff, portly and bespectacled, practices law out of a converted wood-frame house on Main Street in Two Lakes. He is the nominal leader among the contract lawyers appointed by the St. Mary County court to represent indigent defendants brought before the court on charges of criminal sexual conduct (CSC). Richard Nowak, one of Huff's colleagues, says of him, "He's got the most experience out of the contract group. He's got the lion's share of the work." By comparison, Nowak notes that his own appointed criminal practice is a "tiny slice of the pie." Huff began practicing law in St. Mary County in February 1980, two years after Nowak. Brian Muller, another of the county's appointed defense attorneys, began his practice about that same time. So, when we interviewed them in 2003, it was apparent that these lawyers constituted a stable and experienced defense bar.

Huff and Muller had been in practice for about three years, and Nowak about five, when Chief Prosecutor Davis established the child sexual abuse (CSA) investigation protocol. That fact would have an important impact on the professional lives of St. Mary County's defense attorneys because it would make their work on child sexual abuse cases more difficult and largely neutralize their ability to advocate effectively for their clients.

## CASES INCREASE, AND A RESPONSE

"When I first came here," Huff reflected on the protocol's establishment, "the abuse and neglect area of the practice of law primarily involved physical abuse. Rarely if ever did you see a case of sexual abuse. . . . In fact, I don't remember a case of sexual abuse in '80, '81, in that initial period of time. . . . All of a sudden we had this enormous influx of CSC cases." Confronted with this increase, the prosecutors groped for an adequate response. Within only a couple of years, the basic elements of the protocol were in place, even though researchers and practitioners knew little about the phenomenon of child sexual abuse.

· Huff provided his view of the protocol's origin: "I think the protocol itself . . . developed as a result of this influx of cases that all of a sudden people became aware of sexual abuse." The authorities "were kind of floundering around" in those early years, he said. "How do we do this? Who interviews them?" Calling their initial handling of the cases "real amateurish," Huff said, "At the time there was a real reliance on experts, so-called experts, who, in many instances didn't know any more about the subject than we did. . . . We were fighting all sorts of problems. Somebody would make a claim that sexual abuse occurred, and so they would send them over to [a mental-health professional]. . . . Three months [later] we'd get an admission, after seventeen visits with the so-called experts." He is harshly critical of the prosecution's use of these "so-called experts" to aid in the investigation of cases in those early years. "They were self-appointed," he said, his voice growing angry. "They'd handled ten or fifteen of these cases and the next thing you know, they'd be giving seminars. They were giving seminars on how to do these interviews and they had no more training than anybody else." This position, of course, stands in sharp contrast to the perception and characterization of these early educational and training efforts espoused by community social workers and others.

Huff expressed grave concern about the effect of the investigative methods used in those early cases on the criminal-justice process, faulting an "amateurish method of getting to the truth that clearly was prejudicial in many, many instances." He offered no concrete examples, however. While Huff seemed to overstate the frequency of injustice in St. Mary County, nationally it does seem clear in retrospect that there have been occasional miscarriages of justice that grew out of a lack of sophistication in understanding how to investigate and respond to reported incidences of child sexual abuse.

In the mid-1980s, it was not unusual for children to be sent for psychological treatment when sexual abuse was suspected. Professionals did not distinguish clearly between treatment or therapy and forensic assessment. Since then, considerable research has addressed the best methods of assessing the possibility that sexual abuse took place. Today, assessment is clearly distinguished from treatment.

Research has revealed that we should be less concerned about the absolute number of forensic interviews than about repeated interviews by multiple interviewers (Faller, 2007). While the use of extended evaluation is not uncommon today, these interviews are typically limited to about six sessions with the suspected child victim (Faller, 2007; Carnes, Wilson, Nelson-Gardell, 2000). So, if in the mid-1980s, as Huff asserted, children in St. Mary County were being seen seventeen times, it might raise concerns about the possibility that some children's disclosures had been unduly influenced.

Academic researchers have been critical of how those early investigative interviews were conducted because they are concerned that the use of suggestive or leading questions may have led to false allegations of sexual abuse (Myers, 2006; Lyon, 2002a; Ceci and Bruck, 1993, 1995). Courts have shared these concerns, and the use of these questioning techniques by investigators have provided the impetus for a number of appellate courts to overturn convictions obtained in those early years (Myers, 2006; State v. Michaels).

Similarly, Huff made reference to professionals' lack of understanding about the impact of suggestive interviewing on child witnesses: "Much later we find out that five-year-olds can say anything that you teach them to say, and that was basically what happened." Huff was correct to be concerned. Children's suggestibility has been the focus of much research and is perhaps the most intensely debated of the numerous controversies related to interviewing children (Ceci and Bruck, 1993, 1995). As John Myers, a leading legal commentator in the area of child abuse, has pointed out, "In 1983, no one was aware of the dangers of suggestive questions with young children" (Myers, 2006:123). Huff, however, overstated his case when he argued that all young children can be trained to say anything and implied that large numbers of CSA prosecutions were cases in which the child had been taught or coached in what to say. Even the harshest critics of those early interviewing techniques recognize that the vast majority of allegations of child sexual abuse were well founded (Ceci and Bruck, 1995). Other researchers, most notably, Thomas Lyon, have argued persuasively that children's suggestibility has been asserted in the legal context beyond its scientific support (Lyon 2001, 2002a). Huff himself conceded this point: "I'm sure there were some cases that were legitimate cases that got kind of thrown into that, and I'm sure there were people convicted who shouldn't have [been], and I'm sure there were people who went free who shouldn't have."

In the intervening years, the handling of CSA cases has been reshaped by court decisions and social-science research. Based upon what we now understand to have been problematic interviewing techniques, courts have mandated procedural protections to shield suspects and defendants from the injustice that may grow out of improper interviewing. Among them are taint hearings, a pretrial evidentiary procedure designed to consider whether a particular child's disclosure and description of sexual victimization might have been improperly influenced by an interviewer (*State v. Michaels*). Some state legislatures have mandated special procedures aimed at protecting the innocent from the potential mishandling of CSA cases. Michigan law, for instance, requires child protective services (CPS) and law-enforcement personnel to use a nine-stage forensic interviewing protocol whenever children are interviewed about suspected abuse or neglect. These developments have largely come about because of aggressive defense attorneys.

## THE DEFENSE ATTORNEYS AND CREATION OF THE PROTOCOL

Unsurprisingly, in developing the St. Mary protocol, the prosecutor did not consult with the county's defense bar. "We weren't really totally aware that the protocol was being developed," Huff reported. When asked if he'd ever seen the written protocol, Huff responded, "I have never seen anything in writing. What I see is the cases." Despite having not seen the protocol, Huff and the other defense lawyers clearly understood its basic process. "I'm assuming," he explained, that the "child [goes] through the process of an interview that is videotaped. That videotape is then utilized in an interview with the alleged defendant. Most of the time, that is coupled with a situation where a polygraphist is prepared at that particular time to take the person's denial and continue the investigative process through the process of giving a polygraph examination. And then, if failed, that polygraphist continues the investigation process in hopes that they get a confession." In addition to understanding the protocol's basic sequence, the defense bar has absorbed its broader lessons. As Richard Nowak explained, "the idea was [that] we don't want to put this young child through testimony twice. If we've got to put her or him through testimony even once, that's too much."

Given the written protocol for investigating these cases, one would predict that defense attorneys would find ways to use it to their clients' benefit. This does not seem to be the case, based on our observations of two CSC trials in which men were charged with sexual offenses against minors. In the Inman trial, where few of the protocol's requirements were followed, the defense attorney never confronted the investigating police officer with the procedural inconsistency between these requirements and the methods actually employed (see chapter 10). While the attorney (an experienced defender but not one whom we interviewed) pointed out that the police had not carefully inspected the alleged crime scene for evidence, he never referred to the protocol's specification that police do so, a fact that would likely have been more persuasive with the jury because it was a clear violation of an explicit command that this investigative step be taken.

## VIDEOTAPED INTERVIEWS

The videotaped interviews, in Huff's estimation, "do a pretty good job of fixing who, what, when, etc." In theory, the defense could use the videotape to point out inconsistencies between the child's statements about the sexual assault at the time of the interview and at the time of the trial. From the point of view of the defense, however, this form of impeachment is risky at best and typically of little or no actual value to the defendant for several reasons.

Huff described the first reason: "The degree of variance is oftentimes so minor that it's insignificant." In such a case, Huff said, the child will get the benefit of the doubt from the jury. Next, because of the time delay in getting to trial, discrepancies may work in the defendant's favor because after the passage of months or even years, the child is much less certain about the details of what happened. In such cases, "the last thing we want to do is show that videotape because that videotape at that point oftentimes makes it more solid for the prosecution." Finally, the incident the child describes from the witness stand is sometimes less serious than the one she described on the videotape. In such a case, the defendant clearly benefits from not playing the videotape for the jury.

Alternatively, Nowak reported having shown the videotape to the jury, but admitted, "I've never been successful at getting an acquittal." He expressed concern that showing the tape may actually reinforce the child's testimony rather than cast doubt.

## DEFENDANTS' RIGHTS AND REALITIES: SYSTEMIC INEQUALITY

The cases that Huff, Nowak, and Muller handle are typical grist for the American legal system. That is, they involve low-profile, unsophisticated clients who often do not know that they should obtain legal counsel when first confronted by disproportionately powerful law-enforcement authorities and who typically lack the financial resources to do so.

The U.S. Constitution ensures a criminal defendant certain procedural rights that, in theory, tip the scales of justice in favor of the criminal suspect and the criminal defendant. But those rights are quite abstract, and research suggests that as a practical matter they are not as useful to suspects as one might imagine. Even after being read their rights, unsophisticated criminal suspects rarely assert them (Cassell and Hayman, 1996).

Cassell and Hayman (1996) found that 83.7 percent of suspects in a Utah county who were given Miranda warnings waived them and talked to the police, while only 12.1 percent of suspects asserted one or more before they were successfully interrogated. Furthermore, Grisso (1980) compared the rates of understanding of *Miranda* protection by adults and juveniles. He discovered that only 42.3 percent of adults and 23.1 percent of juveniles demonstrated an understanding of all four *Miranda* rights.

As a practical matter, the very law-enforcement officers who have a vested interest in the suspect's waiving his or her rights are charged with advising the suspect of those rights, a fact that leaves unsophisticated suspects vulnerable to manipulation. Experience teaches that law-enforcement officers grudgingly comply with the demands of *Miranda* even as they systematically undermine its intent (Simon, 1991; Leo, 1996; Leo and White, 1999). Officer Ed Duke demonstrated this pro forma compliance in St. Mary County when he recounted how he informs suspects of these crucial rights: "My whole take on *Miranda* is, it's their rights and they're not mine. So, I'll read a *Miranda* first thing, get that shit out of the way. Now we're going to watch a forty-five-minute videotape. And you know what? They have all those constitutional rights that I've made sure to remind them of and protect 'em, and they don't remember a goddamned one of 'em. So you move right on to the interrogation mode."

As Duke's comment illustrates, when the authorities decide to investigate an alleged crime, even in a relatively resource poor community such as St. Mary County, they have the capacity to bring to bear overwhelming resources, knowledge of the process, authority, and power far beyond what the typical criminal defendant could hope to equal. Piled atop these inherent inequalities are the authorities' intentional efforts to undermine the defendant's assertion of his rights. In contrast to the CSA prosecution of, say, Michael Jackson, the international pop music star, with its prominent defendant and battery of skilled defense attorneys with access to the substantial resources necessary to mount a truly aggressive defense, it is these routine cases, with their unknown main characters and their potentially devastating consequences for the defendant, that represent the typical criminal case. These defendants have no realistic access to counsel in the crucial early stages of the investigation, when it would be most helpful, no investigative resources, and no access to expert witnesses. The defendant, of course, is never imbued with the imprimatur of legitimacy that police and prosecutors take for granted (Blumberg, 1967). As Jim Henry noted, people are intimidated by the police and are more likely to cooperate when an officer is present. Thus, when it comes to the practical, as opposed to theoretical, realities of criminal investigation and the allocation of resources, there is a clear imbalance of power between the typical suspect and law-enforcement authorities. It is these routine cases that also provide the best measure of whether the American system of criminal justice lives up to its ideals of fair processes and just outcomes.

## SPEED AND ITS IMPLICATION FOR THE DEFENSE

The St. Mary County protocol is set up to take advantage of the inherent legitimacy held by the state. As Jameson, explained, speed is an essence of the protocol's effectiveness: "One of the tricks of the whole thing is doing it quickly. Probably more than videotaping it was doing it right now, not a week from Tuesday. . . . Suzy tells her teacher that Mom's boyfriend is doing something to her on Tuesday morning, we get the interview Tuesday after lunch and we get to the house before she's supposed to get off the bus and interview him, those are the cases that work the best." He further explained, "Quickness is important for a couple of reasons. Once . . . Mom's boyfriend finds out Suzy talked to the [CPS] worker, he gets to Mom, he gets to Suzy, he gets to a lawyer. . . . As soon as a lawyer comes into the picture, a first-year law student is going to tell him, 'Don't talk to anybody.'" John Hunter, a second prosecutor, agreed with Jameson's point, saying, "They [suspects] don't begin to marshal their defenses until the police are knocking on the door. And so you want that period of time to be—the knocking on the door to the intensive interrogation by the officer—you want those two things to be as close as possible."

Huff understood that law-enforcement authorities were attempting to obtain confessions before suspects employed legal counsel. "The prosecutor doesn't want us involved because if someone's smart enough to pick up the phone and call a lawyer, the first thing we're going to says is, 'Don't you say one word. If there's nothing else you do, don't talk to anybody.' 'Let them prove the case if they have to prove the case, but don't you help them.' And so, yeah, the last guy they want to involve in the process is the defense attorney." Huff summed up the effect of the presence of a defense attorney on the operation of the protocol. "It ceases to exist if the people contact an attorney."

Because no defense attorney is involved in the early stages of the case, most suspects agree to cooperate with the investigation. They submit to what prosecutor Hunter called an "intensive interrogation" by police. Although the protocol required that both the child's interview with CPS and the polygraph be videotaped, the interrogation of the suspect by the police is not videotaped. Almost 38 percent of the suspects confessed before this initial interrogation is concluded (see chapter 1). The practical effect of the protocol's implementation and operation on the defense attorneys is to shift their advocacy in most CSA cases from the question of guilt or innocence of their clients to the question of the sentence to be imposed.

## OVERWHELMING EVIDENCE, BUT A FAIR PROSECUTOR

Very often, by the time Huff gets involved in a case, particularly those to which the court appoints him, there is a mountain of evidence against his client. "Normally when we get the call, it's, 'I've given a confession.'" Saying this, Huff broke into frustrated laughter. "They have her videotaped, and if he takes the stand they're going to rebut the hell out of him."

Nowak described a case where this dynamic was at play. He related a situation in which his client had confessed, before Nowak was appointed, and was sent to prison for nine years. "He was only charged with molesting one of the daughters, but there was evidence that he [had] been through them all. . . . And it never went to trial; again, this was one of those cases you didn't have a leg to stand on . . . the guy had basically confessed to everything that had happened." Overcoming a client's confession is a Sisyphean task. As Drizin and Leo have written, "With the exception of being captured during the commission of a crime (whether by physical apprehension or electronically on videotape), a confession is the most incriminating and persuasive evidence of guilt that the State can bring against a defendant" (2004:921).

Perhaps the most compelling power the state has on its side is its legitimate authority. Under St. Mary's protocol, police officers request that the suspect accompany them to the stationhouse to discuss the allegations leveled by a child and captured on videotape. The suspect is not under arrest. He or she is legally free to decline the police officers' invitation. Despite his prerogative to refuse to cooperate, to the average criminal suspect, taking the trip to the local police station is not a wholly voluntary act precisely because the officer carries such an inherent presumption of authority. As our research in St. Mary County illustrates, almost two-thirds of suspects who cooperate with law enforcement and go to the police station will ultimately confess to a crime (Faller and Henry, 2000). Thus, from the vantage point of the average suspect, that first step across the threshold of his door into willing cooperation with law enforcement is fateful. He rarely invokes the right granted him by the U.S. Constitution not to go along with the police, not to cooperate, to refuse to provide the primary evidence by which the state will convict him.

Despite systemic inequality and a protocol designed to undermine a suspect's access to legal counsel in the crucial early stages of the investigation, the St. Mary County defense bar spoke with one voice in praise for the fairness and honesty of Chief Prosecutor Mark Jameson. Nowak said he was "extremely fair" and that "he ran his prosecutor's office that way." Similarly, Muller said, "He's fair and he's honest." But this individual prosecutor's personal integrity does not change the practical impact of the imbalance of power.

There are several possible reasons for the defense attorneys' sense of the prosecutor. First, this may stem from Jameson's straightforward approach to cases. Jameson does not engage in the sort of activities that many prosecutors do; he readily discloses to the defense the warts on his cases and the foibles committed by law-enforcement officers. Repeatedly, Jameson said during our interview that a case "is what it is." If there are inconsistencies, poor investigations, or weak evidence, he makes no effort to hide these facts. Another possible explanation is that at its core, the protocol is driven by values—individual values as translated into public values. Perhaps these defense attorneys have adjusted their practice to work within a system over which they cannot effect change. Finally, they may perceive the prosecutor to be fair because, as mentioned earlier, in CSA cases they deal with him mostly in terms of negotiating a sentence rather than in determining guilt or innocence. The powerful evidence of a legally obtained confession obviates the need for the defense lawyers to focus on the guilt or innocence phase of the proceeding and to focus instead on the amount of punishment and treatment to be meted out. In this realm, the prosecutors are quite moderate, seeking not to confine defendants for the maximum period but focusing more on rehabilitation and reintegration into the community.

## POLYGRAPH PROBLEMS

State law guarantees a CSC defendant the right to take a polygraph examination. If the suspect does not confess during the initial interrogation by police, he is offered an immediate polygraph examination. Most of those who have not confessed by the conclusion of the initial police interrogation agree to submit to the polygraph examination. By the time the polygraphist is finished with the suspect, the confession rate is 64 percent (Faller and Henry, 2000). "When you've failed it," Huff observed, "that's a powerful tool." He explained that the polygraph was important for both sides in a CSA investigation. Whether to take one and under what circumstances is a complex decision.

"I will almost always—in retained cases always and in contract defender cases I will suggest to the client that despite the fact that they're indigent, I think they should have a private polygraph. . . . It's a difficult situation because I don't want necessarily the prosecutors to be aware of a private polygraph." There is a catch-22 in which an indigent criminal defendant and his counsel often find themselves in their effort to investigate and develop a case for the defendant. "I know I could go to the Circuit Court and secure funds to get a private polygraph," Huff explained, "but everybody and their uncle then knows that my client has taken a polygraph, and if I don't bring forth the results they know he failed it." In Huff's view, going to the court for money to obtain a private polygraph "defeats the purpose of the private polygraph."

"The prosecutor will oftentimes offer a polygraph," Huff said. He sometimes advises his client to submit to the prosecutor's proffered examination. "Polygraphs aren't going to hurt my client," Huff explained, since the prosecutors "already think they're guilty. So we're not trying to sway the prosecutor. He's already made up his mind. He wouldn't have filed charges if he didn't think my client was guilty. The danger of the polygraph is the utilization of it in rebuttal if the defendant says something, and that's where you've got to be careful." Here Huff's concern is with the prosecutor's ability to confront the defendant with inconsistent statements made during the polygraph examination if the defendant testifies in his own defense. Since polygraphs are videotaped, the prosecution can use them if the defendant makes any statement at variance with it during subsequent interrogation or at trial. Moreover, if the defendant mentions during his testimony that he took a polygraph, although its results are not admissible, he can be cross-examined about the test because he opened the door to the prosecutor.

Huff is wary of the state's use of the polygraph. "The protocol itself is troubling to me as a defense attorney because this polygraphist isn't seeking the truth. He's seeking a confession." He goes on to say, "I instruct all of my clients that if they get to a point where the polygraphist ceases to be anything other than a polygraphist—and he starts, 'You failed this polygraph'—at that point, you break off, you stop [and] you say, 'I am not going to say anything further.'" He also doubts that most of his court-appointed clients have the sophistication to submit to a prosecution polygraph. "I suggest strongly to indigent clients that they conduct a private polygraph," he reiterated, "and only as a last resort. If I feel that I have a client who is sufficiently astute to understand when to stop, will I go ahead and allow a polygraph to be conducted by the prosecutor." Indigent clients are by definition poor and, according to attorney Muller, a private polygraph ran about $300 at the time. As already noted, these clients tend to be uneducated, and they often lack the strength of personality that would make a fair match for an interrogator as skilled as polygraphist Rick Rivers.

If Huff's clients follow his instructions and "pass the polygraph, it's a hell of a bargaining tool. . . . You'd have to have a mound of information to justify continuing with the prosecution after a passed polygraph has occurred." To bolster his client's chances in the event of a successful polygraph examination, Huff uses the same polygraphist that the prosecution uses. "We have an advantage here," he explained, "in that the same polygraphist does both, Rick Rivers, and the reason I do that is because if I get Joe Blow down the road . . . the prosecutor doesn't know that guy. And so I know Rick Rivers has the ear of the prosecutor. If I come in with a report indicating that my client has passed a polygraph, if it's Rick Rivers who'd conducted the polygraph, I know full well that prosecutor's going to say, 'Hey, that's as good as done.'" Huff returned to the value of using Rivers to conduct his private polygraphs. "I can call Rick and tomorrow he'll be down here in my office and my guy can sit across that table and take the polygraph. And if I walk in with that polygraph completed by Rick Rivers, it's as good as if it happened in their [the prosecutor's] office, only a whole lot safer." It is safer because the result will be disclosed only if the defense attorney believes it will be helpful to his client's case.

## THE EXPERT WITNESS: JIM HENRY

Huff also expressed concern about the prosecution's use of Jim Henry as an expert witness. "The prosecution is very quick in these cases to utilize the expert testimony of Jim Henry. Jim Henry has testified so many times, he's like the ultimate expert witness. He sits there in his scholarly attire and turns to that jury and he leans over and he's just telling them a story." Huff distinguished Henry from the "experts" that the prosecution relied upon in the early days of the protocol. Muller concurred, describing Henry as an "excellent witness . . . you put a penny in him and you get a dollar's worth out for the prosecution."

Henry does not conduct an evaluation of the child but testifies by way of hypothetical questions to explain aspects of children's reactions to sexual abuse that may seem troubling or counterintuitive to juries of laypeople. In nearly every case that goes to trial, the prosecution calls Henry to explain the psychological processes that contribute to and research that explains the seemingly paradoxical behavior sexually abused children may exhibit. Henry's involvement clearly frustrated and perplexed the St. Mary's defense bar, which was evidenced by Huff's estimate that Henry has testified five hundred times. In a nineteen-year period, from 1988 to 1998, St. Mary County handled some 443 CSA cases, but only eighteen cases actually resulted in a trial (Faller and Henry 2000). Still, Huff described a man who has a wealth of experience and an easy command of volumes of scholarly research that he can bring to bear on the issues presented by the case. Nowak described Henry's demeanor in the courtroom as presenting a real challenge for the defense. "He really, literally testifies to the jury because he does a good presentation. He'll look at the jury in the eye instead of answering questions to the prosecutor directly, he'll just talk to them and it turns into a college lecture." While he has attempted to "block the effect of his testimony," Huff admitted that Henry's testimony is "compelling" and "almost impossible to beat." Muller explained, "I have never seen anybody that's ever cross-examined him, myself included. . . . You can come up with what you think is the best hypothetical in the world . . . and you ain't going to get it." In fact, Nowak claimed, "There is only one question you can ask Henry. Well, two questions I guess. How many times have you testified? And he'll rattle off—I don't know, fifty, a hundred, whatever. [And] how many times have you ever testified for the defense?" The answer is that Henry has testified for the defense in only one criminal case.

Despite their consistent frustration in dealing with Henry's testimony, the defense lawyers seemed to have undertaken little effort to try to counter his devastating contribution to the prosecution. Nowak said he had never asked the court to appoint an expert of his own although he was certain he could locate an expert through a statewide association of defense attorneys "that would probably sink him . . . in a close case." Nowak explained that he believed that the court did not have funds to pay expert witness fees, a rationale often offered to preclude the appointment of an expert witness for an indigent defendant (Uphoff, 1999). Like Nowak, none of the other defense attorneys we interviewed gave any indication that they had sought court appointment of an expert to provide a jury with a different perspective on these issues. In the Inman trial the defendant requested and was granted court funds to retain an expert witness, although no expert actually testified. Moreover, although they recognized the effect Henry's testimony has on the jury, none of the defense attorneys we interviewed indicated that they had ever attempted to have Henry's testimony excluded from trial, because there is no money for a defense expert to meet the state's evidence, because Henry had not seen the complainant, or for any other reason.

## ADDITIONAL CONCERNS

Huff expressed two additional concerns about the county's use of the protocol. The first deals with the interplay and conflicting goals of two public entities involved in cases of intrafamilial child sexual abuse. In these cases, both the state's public child welfare agency and law-enforcement authorities are involved. The two public agencies have very different missions. "You've got [the children's services agency], whose stated goal is to reunite the family—and so they don't really care what's happening criminally—they're off setting up counseling sessions, setting up family skills sessions and taking the child to the counselor. At the same time, they're referred to the prosecutor, whose stated purpose is putting the son-of-a-gun in prison. Sometimes that can be a very confusing situation to the criminal defendant. I have often argued that the [child welfare agency], at that point, has no business sending a criminal defendant [to counseling] because they're an arm of the law, they're an agent of the state in my opinion. And we've run into problems with that where a client will go to a counselor and make all sorts of admissions to a counselor and all of a sudden it becomes evidence [in the criminal case]."

From the defense lawyer's perspective, the client's dual relationship with the state is difficult to manage. If the client does not cooperate with child-welfare officials, he might lose his children to termination of parental rights. If the client does cooperate, he may be confronted with his own words as the primary evidence against him in a criminal prosecution that could send him to prison for decades.

Huff's second concern was with the way the authorities conducted investigations in cases of suspected child sexual abuse, noting, "There's no law that says cops and prosecutors can't lie. And, of course, they do, every day." Huff's point seemed to be that the system of investigating these alleged crimes is unfair to suspects. Huff's concern about the fairness of the system in investigating suspects finds support in Supreme Court precedent (e.g., *Nix v. Williams*), the practical experience of defense attorneys (Dershowitz, 1982), in the academic legal literature (Clark, 2003; Cassell, 1996), and in the interviews our research team conducted with members of the St. Mary County law-enforcement team.

## THE BROADER LEGAL SYSTEM

Courts have long shaped legal doctrine to permit law enforcement officers to engage in treatment of suspects that is arguably dishonest and morally questionable for state actors. For example, in the renowned case *Brewer v. Williams* (1977), the Supreme Court suppressed a suspect's statements, made after he had asserted his Fifth Amendment right to remain silent and after a police officer, ignoring the defendant's request for a lawyer, delivered what has become known as "the Christian burial speech," in which the officer exploited religion to wrangle incriminating statements. From the information provided in those statements, the authorities discovered more incriminating evidence. The Supreme Court held that the statement made by the suspect was taken in violation of *Miranda*, since the suspect had asserted his right to an attorney. The additional evidence was deemed a fruit of the illegal interrogation, and it, too, was suppressed. Despite finding that the police had behaved illegally, the Supreme Court invited the government to argue at the defendant's retrial that the discovery of the evidence that resulted from the statement was inevitable. The government accepted the invitation, and the case made its way back to the Supreme Court, which engrafted onto confession law an "inevitable discovery" exception to the Fifth Amendment's grant of the right to remain silent (*Nix v. Williams*).

Similarly, in *Frazier v. Cupp* (1969), the Supreme Court upheld the admission of a confession even though it was gained only after the police lied to the suspect, telling him that his cousin and codefendant had confessed. The message to law enforcement from the courts has been clear and consistent: manipulate suspects and the courts will protect your case from negative consequences of that behavior.

In his provocative 1982 book *The Best Defense*, Alan Dershowitz discusses at length the lies, half-truths, and deceptive police practices that he has observed in his own legal practice. He sums up his experience by asserting, "It is fair to say the American justice system is built on a foundation of not telling the whole truth" (xix). Sherman J. Clark of the University of Michigan Law School has observed that, "It would have to be admitted that the criminal justice system requires us to do many things of which we can not be proud. . . . We encourage co-conspirators to betray one another. We literally pit brother against brother. We employ undercover officers to lie and gain people's trust so that they can betray them. This is unpleasant stuff, however necessary and justified, and the names we give to those we employ in this dirty business—'rat' and 'narc'—evince our desire to distance ourselves from what we do" (Clark, 2003). Police lies and half-truths are routinely employed when interrogating suspects (Drizin and Leo, 2004).

## THE RELIGIOUS MAN AND HIS RETARDED DAUGHTER

Rick Rivers, universally acclaimed by the county's law-enforcement professionals as a consummate interrogator, described his effort in one case in which a man who professed strong religious convictions was accused of sexually abusing two of his daughters, the second of whom was mentally retarded. We have discussed this case earlier in this book and will discuss it in more depth later, but before doing so, I will briefly address two issues: the impact of this case on our research team's discussions in preparing this manuscript, and my definition of the term "manipulate" and what constitutes "manipulation."

No case or issue that arose during our years of research regarding the St. Mary protocol or writing of this manuscript generated more discussion or dissension than the handling of this case. It is fair to say that members of our research team vehemently disagree about almost every point of discussion regarding the matter. Generally the split has been between the lawyers, arguing that the polygraphist Rick Rivers intentionally manipulated the suspect in order to obtain a confession in a weak case and that this is emblematic of the legal system's excusing questionable behavior by or on behalf of law enforcement; and the clinicians, arguing that the evidence in the case is in fact strong and that Rivers did not manipulate the suspect. We spent hours and had several heated conversations in an effort to sort out our thoughts and feelings about this case.

This deep division led to an exploration of the meanings of "manipulation" or "manipulate." The *American Heritage Dictionary of the English Language* defines "manipulate" as, "To influence or manage shrewdly or deviously." The same dictionary defines "manipulation" as, "Shrewd or devious management, especially for one's own advantage." These are the definitions I and the other lawyers intend to be applied to the use of those terms in the discussion that follows.

Sometime before the investigation at issue, county authorities had mounted a similar investigation when it was alleged that the religiously devout suspect had sexually assaulted another of his daughters. Rivers had been unable to get this man to confess in that earlier case. Despite a recantation by the daughter who was the alleged victim in the first investigation and the lack of a confession by the suspect, the man plead guilty to a lesser offense and received a sentence of nine months in jail. Rivers was convinced that the man had abused both girls. Rivers described his own reaction to the case: "He wouldn't admit, and I just had so much disdain for the guy. I didn't like him. . . . He would roll in his religion, this issue about how honest he was and how he believed in God. And I was just incensed with him because he's such a liar." Of the second daughter, Rivers said, "This girl could never be a witness." Rivers next described how this mentally retarded girl, using an anatomical drawing, had poked a pin into the vaginal area of the drawing to illustrate where her father had hurt her. Rivers then continued:

> What happened was, they brought him in. He says, "Hi. How are you? Nice to see you again." So what happened was—I didn't do a polygraph on him. I sat him in the room and started talking to him. And he was quoting scripture and the law. I had spent some time talking, so I really established a fairly good

rapport with him and I knew there was an emotional investment in this. And I had showed him the videotape [of the interview with his retarded daughter], and one thing led to another. I say, "You know, you're a religious man and I'm religious. And I believe in God." I say, "Do you believe in predestination?" And he says, "Oh, yes." I say, "That's why God probably put you in this room with me. Because he wants you to tell the truth." And he lost it and confessed.

Our team had two major disagreements about this case. The first had to do with the strength of the evidence of the defendant's guilt, and the second with whether Rivers's actions can fairly be characterized as "manipulation" of this suspect.

## HOW STRONG IS THE CASE?

The question of the strength of the legal case against this suspect has two elements. First, the daughter at issue in the first case had recanted her allegations that her father had sexually abused her. Recantation in cases of child sexual abuse is not uncommon. Research has found recantation rates that range from about 4 percent to about one-third of the alleged victims (Faller, 2007; Malloy, Lyon, and Quas, 2007). Some children falsely recant; that is, some children who were sexually abused recant their disclosures. They may do so for a number of reasons: they are threatened by the perpetrator or pressured by unsupportive family members, they may fear the consequences of the disclosure (a parent or loved one may go to prison), or they may feel guilty about the impact upon their family (Haralambie, 1999). Because a recantation may be false, mental-health professionals do not necessarily believe that this weakens the evidence that sexual abuse has taken place. However, whether a recantation is true or false, it presents very serious challenges for the prosecution, which must prove a criminal charge beyond a reasonable doubt. Recantation means that the state's primary witness has told two conflicting stories of what happened (Perlis Marx, 1999). For this reason, the testimony of the retarded girl's sister is likely to be unpersuasive in a legal setting where she would be expected to face a vigorous cross-examination. Additionally, because the second daughter could not testify because of her handicap—indeed, could not even articulate her complaint—the lawyers would describe the case Rivers talked about as one that is legally "weak," and one that suggests an especially cautious approach by state actors. The clinicians, on the other hand, viewing the case through their particular professional lens, do not find that either of these factors weakens the case. Our differing perspective almost certainly influences whether we believe Rivers resorted to manipulation in conducting the interrogation of the suspect.

## WAS RIVERS "MANIPULATIVE"?

Rivers used this case to illustrate how experience taught him that he is more successful in obtaining confessions when he is able to contain his anger at the suspect and treat him or her with respect. But there is another, far darker, lesson to be gleaned from this case. The government's polygraphist—a former police officer trained in methods of interrogation—and lead interrogator of the suspect determined in his own mind that the man "is such a liar." The evidentiary basis for Rivers's conclusion was unclear; his own recitation of the facts of the case makes it clear that the girl was sufficiently retarded that she could not testify. Despite these factors that would suggest a cautious approach to a very difficult case, it was Rivers's view that the suspect was lying when he asserted that he did not abuse his daughter. One of our research team's major disagreements was whether it is fair to characterize Rivers's behavior in this case as "manipulation" or "manipulative." The lawyers say it was; the clinicians disagree. From a defense attorney's perspective, Rivers's manipulation—that is, his shrewd or devious management of this suspect—seems clear. Regardless of whether one believes Rivers to be a religious man (in his interview Rivers described himself as religious, and the lawyers on our team take him at his word), he exploited the man's religiosity by aligning himself with the man as a fellow believer to gain his confidence, and through that confidence a confession. Whether Rivers's actions were "devious," they were certainly "shrewd"—Rivers got a well-defended sex offender to admit his sexual abuse of his defenseless daughter. Practices such as these help explain why Huff insisted that his clients discontinue the polygraph when the polygraph examination becomes an interrogation—indeed, in this case, Rivers did not even attempt to conduct a polygraph, relying instead upon his considerable skill as an interrogator. This is precisely the sort of "unpleasant stuff" to which Clark refers.

Yet, as Huff himself implicitly admitted, such actions by law-enforcement officers or their agents do not violate any legal rights of the criminal suspect when, at another point in the interview, he said, "Our prosecutors are cognizant of a defendant's rights, and will usually bend over backwards to make sure they're protected." It is, of course, these very prosecutors who have developed the CSA investigation protocol and arranged for Rick Rivers to question Huff's potential clients. When asked about his perceptions of the fairness of the county's protocol for handling CSA cases, Nowak replied, "That procedure doesn't bother me that much as far as fairness is concerned. . . . I think they generally do a fairly good job of focusing on the person that is the likely offender without any prejudice to them. Many is the time they do a good job and the person just spills the beans on videotape." Muller makes this point in virtually the same words. "I don't think it's necessarily all based on just the police and police tactics, basically the real coercive questioning and that type of thing. I think they can be awfully persuasive, and I've seen in the videotapes that they are persuasive. But they can be persuasive and still not be coercive. So, I don't want to lay that on the police because I don't think that's fair. I don't think there's a lot of coercive questioning going on."

Whether the police or Rivers, their proxy, are "coercive" in their questioning of suspects depends, of course, upon how one defines "coercive." While in the early part of the twentieth century police questioning was routinely physically coercive, even brutal, police no longer routinely trade in physical assaults to gain confessions from suspects. As the Supreme Court observed in 1966, "modern practice of in-custody interrogation is psychologically rather than physically oriented" (*Miranda v. Arizona*, 448). The court, in that case, summarized the way in which law-enforcement officers conduct interrogations by evaluating the leading textbooks from which police are trained. The majority of the justices first observed that isolating the suspect and being alone with him, in a place with which he is unfamiliar if possible, and most preferably in the interrogator's office, is the first step to successful interrogation (*Miranda v Arizona*, 449). It then went on to explain:

> To highlight the isolation and unfamiliar surroundings, the manuals instruct the police to display an air of confidence in the suspect's guilt and from outward appearance to maintain only an interest in confirming certain details. The guilt of the subject is to be posited as a fact. The interrogator should

direct his comments toward the reasons why the subject committed the act, rather than court failure by asking the subject whether he did it. Like other men, perhaps the subject has had a bad family life, had an unhappy childhood, had too much to drink, had an unrequited desire for women. The officers are instructed to minimize the moral seriousness of the offense, to cast blame on the victim or on society. These tactics are designed to put the subject in a psychological state where his story is but an elaboration of what the police purport to know already—that he is guilty. Explanations to the contrary are dismissed and discouraged.

While manipulation to gain a confession may be a sharp practice, it does not violate the suspect's rights. It is therefore acceptable from a legal perspective. Thus, while these defense attorneys do not entirely trust the police or polygraphist, they know that these officials' handling of suspects is not illegal.

Returning to the case of the religious man, should we care whether Rivers manipulated the suspect during the interrogation if his behavior is not illegal? This question, of course, is a normative one, and reasonable people may disagree—even very strongly—about its answer. On one hand, if the man was not in fact guilty of sexually abusing his daughter, we would all be bothered by man's false confession to a detestable crime. If, on the other hand, he is guilty, how should we view Rivers's behavior? The clinicians believe that Rivers showed himself to be a skilled interrogator doing his job, that he was honest, that he is a religious man himself, and that he smartly found a way to get a sex offender to confess his guilt in a case that would have been extremely difficult, if not impossible, to prove without this confession. The lawyers believe that Rivers was manipulative and that the confession he obtained was legally valid. Even though a guilty offender was apprehended, the lawyers think we should be concerned by Rivers's behavior. They find it problematic for state actors to manipulate suspects in this way, in part because there have been many cases where the suspect doing the confessing is not factually guilty of the crime (Gross et al., 2005; Drizin and Leo, 2004).

## CRIMINAL PROCEEDINGS

The St. Mary protocol has several important impacts on how cases are handled after the investigation is complete and criminal charges are filed.

While not required by either the due-process clause of the Fourteenth Amendment (*Lem Woon v. Oregon*) or by the Fourth Amendment's prohibition against unreasonable seizures (*Gerstein v. Pugh*), every state provides a procedure by which a neutral decision maker reviews a prosecutor's charging decision in felony cases (Kamisar et al., 2002). The purpose of a preliminary examination is to allow an independent determination to be made as to whether there is sufficient evidence that the defendant has committed a crime to allow the case to proceed to trial. In felony cases filed in the state in which St. Mary County is situated, unless waived by both the defendant and the prosecution, the preliminary examination is held in the district court. If the judge finds sufficient evidence that the defendant committed a felony, then she may bind the defendant over to the circuit court, the state's court of general jurisdiction, for further proceedings and trial.

As we have noted, an unwritten aspect of the St. Mary County protocol provided that if defendants assert their right to hold the preliminary examination and the child has to testify, the prosecutors will not subsequently offer the defendant an advantageous plea bargain. While acknowledging that the prosecutor's office considers the preliminary examination a major factor in plea negotiations, Huff observed, "Cases get settled all the time . . . and it isn't true that it always gets worse." However, he agreed that whether the child must testify at a preliminary examination is "a major factor" in the prosecutors' willingness to deal at later stages in the case.

In part because plea negotiations are complicated when the defendant holds a preliminary hearing, Huff is careful in deciding whether or not to proceed with the hearing. "I've talked to many criminal attorneys, [and they say,] 'Boy, you've got to have that prelim.' But let me tell you, in these cases, you have that prelim and you're either going to get a trial or you've precluded any options for your client." Rather than routinely hold the preliminary examination, Huff will do so only when he has a realistic opportunity to have the case dismissed by the court at that early stage in the proceeding or where holding the exam lays the foundation for a later defense at trial. He explained that he holds a preliminary examination where "the defendant tells me absolutely, unequivocally that [he is] innocent of the charge and that there is a sufficient factual discrepancy to justify that." Similarly, he will hold the preliminary hearing in a situation in which the defendant asserted that he was "in California the day it allegedly happened, and by putting that information on the record and establishing that date, you're now setting up that alibi so at trial time, we've got her tied down to a date, time, and place."

Huff pointed out two additional considerations. First, he expressed concern that the child will be strengthened and will gain confidence by the experience of successfully testifying at the preliminary hearing. By holding the preliminary examination, "You're also allowing the child to realize that it isn't as bad as they may have thought. . . . Once they've done it, it's not that hard to do it again."

The second consideration has to do with the reason criminal-defense attorneys typically hold preliminary hearings, establishing a formal record of the witness's testimony that can be used later at the trial to show the witness has changed his or her story. That is, the defense lawyer will use discrepancies in a witness's testimony at the preliminary exam and at the trial in an effort to impeach the witness's credibility, to show she is lying. But Huff asks rhetorically, "How important is impeachment when you're impeaching a six-year-old or a seven-year-old or an eight-year-old?" He answered himself, "It's not important. The jury's going to give the kid the benefit of the doubt 99 percent of the time."

Huff emphasized that mere factual disagreements between the allegations the child makes and the story the defendant tells rarely provide any reason to assert the defendant's right to hold the preliminary examination. Given these considerations, he estimated that he holds the preliminary exam in only about 10 to 15 percent of these cases.

## INNOCENT BUT PROVEN GUILTY?

Probably every criminal defense lawyer has represented a client who was found guilty after trial or who pleaded guilty to get an advantageous sentence and to avoid the possibility of a much harsher penalty being imposed, but who, the lawyer believes, was actually innocent of the charges. The three defense attorneys we spoke to in St. Mary County were no exception. "Somewhere in this state," Huff asserted confidently, "there's a guy in prison who is totally innocent of these charges." He described a case in which a client was charged with sexually assaulting his girlfriend's child. The man, according to Huff, confessed but later denied that his statement was a confession. In essence, the man asserted in his defense at trial that he was simply "going along with what [the police] said because I thought that would be better." This tactic was not successful, and the man was convicted.

Nowak, too, related a case in which he believed an innocent client was convicted. The case was unusual in two respects. First, it was one of the few cases involving a female perpetrator. Second, the case was as much about physical as sexual abuse. "I was convinced the client was innocent," he said. "It was more physical abuse than anything, but it was sexual connotations because what she was accused of doing was basically grabbing the kid by the penis and the genitals and twisting . . . because she'd allegedly got mad at him." Later, after the woman, the boy's stepmother, had served her sentence, the boy, at age twenty-one or twenty-two, recanted.

Similarly, Muller described a case that he was handling at the time we interviewed him. The complainant in the case, whom Muller described as "an accomplished liar," had alleged that his client had sexually abused her. Muller's client took and apparently passed the polygraph. The complainant also requested and was given a polygraph, which she passed. Muller continued, "The girl recanted like two or three times and my guy's adamant that he didn't do anything and he's also adamant that the reason why it's coming forward again is because of the fact that the [girl's] mother is trying to set him up. They're going through a divorce, too, which is part of it." Muller characterized the case as "bothersome" and "difficult" in part because "there's enough there to win and enough to lose. A lot depends on your abilities at that point."

These examples, and Huff's more emphatic assertion that innocent people may have confessed or provided statements that appear to be confessions, is arguably well founded. In the past decade, researchers have uncovered a disquieting number of wrongful convictions, many of which are the result of false confessions (Gross et al., 2005; Dirzin and Leo, 2004). In their 2004 study, Drizin and Leo documented 125 cases in which a criminal defendant falsely confessed, often to very serious crimes. Why would a person falsely confess to a crime he did not commit? A number of commentators have documented the way in which routine police questioning of suspects may lead to false confessions (Scott-Hayard, 2007; Gross et al., 2005; Drizin and Leo, 2004; Fulero and Everington, 2004; Drizin and Colgan, 2004). As already noted, law-enforcement officers routinely use manipulative and psychologically coercive techniques when questioning suspects whom they have deemed to be guilty. Among the techniques are incessant, repetitive questioning, the use of falsified evidence, lies, threats of harsh treatment (if the suspect does not confess), positive inducements, such as promises of favorable treatment, and minimization of the alleged wrongdoing (by, for example, providing the suspect with a reason for engaging in the illegal behavior that minimizes moral responsibility, such as telling a suspect in a case of child sexual abuse that he may have been drunk at the time of the incident or suggesting that the child initiated the incident) to induce a suspect to confess (Gross et al., 2005; Drizin and Leo, 2004; *Miranda v. Arizona*). These coercive techniques are believed to be the primary cause of false confessions (Drizin and Leo, 2004).

False confessions are most likely to occur when one or more of three elements are present in the case. The first element is that the suspect is a juvenile. Both Gross and his colleagues and Drizin and Leo have documented a disproportionate number of juveniles among demonstrably false confessors (Gross et al., 2005; Drizin and Leo, 2004). Juveniles' immaturity, impulsivity, lack of future orientation, and desire to please adults are thought to contribute to their overrepresentation among false confessors because they lack the psychological resources to withstand intensive, manipulative and coercive police interrogation techniques. Juveniles appear to be particularly susceptible to the police use of deception in the interrogation process (Scott-Hayward, 2007).

The second element is that the suspect is interrogated for excessively long periods of time, typically beyond six hours (Gross, 2005). And the third element is that the suspect be developmentally delayed, for such suspects are more likely to falsely confess than suspects who function at normal intelligence (Gross et al., 2005; Drizin and Leo, 2004). Drizin and Leo have suggested a number of characteristics of mentally retarded persons that leave them vulnerable to police interrogation tactics: "Because of their cognitive deficits and limited social skills, the mentally retarded are slow-thinking, easily confused, concrete (as opposed to abstract) thinkers, often lack the ability to appreciate the seriousness of a situation, may not understand the long term consequences of their actions, and tend to have short attention spans, poor memory, and poor impulse control. The mentally retarded tend also to be highly submissive (especially eager to please authority figures), compliant, suggestible, and responsive to stress and pressure" (2004:919–920).

While we cannot say for sure, a number of cases discussed by professionals in St. Mary might lead one to pause and reflect on the possibility of false confessions. Of particular concern in this regard, prosecutor Mark Jameson discussed two cases that involved teens who were or had recently been "special education" students, suggesting the presence of limited cognitive capacity:

> They were able to function in society, so they are not incompetent, but they are low-functioning kids. One boy was having intercourse with his nine-year-old niece. The other boy was doing cunnilingus and other stuff with a nine-year-old niece. The cases weren't related, they were just very similar. . . . They both confessed, one to a police officer and one to Rick Rivers, the polygraph operator.
>
> So, we'll take the first guy. He was living with his aunt, because he wasn't getting along with his parents. He was in jail, you know, scared. So we agreed to put him in a treatment program for mentally retarded sex offenders.
>
> So we let him out on bond, put him with his father . . . and he went through the treatment program for about six months. He pled guilty to assault with intent to commit penetration, which is a ten-year felony offense. . . . We put him in a jail for a year, he's in jail right now, and our local treatment program and then he'll be on probation to follow up with that. Now, intercourse with a nine-year-old is pretty bad stuff. But was the answer to give the guy ten years in prison?
>
> The other boy ultimately pled to assault with intent to commit penetration. We did a psychological evaluation. He went to jail also.

These cases and the reality of false confessions raise several questions. Could these intellectually slow teens, who qualified for a treatment program for mentally retarded offenders, have falsely confessed? Could they have been pressured into admitting more or more serious offenses than they actually committed? Have other innocent persons falsely confessed in St. Mary County? What, if anything, in the conduct of the county's protocol for investigating cases of child sexual abuse might protect against the possibility that a suspect might falsely confess?

Of course, we cannot know the answers to these questions. What we do know about the American criminal-justice system more generally is that some not inconsequential number of suspects have falsely confessed to awful crimes. Therefore, we cannot rule out entirely the possibility that some suspect in St. Mary County might have confessed to a sexual crime against a child that he did not commit.

We have identified no case in which the interrogation by the police, the polygraphist, or the police and polygraphist combined lasted longer than the six-hour threshold that researchers have identified as raising concerns about the possibility of false confessions. Most of the interrogations we have identified lasted less than three hours when the initial police questioning and the polygraphist's interrogation are combined. These findings provide some support that the interrogation methods used in St. Mary County are not unduly conducive to false confessions.

A second group of St. Mary County suspects raises concern. In our examination of 443 court files of CSC charges over a twelve-year period of time, at lease fifty-six of the defendants were eighteen years of age or younger at the time they were alleged to have committed a sex offense. Thirty of these were charged with criminal sexual conduct in the third degree, that is, penetration with a person who is at least thirteen years old but less than sixteen years old, a fifteen-year felony under state law. Another eight were charged with fondling a child between those ages. This suggests that many of these CSC cases involved teenagers engaging in sexual activity with someone within five years of their own age. Forty-seven of them pleaded guilty to an offense to resolve their cases. Four of these defendants received no sentence that we could verify, while one received only probation; we have sentencing information on only forty-two of the remaining defendants. The vast majority of those for whom sentencing information was available (36) were sentenced to either the county jail (25) or prison (11).

Despite numerous cases in which those found guilty of crimes have been subsequently proven innocent, our legal system remains skeptical of a convicted person's protestations of his innocence. Huff described one client's unsuccessful effort to assert his innocence at sentencing and to explain that he was not guilty of the crime. "And, of course, the state of the law today is that *that* in and of itself can be used against him to enhance the sentence; the mere fact that he's not admitting even after that jury trial." The state's sentencing guidelines permit the court to punish more harshly a defendant who continues to maintain his innocence after conviction at trial. "I can't imagine a worse fate than to be accused of such a crime and be innocent because everything you try to do to defend yourself is deemed to be evidence that you did it. . . . Well, can you imagine being an innocent person in that circumstance?"

Huff's concern is understandable. It is clear that at least some innocent persons might be found guilty or enter guilty pleas because the risks of not doing so are too great to bear. For example, some innocent defendants enter guilty pleas because the prosecution makes a favorable plea offer, and the penalties they face if convicted of the offense for which they are charged are draconian. Consider, for example, a hypothetical case in which a seventeen-year-old boy has sexual relations with his sixteen-year-old girlfriend. When the girl's parents discover this, the girl claims she was forced. The parents contact the police and the boy finds himself charged with criminal sexual conduct in the first degree (an offense involving sexual penetration accomplished through the use of force), a major felony, the punishment for which could be life or any number of years in prison. The boy may very well have a viable defense of consent. However, if the prosecutor offers a plea bargain to criminal sexual conduct in the second degree (involving mere sexual contact), and a sentence to time in the county jail followed by treatment in the county's sex-offender treatment program (and, necessarily, placement on the sex-offender registry), the boy might well accept the deal and enter a plea of guilty as a hedge against the possibility of being found guilty at trial and receiving a sentence of decades in prison.

Despite these possibilities, the defense attorneys generally recognized that most of the defendants they represent are in fact guilty. Muller made this point more bluntly. "Most of the ones I've lost, I don't feel too bad about because they were laydowns . . . you know, probably a jerk they had clear and compelling evidence against. My job was basically to protect his constitutional rights, I guess, and hold his hand and go through the whole thing." Still, as Huff pointed out, "the mindset of everyone in the process is that when the child makes the accusation, and if it gets to the point where the protocol has been initiated, nobody has any thought that this might not have happened." The cases that haunt these defense attorneys are those in which the defendant maintains his innocence, goes to trial, and is convicted. Such cases, of course, are the most dependent on the skill of the defense attorney to see that a just result is achieved.

Aside from the general concern that it is possible for innocent people to be wrongly convicted, the defense bar is generally supportive of the use of the protocol. Similarly, they were supportive of the use of the sex-offender evaluation and of community corrections in responding to findings of guilt. As we have noted elsewhere, the sentencing process typically begins with an evaluation of the offender by a mental-health professional who specializes in the assessment and treatment of sex offenders. In the less predatory cases or cases where there is a violation of the law that is less morally culpable (for example, where a seventeen-year-old has nonforcible sexual intercourse with his fifteen-year-old girlfriend and is therefore guilty of statutory rape), the county will often sentence the defendant to serve time in the county jail coupled with a requirement that he attend sex-offender treatment. The defense attorneys were universally supportive of these efforts to keep defendants from going to prison for long periods, although none of them discussed the collateral consequence of being required to register as sex offenders for decades, if not the rest of their lives.

Huff is sometimes able to use the county's commitment to community-based treatment to the benefit of his clients. As an example, he described a case he was handling at the time of our interview. The defendant had a prior conviction as a juvenile that was related to a sex offense, but he had admitted to the police his involvement with the current charge, too. Huff worked out a contingent plea with the prosecutor by which the client would at the very least admit to a high misdemeanor sex offense, which would expose him to two years of incarceration. However, they have agreed that the defendant will have a sex-offender evaluation by Mark Reggio before the guilty plea is actually taken. If the client does well in the testing, the deal would be made even more advantageous to him by allowing him to plead to an attempted criminal sexual contact offense, which would expose the defendant to a maximum of only thirty days in jail. Huff explained his communication to the client: "I say, 'Look, there is some risk here. If Reggio says you're a predatory pedophile, they're not going to treat you very kindly.' Remember, sometimes that risk is well worth it because that's the only hope they have."

Making such difficult choices was a theme in our discussions with the defense lawyers. Huff described another case with a defendant who was "very, very slow" and in which there were limited options for the defense:

> I have another one that's pending right now where the guy did it. And it's his second time. It's not a second offender, but he had a similar situation as a juvenile when he was like nine or ten years old. He was the aggressor with his sister, who was, I think, six or seven at the time. And they dealt with it as a CSC case even though it was not settled as a CSC case. So he

has no record. He's not listed as a sex offender. The incident happened. He acknowledges, "What the kid says is true. That's what I did." Well, what do you do with him? Trial's not going to help you. And so you tell him, here's what the prosecution says. If this is some kind of aberration that's only going to happen this time, and Mark Reggio says, "Yeah, I'll take you in this program because I think we can work with you," then that's the best you're going to get from anybody. That's the best thing you can do for the guy no matter what he pleads to.

Huff indicated that he advised the client to pursue the plea and the evaluation because he was confident that there was not a viable defense and that his client would lose a trial.

Many rights afforded the defendant are rendered moot by the realities of the legal system. For example, if a defendant pleads or is convicted after trial, he retains the right to object to the sex-offender evaluation. Huff says, "But if I object to it, the judge is going to assume the worst, and my guy gets body-slammed anyway. So you go ahead and subject him to it and hope maybe there's some good that comes out of it."

These defense attorneys evince an intimate knowledge of the other players in the local criminal-justice system. They have all worked together, albeit as adversaries, for many years. As in any small-town setting, the insular nature of the practice with its relatively few players may work to either the advantage or the disadvantage of criminal defendants. On one hand, knowing the system and its players may assist the lawyer in predicting the most likely outcome of a case based upon an assessment of the various options presented. Alternatively, it may work against the defendant because the attorneys may be reluctant to be too aggressive in any given case, not wanting to offend the judge or the prosecutors with whom they must work every day, and whom they rely upon, in the case of the judge, for appointment to cases (Blumberg, 1967). Still another possibility is that the defense attorneys—consciously or unconsciously—help to enact and reinforce the community's normalized sense of justice.

## CONCLUSION

Court-appointed defense attorneys in St. Mary County face numerous obstacles when representing defendants in CSA cases. Not the least of

# Victim and Offender Treatment and Therapeutic Justice

# NINE

KATHLEEN COULBORN FALLER

I don't see sex offenders as being horrible, terrible, villainous people. I've always seen them as individuals with a problem. I've respected the person but detested the pathology.

—Mark Reggio

I'm not sure what the dynamic is that leads people to do these things. It's because they're not emotionally healthy, obviously, not because they're evil.

—Judge Richter

Treatment is an important component of a comprehensive response to child sexual abuse (CSA). Victims deserve treatment; offenders need it. In St. Mary County, we found what we have termed "therapeutic justice," which is broader than mere therapy. Therapeutic justice is embodied in the protocol, in victim advocacy, in treatment for victims, and in community-based treatment for those offenders who satisfy the screening criteria. Therapeutic justice is embedded in a community compact about management of sexual-abuse allegations, which can be characterized as normative justice. This chapter describes treatment and supportive services for victims and the screening process and sentencing alternatives for convicted sex offenders.

I discuss victim treatment first because it came first, describing what we learned about treatment for children and their supportive caretakers and relating these findings to best practice in victim treatment. At the national level, until quite recently, the assumption was that therapists could do whatever would help victims, but that offender treatment required standards, qualifications, and oversight. St. Mary's victim and offender treatment reflects this perspective.

Placing priority on successful CSA prosecution in St. Mary County resulted in a disproportionate number of sex offenders in need of a sentence. Using court file data from St. Mary County over ten years, we compared the proportion of the St. Mary County population sentenced for a sex offense to one other study, one involving the State of Rhode Island (Cheit and Goldschmidt, 1997). St. Mary sentenced its citizens for child sexual abuse at 4.2 times the rate of Rhode Island (Faller, Birdsall, and Vandervort, 2006). Comparable statistics were reported by Prosecutor John Hunter, who noted that in 2002 St. Mary had the same number of criminal sexual assault convictions as an adjacent county that is 3.8 times St. Mary's size.

To provide therapeutic justice, St. Mary County had to develop a strategy for screening convicted offenders and intervention alternatives to state prison. These alternatives included a combination of treatment, up to a year in jail, and up to five years on probation. Thus, treatment for offenders emerged as an afterthought to the protocol, but it became an important complement.

## VICTIMS COME FIRST

Professionals in St. Mary County told us that even before the development of the protocol, there was support for child abuse victims. Services included advocacy, support, and treatment.

### Victim Advocacy

Laura Cook, the county's victim advocate, asserted that St. Mary County was provictim even before 1984, when the U.S. Congress passed the Victims of Crimes Act (VOCA). VOCA provides a support person for a crime victim and treatment for victims who are to testify in a criminal proceeding (U.S. Department of Justice Office of Victims of Crimes, 2004). As the reference suggests, this program is deeply entrenched in the criminal justice system. One of the dilemmas of the statute is that, if there is not enough evidence for a criminal case, the victim cannot receive treatment funds. Nevertheless, it is a federal source of funding for victim advocacy, treatment, and other services. Communities design and administer their own programs, which means some are flexible and generous and others are more rigid and begrudging.

Cook, a grandmother and lifelong resident of St. Mary County, had spent fifteen years in the prosecutor's office and had worked with all types of crime victims. But, she observed, "I would say that some of the longest conversations are with a child victim of either sexual assault or physical assault." She does not possess professional training for this position, and, indeed, started in the prosecutor's office as a clerical staff satisfying procedural requirements for the federally funded VOCA program—sending notices of hearings and trials, and even transporting witnesses to assure they show up in court.

Her lack of professional reserve was evident in her interview. She spoke of a case in which the defense attorney claimed the sexual abuse was, "you know, her [the victim's] idea." Cook's reaction was, "Yeah, right. Let me shoot you in the head." By her own admission, when Cook started working for the prosecutor's office, she "was fairly clueless about the legal system . . . everything was like a big surprise to me every day. Like, five hundred times a day there was a surprise." She added, "I think that's also valuable that maybe I do have that man-on-the-street perspective instead of the legal [one]."

She said that she spent "all day on the phone," frequently fielding calls from "screamers." In short, she talked to the victims, to be sure, but she especially talked to their caretakers. So although her work involved making sure victims obtain treatment and other resources for which they are eligible, a great deal of her role involved seeing that victims and their caretakers got accurate and timely information about the criminal case and court process. Typical issues that concern victims and their caretakers include explaining, she said, "why someone is out on bond; why they're not arrested yet; why the case hasn't been charged yet; why it wasn't charged more seriously." But they can also include fielding questions about the relative power and status of parties to a proceeding: "Well, *he* knows everybody. They're not going to arrest *him* because he's a big shot and he knows this and that." Finally, a common complaint is that the child's videotaped initial statement about the sexual abuse cannot be employed in lieu of taking the witness stand. As a nonlawyer, this complaint resonated with her. Indeed, these perceived injustices are common in sex crimes nationally. Occasionally, Cook's role in court on CSA cases was to serve as a support person for the child. She typically played this role only when the parent or another family member could not be present during the child's testimony because the relative was also going to testify. More commonly her role was to introduce the child to the courtroom and its personnel so that the daunting and unfamiliar process at least became the "devil you know."

As Cook described her roles and perspective, her multiple identities were apparent. The way these identities intersect and connect her to the community is not uncommon in small communities such as St. Mary. So is her lack of professional training for the pivotal role she plays in the lives of victimized children and their families.

## Victim and Supportive Caretaker Treatment

Susan Connor was the therapist identified by others in the community as the key person to interview about victim treatment. Connor had been St. Mary County's sexual-abuse-prevention education specialist and was the first therapist to provide treatment for victims and nonoffending parents. Donna Wagner, a children's-services pioneer and Jim Henry's supervisor, pointed out how "sweet" that was because Connor already knew about the dynamics and manifestations of sexual abuse. Connor was also actively involved in the early development of the protocol. She noted that, small as St. Mary County was, there were therapists who would never touch a sexual abuse case. "But I knew by that time I was hooked on these kids. I wanted something good and I knew we had to do the legal process [to attain the good]."

Connor holds a master's degree in social work, and in 1984 she "was invited to interview for the 'female half' of the child sexual abuse contract that Children's Services had implemented the year before," the protocol was actually developed. Initially Connor partnered with an ex–St. Mary County child protective services (CPS) worker. Connor treated the girl victims, and her male counterpart treated the boys.

Connor described their efforts to orchestrate the child's treatment with the child's testimony. She longed for the good old days of the protocol's beginnings when Jane Jacobson, the only female prosecutor to handle CSA cases, would prepare kids to testify and CPS workers, with administrative support, were stretching boundaries. Conner thought there was a "window of opportunity" when the child's testimony would have maximal effect in court. During that window, the child was still emotionally connected to the sexual victimization but also emotionally capable of taking the witness stand and surviving direct examination and cross-examination. Direct examination requires telling the painful history of abuse, and cross-examination involves having the history challenged by the defense.

Wagner provided additional history of victim treatment in St. Mary County. She said that community mental health (CMH) therapists believed that "they have a different mission than we do; they're trying to keep people out of state hospital." But as children's-services supervisor, she believed CMH's responsibility was to provide sexual abuse treatment. She explained how her view prevailed. "What helped us out with that, frankly, is the supervisor from CMH married one of my foster care workers and then you start to cross-fertilize, and then they started to understand what we needed." Wagner's observation underscores the importance of personal connections, especially in small communities. The current CPS supervisor, Carol Bragg, echoed Wagner's positive appraisal of the CMH clinicians, but noted that they can serve only families receiving Medicaid, which means that they have income just above the poverty level; thus, only poor children qualify for treatment at CMH centers. Wagner added, "some private sector people" thought "we could make some money here."

Wagner and Cook, when asked about successful victim advocacy and treatment, described the same case. It involved a three-year-old girl who was a victim of first-degree criminal sexual conduct (CSC) by her father. The little girl's interview was videotaped, and she made a disclosure. She was removed from the home and placed in a supportive foster home. At the time, the three-year-old did not have the verbal capacity to testify in criminal court. The prosecutor, therefore, did not file criminal charges against her father. Eventually parental rights were terminated, and the girl's foster mother adopted her.

Although the little girl was technically safe, the adoptive mother "was on pins and needles, wondering if that guy was out in the community or what's going to happen to him," according to Wagner, who further reported that she "kept us all motivated with her phone calls and what's happening next? 'I just want you to know how the child's feeling,'" the concerned new parent would say to the advocates. Wagner recognized the significance of this subtle pressure. "There's a lot of parties to keep these things going. . . . Mothers are a big one. And this mother was motivated to see this man behind bars. And the child had counseling."

Cook made the following observations about the same case: "We did not go to trial until she was five, while she was in therapy." In describing her role, Cook said, "She came [in] when she was real little, when she was three years, so, you know, to say 'Hi.' We would take her into the courtroom a few times, let her set up some chairs." When the child was five and her therapist thought she could testify, the father was charged. There were procedural delays, but eventually the father went to prison, the entire process taking about eight years. In larger communities, with less stability among professionals, this case might have fallen through the cracks.

Although professionals noted that treatment and victim advocacy played pivotal roles, they all also acknowledged the importance of caretaker advocacy and support on the long road to therapeutic justice. The centrality of the supportive caretaker is well documented in the research literature. Caretaker support precipitates sexual-abuse disclosure and aids victim recovery (see Bolen and Lamb, 2002, 2004, 2007a, 2007b; Everson et al., 1991; Hershkowitz, Lanes, and Lamb, 2007; Lawson and Chaffin, 1992). Given the vital role of the child's primary caretaker, findings from the St. Mary County court file data are instructive. Most children (80.8 percent) initially reported their abuse to someone other than mandated investigators (that is, not to CPS workers or police), and 54.8 percent of the time, this report was to a primary caretaker. More than three-fourths (79.3 percent) of nonoffending parents are described in the criminal file as believing their children's statement about sexual abuse and supporting their children (Faller and Henry, 2000).

## Best Practice in Treatment of Victims of Sexual Abuse

None of the professionals we interviewed described specific treatment approaches. This was true even of Susan Connor and is fairly typical nationally. Until recently, victim treatment programs have derived from the "practice wisdom" rather than research. Some clinicians wrote about their techniques, which were then adapted and adopted by other clinicians (see Ciottone and Madonna, 1996; Gil, 1991; Karp, 1996).

Beginning in the 1990s, however, the federal government began funding more scientifically based treatment for children traumatized by sexual abuse. First, the National Center on Child Abuse and Neglect, and later the National Institute of Mental Health, supported research on effective treatment of sexually abused children. Several university-based sexual assault and trauma treatment centers received grants to conduct this research.

The research into best practice built upon studies of the impact of sexual abuse and treatment models, primarily behavioral interventions, which are successful with other problems. The pioneering sites for the treatment research are the CARES Institute and the Center for Traumatic Stress in Children and Adolescents. The treatment is called trauma-focused cognitive behavior therapy (TF-CBT; see Cohen and Mannarino, 1996; Cohen, Berliner, and Mannarino, 2000; Cohen, Mannarino, and Deblinger, 2006; Cohen et al., 2000; Deblinger, Lippmann, and Steer, 1996; Deblinger, Steer, and Lippmann, 1999; Deblinger and Heflin, 1996; Deblinger, Mannarino, Cohen, and Steer, 2006).

TF-CBT is a short-term treatment of twelve to sixteen individual sessions for the child and caretaker, followed by joint sessions for them. Content for sessions includes didactic material and exercises focused on the following issues:

- Psychoeducation about children's reactions to trauma
- Identification and copying with trauma-related emotions (anger, shame, fear)
- Stress-management skills for children and parents
- Recognition of the connections between thoughts, feelings, and behaviors
- Development of a trauma narrative (written or pictorial)
- Parent-child communication about the trauma
- Modifying inaccurate or unhelpful trauma-related thoughts (for example, the abuse was my fault)
- Parenting skills

TF-CBT has been demonstrated to be more effective than child-centered supportive treatment (CCT), a version of which clinicians in St. Mary County were providing. These outcomes were found in a multi-site study, and positive effects were sustained at follow-up in a randomized trial involving 229 children and caretakers. Both treatment groups improved, but TF-CBT resulted in significantly greater improvements immediately (Cohen et al., 2004) and in the longer term (Deblinger et al., 2006) for children and their caretakers.

In addition, TF-CBT has been externally evaluated. Saunders, Berliner, and Hanson (2003), in a review of evidence to support treatments for child physical and sexual abuse for the Department of Justice, found TF-CBT to have the most research support for sexually abused children. Examining treatment outcomes, researchers found that TF-CBT was the only treatment that was "well supported, efficacious." Similarly, the National Child Traumatic Stress Network (NCTSN) undertook a review of "empirically supported treatments and promising practices." TF-CBT is effective in the treatment of sexual abuse with children from the ages of three to eighteen, both males and females, and with Caucasian, African American, and Latino populations. Altogether about a thousand child/caretaker dyads have participated in the research on TF-CBT.

Because of the efficacy of TF-CBT, NCTSN supports a free Web-based ten-hour course that can lead to positive, cost-effective treatment outcomes for children and their caretakers nationally, but also potentially in small communities such as St. Mary County. Moreover, Jim Henry now directs a trauma-treatment center that provides TF-CBT treatment and professional training. This has included training in TF-CBT to CMH professionals in ten counties, including St. Mary.

## TREATMENT OF SEX OFFENDERS

In St. Mary County, community-based treatment of sex offenders was an outgrowth of the focus on therapeutic jurisprudence, but it was not included initially in the protocol. However, not all sex offenders are treatable in the community.

When Mark Jameson became chief prosecutor, he provided a kinder, gentler leadership than Charles Davis. Jameson thought beyond the courtroom, the jailhouse, and the state prison. As Police Officer Ed Duke described him, "Mark came in more approachable, more laid-back, certainly, more emphasis on rehabilitation certainly has been one of Mark's legacies."

Jameson was well aware from his accumulating firsthand experience that all sex offenders were not equal. Some needed and deserved to be locked up; others did not. He worried about the ultimate consequence of a protocol that obtained a confession, then a plea, that then resulted in a prison sentence for sex offenders who were treatable. Speaking of the development of offender treatment in St. Mary County, he observed, "Treatment in prison wasn't very good. I don't even know if it existed, to tell you the truth."

Officer Duke expressed the same concern in less polite terms. "If you think you're gonna send somebody to the state prison system to get them rehabilitated, you're full of more shit than a crippled coon. It's just ain't going to work that way." The point is well taken. Prison-based treatment is minimal, and arguably prison culture is antithetical to sex-offender treatment goals of openness and honesty. For the good of the offender and the good of the community, St. Mary needed a diversion program for some sex offenders.

## Developing a Strategy Through Creative Use of Resources

This developing awareness of different types of offenders and limited rehabilitation resources in prisons inspired Jameson's treatment innovation. Among the earliest challenges he faced was finding funding and a facility. He first sought state community corrections funds, intended for use with nondangerous felons, for the evaluation and treatment of sex offenders. He encountered obstacles at both local and state levels.

Local opposition came from the Two Lakes community corrections facility, where Jameson wanted to locate the sex offender treatment program. It housed a program for young felons—"B and E [breaking and entering] boys," or, as Jameson noted, "Dirty white boys, we call them. They go out and break into some houses and then they end up [in the intervention program]—it's a wonderful program. We are fortunate to have it. The judges like it, the lawyers like it, the cops like it, little old ladies in Two Lakes like it. It's an excellent program. But they say, 'We aren't going to take sex offenders.'" Eventually Jameson overcame their reluctance.

At the state level, Jameson encountered resistance from the Department of Corrections. Jameson reported, "So we started doing this and we were going on our merry way and being successful and they said, 'You can't use the money for this on violent offenders; these are violent offenders and this is for nonviolent offenders.' John Stout was the director of the Department of Corrections, and he was sort of a blustery guy who'd been from Chicago's Corrections Department. So I went to the State Board and said we want to use this for this purpose and we're not diverting violent offenders from prison. . . . So, grudgingly, like [by a] 6–5 [vote] they allowed us to use the money for that purpose. Then later on they decided it was diverting people from prison and they held us out as a model for other counties to use the money for sex offender treatment, and Mark Reggio [the St. Mary County sex offender therapist] actually came and spoke at the state conference about how our program works." Once again St. Mary County was a leader in innovations involving handling CSA cases, in this instance in offender treatment.

As with other aspects of the St. Mary County protocol that shift the burden in child sexual abuse cases to professionals, the structure and the success of the sex-offender treatment program centered on an individual—Mark Reggio, a psychologist who worked for CMH for seventeen years doing sex-offender work and then, tired of the paperwork, exited the public sector but continued doing sex-offender evaluations and treatment. We interviewed him in the dilapidated storefront where the County Probation Department had given him an office.

Before moving to St. Mary County, Reggio worked in a sex offender program in Oregon directed by Barry Maletzky, one of the pioneers in sex offender treatment (Maletzky, 1991). Reggio had also been influenced by William Marshall, an internationally recognized expert who is emeritus professor of psychology at Queens University in Ontario and past president of Association for the Treatment of Sexual Abusers (ATSA). Bill Marshall has been responsible for developing and evaluating sex-offender treatment programs in Canada, Australia, and other countries (Barbaree, Marshall, and Hudson, 1993; Marshall Laws, and Barbaree, 1990; Marshall, 1989). Interestingly, these two leaders in sex-offender work represent divergent views about conducting treatment—sometimes called the hardnosed and the softhearted approaches. Maletzky's treatment relied heavily on aversive conditioning, for example, associating deviant sexual fantasies with noxious odors, tastes, and electrical shock, and he put little emphasis on developing offender empathy for their victims, finding empathy enhancement more useful with adolescent offenders (Maletzky, 1991). Marshall, on the other hand, emphasized the importance of offender attachment difficulties and their deficits in social skills (see Webster et al., 2005), and, although he also uses behavioral interventions, the emphasis is on cognitive-behavioral strategies as opposed to aversive conditioning.

Reggio also joined the Association for the Treatment of Sexual Abusers (ATSA), the North American organization for sex-offender therapists. Begun in the late 1970s, ATSA brought together frontline professionals who assess and treat sex offenders in corrections facilities, residential programs, and the community, and researchers who have developed and are evaluating interventions with sex offenders. These professionals have been greatly concerned with best practice standards, educational requirements, and mechanisms for assuring adherence to them by sex offender professionals. By 2009, ATSA was holding its twenty-eighth annual conference.

Thus, Reggio was grounded in existing knowledge when he crafted sex-offender intervention for St. Mary County and has continued to update that knowledge (and modify his practice). Both hardnosed and softhearted influences were apparent as he talked about his practice. Moreover, he articulated how he thought St. Mary practice was consistent with and diverged from the ATSA guidelines.

As he spoke of sex offenders, the softhearted approach was apparent. Reggio has never seen them "as being horrible, terrible, villainous people. I've always seen them as individuals with a problem. I've respected the person but detested the pathology." Reggio expressed concern for offenders' "health," describing them as engaging in behaviors that are unhealthy for themselves, their victims, and the community. His view echoed that of Judge Richter, who said, "I'm not sure what the dynamic is that leads people to do these things. It's because they're not emotionally healthy obviously not because they're evil." These opinions suggest a kind of meeting of the minds of the judge, who is often responsible for sentencing, and the therapist, who is responsible for assessments and treatment.

On the other hand, the hardnosed approach is reflected in the narrow eligibility for community-based treatment in St. Mary County. As Reggio says, "CSC one or three, you know they're sent to prison." (These charges involve penetration.) Thus, offenders must have only committed fondling offenses to stay in the community and receive treatment. The court file data indicate greater flexibility than that was exercised. It could be, however, that the conviction was for a less serious offense, allowing for a community-based sentence. Nonetheless, close to two-thirds of suspects whose initial charge involved some sort of penetration (oral, anal, vaginal, digital, or combinations of penetration) received jail with treatment and/or probation.

Illustrative is a fifty-eight-year-old man who was the boyfriend of his fifteen-year-old victim's grandmother. He initially denied sexual abuse to law enforcement but tearfully confessed to polygraphist Rick Rivers before being hooked up to the polygraph machine. Although in this session he continued to describe his victim as tempting him and not resisting his abusive behaviors, he admitted to virtually all acts she described, which included digital penetration of her vagina and her performing oral sex on him. He expressed relief after unburdening himself of the secrecy and denial. He said he knew what he did wasn't right; "it was not him." He had no prior convictions, he pleaded, and he did not go to trial. He received two years' probation, six months in jail, and sex-offender treatment.

In addition, statutory rape situations are eligible for community-based treatment. Reggio described them as "CSC offenses where the males are like seventeen or eighteen and the females are fifteen. And so, you know, I have a little bit of queasiness about dealing with them" as penetration sex offenses. This is a judicious handling of such cases. Some communities ignore them, even though the sexual relationships can be exploitive. Other communities treat them severely, criminally prosecuting the boyfriends and even compelling the girls to testify. St. Mary has found a middle ground by providing these young men treatment.

Like much of the community's approach to CSA cases, Reggio regarded himself as part of a team. St. Mary had very good probation officers, he noted, who "really stay on top of the CSC offenders. . . . We like one another, we respect one another, and I've been very fortunate. We listen to one another." This team approach increased Reggio's confidence that the community is safe while the offenders receive treatment.

## THE IMPACT OF THE ASSOCIATION FOR THE TREATMENT OF SEXUAL ABUSERS

Reggio was an enthusiastic member of ATSA from 1990 to 1995, but he ended his membership over disputes regarding two policies. He still attends their annual conferences, however, and finds them very useful in keeping up on state-of-the-art sex-offender treatment. First, Reggio disputed ATSA's policy that held that an offender who did not admit to his offense was not treatable. "I didn't agree with that. I mean I felt it was kind of healthy that if an individual does something wrong and they recognize it's wrong and they're in trouble for it, the healthy response is to say, 'No. You know I didn't do it.'" The challenge of treatment was to get offenders to admit their sex offenses and take responsibility for them. If they fail to do this, then "there is a problem." In actuality, ATSA policy, as reflected in the *ATSA Practitioner's Handbook* (ATSA, 1993), is fairly consistent with Reggio's philosophy:

> 19. Most sex offenders enter the system with varying degrees of denial regarding their behavior. Overcoming denial is a gradual process achieved in treatment. The existence of some degree of denial should not preclude an offender entering treatment, although the degree of denial should be a factor in identifying the most appropriate form and location of treatment.
>
> 20. Sex offender treatment is unlikely to be successful unless the offender admits his behavior. Community-based treatment is not appropriate for offenders who continue to demonstrate complete denial after a trial period of treatment.

Reggio may have had a different impression because, for ATSA, hammering out a policy on sex offenders who are in denial involved numerous clashes and lively debate. Those therapists who had the luxury of only taking the confessed offenders into treatment advocated narrow treatment eligibility as ATSA policy, and those who, like Reggio, had responsibilities for both the confessed and the nonconfessed took a different view. ATSA current policy reflects the field's consensus as well as Reggio's view.

Nevertheless, sex-offender therapists may encounter serious dilemmas as denying and minimizing offenders try to come clean. Often their known sex crimes are the tip of the iceberg when compared with those crimes that are actually committed. Knowing the full extent of the offender's problem is vital to appropriate treatment, and their coming clean is generally a positive sign in treatment. Yet, without some guarantee that full confession will not result in additional prosecution and incarceration, it would be foolhardy for offenders in treatment to make such admissions.

Gene Abel and Judith Becker encountered this dilemma in their pioneering study of the extent and variety of deviant sexual acts among offenders who were in treatment and voluntarily participated in their study (Becker et al., 1987). To maximize the likelihood that their 561 participants would be candid, they and their colleagues went to great lengths to guarantee confidentiality and protect participants from additional legal intervention. They obtained a certificate of confidentiality from the federal government, gathered information about types of crimes without identifying information, using numbers instead of names, and put the master list of names and numbers in safekeeping with fellow researcher Bill Marshall in Canada.

Their findings were groundbreaking and myth-shattering. Paraphiliacs (persons with deviant sexual tastes and arousal) do not stick to one form of deviant behavior. On average they commit two types of deviant sexual behaviors and 520 deviant acts, but the number of acts and victims varied by the type of deviant behavior. For instance, nonincestuous child molesters who victimize boys committed on average 282 acts, compared to those who victimize girls, who committed 23. Additional important findings are that incestuous fathers were almost four times more likely to abuse girls than boys, and half of incest offenders also sexually abused children outside the home. Most offenders in the study began their sexual deviancy in adolescence (Becker et al., 1987).

Reggio was surely aware of the findings of Abel and Becker and the ATSA practice principle that "community safety takes precedence over any conflicting consideration and ultimately is in the best interest of the offender" (ATSA, 1993:3). St. Mary's policy regarding additional offenses discovered during treatment, like other elements of its policy and practice, evolved from an individual case. In the early 1990s, when group treatment took place at the courthouse annex, Reggio said that a group member came to him after group. The man said, "Mark, you know I have other victims, but I'm afraid to say anything." This prompted Reggio to consult Mark Jameson, the prosecutor, and they arrived at a mutual understanding.

Reggio reported, "In treatment, they disclose other victims and the understanding was that I will tell the prosecuting attorney. The prosecuting attorney will notify the victim's family, but the offender will not be punished for advancing the treatment. And to me, that is just that's amazing; I mean, that's just wonderful." In short, the therapist and prosecutor found a way to promote the interests of the victim, the offender, and the community at once.

This policy of informing the prosecutor and the victim's family, but not punishing the offender for progress in treatment is amazing and wonderful. It also makes sense in a small community with vigilant probation officers in constant communication with the therapist. These professionals, with prosecutor oversight, can manage fifty-five to sixty sex offenders. This practice does not appear in the protocol but is one of several unwritten understandings that make the protocol work. Reggio was unsure whether this practice would continue under a new chief prosecutor.

The second dispute Reggio had with ATSA had to do with when, in a criminal case, a sex-offender evaluation should occur. Reggio said, "ATSA ethical standards won't allow you to provide an evaluation or conduct an evaluation that's pre-adjudication. Their philosophy is that you shouldn't become involved in the judicial system until after the person has pled or has been convicted." In their *Practitioners Handbook* and their *Professional Code of Ethics*, ATSA does not address this issue directly. These two documents refer to voluntary (nonadjudicated) and involuntary (adjudicated) clients. So again, Reggio may be mistaken about ATSA's official position. He appeared to be referring to the questionable practice of defense experts evaluating their client prior to adjudication and declaring that the client does not fit the profile of a sex offender, which ATSA does not support, simply because there is no one profile for sex offenders (see Hanson, 2003). There are many different profiles.

## THE SCREENING PROCESS

Most offenders are referred to Reggio after conviction, but before sentencing. Thus, he says, "My job was then to do an evaluation and assess his degree of pathology and make treatment recommendations. And if the judge decided to keep them in the community, then would I be able to treat them?"

Of the 414 court file cases on which offender evaluation data are available from the court files, 256 (61.2 percent) received an evaluation by Reggio. Receiving a sex-offender evaluation before sentencing was positively associated with having confessed, with having been charged with a more serious sex offense, and with having pleaded. However, severity of the offender's sentence was unrelated to having a presentence evaluation. This finding, in part, reflects the elimination from the analysis of seventy-nine cases with no sentence. The no-sentence cases include ones in which the suspect passed the polygraph (see the chapter 6) as well as other cases where the prosecutor decided not to go forward, for example when evidence was inconclusive, or children were unable to testify.

Reggio appeared to conduct a comprehensive sex offender assessment, which included widely used standardized measures and an in-depth interview. In the beginning of sex-offender treatment in the United States, there were no sex-offender-specific assessment instruments. Thus, he said, "I would give the IQ test, the Millon [2005] and the Minnesota Multiphasic Personality Inventory [MMPI-II]." The two latter tests both assess psychiatric diagnoses and personality disorders. The Millon has been widely used by sex-offender evaluators and therapists, since it measures twenty-two personality disorders. Sex offenders with personality disorders, especially those with antisocial personality disorder, are considered to have poorer prognoses (Salter, 2003). The MMPI-II is perhaps even more widely employed on cases in litigation, including sexual abuse cases. Although widely accepted as a measure of psychiatric diagnoses on Axis I and Axis II, the MMPI originally was normed in the 1950s on white Minnesotans. MMPI-II, the more recent version (1989), has a broader normative population and a different scoring system. Thus, in the beginning, Reggio followed state-of-the-art practice, but that practice had limitations.

Reggio's current screening practice reflects advances in sex-offender assessment strategies and risk assessment, which support the use of standardized measures that are sex-offender specific and actuarial data (ATSA, n.d.). For example, he uses the Shipley Scales, risk assessment measures developed by Robert Freeman-Longo, another former ATSA president, a measure of empathy, and the Psychopathy Check-List-Revised (PCL-R) developed by Hare (2005), when he is concerned that he is dealing with an individual who has antisocial personality disorder. Hare, a psychologist at the University of British Columbia, has dedicated his career to the development of the PCL-R, a vastly superior instrument for detecting psychopathy— or antisocial personality disorder, as it is currently referred to in the American Psychiatric Association's *Diagnostic and Statistical Manual* (DSM-IV)—in sexual offenders and other criminals.

Reggio continues to conduct an in-depth interview and to compare the offender's disclosures to the police report. Based upon this evaluation process, he said, "I'll come up with a diagnosis, a prognosis, and with some treatment recommendations." Reggio's integration of findings from standardized measures, actuarial predictors of risk, and his clinical interview represent current best practice.

Reggio also said, "The defense attorneys, I think, have learned to respect the treatment component of it to where they're trying to not only legally look out for the best interest of their client but also look out for the health of their client." In fact, defense attorney, Richard Nowak, confirmed that penalties were "tailored" to fit offenders' needs: "What does this deserve? Does this deserve counseling as opposed to anything else?" He goes on to provide an example that "stands out most" in his mind. In this case, Jameson, the prosecutor, "didn't view it as merited a lot of jail time. And it involved a dad that started carrying on with a fifteen-year-old babysitter. It was settled. It was settled and the type of sentence included a lot of counseling." Nowak continued, "I know that individual now and he's out and about and for all appearances appears to be a law-abiding member of the community."

Concern about the health of sex offenders was a recurrent theme in Reggio's interview. Interestingly, this mindset toward sex offenders is very similar to that articulated by Rick Rivers, the polygraphist, and that of Judge Richter. This similarity was not lost on the researchers, who also noted that all three of these men held the trust of the community. What they think, in Rivers's case (whether the person sexually abused a child), in Reggio's case (what sort of treatment/intervention is required), and in Judge Richter's case (an appropriate sentence for a sex offense), are the community decision points. Thus, this triad of individuals permits the case to be resolved—from start to finish—among professionals without relying heavily on the child's participation. Furthermore, institutional players such as prosecutor Jameson and defense attorney Nowak seem to have incorporated this dependence on key professionals into their everyday practices with CSC cases.

## THE SENTENCE FITS THE SERIOUSNESS OF THE CRIME

From our interviews with St. Mary County professionals, our review of the protocol, and the court file data, a therapeutic and social justice question emerged. Does the quick law-enforcement response required by the protocol, embodied in seeking a suspect confession as soon as possible after the child discloses and before he or she has a chance to "lawyer up," result in injustice? We knew from an analysis of the court file data that having a court-appointed attorney, a proxy for being poor, was a predictor of confession (Faller et al., 2001). Of course, it can be argued that confession is good for the offender, because it relieves the offender of the burden of harboring a secret, is a precursor to rehabilitation, and relieves the child of the burden of testifying. But does confession and having a court-appointed attorney disadvantage the suspect in sentencing? The court file data indicated that confession and having a court-appointed attorney *did not* result in more severe sentences. Analyzing ten years of data on 218 male offenders, who received sentences, predictors of a more severe sentence were the seriousness of the sex crime (penetration, more instances of abuse), prior conviction of a sex crime, and young age of the victim. Moreover, despite the single-mindedness with which St. Mary County pursues sex offenders, the actual sentences were not all that severe. From data from 1988 to 1998, the figures were: jail, probation, or both: 127 offenders (58.3 percent); 1–5 years in prison: 43 offenders (19.7 percent); five or more years in prison 48 offenders (22.0 percent) (Faller, Birdsall, and Vandervort, 2006); more recent data are in keeping with these distributions. Thus, the majority of convicted sex offenders stayed in the community. The data do not tell us whether the sentence included sex-offender treatment, but it is probably safe to assume that most community sentences did.

These findings support a conclusion that professionals in St. Mary County enact normative justice through a community compact that does not merely support sexual abuse victims but also supports just sex-offender treatment, allowing those who have committed lesser sex crimes to stay in the community and receive treatment.

## THE TREATMENT PROTOCOL

Reggio designed a sixteen-session group treatment program for sex offenders that meets weekly for an hour and a half and is consistent with state-of-the-art practice. After offenders completed the group treatment, he wrote a discharge summary that might recommend weekly or biweekly individual treatment. Most offenders received five years of probation, a sentence to treatment, and up to a year in the county jail. Judge Richter pointed out that having 173 jail beds and a probation center facilitates therapeutic justice. The county had the capacity to lock people up.

Reggio described the structure of his group treatment program: "The treatment format is set up, the first session is group rules, expectations, introduction. Second session we go over the format that I'm going to use in the treatment, which is . . . essentially Anatomy of a Crime." To elucidate this anatomy, Reggio used David Finkelhor's four preconditions to sexual offending:

1. emotional congruence—why the adult has an emotional need to relate to a child;
2. sexual arousal—why the adult is sexually aroused by a child;
3. blockage—why alternative sources of sexual and emotional gratification are not available; and
4. disinhibition—why the adult is not deterred by normal prohibitions against sexual offending.

These four preconditions derive from a review of eighty-one articles on risk factors for sexual offending against children conducted by Araji and Finkelhor, first published in 1985, with a later version appearing in a groundbreaking book published in 1986 (Finkelhor et al., *Sourcebook on Child Sexual Abuse*).

Finkelhor, a sociologist at the University of New Hampshire, is arguably the most important modern researcher and theorist about child sexual abuse and child victimization. The four-preconditions model not only encompasses the spectrum of factors studied and found significant in sexual offending, but it also demonstrates that, in almost all cases, multiple factors, from a history of abuse as a child to being drunk at the time, play a role in sexual offending.

Reggio noted, "I added a fifth component: the target's going to be an individual child." In his opinion, it was crucial to focus treatment of sex offenders upon their process of selecting and grooming a victim.

Following the general presentation of the model in the second session, Reggio examined in depth "specific precursors to offending: history of abuse, alcoholism, intimacy, dating habits, sexual confusion, sexual role confusion. I mean there's the whole gambit of things we look at. And every session I start out presenting some material." An example he cited for the topic of sexual addiction, Patrick Carnes's information, again demonstrates his knowledge of the sex-offender literature (Carnes, 1990).

The second part of the offender-treatment sessions involved an offender describing his sexual abuse. Reggio said, "And then one of the group members goes over his offense. Reggio indicated that he relied heavily on the group to confront the individual who describes his offense, but he structured this involvement by requiring each group member to ask one question, thus ensuring that all group members contributed, but that the contribution was not burdensome. This questioning is a strategy to assist the individual who is describing his offense in addressing his "cognitive distortions" or "thinking errors" (denial or minimization or rationalization). Reggio also used the police report, which contains the child's disclosure and any other evidence (for instance, medical findings and crime scene findings), again asking the group to query any inconsistencies between the individual's admission to the group and the child's disclosure and other evidence.

Reggio described his approach to another common issue in sex-offender treatment, empathy development. He assists offenders in empathy development, relying not on the victims' disclosures or professionally produced materials on the impact of sexual abuse, but rather on popular films—for example, *Lolita* and *The General's Daughter*. Using these films, he assisted group members with empathy insights by asking them to put themselves in various actors' shoes.

The last sessions focus on relapse prevention, a treatment technique that assumes offenders experience a series of emotions (anger, loneliness, self-pity), cognitions (I deserve something to make me feel better; the child isn't a virgin), and behaviors (getting drunk, going into the child's room) that precede the offense (see Laws, Hudson, and Ward, 2000; Marques et al., 2005). Relapse prevention involves identifying key decision/action points and developing strategies for disrupting these responses or the offense cycle. Reggio said, "Each one of them is required to put down [in writing] their offense cycle: 'What are you going to do to disrupt your cycle?' You know, 'Who are you going to use as a resource? Where are you going to go? How are you going to know when you're starting your cycle again?'" Relapse prevention has its supporters (see ATSA, 2001; Laws et al., 2000) and detractors (see DeClue, 2002); its effectiveness related to offender treatment, which will be discussed next, is controversial.

## HOW SUCCESSFUL IS OFFENDER TREATMENT?

One would think that after thirty years of research, the question of offender treatment effectiveness could be readily answered. It cannot; offender treatment outcome is a contested issue. In 1989, Furby, Weinrott, and Blackshaw reviewed existing outcome studies and concluded that treatment was not more effective than no treatment. More recent findings are more varied. Some demonstrate positive effects of treatment (Hanson et al., 2002), and others demonstrate no effect (Marques et al., 2000). Moreover, there are disagreements about the interpretation of existing treatment outcome studies. The most comprehensive study, a recent meta-analysis of sixty-one studies of treatment outcomes with more than nine thousand offenders, conducted by Hanson and colleagues (2002), found modest positive effects of treatment, mostly of treatments based upon behavioral strategies.

What is an appropriate research design for studying the effectiveness of sex offender treatment? The gold standard for determining the efficacy and effectiveness of a treatment is a randomized control clinical trial. This involves screening subjects into the intervention (for example, defining them as sex offenders) and then randomly assigning them to either the treatment being tested or an alternative (no treatment or another, presumably less effective, treatment). Because of community reactions to sexual abuse, professionals cannot contemplate randomized assignment of sex offenders to no treatment as an alternative to treatment, and then compare the two groups. So, to date, there are no rigorous randomized control trials of sex offenders involving no treatment. Typically, treatment is compared to a nonrandom group that receives no treatment, either because group members refuse it or because treatment is not available. Studies also have compared those who complete treatment to those who do not. Not surprisingly, studies using these two comparison groups find that treated sex offenders recidivate at lower rates (see DeClue, 2002; Maletsky and Steinhauser, 2002).

There is one exception to the lack of randomized control trials, a randomized control study of incarcerated sex offenders, testing cognitive behavioral treatment with relapse prevention (RP), against two groups who received traditional prison treatment (Marques et al., 2005). These researchers examined findings on 704 sex offenders: 259 randomly assigned to the treatment (RP) condition, 225 randomly assigned to the volunteer control (VC) condition, and 220 selected for the nonvolunteer control (NVC) condition. These three groups of offenders were followed over eight years, and no significant difference was found in recidivism rates among treatment conditions; RP: 21.9 percent reoffended; VC: 17.2 percent reoffended; and NVC: 20.6 percent reoffended. Indeed, the treated group recidivated at a marginally higher but nonsignificant rate, a sobering finding.

What are actual reoffense rates? Popular opinion is that virtually all sex offenders "do it again," even with treatment (ATSA, n.d.b.); thus the popularity of sex-offender notification laws, even though these laws have yet to demonstrate a positive impact on recidivism (ATSA, n.d.c.). The statistics from the study by Marques and colleagues suggest that about a fifth of treated child molesters reoffend. It is worth noting that these offenders are incarcerated child molesters at Atascadero State Hospital in California, a maximum-security facility. Thus, these persons had committed serious sex crimes.

The meta-analysis by Hanson and colleagues (2002), mentioned earlier, found lower rates of recidivism, 12.3 percent for treated sex offenders and 16.8 percent for those in comparison groups. Reggio estimates that he has recidivism rates are between 10 and 15 percent, thus in the expected range for treated offenders. Maletzky, one of Reggio's mentors in Oregon, conducted a twenty-five-year follow-up study of 7,275 sex offenders treated in his program and found a 10 percent recidivism rate (Maletzky and Steinhauser, 2002).

But not all sex offenders are equal in terms of future risk. Many studies include rapists of peers as well as child molesters. Child molesters are divided into those who sexually abused boys, girls, and both boys and girls. Child molesters are further divided between those committing extrafamilial and intrafamilial sexual abuse. Although studies vary somewhat in their findings, research suggests that rapists (20 percent–50 percent) (Hanson et al., 2002; Maletzky and Steinhauser, 2002) and extrafamilial sexual abusers of boys (40 percent) (Hanson et al., 2002) are at high risk for reoffense. Reggio describes his concern about risk for reoffense among incest offenders, who are found in most studies to be relatively low-risk (10 percent). However, Reggio identifies a specific group of incest offenders, those for whom incest is intergenerational and "a way of life." Although rarely differentiated in studies of treatment outcomes, his observation is supported by practice. One of the problems in polyincest cases (families with two or more sexual-abuse relationships) is that there are so many sexualized relationships it is difficult to break the cycle of incest without breaking up the family (Faller, 1991).

Reoffenses can go undetected, and therefore unstudied. A further question is, "Is getting caught again a definition of reoffense or is being convicted?" For example, Maletzky concluded that being charged with another sex offense should be the definition of recidivism, not being convicted (Maletzky and Steinhauser, 2002). Furthermore, Marshall and Barbaree, who are in the softhearted camp, concluded that the reconviction rate should be multiplied by 2.4 in order to calculate actual detected reoffenses. This conclusion was based upon follow-up contacts with the formal and informal social networks of treated offenders (Barbaree and Marshall, 1998).

Another issue is how long sex offenders should be followed after treatment before determining that they are not going to reoffend (Marques, 1999). Initial studies of model treatment programs followed up sex offenders for a year or two after discharge and found quite low reoffense rates—for example, 4 percent (Maletzky, 1991). Hanson and colleagues (2002), however, in their meta-analysis followed up untreated but formerly incarcerated sex offenders fifteen to thirty years after discharge and found that 42 percent had committed a new sex offense. Offenders varied in terms of their level of risk. If the offender was never married, had a sex-offense conviction prior to the instant offense, had boy victims, and was sexually aroused to children, the reoffense rate rose to 77 percent.

St. Mary County does not use the penile plethysmograph, used in many large sex-offender treatment programs but rarely in small, community-based programs. This is a mechanism that is placed around the offender's penis and used to measure his arousal to deviant and non-deviant sexual-stimulus material. In treatment, it is used as one of several measures of progress. In follow-up, the plethysmograph is used, again among other measures, to detect deviant arousal—an index of "backsliding."

In our examination of St. Mary court file data, we could track three of these four factors that are predictive of high reoffense rates—having boy victims, prior convictions, and multiple victims. We identified twelve offenders with multiple boy victims and prior convictions. All twelve of these individuals went to prison.

## CONCLUSION

Treatment and therapeutic justice when adults sexually abuse children are not straightforward. St. Mary County has developed some fair solutions to the challenges and dilemmas of placing a priority on criminal prosecution of child sexual abuse, but also on normative justice.

Sex-offender treatment in St. Mary County has been subjected to more scrutiny and held to higher standards than has victim treatment. This differential response is consistent with national trends. The implicit assumption is that if victims are safe, the specific treatment they receive for their trauma is of secondary importance. In contrast, offender treatment must meet best-practice standards to assure community safety and prevent reoffenses (see ATSA, n.d.b.).

The lesser standard for victim treatment may change in St. Mary County, however. Now there is readily available evidence-based treatment, trauma-focused cognitive behavior therapy. Moreover, the National Child Traumatic Stress Network (NCTSN), with the support of the federal government, is engaging in ongoing review and development of effective treatment for child sexual abuse and other child trauma (National Child Traumatic Stress Network, 2008).

On the other hand, sex-offender treatment in St. Mary County reflects an adaptation of best practice. Most professionals would agree with the decisions made in St. Mary County. An approach that involves differential response to sexual offenders, community-based punishment and treatment for some sex offenders, and careful monitoring of convicted offenders who are in the community are components of an appropriate response and reflect normative justice.

The Overall Process and
Concluding Lessons

**PART 3**

People, Protocol, and Process          **TEN**

*The Inman Case*

KAREN M. STALLER

Unlike the ones that have come before, this chapter follows the life history of a single St. Mary case from initial incident to final outcome. Admittedly, this case does not illustrate the optimal operation of the protocol—which in the best of circumstances would not have required a child victim to testify at a criminal trial. In doing so, it highlights some of the difficulties facing prosecutors elsewhere. However, this case does illustrate the tenacious and dedicated nature of the St. Mary's prosecutor's office even thirty years after the development of the initial protocol. In the end, it illustrates what making child sexual abuse (CSA) prosecutions a priority looks like in practice.

## THE INVESTIGATION

On the sweltering summer afternoon of July 3, 2002, twelve-year-old Takisha Johnson voluntarily climbed into the front seat of Tommy Inman's red van. Their accounts of what occurred next overlap considerably, but they differ in one particularly significant aspect. Nonetheless, there is absolutely no doubt that on the eve of the July 4 holiday, as the thermometer began receding from the ninety-nine-degree mark, sixth-grader Takisha rode off alone with forty-eight-year-old Inman.

Corporal James Ford would first learn these names the next morning when he arrived at the Augustine stationhouse at 7:00 a.m. for the start of his twelve-hour holiday shift. A twenty-three-year veteran of the police force, Ford began his day reading his colleagues' reports from the night before. They included the record of a complaint filed by Melissa Johnson, who told his department's patrol division lieutenant that her daughter, Takisha, was late coming home and had driven off with a man whom her daughter's playmates identified as Thomas Inman. Several hours later, at around 9:30 p.m., Ms. Johnson spoke to the same officer again, this time telling him that Inman had given her daughter a ride and she was now safely home. The lieutenant closed the missing-person case.

July 4 was a busy day in the small village of Augustine in St. Mary County. There was a parade at 11:00 in the morning, and the annual fireworks display began at dusk. Ford would later say it was one of the busiest days of the year, in part because the holiday "kind of doubles the size of Augustine." It was between these two big community events, at around 2:00 in the afternoon, that Ford received a call from Ms. Johnson, reporting that Thomas Inman had sexually assaulted her daughter the evening before. Ford asked Johnson to bring Takisha down to the stationhouse.

There was a time in the 1980s when a trio of professionals known as the Sex Busters would have leaped into action. Had Ms. Johnson called during their reign and State Trooper Ed Williams caught the case, he would have picked up the phone immediately and called in his friend, child protective services (CPS) worker Jim Henry, to accompany him on a criminal sexual conduct (CSC) investigation. Henry would have joined on—holiday or not—and interviewed the child in front of a video camera. Inman would have been interrogated that day, and if that pressure were not enough, Rick Rivers would have been waiting in the wings, ready to hook Inman up to his polygraph machine. The result, more often than not, was some sort of confession.

However, Jim Henry was no longer a CPS worker in the county, and Williams had retired from the force. Ford had been exclusively in charge of cases of CSC with a child for his small department for almost two years. An affable, sincere, soft-spoken, and thoughtful man, Ford had a pragmatic attitude about his work and had learned from experience. He asked for help when he needed it, but it was a holiday, and he didn't have very much information, so talking directly with the victim and her mother by himself made sense to him.

Ms. Johnson arrived with two of her three children—Takisha and her younger sister, Cleo—promptly at 3:00 p.m. Ford deposited Cleo in a waiting room and sat down to talk with Takisha and her mother. Ms. Johnson began relaying her daughter's account—one that she herself had first heard just a bit earlier that morning—to Ford. Its essence was that Thomas Inman had driven Takisha to an isolated wooded area the night before and sexually assaulted her. At this point in Ms. Johnson's account, Takisha started to cry.

Ford faced some professional decisions about how to proceed. He had been listening to Ms. Johnson, directing his questions to her. He now decided he needed to talk to Takisha alone, calm her down, and get the kind of information that would allow him to proceed with an investigation. Ford escorted Ms. Johnson out of the room. Once alone with Takisha, he reassured her that "everything was okay" and that he just "needed from her exactly where this happened at" and "kind of a brief synopsis of what happened," adding that he only wanted to know what "she could tell me at that time." He did not want to push the tearful girl to tell him everything. Later, he said that although he frequently interviews the victim himself, "I felt that with just talking with Takisha . . . I felt maybe a female would be better suited to do the interview than myself." So his plan involved calling CPS and asking if one of their social workers would assist him by doing the videotaped forensic interview with Takisha.

In the meantime, Takisha had calmed down a bit, but not completely. She couldn't say exactly where the assault had occurred. She and her family had just moved to the area about eight months earlier, and street names and places were unfamiliar to her. She just knew Inman had taken her down a dirt road in a wooded area and had dragged her up and down a hill, repeatedly assaulting her. At this point, Ford decided to focus his immediate investigation on locating the site of the crime, postponing his call to CPS about the interview. Establishing venue (the location at which the alleged crime took place) was a critical component of any criminal investigation, and something he could do immediately.

## FINDING THE SCENE: CRIMINAL INVESTIGATION

Takisha remembered driving by a skateboard park, and she knew the address of her friend's house and therefore could identify the exact location where she had gotten into Inman's van. That spot wasn't very far from the police station, and there was a skateboard park about a quarter of a block away. Ford led Takisha out the doors of the stationhouse and pointed to the skateboard park down the street. She confirmed that it was the one they had driven past the night before.

Ford asked Takisha if she would drive around with him in order to see if she could remember the route Inman had taken. Takisha was fearful about getting into the patrol car with the officer alone and asked if her sister could come along. Ford thought that was a very good idea, so, with the two girls in the back seat of his patrol car, he set out in search of a spot that Takisha might be able to identify. Had Jim Henry been present to advise Ford, he would undoubtedly have warned against reenacting the experience of the evening before by putting this child in his car and driving to the site of the assault. Any other social worker would have given the same warning.

The process was one of trial and error. At times something would look familiar to Takisha; then they would reach the next corner, and nothing would look familiar. However, in bits and pieces she began remembering things. There was a dam and some railroad tracks. Ford considered where the little village had dams and railroad tracks. Topple Dam, off Main Street, seemed a likely possibility. They got to the nearby railroad tracks and Takisha remembered a large sign reading F. M. Copper Company. Ford drove behind the Copper Company to a wooded area and asked Takisha if it looked familiar. It didn't, but Takisha suddenly remembered a small bridge with people fishing off it. Ford thought about it. The southbound railroad tracks again lined up with Main Street—there was another intersection that could be helpful. He turned the car around and drove to that intersection. When he stopped, Takisha recognized it and wordlessly signaled for him to make a left-hand turn. The officer swung the car left, and there was a little bridge. The area looked familiar to Takisha, reported Ford, so, "I went up and there's an access road here. It's kind of an offshoot. On the left hand side is a dirt, gravel, and it goes back toward Triplex. When I got to this intersection I stopped. 'Does anything look familiar?' And she pointed left again, so I started going down this road." It was at this point, according to Ford, that Takisha's little sister Cleo abruptly piped up from the backseat that her big sister wanted to return home *now*. Ford described the moment, "When I got approximately halfway down the road, I kind of slowed down, and I looked back and Takisha was crying, trembling, tears were running. She was—she looked terrified, and I thought to myself, maybe I found the area. Maybe she remembers. So I did not go all the way back. What I did is I stopped because I wanted to get her back to her mother and our office."

So Ford didn't drive Takisha deeper into the woods and down the road that seemed to lead to the site of her assault. Instead, he turned his patrol car around and headed back to the stationhouse. Much later, Ford would testify that the area he came upon—and then backed away from—had a dirt road with trees, an embankment, an old bridge off of which people fished, and railroad tracks. In short, the spot where Takisha started to cry contained all the features she had independently offered him for his search. Nonetheless, in the eyes of the law there would be questions about whether the venue of the crime was ever sufficiently established.

## THE MEDICAL INVESTIGATION AND CPS CALL

When they returned, Ford asked Ms. Johnson to take Takisha straight to the emergency room of the Two Lakes Hospital. After they drove off, Ford turned to his second order of business. He called the on-duty CPS worker, Sue Hamilton, and asked if she would do a "courtesy" CSC interview for him. It was a "courtesy" interview because this case was exclusively a criminal matter, and it did not invoke CPS's jurisdiction because the alleged perpetrator and victim did not live together. Nonetheless, had former CPS worker Jim Henry received the call, most likely he would have dropped everything in order to videotape the victim so that the suspect could be confronted immediately with the videotape of a traumatized child. In this case, that did not happen. Ford and Hamilton scheduled the CSC interview for the next morning, a business day, Friday, July 5. This was certainly in accordance with the rules as written in the St. Mary County protocol, but it somehow violated the spirit of that rapid interdisciplinary response that had characterized the policy's execution in earlier years. Immediacy, speed, surprise, catching both victim and alleged perpetrator in the emotions of the moment had historically given the protocol its bite.

After that phone call, other tasks occupied Ford's attention for the remainder of his shift. At the end of it, he headed home for a long holiday weekend and did not return to the office again until Monday, July 8. By then, Inman had been arrested for a parole violation but had not yet been charged on any CSC counts. The county's investigation protocol charges law enforcement with the task of immediately collecting additional evidence. However, neither Ford nor anyone else in his department did any further investigation. Inman's defense attorney, Mike Oakley, would capitalize on a long list of these omissions.

## A CPS CASE: PHYSICAL ABUSE

An hour after receiving Ford's call, CPS worker Sue Hamilton received yet another phone call during her holiday shift. This one came from the hospital staff at the Two Lakes emergency room. A staffer told her that they were "having a rape kit completed and there was some evidence of physical abuse" perpetrated by the child's mother. As mandated child abuse reporters, the hospital staff was requesting that Hamilton come over immediately to investigate the physical abuse allegation. Hamilton quickly learned that the victim was Takisha Johnson.

The hospital staff told Hamilton that Johnson knew they were calling CPS about the bruises on Takisha's body. An irritated Ms. Johnson demanded to know why they were treating *her* like a criminal when a strange man had sexually assaulted her daughter. By the time Hamilton had arrived at the hospital, Ms. Johnson had already stormed off, taking Takisha with her, against the stern instructions of the hospital staff. Even so, both Takisha and her mother had told the same story about the source of the welts and bruises on Takisha's body. Ms. Johnson had been angry when her daughter returned home, after her curfew, on the night of July 3 and had punished Takisha by hitting her with an electric cord.

Unlike the "courtesy" interview that Hamilton was going to do the next day for Ford, these allegations fell squarely within her professional mandate. She got to work immediately. Hamilton spent the next part of her July 4 holiday tracking down Ms. Johnson, who reluctantly but eventually consented to return to the police station for the second time that day.

For the fourth time in less than four or five hours, traumatized twelve-year-old Takisha told her story. Hamilton said later that although the July 4 interview "was primarily for the physical abuse," when she had asked how it occurred, Takisha had not only reported that her mother was angry because she missed curfew and had hit her but had also recounted her sexual victimization.

In her interview with Hamilton, Ms. Johnson was apologetic and remorseful about losing her temper. She explained that while curfew was an issue, she had been more worried and angry that her daughter had driven off with a strange man and lied to her about it. Ms. Johnson confessed to being scared and frustrated. At the end of the interview, Hamilton recommended that Ms. Johnson attend some parenting classes, but having no immediate concerns about Takisha's physical safety, she sent them both home. Nonetheless, this professional decision did not deter Inman's attorney from arguing at trial that the real villain in this matter was not his client but Takisha's own mother, with her "poor parenting skills" and her "anger management problems."

By late afternoon on July 4, Takisha and her mom had spent most of their holiday talking to professionals from the police department, hospital, and CPS systems. Takisha had told her story four times in less than twenty-four hours—three times to complete strangers (a police officer, a nurse, and a social worker)—yet there was no videotaped CSC interview as required by the county protocol. That was scheduled the next day. It marked the fifth time, in less than forty-eight hours, that Takisha had to retell the details of her sexual attack for the benefit of adults and the institutions they represented. This time, the tired child told her story tearlessly and without emotion in front of a camera.

After the interview Hamilton kept the videotape until Ford returned to work on Monday, July 8. Given that the county prosecutor's protocol for investigating CSA cases was predicated, in part, on speed and surprise, precious time had already slipped away.

## WHAT THE PROSECUTION KNEW

By the time St. Mary County Chief Prosecutor Mark Jameson got wind of this case, it was clear that things were not going smoothly. Jameson, who always wanted to know immediately when there was a CSC case brewing under his watch, didn't hear about this one until July 8 or 9. By then, Inman had already been arrested for a parole violation, but he would not be charged with three first-degree felony counts of CSC until July 11. Jameson would later characterize this case—in his understated way—as "sticky."

Inman had had plenty of time between July 3 and July 11 to rally his personal defenses. There was no swift confrontation with an emotionally charged videotape; there was no offer of a polygraph. No pressure was placed on Inman to confess on July 4 when the facts first came to light. Inman was appointed a well-respected defense attorney, Mike Oakley. The pair refused to waive preliminary examination. So on July 30, 2002, Takisha had to appear in open court and tell her story again, this time in a public courtroom. The judge warned the prosecutor's office that venue was going to be a problem. It was not clear that the exact location of the alleged crime could be established. Prosecutor Jameson pressed forward.

By the time the trial was on the horizon, in late December 2002, Jameson's office had already obtained thirty-nine CSC convictions that year, and an additional thirteen cases were pending. Another nine had been dismissed. Of those dismissed, one suspect pleaded to other felonies, one had died, and in another the victim had run away from home and could not be found. Of the remaining six dismissals, Jameson believed that only one of them had not actually committed the offense. His thirty-nine CSC convictions were out of a total of three hundred felony convictions in the county during that same period. In short, 13 percent of all felony convictions in St. Mary County in 2002 involved CSC incidents. If Jameson was right about the nine dismissals, then—at very minimum—there were forty-seven child victims of sexual assaults in the county in less than one year, without including the thirteen pending cases. Some of these situations undoubtedly involved more than one child. Furthermore, there is good reason to suspect that some of these perpetrators (perhaps even more than "some") were recidivists who weren't caught earlier. All told, that was a substantial number of child victims for a small community. Of course, when the protocol functioned efficiently, these cases did not go to trial. Jameson estimated that, on average, he took four CSC cases to trial a year. However, he quickly put that into perspective given his twenty-year career, "That's a lot of CSC trials and a lot of kids."

The Inman case was one of the few going all the way to trial, and in Jameson's own assessment the need to do so was because the case "to some extent got screwed up." Nonetheless, weaknesses and all, Jameson was not going to quit on this victim. It was this county's mission to see through even the most difficult cases as it had for decades. All he could do about the state of his evidence was shrug his shoulders and utter his oft-repeated mantra, "It is what it is."

Jameson knew much more about Inman than his jury would ever learn. In this small community, with its lifelong residents and inter-twining family histories, it was hard not to cross paths with everybody at some point. So it was with Jameson and the Inman family. Jameson had attended high school with Inman's brother. He was also very famil-iar with Inman's stepsister, Catherine. Catherine was, in Jameson's view, a "sad" case. In stark contrast to Catherine, Jameson character-ized Thomas Inman as an "evil" man. Even though Jameson's job was pursuing bad people, this characterization of Inman coming from the ever-polite and respectful prosecutor seemed oddly out of place until he provided his supporting evidence. That came in the form of a story about Catherine.

"Years ago," as Jameson told it, "there was a lady named Catherine Henley," who was in a "very stormy relationship with her husband Lloyd." They had nine kids, including a beautiful little three-year-old girl named Princess Veronica. One night, following Lloyd's release from jail for bat-tering Catherine, the pair got high. Princess Veronica, who had been traumatized by a series of recent events, "pooped her pants," for which her parents placed her on the toilet in the bathroom and abandoned her there. She eventually fell in and died of "positional asphyxiation." The couple wrapped up the little girl's lifeless body and placed it in the trunk of their car and drove around for the next seven months until Catherine got into an automobile accident. Afterward, Catherine and Lloyd went "to the wrecker yard" and retrieved "the little body out" of the trunk and buried her. Catherine and Lloyd continued to fight, or as Jameson put it, "go at it hammer and tongs." One day after one such dispute, Lloyd walked into the sheriff's office and said, "I want to tell you where a body is buried." The police, with the help of a cadaver dog, found Veronica's body, which had been buried for two years. In the aftermath, among other things, Catherine went to prison. In spite of everything, however, Jameson had sympathy for Catherine. "Poor Catherine was a pretty pathetic case herself. She had nine kids, but she was only about twenty-six years old. A pretty girl, and kind of nice, too."

Jameson was even sympathetic to Lloyd and the couple's complicated lives. He contrasted them with his own upbringing in St. Mary County:

> I grew up in Two Lakes from a white lower-middle class family—mom, dad, two sisters—you know, Beaver Cleaver time. And everyone doesn't function like that. And so here are these people that are so dysfunctional, they accidentally killed this child, put it in the trunk, drive around with it, and it's hard for people to, to—how can someone do that? But to them it didn't seem all that abnormal. And Catherine and Lloyd loved each other, but hated each other and . . . were screwed up. Still are, but, you know, if you are respectful to them the dividend is, she'll write you a letter from prison. She doesn't hate me, she doesn't resent me, she knows what happened and she's just sad. Now, there are a lot of evil bad people. This guy [Inman] next week is one of the evil ones. Catherine is just one of the sad ones.

What links these two tales together is the letter that Catherine had sent Jameson from prison just two months before the start of the Inman trial. According to Jameson, it read:

> Dear Mr. Jameson. Thomas Inman did this to me when I was ten years old. Please don't let him do this anymore. We have the same mother and we are stepsiblings. He used to come in my bed when I was 10 and does these bad things to me and I was only 10 and nobody would believe. I know you will believe me and I want you to do something. I don't want you to let him do this anymore.

The characterization of Inman as evil was easy for Jameson. All he had to do was fill in the blanks. Inman was never charged—nor ever would be—for the sexual abuse of his stepsister, Catherine, as a child. In believing Catherine, Jameson necessarily also believed that Inman got away with sexually assaulting her when she was only ten. Takisha, Jameson noted, is "another twelve-year-old girl who's just like Catherine was twenty years ago." It was unlikely these were just two isolated incidents separated by two decades—the more probable hypothesis was that there were plenty of other similar victims out there. So for Jameson, who had made prosecuting CSA cases a priority—in part because he believed if he intervened he could prevent the victimization of other children—

this was the worst kind of case. It harbored the possibility that a recidivist-perpetrator had been unimpeded for decades.

So in December 2002, Jameson was about to start a trial firmly convinced he was prosecuting an evil man, but also knowing that he was doing so in a case where the usual effectiveness of the protocol was not evident. Had a more aggressive social worker, like Jim Henry, and a more single-mindedly determined officer, like Ed Williams, conducted the investigation, their combined interdisciplinary efforts might have changed the way events unfolded and have better protected Takisha. Nonetheless, Jameson was going to rely on former CPS worker Jim Henry even now, this time as an expert witness to help explain some of the case's messy features to the jury.

Jameson had charged Inman with three felony counts of CSC with a child: one involving digital penetration, the second penile penetration, and the third fellatio. So, in the midst of packing for his move upstairs for his new job as judge, Jameson had also prepared Takisha for a trial. Among other things they had watched the videotape of her interview with Sue Hamilton and talked about testifying, in open court and in front of Tommy Inman, about what he had done to her.

## THE TRIAL: COMPETING NARRATIVES OF A "ROAD TRIP"

### Picking Jurors

At 8:00 a.m. on the first morning of what would be the three-day Inman trial, the upstairs hallway was already swarming with prospective jurors. When the courtroom doors opened a few minutes later, they quickly filled all the vacant seats on the hard, pewlike benches in the small courtroom. Thomas Inman was sitting at the defense attorney's table on the left side of the courtroom next to his attorney, Mike Oakley. Inman was a slender, balding middle-aged African American man, comfortably dressed in a gray sweat suit and wearing black-rimmed reading glasses. It was impossible not to notice immediately that his right ear had been cleanly—almost surgically—sliced in half. He had other scars on his face and neck, as though his personal history might be recorded in layers of scar tissue.

Inman was upbeat, even gregarious. It was a confidence that did not wane at any point over the next three days. In fact, during breaks he would banter with anyone present in the courtroom, and at times that included the prosecutor, police officers, court officers, spectators, and members of our research team.

The case was being tried in front of Judge Richter, who had sat on the bench for the last twenty years and had been the chief prosecuting attorney in St. Mary County before he was judge. The first order of business was selecting a jury from among the crowd. It was a process that took the whole morning as jurors were excused for one reason or another. It was inevitable that in this small county a random group of prospective jurors would know—personally or professionally—people connected with the proceedings. This led to several being excused. Jameson unexpectedly profited from this interconnectedness when Judge Richter ticked Jim Henry's name off on the witness list. A potential juror responded that he did, in fact, know Henry both personally and socially. So the judge asked, "If Dr. Henry does testify in this case, would you give greater weight to his evidence because you know him?" The potential juror quickly and confidently answered, "Yes, I would." The judge promptly thanked him and sent him on his way. However, this was too good a tidbit for an experienced trial attorney like Jameson to pass up. He used this unexpected endorsement of his star expert witness in his opening statement.

Ultimately, when the jury selection was finalized, Jameson knew about half of them personally. He privately worried because the judge had excused so many women, because he saw no "leader" in the group, and because they were all white. In fact, the entire jury pool had been white, while both defendant and victim were African American. This was a recurring problem in St. Mary County, and the defense attorney had raised the issue in what was a standard defense counsel's motion. In an equally standard response, the judge denied the motion and continued with the trial. In this proceeding a trio of white men supervised the administration of justice over a black man who would be judged by twelve white jurors.

## Opening Statements

The differing styles of Prosecutor Jameson and Defense Attorney Oakley became even more evident as the two presented their opening statements for the impaneled jury. Jameson was a regal presence in the courtroom. He walked slowly into the empty space before the jury and spoke without notes. His opening statement was carefully constructed to paint a compelling and coherent version of what had happened. He told the story, in part, by switching voices and performing dialogue with the major cast of characters. In doing so, he advised the jurors of what they would hear, putting a positive spin on some things that could weaken his case and omitting other things altogether.

He prepared the jury for the fact that Takisha's mother was frantic, worried, and angry on the night of July 3, that Takisha initially lied about where she had been and was punished for it. Yet Jameson also described a remorseful mother who spent the night awake, waiting for daylight, so she could ask her daughter, more calmly, what had happened the day before.

He reminded the jurors no fewer than eight times that soft-spoken Takisha was only twelve years old and prepared them for her quiet demeanor. But he also recited the litany of performances Takisha had already been through: "Takisha had to tell this story to her mother, to Corporal Ford, to the doctor and the nurse, to the protective services worker, to me, and now she's going to come in and tell you." He underscored this list with his punch line, "She's twelve years old."

He noted that a doctor had found evidence of abrasions in Takisha's vagina but left out, for the moment, the fact that no other physical evidence—no seminal fluid, sperm cells, or foreign hairs—was found on Takisha's body.

Jameson explained that Takisha's delay in disclosure was not unusual. "Now, we're going to call a witness. His name is Jim Henry. You heard a little bit about him. One of our jurors knew him, and that juror was excused. Jim Henry is a former protective services worker here, and he's now a professor at State University, and I'm going to ask him some questions. Would a child come right back and tell their mother what happened? In this case Takisha did not. Mr. Henry is going to tell you that isn't an unusual circumstance."

Jameson highlighted, for public consumption, his confidence in Police Corporal Ford, saying that he had "done a number of investigations of criminal sexual conduct cases for the Augustine Police Department." He explained away Ford's delay in securing Takisha's full account of the facts: "He thought, 'I better get a female protective services worker and do the interview with this child.'" Finally, he praised the quality of Ford's police work: "What a good investigator you have, to take the girl to Two Lakes Hospital for a medical examination." He did not bother to warn the jury that neither Ford nor any of his colleagues had failed to do a long list of things that they should certainly have done.

Defense attorney Mike Oakley had consulted with Inman throughout Jameson's opening statement (a practice he continued throughout the trial, exhibiting extreme attentiveness to his client). At the start of his opening statement, Oakley lugged a three-ring trial notebook to the lectern. It was a standard method for organizing a case for trial, and the tool reflected his careful preparation. Although an experienced trail attorney, Oakley did not appear as being at ease with the setting, as had his prosecutorial counterpart. He delivered his entire opening statement standing behind the lectern—alternatively leaning on it or clasping and unclasping his hands behind his back—rather than prowling around the open space in front of the jury, as Jameson had. He consulted his huge trial notebook frequently, unlike Jameson, who worked from memory. Nonetheless, it was clear that he, too, was well prepared for this trial.

Unlike Jameson, Oakley spent no time spinning out his version of Inman's story. Instead, he reminded the jurors that Inman was exercising his constitutionally protected right to have a trial by jury and that the prosecutor's office had the burden of proof. It was a heavy burden at that—beyond a reasonable doubt. He asked the jury to keep an open mind throughout using a metaphor of a sponge, "Don't reach any conclusions at this point. Just listen and watch, store things in that big sponge."

He reminded the jury that the testimony of most of the witnesses would be circumstantial and that only two people—Takisha and Tommy—could talk about what actually happened. Surprisingly—since defendants in criminal proceedings rarely take the witness stand— Oakley promised that Inman was "going to share with you his story in this case," adding, "He has a very good memory of what went on July 3, 2002." As for Takisha and Inman's time together, Oakley promised the jury, "Mr. Inman will tell you that at about 7:15, he and Takisha left in his van to go driving around. Sometimes they call this a road trip, but you can reach your own conclusions."

So the two stories with their crucial differences were laid out for the jury. Everyone agreed Inman had driven Takisha around on the evening of July 3. The only question was whether the "road trip" included a sexual assault.

## First Witnesses: Friend and Mother

Jameson's first witness was Takisha's friend, Faith Fox. For a thirteen-year-old, Faith demonstrated exceptional poise and self-confidence on the witness stand, at one point during cross-examination demanding that the defense attorney define the word "acquaintance" before she would answer his question. This fiery, self-assurance was a characteristic that Inman himself would find fault with when he later took the witness stand.

Faith testified that she was an eighth grader and that in July 2002, she had been living with her grandmother, Nicky Bass (who would later testify on behalf of Inman), her mother, her two sisters, Cassie and Reece, and "Tommy" (Inman). Faith testified that her friend, Takisha, was in sixth grade.

On the afternoon of July 3, she and Takisha had bought snacks at a local gas station and had settled down to play cards on a folding table in the yard. They were switching games so that Takisha's sister Cleo could join in, when Tommy pulled up in his van at around 2:00 or 3:00 p.m. Tommy asked Takisha to go someplace with him. Faith said she thought her friend appeared reluctant to go, so she asked Tommy if she could come along, but Tommy had said no. Faith figured Tommy was going to the store because he turned left at the end of the street and headed toward town.

At about 6:00 p.m., by Faith's estimation, Takisha's older brother Andy appeared, looking for his sisters, and she told him that Takisha had driven off with Tommy. Together, the children headed toward the Johnson apartment to inform Takisha's mother when they came upon her driving toward them. After learning of Takisha's disappearance, Ms. Johnson ordered her two children into the car and departed for the police station, leaving Faith behind.

At about 7:00 or 8:00 p.m., Faith tried telephoning her friend Takisha, but no one answered. She testified that Tommy returned about twenty minutes later and was informed that the police were looking for him for "taking that little girl." Tommy responded that he wasn't concerned because he had already dropped Takisha off at her apartment. After hearing all this, Faith trotted back inside and tried calling her friend again.

This time Ms. Johnson answered but said that Takisha was "not allowed to be on the phone."

On cross-examination, the defense attorney elicited some more information from Faith. Tommy had come and gone from the house earlier in the day. He had been doing some maintenance work on someone's car. Faith said they had asked Tommy for money, which he had given them. His gift was the source of funds for their afternoon snacks. She reported that Tommy continued working on a car in the driveway and at one point took the kids to the auto parts store to get supplies. He actually had wanted Faith to go into the store to buy something for him—plugs or something—but she had refused.

Jameson's second witness was a very pretty and credible Ms. Johnson. She and her three children had moved from another state, seven or eight months before the incident. She testified that Takisha was playing with her friend Faith on July 3. Although Ms. Johnson did not know Faith's mom well, she knew Faith and where Faith lived. On the afternoon of July 3, Ms. Johnson received a telephone call from her son saying that Takisha had gotten into the car of a man named Tommy. Ms. Johnson instructed him to return home immediately. She waited nervously for about fifteen minutes but, being too impatient to wait longer, got into her car and drove toward Faith's house. She saw Andy, Cleo, and Faith walking in her direction. She asked them for Tommy's full name and was told that it was Thomas Inman. She instructed her two children to get into the car and headed directly to the police station.

Ms. Johnson arrived at the stationhouse at about 4:00 p.m. and told an officer that her daughter had gotten into a burgundy vanlike car with Thomas Inman. The police were already familiar with Inman and knew exactly where he lived. They promised to look into the matter, sending her back home in case Takisha returned. At about 9:00 p.m., Takisha did return, but according to Ms. Johnson she "had an attitude." The mother testified she had been angry, scared, and relieved all at once. When asked, Takisha reported she had been at her friend "Barbie's house." Ms Johnson accused her daughter of lying, pulled out an extension cord, and hit her on her bare arms. Then she sent Takisha to bed. Shortly thereafter, Ms. Johnson telephoned the police and informed them that her daughter had returned home safely.

It was sometime later that Ms. Johnson began to realize that something felt wrong. She knew that Takisha had driven off with Tommy and did not believe Takisha's story about Barbie because the two girls had recently had a falling out and weren't speaking to each other. It didn't make sense that Takisha would lie. Ms. Johnson testified that having "got over my anger" she "sat up" all night waiting for daybreak. On July 4 she "sent my two kids off to the store, so I can have time with Takisha." She sat Takisha down and told her, "I'm not mad at you, but something is not right. I won't be mad at you, just tell me the truth. Did you go somewhere with Tommy? Did he take you somewhere?"

According to Ms. Johnson, Takisha "said 'yes' and then that's when it just—it was just a rush. She said, 'Mama, he took me to some woods and he. . . .'" At this point, Ms. Johnson broke down on the witness stand and began to cry. Oakley made his first objection of the day. It was an objection that appeared to be aimed as much to stem the flow of tears as to the nature of the testimony. As Jameson responded to the objection addressing the judge directly, Ms. Johnson composed herself. It was a spontaneous unscripted moment that rang emotionally true for those of us sitting in the courtroom watching.

Ms. Johnson continued to recount the events of July 4, including going to the police station. She observed that Takisha was in tears when she returned with Ford and Cleo from their ride in his patrol car. She also recounted her experience at the hospital, including being questioned about the bruises on Takisha's body. After a long wait, Ms. Johnson left the hospital, admitting she did so against the wishes of the doctor. She noted she had left her son home alone and needed to get back to him.

On cross-examination, Oakley asked Ms. Johnson about the beating. He wanted to know if Ms. Johnson had fled the hospital because she knew that the bruises were going to be investigated and feared prosecution for it. Oakley pushed her on her knowledge of Inman's relationship with Takisha. When asked whether it was true that "your daughter has done overnights at the home that Mr. Inman lives in," Ms. Johnson quickly corrected the impression, saying, "She stayed with Faith and her grandmother." She denied knowing that Mr. Inman had taken Takisha and the other kids to the movies and ice-skating. Finally, the defense attorney wanted to know why Ms. Johnson had not bothered to take Takisha's clothing down to the police department or to the hospital. The lack of attention to the clothing that Takisha was wearing on July 3 was a recurring theme in Oakley's questioning. No one had thought to gather this evidence.

## Takisha's Testimony

Not surprisingly, the most dramatic testimony of the day came directly from Takisha. She testified that she was twelve, had lived in Augustine in July 2002, and had been in sixth grade. She identified Thomas Inman, noting that she knew him and that he had lived in the same house as her friend Faith. Then the harder questions began to flow:

> Was there a day when you got in a car and went for a ride with Tommy?
> Yes.
> Do you remember that day?
> Yes.

Like Faith, Takisha testified that they had been playing cards, and that they went to the store. Later that day, Tommy pulled into the driveway in a burgundy minivan and asked Takisha if she would "do him a favor."

> Did he tell you what the favor was?
> No.
> Did he ask you to do something?
> No.

Nonetheless, when requested, the child climbed into the passenger seat of the burgundy minivan.

> Did you know what you were going to do?
> No.
> Did you know where you were going?
> No.

She testified that Tommy drove her to "someplace with a lot of trees" but that she could not say exactly how they got to this place or where it was. They eventually turned down a sandy or dirt road and he parked the van at the top of a hill between some trees. She testified that at this point, Tommy grabbed her and she tried to push him off. He climbed over to the passenger seat and "yanked down" the Capri pants she was wearing to her ankles. Next he did the same with her underpants. He then removed his pants.

What happened next?

He tried to stick his penis in me.

And where did he try to stick it?

In my vagina.

Did that hurt?

Yes.

Was he able to get it in there?

Yes, but not all the way.

And were you pushing at him?

Yes.

What happened next?

He lit this thing and started smoking.

Was he still over above you?

Yes.

And what was this thing?

I don't know.

What did he light it with?

A lighter.

Was it like a cigarette?

No, it was in a glass tube kinda thing.

And he was smoking this thing out of a glass tube?

Yes.

Did it make smoke?

Yes.

What did he do with the smoke?

He blew it in my face.

What happened next?

Then . . . then he made me suck his penis.

This went on and on. Takisha responses were clipped, almost emotionless, but she described what felt to those of us listening like an endless afternoon of repeated victimization. He put his penis in her mouth again; he started "smoking that thing again." Jameson repeatedly asked if "anything came out" of Tommy's penis. Takisha repeatedly said, "No." Finally Inman opened the car door.

Did you get out of the car?

No, he pulled me out of the car.

Did you still have your pants down around your ankles?
When he pulled me out, he took off my pants all the way.

According to Takisha, Inman dragged the partially naked and bare-foot girl down a hill and "made me suck his penis again." He pulled her back up the hill, put her back in the car and "stuck his finger in my vagina." He "started smoking that thing again." When Jameson then asked, "Did he say anything then?" He got the longest burst of uninterrupted testimony he would get from Takisha all day:

> I said, "Could I go home?" And he said—he said, "I'm going to fuck you all
> night." And he said, "You can't go home until you give me good head or
> unless—unless I get my penis in you."
> Then what happened?
> Then he tried to stick his penis in me again.

Takisha told the jury she tried to keep her legs shut but he "kept on screaming at me, 'Open up your legs'" and made her open them. He kept trying to stick his penis in her.

> Did he get it even partway?
> Yes.
> Did that hurt?
> Yes.
> Did he stop?
> No.
> What did he do then, next?
> He stuck his finger in me again.
> How long did all this take?
> I don't know.
> What happened after he stuck his fingers in you again?
> I said, "Could I go home?" And he said, "Yeah."

Inman asked Takisha if she could walk home by herself. She said she didn't know where she was or how to get home. Takisha testified that rather than drive her directly home—and knowing she had a curfew—Inman drove her around Two Lakes, "asking people do they know somebody who sells something," but she didn't know what he wanted to buy. More than once, he stopped at an apartment trying to purchase something. Finally, he stopped at a Shell gas station and bought a forty-ounce bottle of beer. Then, and only then, did he drive her close to her home. Before letting her go, he asked her, "What do I want for me not to tell anybody?" She asked only to be allowed to go home. He let her go.

Takisha went straight home, but she was afraid she was going to be in trouble for missing curfew. Takisha testified that her mother was mad and admitted lying to her about being at Barbie's house.

> Why did you say that?
> I was scared.
> Did your mom believe you?
> I don't know.

Takisha testified that she was "spanked" with an extension cord, that it hurt, and that she had cried. She admitted that she wanted to tell her mother what had happened but that she was sent to bed. The next morning, in keeping with her mother's testimony, Takisha got a chance to talk to her now calmer and repentant mother.

> Did you tell her?
> Yes.
> Was that the first time you told anybody?
> Yes.
> Was it hard to tell her?
> Yes.
> Did you cry?
> Yes.
> Did she cry?
> Yes.
> Did you tell her everything or just part of it?
> Part.
> What happened when you told her?
> She called the police.

Takisha testified about meeting Ford and going to the hospital for an examination that included checking her "private area" and into her "vagina." When asked, she told the doctor about the bruises on her arms. Takisha recalled talking to a CPS worker the next day about everything that had happened.

On cross-examination, Inman's attorney gently focused on some inconsistencies in Takisha's various accounts of the day, which included two interviews with Sue Hamilton (one on July 4 recorded in a written report and a second on July 5 recorded by videotape) and Takisha's testimony at the preliminary examination on July 30. Specifically, Oakley focused on the number of times Tommy had dragged Takisha up and down the hill and whether or not he had "grabbed her by the throat" or by the shoulders. Finally, Oakley wanted to know why Takisha hadn't asked for help at the gas station or tried to run away.

> Is it true that Tommy went in and paid for the gas?
> Yes.
> And he left you outside in the van?
> Yes.
> Did you ever ask anybody for help?
> No.
> Did you think about running away?
> Yes.
> Did you ever try and run away?
> Well, he had me with a lot of trees.
> No, when you were at the gas station.
> No.

Finally, and predictably, Oakley homed in on Takisha's inability to identify the exact location of the assault.

> Do you really know where this happened, other than it was around some trees?
> Yes.
> You know where it happened?
> Yes.
> Where did it happen?
> I know—I know how it looks when I get there but don't know how to get there.

## The Expert: Jim Henry

Social worker Jim Henry was called next. He strode confidently—as he had undoubtedly done over the decades—to the witness stand. The courtroom players—including judge, defense attorney, and prosecutor—knew him very well. Even the local newspaper reporter complained to us during a break that Henry always said the same old thing. Of course he did. Henry spoke not only from the social-science research literature, but also from twenty years of experience working on cases like this, and from a child advocate's perspective.

Jameson quickly established Henry's credentials, and he was qualified as an expert witness for the purposes of the trial, just as he had been many times before. Jameson confirmed that Henry did not know the victim and had been given only what he described as a "very sketchy, two-minute overview of some brief details" about the case. Henry's testimony was delivered in the form of responses to a series of "hypothetical" situations that followed the fact pattern of the prosecutor's version of the events. Among other things, Henry established that it was not unusual for a child to delay disclosure or to lie when confronted by an adult. It was particularly understandable that a child would delay disclosing when confronted by an already angry mother. So when asked if it would surprise him that a child did not disclose in Jameson's hypothetical situation, Henry argued that between the mother's anger and the child's sense that she had done something wrong there was "a significant barrier to that disclosure."

Jameson continued the unfolding hypothetical, suggesting that an angry mother calms down by the next day. She asks her child once again what happened and this time gets a different story. Said Henry:

> The key piece is Mother's ability to communicate that I really want to know and no matter what you say happened, I love you. No matter what you say has occurred to you, it's okay, and so the way that the mother or a mother would approach their child really sets the stage for being able, potentially, and again it's potentially, for that child to disclose.

Henry noted that disclosure was a process, and therefore incremental disclosure could and should be expected.

On cross-examination, Oakley was quick and to the point, asking only four questions. He established that Henry had testified as an expert witness twenty-five times before—twenty-four of those times for the prosecution—and that he had never personally met Takisha Johnson.

## Medical Evidence and the Lack Thereof

The final witness of the day was the doctor who examined Takisha at Two Lakes Hospital, an emergency-room physician who had done a full physical exam. He reporting finding some injury to her vagina, including abrasions and scrapes that were consistent with injury—possibly by a fingernail—from the day before. He also testified to finding no other physical evidence of sexual assault. Finally, he reported finding bruises on Takisha's body that both Takisha and her mother had explained were from the beating inflicted the evening before. The doctor testified that he had asked Ms. Johnson to wait until the CPS worker arrived. In fact, he had followed her out to the parking lot, demanding that she stay. However, she had driven off after saying that she needed to get home to her son.

## THE TRIAL: DAY TWO

Jameson started the second day of the trial with a forensic scientist from the state police laboratory. She had received and processed the sexual-assault kit sent to the lab. Summarizing her testimony, Jameson said, "So basically you didn't find anything in this case, did you?" Her response was, "That is correct." She admitted that her lab findings could be consistent with a case in which no ejaculation had taken place. Indeed, St. Mary County's written protocol reminds its users, in boldface type, that "contrary to popular opinion, sexual abuse can occur without leaving any obvious or lasting hymeneal or vaginal findings." Nonetheless, for a jury looking to be convinced beyond a reasonable doubt, this was not easily accepted. The only medical evidence supporting Takisha's claim were Dr. Worden's findings of scrapes and abrasions, which could be consistent with digital penetration.

## Corporal Ford

Jameson's last witness before resting his case was Corporal Ford. Ford gave a detailed account of driving Takisha around trying to locate the exact site of the assault. Using a large aerial photograph, a yardstick pointer, and pushpins to mark significant spots, he traced his route with Takisha and marked the point where she had cried and he had turned around. In addition, he testified that he had directed Ms. Johnson to the hospital and sent the resulting sexual-assault kit to the crime lab. Finally, he testified that he had scheduled the CSC interview with Sue Hamilton for the following day because he thought Takisha was better off talking to a female interviewer.

On cross-examination, Oakley predictably highlighted the ambiguity of the location of the crime and a long laundry list of investigatory failures. Oakley quickly established that the village had four or five bridges and at least two dams, and that Ford had not bothered to visit these other possible sites.

> In your driving around with Takisha, is it correct that she never said, "This is the spot. This is the location?"
> Right. That is correct. She did not.

Oakley also underscored the failure of the police to collect any additional evidence. There were no photographs taken of Takisha. No physical evidence samples were taken from Inman. Ford never went back to the alleged scene of the crime to check for tire tracks or get out of his patrol car to look for footprints. He never collected clothing. He did not look inside Inman's van. It was, all told, a pretty long list of omissions. The officer readily and honestly admitted that "typical" or "common" police work would have included these actions.

At the close of this testimony, Jameson rested his case. Mike Oakley made the predictable motion for a directed verdict of not guilty. Specifically, he argued that the issue of venue was not established. The judge, however, thought differently. Richter responded that the jury could find beyond reasonable doubt that the venue was established within St. Mary County, even if not specifically in the village of Augustine. He denied the motion. The trial continued.

## Inman's Defense

Oakley opened Inman's defense with the nurse from Two Lakes Hospital who had assisted Dr. Worden. The nurse testified that Takisha had complained of pain "in her privates" but also that she observed "numerous welts and bruises" on Takisha's body and that Ms. Johnson admitted she had "whooped" her daughter. The nurse was followed by a series of witnesses who testified as to Inman's activities on the morning of July 3. But only testimony as to the period in question—other than Takisha's—came from Thomas Inman himself.

Inman testified in detail about what he did on the morning of July 3. His description became less coherent about his activities later in the day, although by his own admission by that time he had smoked crack cocaine and consumed at least three forty-ounce bottles of malt liquor.

At about 2:10 p.m. on July 3, Inman drove over to his mother's house to pick up his sister to drive her to work. Inman sat in the car listening to the radio and waiting for her; when she didn't appear, he drove back home. This was between 2:30 and 2:35. He entered the house, "And I told Nicky, 'If my sister calls, to let me know, and I'll come back down and I'll take her to work.'" Inman retreated to his room, waited until 3:00, and then started smoking crack cocaine that he had obtained earlier in the day. He said, "I stayed upstairs for about an hour, okay, doing the drugs and at around four o'clock, I washed up, brushed my teeth, cleaned my hair up, and came downstairs around 4:15."

Next he drove to an auto parts store for supplies. On the way home, he stopped at an "Arab" mini-mart store for two forty-ounce bottles of beer. When he got home, the children (Takisha, Faith, Cleo, and Cassie) were there. He gave each of them $2. It was 5:00 p.m. At this point, Inman testified:

> No one's memory is perfect, okay? Yesterday, when Faith testified, she brought a memory back to me that I had forgotten . . . and I have no idea about how I asked the kids to come with me, but I drove to the auto parts place and . . . asked Faith to go in and buy me a spark plug gauge.

Inman confirmed that Faith refused to make the purchase, so he went in himself. When asked why he had requested that Faith do this task for him, he said, "I was tired. I was still working on the car, probably was disarrayed, probably was a little drunk—more definitely [than] probably a little drunk, so I wanted her to go in."

They returned home, he worked on the car some more, and he cleaned up. It was now 6:30 p.m. "What did you do after you cleaned up?" asked his attorney. Said Inman, "This is a gray area, on shady time, but somewhere between six-thirty and seven o'clock, I got in my van and left." No one was with him at the time, and Inman says he drove around Augustine looking to buy more drugs. By what Inman called his "best estimate," this took about an hour or so, and he returned back home "between seven-thirty, eight o'clock. Again, like I say, nobody's memory is perfect, but it was around about that time." Faith, Cleo, and Takisha were sitting at the table in the yard when he returned. Inman testified that he "rolled my window down and I motioned to Takisha to come over to the car." She did and he asked her, "Would she like to do me a favor?" She said 'Yeah' and opened the door." Inman continued, "When she opened the door, and then I asked her, and this is another shaded area because I try to play it in my mind whether I asked Takisha to drive my van to Two Lakes, or did I ask her to drive this car to Two Lakes for me, and Takisha said, 'Yeah sure. I can do that.'"

His attorney followed with other questions:

Did Takisha drive anything?
No. Takisha, when the door was open, jumped in the passenger seat.
What did you do?
I vaguely remember, and this is vaguely. I vaguely remember Faith yelling,
    "Where are you going?" And I vaguely remember Takisha yelling back,
    "I don't know, but I'll be back in a few minutes."

Inman testified that he drove back to Two Lakes and spent thirty minutes "driving around looking for some cocaine." Then, "at around 8:30 Takisha started telling me that she needed to get home, and she needed to be home by nine o'clock. She said this several times, and I told Takisha I'll get her home in plenty of time. I made one more run around 'A' Street [a drug area] and when I didn't see anybody I know I drove—that would be north, I guess, State Street to Shell gas station."

At the gas station, Inman says he left Takisha in the van, bought gas and a couple of sodas. He then drove Takisha back to her apartment complex area. "I backed my van to that area right there, which was facing the door. No sooner than I had parked my van, Takisha had opened the door then went out and went hurriedly to the door." It was, reported Inman, 9:08. Inman testified that he was not concerned that it was past Takisha's curfew because "it's only a few minutes past nine; she would be all right."

Back at his house, Inman was informed that the police had been looking for him. "I said, 'For what?'" They responded, 'For having that kid in the car with you.'" Inman testified that he figured it was "okay" because he had "just dropped her off." He didn't call the police nor did he try to contact Takisha's mother.

On the witness stand, Inman explicitly denied ever touching Takisha, grabbing her, exposing his penis, pulling down her pants, touching her vaginal area, putting his penis in her mouth, blowing smoke in her face, stopping in a wooded area, and offering her gifts or money in exchange for not telling anyone what happened. Inman did admit to having been convicted on burglary charges in both 1993 and 1994 and having served his "punishment."

On cross-examination, Jameson focused on getting the defendant to account again, slowly and in great detail, his drug and alcohol consumption over the course of the day. Jameson asked for this account out of sequence, in part, he later explained, to test the clarity and consistency of Inman's story. Furthermore, Jameson was incredulous about Inman's basic plotline, first, because it involved looking for crack in one area of town, driving all the way home just to pick up a child in order to head out immediately to look for crack again, and second, because the "favor" he wanted from Takisha seemed to involve asking an unlicensed twelve-year-old to drive one of his cars.

> Now why were you going to do that?
> Drive the other car into Two Lakes?
> Yes.
> This may sound dumb, okay, at first was one scenario, but it may be another one, but the purpose I wanted Takisha to go to Two Lakes for me was originally to make sure that I could drive up here and back.
> Were you going to have this twelve-year-old girl drive your van?
> Yes, sir.
> Because you were either too drunk or too high?
> Yes, sir.
> Why did you ask her?

At this point, Jameson got an unexpected gift from the defendant while explaining why Takisha was a better traveling companion than her playmate Faith. Jameson would highlight this response in his closing argument. "Why did you ask her?" Jameson inquired. Inman responded:

> Cleo's too young and Faith, the best term I can say, is a problem child. Faith always mouths back to someone. Faith cusses out her grandmother, beats the other kids up. She dirties her room up, and one of the other few things that Faith does is Faith tells everything.
> So you asked Takisha?
> Yes, sir. I did.

So in the end, Inman corroborated virtually every element of Takisha Johnson's story with the exception of the detour down a dirt road into a wooded area and the multiple assaults that Takisha had repeatedly told adults —including her mother, police officers, doctors, nurses, prosecutors, social workers, judges, and now a jury—had happened there.

Mike Oakley called one final witness, social worker Sue Hamilton, although after Inman's testimony her appearance seemed anticlimactic. Oakley focused on the two versions of Takisha's story that Hamilton had heard; one on July 4, which was not videotaped, and the other on July 5, which was. Although Hamilton testified that the two stories were "pretty consistent," Oakley pushed her on the several inconsistencies. The most significant were that in one account Takisha said she had been sodomized (a fact that Takisha had confirmed on the witness stand, but that was not a crime with which Inman had been charged) and that Takisha may have (although Hamilton could not remember for sure) made inconsistent statements about how many times Inman dragged her up and down the embankment. Oakley was incredulous, "Do you think a trip up and down a hill of [sic] every sexual act would be a significant act to a twelve-year-old?" Hamilton agreed it would. Nonetheless, when Oakley confronted her directly—"Would you expect a twelve-year-old to remember the number of times that happened?"—his witness's response was less than he probably hoped for: "It depends. I don't know." Still, he had made his point for the jury—that if Takisha was telling the truth, the nature of the sexual attack and number of trips up and down a hill should have been consistent in each and every one of Takisha's eight or so reports of the incident. He was planting seeds of doubt directed at the beyond-reasonable-doubt standard.

## DAY THREE: CLOSING ARGUMENTS AND VERDICT

The final day was reserved mostly for closing statements. Jameson first reiterated the charges: three counts of felony CSC with a child, one involving "digital penetration of the vagina," the second involving "penile penetration of the vagina," and the final count of fellatio. He reminded the jury that the sexual act need not have been completed to find the defendant guilty, nor was it necessary for semen to have been ejaculated.

Jameson focused on the shifting, multidimensional natures of power, control, and truth. As he walked through the evidence, he talked about power as it related to Takisha, power and control as it related to Inman, and finally power as it rested in the hands of the jury. He also implied that the jury should consider the temporal nature of these constructs. What were they on July 3? What were they doing today?

Jameson started his argument. "She was twelve years old. She still is, and on the third of July, she was not in control of any part of that situation. She didn't have any power. She didn't have any control. The defendant had the power and the defendant had the control." On the other hand, he pointed out that "in the witness chair she has the power of the truth" and asked them why she would lie. Jameson invited the jury to ponder the question, "Why would she say he put his penis in her mouth and his finger in her vagina and tried to penetrate her in the vagina? Why would she say that?" There seemed to be no explanation, no other motivation, than to tell the truth.

Jameson anticipated an argument that Oakley would seize upon in a moment: Why didn't Takisha tell her mother the truth immediately? After all she probably could have "spared herself the whipping." Jameson turned to his expert witness and social worker, "But you remember what Dr. Henry said. Kids don't tell right away." He went on to highlight Henry's testimony, anticipating the argument that Takisha told multiple versions of the story, and to put that problem into context:

> Dr. Henry also told you that this is a process. It's a lot of information to deal with, and it comes out in a process which you heard here. The girl had to tell

this story a lot. She told Mom. She started to tell Officer Ford. She told the nurse and maybe a little bit to the doctor. Then she told Sue Hamilton, the protective services worker. Then she told Sue Hamilton again the next day. Then she told me. Then she told you. This isn't something that she enjoyed talking about, and I asked her to come in here and raise her hand and swear an oath and tell you what happened to her, and you saw it.

He underscored her age, as he had in his opening statement: "She gives you her twelve-year-old version of the events that happened to her." He corrected his own statement, for the benefit of the jury, to enhance her credibility: "She says he's smoking crack in the van. Excuse me." He pauses. "She doesn't say that. She doesn't know what she's describing. 'He had a little glass tube, and he was blowing it in my face and then he did it again.' She doesn't say he was using cocaine. She describes what she saw."

He invited the jury to use its observational powers, but also to remember the differences between Inman on July 3 and Inman today. "He's not polite, articulate Tommy Inman. He's drunk and he's stoned." Jameson used this fact to point out the difference between Inman and Takisha, then and now. "Several times during his testimony he said, 'Well, that's a little hazy or maybe this part is a little bit unclear, or this is a little hazy.' She wasn't hazy or unclear. She wasn't high. She wasn't drunk. She was just a little twelve-year-old girl that got in a car she shouldn't have."

Jameson also seized on what he could from Inman's own testimony. Chief among these was the gift Jameson had unexpectedly received when Inman explained why he had selected Takisha as a companion over Faith. Jameson asked, rhetorically, would Inman allow Faith to come along? "No," he answers his own question, "Faith is disrespectful. Faith is mouthy and the defendant says Faith talks. Faith talks, so Faith has to stay there and he takes quiet, shy, sweet little Takisha, and she gets in the van."

Jameson focused on the issue of Inman's power: "She says again and again, 'I need to go home.' And he takes her home when he's ready because he's got the power, and he's got the control." Finally, Jameson concluded that the power now rested in the hands of the jury. "And now you've got the power. You've got the control. You're gonna go back in the jury room in just a few minutes and exercise that power and control, and it's not a punishment control or a punishment power. . . . Your job and your power is finding the truth, and the truth in this case is that the defendant is guilty of three counts of criminal sexual conduct in the first degree. . . . You go back there and exercise your power and your control."

Oakley began where Jameson left off. He thanked the jurors for their time and attention. He reminded them that the burden of proof was on the state. Ultimately, he also agreed with Jameson. "This case is essentially a trial about who you believe." So he began his substantive argument by assessing the character of the two main players, arguing that Takisha "has a history of lying" and was "whipped" for it. In comparison, his client "testified very candidly. He told you the good and the bad. He's been in trouble before. He used drugs. He's used alcohol. That's the neat thing about our system; it's based upon the truth. You can't just fabricate what looks good. You've got to tell it all, and that's what Mr. Inman did."

Oakley asked the jury to consider what was clear and unclear to them but then walked through the evidence based on his interpretations of clarity. He argued that some things were very clear. It was clear that Ms. Johnson had assaulted her daughter. It was clear that Takisha "told a different story to different people," which, he argued, contained "significant inconsistencies." It was clear, he said, that there was nothing wrong with Takisha when she returned home on the night of July 3. It was clear that Takisha lied to her mother. Then Oakley turned to Jim Henry. "We've all known Dr. Henry for years, and he has his PhD." But, he argued, Henry's opinion defied common sense. Why wouldn't Takisha have told the truth rather than get a beating? "I submit that if she was ever going to tell the truth of what happened, that was the time to do it. It was almost like torture. She could have stopped the beating at any moment by telling her mother what happened. Did she do it?"

Oakley asked the jury to consider what they had observed in the courtroom. "Did she show the type of reaction and the type of emotion you would expect to see from a person who had been sexually assaulted? Did she seem mechanical and rehearsed?" He asked the jury to reflect on Takisha's behavior on July 3 as well. "Reflect on what she did or didn't do. She didn't run away. She didn't cry for help. She didn't go into the store and ask for help. . . . Is that the conduct of somebody who has just been assaulted?" He repeatedly referred to the physical abuse marks inflicted by Takisha's mother and only briefly to the "superficial tears and abrasions in her vagina area."

He built an argument that the real villain—or at least an alternative possibility worthy of creating reasonable doubt—was Takisha's mother.

"It's Mr. Inman's theory that we're here today because this has all been formulated by Melissa Johnson as a cover-up, to deflect from Melissa Johnson. I submit that she has anger problems and parenting deficiencies. Her daughter was caught in a lie and she lost control." So he posited an alternative. "Takisha is intimidated not by Thomas Inman, who committed the alleged sexual assault." Instead, he said, Takisha was fearful of her mother.

Oakley went through the litany of things that were missing. There was no investigation of Takisha's clothing, none of the crime scene or of the van; no biological samples were take from Inman; no indication of STD or HIV; no neck or mouth injuries; no photographs of the victim or the crime scene; and no consistent time frame.

Finally he turned to the issue of Inman's moral character, "You don't need to like him. By his own testimony, he used drugs and alcohol and drove a minor around in a van." But he admonished the jury to remember, "That isn't what he's charged with."

## A Road Trip with Sexual Assaults—or Not

In the end—as is frequently the case in matters of child sexual abuse—the evidence mostly boiled down to the word of one adult against one child. There was some circumstantial evidence and limited medical evidence of abrasions, but mostly it was just two different narrative accounts of what happened on July 3. It was undisputed that Inman had consumed at least three forty-ounce bottles of malt liquor and had smoked crack; that Inman invited Takisha into his van in preference to Faith; that Takisha and Inman drove around in his van while he was looking to buy crack cocaine (although Takisha could only report he wanted to "buy something"); that Takisha repeatedly asked to go home, and that she told him of her impending curfew. The only thing really in dispute was whether their "road trip" included a detour into a wooded area for a series of sexual assaults. She said it did. He said it did not.

## THE VERDICT

On the morning of December 19, 2002, the jury began its deliberations. Less than five hours later, it delivered its verdict form to the court clerk. The form was read aloud in the courtroom for the record:

The members of the jury find Thomas E. Inman:
> as to Count 1, guilty of criminal sexual conduct, digital penetration;
> as to Count 2, not guilty to criminal sexual contact, penile penetration;
> as to Count 3, not guilty, criminal sexual contact, fellatio.

So the "truth" as the jury determined it to be was that Inman was guilty of only one of the three types of assaults alleged. Or at least only one had been proven to them beyond a reasonable doubt. It was the one in which there was some physical evidence—those abrasions—to buttress twelve-year-old Takisha Johnson's word. The fact that there was no trace evidence—even though medical experts said that this could be consistent with a rape in which there was no ejaculation—rendered Takisha's account insufficiently persuasive.

Jameson later commented the verdict was "clearly a compromise." It is a bit odd, when you stopped to think about it. First, the jury had to make a decision about the nature of the "road trip." Did it involve a detour into a wooded area or not? Apparently, the jury believed Takisha because it found Inman guilty on the first count. But what of the other two counts? Did it think Takisha made up that part? Why would she lie about having a penis thrust into her mouth or vagina? Why did the jury need more evidence to believe her account of what happened in that wooded area? The most logical explanation is that without physical evidence, the jury was not persuaded beyond reasonable doubt. Therein lies one of many problems that prosecutors face in pursuing CSA offenders. Frequently there is little or no physical evidence. Invariably, cases rest on the word of the child versus the word of an adult. And we might ask—as Jameson would—in such a showdown, who has the power?

Inman was sentenced as a fourth-offense habitual offender and received a forty- to seventy-five-year sentence in prison. He appealed based on several arguments, including that he had been denied effective assistance of counsel, as well as an impartial jury because of the lack of African Americans in the jury pool. He lost his appeal, and the trial court conviction was affirmed.

Inman's case was Jameson's last trial as chief prosecutor in St. Mary County, closing one chapter in Jameson's career and opening another. But it was undeniably fitting that his grand finale was a difficult CSC case. It was equally fitting that social worker Jim Henry had testified as his expert witness. It was Henry and his fellow Sex Busters who had breathed life into the prosecutor's original protocol, convincing everyone of the importance of protecting kids and working together. It was through this joint effort over twenty years that Jameson had learned so much from Henry about the dynamics of child sexual abuse that it helped him present difficult cases to the jury. In turn, Henry had learned so much from Jameson and other prosecutors about the criminal justice system that he could help them win these cases. Jameson and Henry shared a zealous dedication to children and were unified in their commitment to seeking justice on their behalf. Perhaps most fitting of all, however, was that in the Inman case, which prosecutors in many jurisdictions would have abandoned as unwinnable well before trial, Jameson obtained a conviction.

# Conclusions from the Study
# of St. Mary County

KAREN M. STALLER

ELEVEN

I tend to think maybe we inspire by example.

—Judge George Richter

The story of St. Mary County, as told in these pages, builds on the idea that there is value in studying the particulars of a single case. Such studies can illustrate how professional practices operate in the real world and how actors understand their world and make choices, and therefore speak to the values and priorities that undergird their decision making. This, in turn, reveals the inner workings of bigger, value-laden concepts, such as the notion of "justice."

Case studies are generally credited with having at least three basic strengths relative to other methods. First, they are able to answer how-and-why questions (not *does* something work but *how* and *why* does it work the way it does?). In St. Mary County, we sought to understand how and why the community was so successful in prosecuting child sexual abuse (CSA) cases. We answer those questions below by considering the "perfect storm" elements—biographical, geographical, political, and historical—that coincided to produce the County's success.

Second, case studies are credited with being able to capture the subjective worldview of the participants, which, in turn, provides an interpretative framework for understanding common practices and actions.

This is sometimes referred to as examining the case from the "inside out" (Gillham, 2000:11). Such inside out examinations are significant because individuals base their actions, in part, on their personal belief systems and their understandings of the world. As Hilary Bradbury and Peter Reason have argued, "People are agents who act in the world on the basis of their own sense making; human community involves mutual sense making and collective action Therefore, the only way to understand community sense-making is to start from some appreciation for the agency of individual actors and their place in social settings and organizations" (2003:203). We examine the belief systems of the important players in key roles in St. Mary County (attorneys, law-enforcement agents, and social workers), and we consider how their subjective interpretation of the world helps to explain their actions in order to construct an understanding of community sense-making in tackling CSA cases. In this day and age of commitment to "evidence-based practice" and "best evidence," it is critical to understand that in real-world practice individual agents not only will proceed based on an informed reading of the scholarly literature produced in the academy but also will take action partly based on their values, beliefs, and accumulated practice wisdom. In the section on subjectivities in operation in this chapter, we examine some of these important belief systems and consider how they appear to inform practices in St. Mary County.

Third, case studies can contribute to understanding important public values. Or as sociologist David Thatcher (2006) has noted, "the normative case study rests on the assumption that we can make better judgments about values by reflecting on actual cases." In the section on working with probabilities and uncertainties in the service of justice, we examine the operation of "justice" in St. Mary County as it applies to CSA criminal investigations and prosecution. We identify the key elements employed in shifting the burden in CSA cases away from the child victim and onto the shoulders of professional practitioners and other adults. In doing so, we consider the values that underpin the community's practice of justice as it relates to both child victims and defendants. In this section, we also identify some of the larger issues that must be dealt with when balancing uncertainties in the quest for justice. This includes looking at the darker side of making a given set of choices.

Finally, we suggest what practitioners in other communities might take away as lessons learned from this in-depth and contextual study of St. Mary County.

## A PERFECT STORM: PLACE, POLICIES, AND PERSONALITIES

Exemplar cases are the product of a constellation of forces that are not easily separated from one another. St. Mary County and its sexual-abuse investigatory practices are no exception. Although we have told the St. Mary story in detail on previous pages, here we summarize some of those critical contextual factors that produced the results they did. As with any perfect storm, the synchronicity of factors coming together is what matters to the outcome.

### Historical Context

Historical context is important, and several historical factors played a significant role in the St. Mary experience. We take note of four. First, federal legislative policy set the stage for action at the state and local-community levels on matters of child sexual abuse in the early 1980s. As noted several times in our text, the Child Abuse Prevention and Treatment Act (CAPTA) was enacted in 1974. It provided support to states for the prevention, assessment, investigation, and treatment of child abuse generally. However, it was not until 1981 that the act was amended to include sexual abuse on the list of forms of maltreatment that must be reported. This addition of sexual abuse specifically in the early 1980s played a role in creating the "tsunami" of CSA cases reported by practitioners in St. Mary County in the early 1980s.

Federal and state attention to the problem raised community consciousness and made funding available for community education. As local practitioners began education programs about child sexual abuse and the prosecutor's office began enforcing laws that mandated its reporting, not surprisingly, there was a dramatic increase in the number of cases. This created the particular context in which St. Mary found itself experimenting with how to handle these newly surfacing cases. While virtually all state and local communities in the United States were faced with the problem of what to do or not do, St. Mary County proactively took up the challenge from the earliest moment.

Second, in conjunction with federal recognition of the problem, there was growing public and media attention to child sexual abuse in the 1980s. To the extent that prosecutors before the 1980s had had trouble prosecuting CSA cases because the public was loath to believe that such behaviors existed (for example, as reported by Judge Richter in earlier chapters); with growing public awareness came increasing (if grudging) acceptance that sexual abuse of children actually did occur. This created a context in which prosecution of these cases was possible. Arguably, the public discourse needed to be familiar enough to the pool of jurors that they were willing to entertain the possibility of the crime. Again, the public was primed to do this in the early 1980s at the time St. Mary began to affirmatively and aggressively prosecuting criminal sexual conduct (CSC) cases.

Third, we raise some observations about the state of technology in the early and mid-1980s in order to appreciate more fully the significance of St. Mary's actions. Given the fact that today people can whip out a cell phone, digitally record moving images, and email those images around the globe in a matter of seconds, it is easy to forget about of the relatively primitive state of technology in the early and mid-1980s. Specifically, the introduction of video recorders or camcorders (which captured both *visual* as well as *audio* recording by means of a single hand-held device) first occurred in the late 1970s. The famous format wars between VHS and Betamax were in full swing in the early 1980s. Picking between these different formats was risky because it was unclear which would ultimately dominate. Furthermore, this cutting-edge equipment came with a hefty price tag: one representative VHS model in 1977 cost $1,060, which, adjusted for inflation, would be more than $3,800 in 2008 dollars. While we will consider St. Mary's applied and creative use of this equipment further, at the moment we merely take note of the infancy of this technology at the time St. Mary began to experiment with it.

Finally, and bit more tenuously, we make one more historical observation. Several important community leaders including Charles Davis (prosecutor) and Rick Rivers (polygraph operator)—who spearheaded the earliest efforts of seeking justice in CSA cases—were Marines and served in Vietnam War. While Rivers was the only one to link his personal biography, war, and postwar experiences with his understanding of child sexual abuse, it is plausible that something about the sense of mission and a deep commitment to it may have informed the others as well. In particular, Rivers talked about his willingness to separate "bad acts" from the individual people who committed them without passing moral judgment. He attributed his success as a polygraphist to his ability to do so. Being able to separate moral judgment of persons from their behavior is almost certainly a necessary survival strategy for combat veterans, and one that would also serve those working with sexual offenders against children as well.

## Powerful Personalities

That a set of forceful and energetic individuals gathered in one historical moment in St. Mary County and made an impact is indisputable. These passionate professionals were scattered across several different institutional systems and in a variety of different roles. Together, however, they were responsible for setting into motion the original investigatory initiatives in CSA cases and carrying them forward. Perhaps most significantly, this included the charismatic, take-charge prosecutor, Charles Davis, who forged ahead with coordinating an organized community response and committing policy to paper. However, it also included children-services personnel such as CPS supervisor Donna Wagner and other community leaders, who were deeply committed to educating the public and combating the problem of child sexual abuse. It included a local barber, Chris Kovac, who was savvy enough to convince his law-enforcement patrons of the value of this new hobby called videography. Of course, it also included the colorful interdisciplinary group dubbed the "Sex Busters," an unlikely combination of a hippie-pacifist, an ex-marine, and a no-nonsense cop. They were interdisciplinary colleagues, but they were also friends who frequently ended a difficult day over beer. In doing so, they continued—even after business hours—to process their experiences and integrate their working understandings of child sexual abuse in an intense, loyal, tight knit, and supportive interdisciplinary group.

The community was willing to work with unlikely combinations of individual actors in order to solve the problem of child sexual abuse. In each case, these particular individuals appeared to go beyond doing merely an adequate job and insisted on going the extra mile. Together, they generated dynamic energy in their mission to protect children and prosecute sexual offenders.

## Strong Leadership and Institutional Support

There was unanimous consensus that Chief Prosecutor Charles Davis provided extremely strong and unifying leadership in getting the original

CSA protocol off the ground. However, it is also clear that the institutional support for the mission of protecting children from child sexual abuse and prosecuting offenders extended well beyond the prosecutor's office and included law-enforcement agencies and CPS. In both agencies, supervisors were willing to permit frontline workers to stretch the boundaries of their professional practice in order to provide timely, comprehensive, consistent, and rigorous investigations and interventions in matters of child sexual abuse. These supervisors endorsed a flexible approach to individual role assignments and permitted frontline workers discretion in their work priorities when it came to CSA cases. So, for example, paperwork could be temporarily postponed if the priorities of a team investigation so dictated. Furthermore, as Donna Wagner observed, supervisors were willing to take the heat for frontline workers' actions, thereby providing protection for them when necessary. This prioritization and flexibility resulted in fluid service delivery, unlike the rule-bound and tightly regulated service domains more often seen today. St. Mary's approach stemmed from a desire to serve better the greater public good—as defined by the practitioners of the community—of putting children first. They incorporated these child-centered values into everyday practice.

## Innovation, Experimentation, and Risk Taking

Evident from the earliest days in St. Mary was a willingness of the practitioners in this community to experiment and take risks. A culture was incubated that had practitioners striving for excellence but that also permitted room for failure. The history of the protocol itself involved experimenting with audio and video recording, as well as wiring children to capture incriminating statements by suspects. The video recording flourished and was ultimately incorporated as written policy, while wiring children perished as being detrimental to them and too cumbersome during fast-paced investigations. But the point is that in the quest for better ways to protect children, to secure prosecutions, and to serve community well-being, it was always worth the initial gamble. The failures were embraced as a necessary part of paving a road to best practices.

This spirit of experimentation was never really stifled even as practices became institutionalized. For example, after the sexual-abuse investigatory protocol became written policy, professionals still tinkered with its implementation. Additional, informal practices also began to supplement the written "protocol." These included, for example, the practice of removing plea-bargaining opportunities from the table if a suspect insisted on having a child victim testify at a preliminary hearing. This was a value-based decision that was used to further protect the child's best interests. Additionally, as the caseload of convictions began to grow, the community introduced offender evaluation and treatment programs in order to sort out really bad offenders from those potentially less threatening and to tailor responses accordingly. In doing so, it sought to protect the community better, but also to deliver a more nuanced form of justice. Therefore, the protocol was never a static instrument. Rather, it was a flexible tool that provided a solid set of investigatory steps and allowed further interpretive practices to supplement its procedures.

## Building "Best" Practices in a Void

The community embraced the idea of learning from its members and showed deep respect for the expertise of others. They built on successes in a systematic and progressive manner. Police officers "stole" good questions from other officers. Videotape interviews were used to improve interviewing practice of both CPS workers and police officers. The use of videotapes for peer review (both intradisciplinary and interdisciplinary) seemed to have heightened practitioners' self-awareness and improved their techniques. There was a willingness to forge new practices in a virtual void of established procedures. Together, the prosecutors, police officers, and CPS workers developed strategies that contributed to successful outcomes.

In addition, the level of respect for other practitioners in the community remained extremely high. Prosecutors spoke positively about defense attorneys; defense attorneys called prosecutors fair. Law-enforcement officers deferred to the expertise of social workers when interviewing children. Everyone from prosecutors to defense attorneys spoke highly of polygraph operators and the offender therapist. While some of these words of tribute might have derived from social-desirability bias when speaking to research team members, it certainly appeared to those studying the community that there was an uncommonly deep general appreciation for professional practitioners from other disciplines.

## Demanding Excellence and Ensuring Transparency

Universally, community members commented on Davis's demand for excellence. However, this demand was not limited to just the people directly under Davis's reach, but extended to include CPS workers, polygraph operators, and law-enforcement agents. All of them, to some extent, had to answer to the prosecutor's standards. Furthermore, it was under Davis's leadership that the practice of videotaping both the polygraph and the child forensic interview sessions was begun. These videotapes were readily available in the event allegations were made about the legality or fairness of the process. This speaks to considerable transparency in how professionals conducted themselves in CSC criminal investigations. So, to the extent that criminal investigations, which are shrouded in secrecy, give rise to suspicions about fairness, transparency practically invites opponents to critically examine the fairness of the process. Remarkably, in St. Mary County there have been virtually no complaints in this regard.

## Capitalizing on Technology and Resources

This community repeatedly demonstrated its willingness to capitalize on whatever resources came its way. This included accepting the invitation of a local barber to begin videotaping expert testimony, crime scenes, and child interviews for use in the court proceedings when this technology was in its infancy. Community professionals saw the possibility in the routine use of videotaping and routine use of polygraph tests and they cultivated relationships with individuals who owned equipment at the same time relying on their talents in operating it. The prosecutor's office put these experts under contract and purchased their services while not bothering to go to the expense of investing in its own expensive equipment (neither video nor polygraph instruments). Thus, the community capitalized on both technological advances and the human capital that was readily available within the county's boundaries. Another example of using resources at hand includes the decision to invite former Sex Buster, Jim Henry, back to testify as an expert witness in CSC trials. Few jurisdictions of this size so routinely use the testimony of a sexual-abuse expert as a basic component of its criminal trials.

Together, the community saw the possibilities in technology and personal resources. It experimented with them, capitalized on them, and then cultivated the individual interests and expertise of talented individuals (be that a barber with a video machine, a young scholar as expert, or a polygraph operator with a particular talent for obtaining confessions). It is perhaps in this way, that a financially resource-poor community was able to enhance its practices without the usual influx of extra funding.

## Mandates and Missions

Early on, Charles Davis saw the benefit of an interdisciplinary team whose constituent members got what they needed to be professionally successful: police officers got "confessions," prosecutors got "convictions," and CPS workers got "safe children." He also cultivated and encouraged the interdisciplinary work and practice that allowed a team of three individuals (the Sex Busters) to develop a particular area of specialized knowledge and expertise handling CSA investigations at the same time, exposing each one to the sensibilities and needs of the other team members. This interdisciplinary sensitivity spread to others. The polygraph operators and law-enforcement officers began to understand the significance of keeping children safe, while the CPS workers began to understand the special needs of the criminal justice system. This is deeply reflected in the interviews in which individual agents spoke across disciplinary boundaries in describing their primary objectives and missions. For example, police officers such as this one readily contextualized their job pursuing criminals alongside CPS mandates:

> I think cops across the board are focused on the bad guy. They want to make life miserable for him, piss on his parade. I'm still concerned about what's going to happen to this guy—but I'm not so concerned anymore because now I have other concerns that point in the other directions to my victim; their support group, be it grandma, grandpa, mom, older brothers and sisters, younger brothers and sisters, that type of thing.

Not surprisingly, these interdisciplinary tactics and the implementation of an aggressive investigatory policy led to more confessions and convictions in St. Mary County and created a secondary dilemma. As St. Mary became increasingly successful, it also discovered that not all offenders were cut from the same cloth. The question arose: How are we to sort out the really serious offenders from those who posed less of a risk for the community? Most notably under Mark Jameson's reign, the prosecutor's office began to rely heavily on evaluations, treatment, and sentencing differentials to sort out the serious offenders from those less serious and treat them accordingly. This nuanced approach stands in sharp contrast with practices in place in many U.S. communities today, which are increasingly rigid and punitive in their approach to sexual offenders, often not drawing even the subtlest distinction *between* offenses and *among* offenders.

## Small Town Homogeneity and Stability

St. Mary County is a small, mostly rural, community with a homogeneous and stable population. We offer two reasons this might be significant. First, the professional practitioners in the community were remarkably stable over decades. Prosecutors have made orderly progression from law intern, to assistant prosecutor, to chief prosecutor and finally to judgeships. Key defense attorneys, police officers, therapists, and polygraph operators have been around equally long periods of time. This resulted in a very stable professional-practice community.

Second, there were many overlapping relationships among key players. For example the victim's advocate ran a towing business; the children of a prosecutor and defense attorney dated in high school; the barber cut the hair of the local law-enforcement officers, everyone gathered in at the same restaurant for soup at midday or the same bar for beer at the end of the day; and the state trooper became the county fair commissioner. These intersections suggest a community in which knowledge about people and events may move in unanticipated ways and through informal channels. The prosecutors, for example, spoke of going to high school with a suspect or knowing the families of their jurors. While some might find this coziness uncomfortable, it nonetheless provided a context where interdependency, some conformity to community norms, and responsiveness to others were critical to general community well-being.

## Summary

In short, in this section on the "perfect storm" in St. Mary County, we have identified how the historical context; powerful personalities; strong leadership and institutional support; embracing a spirit of innovation, experimentation, and risk-taking; building a system of best practice through experimentation in a void; demanding excellence and ensuring transparency; capitalizing on all available resources and new technologies; understanding and rewarding the mandates and the missions of all the professionals on the investigatory team; and operating in the context of a homogeneous and stable small town all played a part in creating a perfect storm in which these CSA investigatory practices developed and flourished. However, these factors and characteristics are primarily descriptive in nature and do not necessarily enlighten us as to the motivations or belief systems of community agents that would help explain community practices. We turn to some of those key elements next.

## SUBJECTIVITIES IN OPERATION

A second particular benefit of case-study research is its ability to get at subjectivities and personal belief systems that inform action. In this section, we examine four seemingly commonly held views. The first is that Chief Prosecutor Mark Jameson was extremely fair in the operation of the prosecutor's office. Second, the community professionals expressed a shared readiness to believe children's disclosures about sexual abuse and a common understanding of the general nature of child sexual abuse, including its dynamics and characteristics. Third, among law enforcement agents and the primary polygraph operator, Rick Rivers, there were generally held beliefs that most sexual offenses against children were the result of opportunistic circumstances rather than deep-seated criminality and that these offenders were relieved by confessing to their sins. Fourth, flowing from this general view of offenders was the belief that the community was best protected in the long run by sorting offenders by the seriousness of their behavior and tailoring sentences and treatment accordingly.

In the following section we briefly examine each of these factors. We ask the reader to recognize that these opinions may or may not be scientifically verifiable. Nonetheless, these beliefs were shared among key professional practitioners and informed the way they went about their business and thus help to explain the community's professional practice environment. By examining these attitudes we can begin to make sense of the community's approach to CSA investigations and prosecutions.

## A "Fair and Honest" Prosecutor's Office

The tone and tenor of every prosecutor's office in the United States can be described with any number of adjectives and often reflect the temperament of its chief prosecutor: aggressive, unyielding, adversarial, tough, diplomatic, or politically motivated. A stable force in the St. Mary prosecutor's office from 1982 to 2002 and chief prosecutor from 1992 to 2002, Mark Jameson's prosecutorial tone was uniformly described as "fair." Prosecutors and defense attorneys alike offer this assessment. Most notably, defense attorney Richard Nowak said, "Jameson was willing to see two sides . . . [he] was extremely fair . . . he ran his prosecutor's office that way. He had to be hard where he had to be hard." Another defense attorney, Brian Muller, echoed this sentiment by calling Jameson "fair and honest." This stands in relatively sharp contrast with Nowak's concern that Jameson's successor as chief prosecutor, John Hunter, "may just prosecute for the sheer joy of it." While still describing Hunter as "fair," Nowak voiced a concern that was echoed by other community members, namely that the basic "tone" of the prosecutor's office was going to shift under new leadership. We might anticipate that a shift in basic tone could lead to adjustments in practice across all professional positions including CPS, law enforcement as well as the defense bar.

We offer three additional observations to support the assessment of practitioners that Jameson's approach to justice was basically fair. The first comes from Jameson's own mantra, "It is what it is," which encapsulated his personal philosophy, a pragmatic approach toward handling CSC cases. The second again comes from his personal belief system; Jameson saw his primary job responsibility as getting all parties in a criminal proceeding to acknowledge what happened. For him, this process of acknowledgment was central to the entire justice endeavor. Third, building on this belief that acknowledgment was critical, came the conviction that the community was best served by making individual assessments regarding the seriousness of each offender's risk to the public and tailoring responses accordingly. This personal philosophy about the operation of the criminal-justice system goes far in explaining why he was perceived in the community as running a "fair" prosecutor's office.

Jameson repeatedly resorted to his mantra. By "it is what it is," he meant that he took cases as they came, problems and all. Rather than attempting to diffuse, hide, or minimize facts or circumstances that weaken a particular case in a quest to win, Jameson believed that justice prevailed when cases, with all their complexity and contradictions, were presented as is. In a classic comment that we have used elsewhere, Jameson said, "My attitude has always been that *it is what it is*. If the kid said it happened on Tuesday in Mom's bed on the tape and in court that she said it happened on Saturday on the couch, well, it's inconsistent, but shouldn't you be fair to the defendant also?"

This belief in being fair to both sides was also evident in Jameson's articulation of his primary job responsibility as being to get both victim and offender to a place of mutual acknowledgment of what happened. Jameson summed up this general theory in the following long reflection on a series of "bad acts" and the actor/victims' relationship to them:

> Winona Ryder stole $4,800 worth of stuff. We went through all this rigmarole about $200,000 defense [over whether] she had permission [to take the goods] or she was rehearsing a role—we went through all that—and it boiled down to she did it. She should have walked in on day one and said, "I did it, I got a prescription drug problem, I need help," and everyone would have had a lot more respect for her. But all these people, be it Bill Clinton, or Enron executives, or Charles Manson, or whoever they are, they did a bad thing to someone else. And that person needs to be acknowledged as a victim, and the guy who did it needs to be acknowledged he's the person that did it. That's my job.

We take particular note of these observations because to the extent that community members—particularly the defense bar—perceived the chief prosecutor's office operating from a position of "fairness" rather than primarily from an adversarial position, it helps explain the willingness of the defense bar to forgo hypervigilant or overly aggressive defense strategies as part of their standard practice. If they generally believe that justice was served fairly in the end, this context may explain some appearance of complacency in the defense of their clients. While we do not mean to suggest that the defense attorneys were not doing their jobs, we do suggest that defense attorneys (or any other practitioners, for that matter) will modify their behaviors based on the perceived environment in which they operate.

Believing Children's Disclosures and Understanding the Dynamics
of Sexual Abuse

Together, the prosecutors, law enforcement agents, and CPS workers
bought into the mandate that child protection was a priority. Prosecutor
John Hunter called this commitment to the child the "hallmark of the way
we do things." Furthermore, these professionals uniformly believed that a
child's disclosure indicated that *something* had happened. They maintained
this inclination toward believing in the child's inherent credibility even
when a public backlash of doubt swirled actively in other communities and
in other forums in the United States. In addition, police officers incorporated this belief in ways that motivated them and informed their work.

Over time, those professionals in St. Mary County charged with
investigating and prosecuting CSC cases came to accept children's
accounts, even if they were recounted in a manner that was not consistent with adult narrations of victimization. In the words of one police
officer describing his transformation toward believing children:

Early on in this, I would see these videotapes or talk to these kids and it's
like, Jesus Christ, I don't know whether to believe this kid or not. You know
what I found out? Ninety-nine percent of them are telling the truth. When
you get done sucking on the perpetrator's nose . . . he's told you exactly the
same thing that little Susie told you. I mean, it just blows your mind.

To the extent that investigating police officers in St. Mary County
started from a presumption that 99 percent of their child victims were
telling the truth and that it required only serious police interrogation
to get a suspect to acknowledge this basic truth, children—even poor
narrators—were afforded a privileged starting position.

Because practitioners in St. Mary started from a position of believing the child that something had happened, problematic aspects of the
child's accounting of the incident did not deter them. Prosecutor Hunter
expressed a well-developed personal philosophy about truth, the narration of accounts about the truth (by both children and adults), and
justice. Although other community professionals might not share his
exact articulation, his basic willingness to separate out what he called
the "kernel of the insult" from narrative details was commonly shared.
Hunter said, "You could show a videotape to a child a dozen times [and

still always get] some testimony in direct conflict of what's on that videotape." Like Jameson, he accepted that these conflicts were "just part of the process" and must be dealt with. That said, however, he believed that showing the videotape to the child witness was effective in "cementing the recollection" of what happened and both "solidifying and creating memories as much as it is refreshing." He dismissed the notion that any witness—child or adult—could actually recount and recall the truth as it would be recorded by an outside video monitor instead, "what we're doing" Hunter said "is not really displaying the absolute truth. A lot of what we're doing is solidifying the witness's current belief as to the truth. You know that the action, any actual events of a crime, that's the absolute. And by the time we get to trial, what we really get is the witness's best attempt to recall that. It's only the witness's opinion as to what happened by that time. In the end, "the videotape solidifies the victim's opinion as to what happened and it makes it more truthful in the victim's mind and makes that victim more convincing as they tell it to the jury, even though that videotape also contains inaccuracies, as compared to the absolute activity." Hunter noted that most jurors do not understand this, most prosecutors would not say it out loud, and you certainly would not see reference to it in "trial preparation books." It was, nonetheless, in his view, an accurate portrayal of what happened at trial. He was quick to recognize that "all of these witnesses are doing their very, very best to be truthful. They are being honest. They [really] are. And the heart of the insult is accurate." For our purposes, it was Hunter's idea about the "heart of the insult" which was particularly significant. When applying this concept directly to a child victim he argued that while the details offered to tell a complete story are "probably wrong" the only really significant factor is that, "the kernel of the insult remains with that child."

In short, the general willingness of law-enforcement agents, prosecutors, and CPS workers to accept the "kernel" or "heart" of the "insult" as central, truthful, and actionable—whether or not the child had narrated the rest of his or her account with the kind of stability and consistency preferred by adults—was shared throughout the St. Mary practice community. In the view of its constituents, this "kernel" was and should be actionable no matter what the surrounding circumstances. This is very different from the case in jurisdictions where the prosecutor's office is keeping an eye on the burden of proof and the viability of winning at trial as a gauge by which to assess the child's narration.

As law-enforcement agents in St. Mary County incorporated this belief in children into their professional practice, it fundamentally influenced and shaped the way they approached criminal investigations of child sexual abuse. For example, one officer noted, "I want to make sure I'm doing it [the interview] right, because if I'm not doing it right I'm cheating the victim. I'm not getting the right information." Police officers worried that if they failed in their interrogations of suspects in the early stages of investigation, they might well be sending a child victim back into an environment where she would continue to be abused. "The tragic results of an investigative blunder," said one officer, "are that we could potentially send the victim back home or back into an environment with the offender. This has lifelong consequences for the victim." This kind of outcome particularly violated police officers' sensibilities about protecting the public.

## Beliefs About CSA Offenders

Second, for the most part polygraph operators and law-enforcement agents shared two deeply held beliefs: the first was that most sexual acts against children were opportunistic, and the second was that these offenders wanted to confess. As for the opportunistic nature of sexual offending against children, both prosecutor Hunter and police officer Williams similarly pointed to this characterization. For example, Hunter said, "I think there is an awful lot more of that sort of criminal sexual behavior that goes on all the time. Just momentary lapse, a momentary fondling." Similarly, Williams hypothesized that most offenders in St. Mary are not pedophiles, but instead child sexual abuse was a "circumstantial thing and they were in a situation that aroused [them] and they didn't have the power to say no."

With this characterization of offenders as agents who acted impulsively in circumstances where they were easily aroused and with insufficient personal gumption to resist temptation came a belief that perpetrators felt guilty about their behavior and were relieved by confessing. Confessions were believed to serve a therapeutic function. Ed Williams picked up on this line of reasoning: "Most of the people we had just felt guilty. They really felt they needed to tell somebody. You could see them take a big sigh of relief that they told somebody and that they got it out. And it was probably a healing thing for them."

At odds with the view that offenders were primarily opportunistic, Chief Prosecutor Mark Jameson articulated his own equally deeply held convictions about offenders and their acts: "I have two rules of thumb that I tell people are almost always true. It's almost always true that they did it to somebody else. There are more victims out there than you know and it's almost always true that somebody did it to them." This worldview rested on two critical beliefs that differed significantly from those expressed by law-enforcement agents: first, that sexually offending is to some extent a learned behavior, and second, that in all likelihood individual sexual offenders who came to the attention of the prosecutor's office had offended with other children.

What is particularly interesting about Jameson's view was he particularized the idea that what we see is the tip of the iceberg of sexual offending against children by applying the theory to individual actors. If you believe that the individual suspect you have in your custody, was victimized as a child, has victimized the particular child for which he is facing charges, has probably victimized other children that the prosecutor's office doesn't know about, and, by extension, is likely to victimize other children in the future, you are likely to favor interventions that try to break the cycle of abuse rather than ones that merely punish individuals for the specific act for which he was caught. In part because of this worldview, Jameson led the way in developing assessment and treatment options for offenders in St. Mary County.

## Long-Run Community Protection

Perhaps most significant of all, given these attitudes toward offenders, practitioners began to redefine the very notion of public safety and to focus on long rather than short-term outcomes. Simply punishing an offender for one bad act ceased to be the exclusive focus. Instead, there was intense focus at the earliest stages of the case in doing assessments that sorted out the really bad guys from the "circumstantial" or "bad judgment" offender, tailoring the appropriate treatment response, and relying on the belief that this would reduce reoffending or relapses in the future. There was a significant shift in focus from framing the pertinent question away from how to send someone away to how best to protect the community overall. As Hunter put it, "You have to answer the question of how you are going to protect society when he gets out."

Under Jameson's reign, the community started with this question. As reported by a police officer, "You go in and talk to Jameson, who will ask, 'What's the best course of action to make sure that this guy doesn't come back and reoffend?' That's kind of—from my perspective—that's how it's changed the most is the way the total system deals with these perpetrators."

Indeed, the answer to this question relied largely on the ability of the professionals to sort out the pedophiles or hardcore criminals from the circumstantial offenders. Or, as Jameson framed it, "The trick with the evaluations is to try to find the dangerous guys from the treatable guys." Clearly, that is where Jameson's leadership took the community. Virtually all the professionals spoke about the attempt to do this sorting early on and to adjust the sentencing appropriately. Similarly, the defense bar bought into this "fair" treatment of offenders. Said one defense attorney of the community response, "I think we try to tailor the response more than anything and [ask], 'What does this deserve?' Does this deserve the counseling as opposed to anything else?" St. Mary County police officers noted that they go beyond the "just hook 'em and book 'em and don't look back" approach that characterizes many law-enforcement jurisdictions. Instead, in St. Mary County, "they have to go through just a myriad of programs. You know, you may only get a four-year prison sentence mandatory supervised probation, but you have to go talk to Mark Reggio and do all these other programs."

Professionals in the community settled on the fact that the best hope for community well-being in the long run was to get treatment for offenders. Most made one critical further assumption about treatment: they assumed that it worked. Or, at very least, they assumed that treatment worked better than punishment alone. This was true for both police officers and prosecutors. Said one officer, "I'm convinced they don't want to reoffend. That way you make sure they don't reoffend is you plug them [into] programs we have here and, by God, they don't reoffend. Many, many of them don't reoffend." He understood treatment to be preferable to incarceration alone "because realistically, they're not going to spend the rest of their life in a box. And if all you've done is put him in a cage, and let him pace, when he gets out, he's going to be a wild animal, okay?" Prosecutor Hunter offered support for this position as well:

I really think success in [a] CSC case is usually six or seven times out of ten rehabilitation of the offender. And I think that our Community Corrections

Program has just a superb approach to that. We've had for the first time since 1999—I could brag to parents of victims who've never had somebody successfully complete that program, reoffend. I only have had, in 1999, we had a reoffender and then we had another one or two since, and that's just phenomenal. I don't know that it's something you cure, but it's something that at least you instill a respect and a fear of the system to where they're afraid to do it anymore.

The county was very good at shaping sentences that were consistent with the crimes and that really took the best interests of the victim, the community, and the offender into consideration.

This treatment approach gave rise to a secondary thorny criminal-practice problem. What to do with offenders who confessed to additional criminal acts with their child victim or to additional victims during the course of treatment? Should they be criminally prosecuted for the additional crimes? St. Mary again displayed a very common sense approach to this dilemma: it encouraged the offender to disclose but protected him from additional criminal charges. The prosecutor then notified the victim's family so the victim could receive treatment. This was in sharp contrast to a U.S. Supreme Court case, *McKune v. Lile*, in which a prisoner refused to engage in treatment because he was not insulated from further prosecution for full disclosure. The prisoner was in essence punished for not participating in the treatment program, and the Court approved this approach. The problem, of course, was that the offender was not going to get treatment, and the other victims might not be known or be receiving treatment either.

While most of the professionals we spoke with bought into the belief that treatment was successful and the community was protected, Jameson who initiated the treatment program was not naïve, "It isn't as easy as that. Because the dirty secret is, I don't even know whether treatment works. It may all be as effective as flipping a coin. But I'm willing to take that risk with a certain kind of offenders and try to change their behavior."

## WORKING WITH UNCERTAINTY IN THE SERVICE OF JUSTICE

All professional practitioners associated with the criminal-justice system end up constructing justice through the choices and priorities they favor during the course of daily practice. In this study, we attempted to open the "black box" of criminal-justice practices by showing how uncertainties about the absolute nature of truth, disagreements stemming from disciplinary perspectives, and the subjective beliefs of all the people associated with the system operate as they carry out their professional duties.

Some of this boils down to a question of probabilities. Probabilities, of course, provide us with the hopeful possibility that we get things right (on average) more often than we get things wrong. In the world of public policy and the practice of law, that is about as good as we can do. However, at the individual level probabilities are problematic. They work against minority voices—the innocent man who is treated as guilty or the abused child who is accused of lying. When truth is uncertain, how should we approach justice? How do we go about balancing the relative risks of mistakes when weighing them against probable certainties? In the end, the answer has something to do with our values.

The St. Mary community of practitioners has seemingly come to some consensus about the social risks associated with child sexual abuse (including the possibility of sending a child home with a perpetrator, the possibility that there are other victims out there and; the likelihood of reoffending) and the type of errors associated with legal risks with getting it wrong (either because of false confessions or wrongful convictions). It has made some decisions about how it wants its system of justice to work when dealing with child victims. Thatcher (2006) noted that "case studies can contribute to normative theory—to the more-or-less integrated networks of normative convictions that we rely on when we try to answer the difficult ethical questions we encounter in our personal and professional lives." We attempt to understand how that integrated network of normative convictions contributes to St. Mary's mission of seeking justice for child victims.

## NORMATIVE JUSTICE: SHIFTING THE BURDEN/SHOULDERING THE RESPONSIBILITY

St. Mary County chose to define excellence differently from many jurisdictions. In its desire to "balance between assignment of responsibility and protection of the victim" (Jameson), the county expanded the scope of protecting the victim in ways that went well beyond just the harm done by a particular criminal act, but rather to consider *additional* harms that were inflicted as a byproduct of the criminal-justice system (such as repeatedly having to testify) and *potential* harms that might befall the victim if adult professional practitioners did not do their jobs correctly (such as sending them home with an abuser). "It's our commitment to the child," said Prosecutor Hunter about assessing excellence, "it's not a rigid won-loss percentage, it's not a rigid get the maximum conviction and it's not a rigid take it all the way and lose it. It's just to do our best for the child, whatever we believe that to be. And according to the criteria that many prosecutors' offices set for themselves, that's not excellence. But according to the criteria that we set for ourselves, which is to try to obtain some safety for society with balance with what it gives trauma to the child, I think our approach is pretty effective."

There is nothing illegal about any of the practices used in St. Mary County. Nonetheless, as we have maintained throughout this book, the arrangement of practices maximized the advantages in favor of the child victim by trying to minimize the child's burden in carrying the case and shifting that burden onto the shoulders of the professional practice community. Although we have made these arguments at length in the text, we summarize some of the key points here.

## Privileging the Child's Account

As noted, St. Mary County decided to believe the child's word no matter how problematic the narrative account, if the child provided at least the kernel of truth that a criminal offense had occurred. In doing so, it used the child's version of the facts to confront the suspect directly and pressure him or her into full or partial confessions. This also meant that the primary focus was on the first forensic interview and all efforts were made to deter any future retellings.

## Speed and Surprise

In its heyday, speed and surprise were important factors in investigating allegations of child sexual abuse. There were at least three reasons for this. First, practitioners wanted to protect children from continued exposure to offenders (and therefore wanted offenders at the police station before children got off the afternoon school bus). Second, they believed that speed and surprise benefited their investigation by not allowing time for the suspect to summon up personal defenses, enlist the help of other adults, create counternarratives, or take the prudent action of calling an attorney. Third, it decreased the likelihood that the suspect or other adults would put pressure on the child to recant or otherwise silence him or her.

## Up-Front Work

CPS workers, polygraphists, law enforcement agents and prosecutors all agreed that doing the extra work at the front end of cases would ultimately save time in the long run and produce better securities for the child.

## Trust in Polygraph Magician Rick Rivers

The community of professional practitioners accepted the notion that polygraph operator, Rick Rivers, got to the truth, and his word relative to the guilt or innocence of a suspect was binding. He did not play sides and could be employed by defense attorneys as well as prosecutors. In so investing in Rivers, the community delegated considerable authority to him in determining probable guilt before a case moved forward or ever got to trial. In a sense, then, Rick Rivers was the ultimate purveyor of truth for the community and played a major role in its system of justice in CSC cases.

## Child-Centered and Holistic Case Handling

There was agreement among professionals that the best interest of the child came first. Therefore, the community exhibited a very child-centered approach. Given this child-centered approach, the professional actors orbited around the child and the child's case in ways that were very different than if each actor considered his or her specific and limited role in relation to the case. Arrangements were made around the child, rather than around the institutional practices of the various parts of the child welfare, criminal justice and family court systems.

## Creating Incentives for Certain Behaviors

St. Mary County created rewards and incentives for certain behaviors and disincentives for others. As noted earlier, suspects who made children testify at preliminary examination usually lost their opportunity to plea-bargain. Suspects who confessed to crimes and expressed regret were usually rewarded with less punitive sentencing and better treatment options.

## Graduated Sentencing Structure

By creating a graduated and responsive sentencing structure for those who confessed to CSC cases, the system created some additional built-in protections for child victims in that suspects might be less inclined to gamble by going to trial if they thought they were getting a decent deal up front. It also created protections for defendants and their attorneys because they had more information that could be used in making informed decisions about the handling of the cases.

## Considering Relative Power Relationships

Our research team believes that children start by being disadvantaged relative to power structures in the criminal justice system in four overlapping ways. First, children are less powerful than adults. Second, sexually abused children are often dependent on their abusers as caretakers, teachers, scoutmasters, or in other roles of authority, making them particularly vulnerable. Third, victims in the criminal-justice system are generally in a less protected position than suspects vis-à-vis the relative burdens at play. Finally, child victims are in a particularly vulnerable position relative to adult suspects because of their inability to fully understand and hold their own in a system that favors adults. In short, these overlapping privileges generally favor adult suspects and greatly disadvantage children. St. Mary County has gone to great pains to protect children by leveling the playing field, in every way possible, in its investigation and prosecution of CSC cases.

Taken together, privileging the child's account, speed and surprise, working hard at the front end of cases, putting faith in the polygraphist, utilizing child-centered and holistic investigatory and prosecution practices, creating incentives for certain child-protective behaviors, creating a system of moderating punishment relative to the criminal offense, and considering relative power relationships, helped St. Mary County shift the burden in CSC cases away from children and to adult professionals. In addition, and very significantly, professionals, particularly prosecutors and police officers, expanded their definition of community safety to include being concerned with other unknown victims and potential future victims of individual perpetrators. Thus, the basic scope of public safety encompassed a broad view of professional responsibilities and possible interventions.

## DARK CLOUDS: SOME POTENTIAL DISADVANTAGES

This constellation of choices about how to proceed in investigating and prosecuting child sexual abuse in St. Mary County also had negative consequences. We offer four possible aspects of the practices that may be considered "dark clouds": class and race bias, deference to the polygraph test, reliance on the therapeutic model, and disciplinary disagreements.

### Class and Race Bias

St. Mary County relied quite heavily on obtaining confessions from uneducated, often poor suspects. It is unlikely that the use of speed, surprise and upfront polygraph tests would have worked as well with a more educated, more privileged, and better-resourced offender. For example, the idea that speed permits police officers to interrogate suspects before they have the opportunity to "marshal" their defenses or talk to an attorney is illustrative of the ways that the county's system uses suspects' lack of sophistication and access against them. To that end, questions arise as to the class bias in the prosecution of CSA cases in the county, although this disadvantage likely exists in other jurisdictions as well.

According to our statistics, a disproportional number of African American offenders were prosecuted when compared to countywide demographics. Our statistics indicate that 8.3 percent of St. Mary offenders were African American, while the census reflects a countywide population of less than 3 percent. Although we saw no overt evidence of racial bias, and racial factors may be conflated with that of socioeconomic status, it nonetheless is a troubling replication of the racial disparities reflected in the prison population and criminal justice system in general. In St. Mary County, African American defendants routinely record objections in pretrial motions about the lack of racial diversity in the jury pool, but these objections are routinely denied and denials upheld on appeal. The Inman case serves as an example where such a motion was made. Both the defendant and victim in that case were African American, while the prosecutor, judge, defense attorney, and members of the jury were white.

In short, powerful, educated white men in the community enforce sexual norms on less powerful men, many of them people of color. Despite disparities in prosecution rates, there seemed to be an unspoken assumption that the poor, the undereducated and people of color were fairly treated and that institutional forms of racism were not in play.

## Deference to the Polygraph Test

The polygraph test was afforded considerable weight and polygraph operators granted considerable authority. As noted throughout this book, much deference was given to polygraph results, particularly when the much-trusted Rick Rivers conducted the polygraph session. While there is no disputing Rivers's skill, there are serious questions about the scientific accuracy of the polygraph. In addition, to the extent that polygraph exams do work, they are not likely to detect sociopaths, pathological liars, or other practiced schemers. The county's heavy reliance on polygraph outcomes in order to decide whether to move forward or discontinue a case raises concerns. In many cases, Rivers actually elicits confessions or partial confessions without even running the polygraph charts. It is perhaps this county's reliance on him as a master interrogator (with the threat of a polygraph test) that has influenced the outcomes. Nonetheless, the central role of the test or the threat of the test is arguably misplaced.

## Reliance on the Therapeutic Model

St. Mary County's use of a responsive sentencing structure relied heavily upon therapeutic models that emphasize the importance of confession as the first step of recovery and rehabilitation. Much like the Alcoholics Anonymous (AA) model, therapeutic models of sexual offender treatment usually require that the offender articulate that he has a problem as a prerequisite for intervention. Failure to acknowledge or denial of the problem is considered symptomatic of the problem itself. St. Mary assumed that confession was a first step in treatment. This could pose serious obstacles for the person who was wrongly accused. His insistence on his innocence could then be characterized as resistance to treatment rather than a truthful declaration.

## Disciplinary Arguments

Clearly, our tale of St. Mary County is told primarily from the perspective of the prosecution, although we have tried to do justice to the defense bar. We have also attempted to be transparent about disciplinary disputes. That said, however, we take note of the very real differences in practice orientation that might lead readers to be critical of the practices and choices made in St. Mary County. We hope that, even if readers disagree with St. Mary's choices or our interpretation of those choices, we have at least laid out the points of tension for public discussion. Other communities may choose a different constellation of procedures and working relations, but all must wrestle with the basic underlying questions and make choices about their own priorities and values. In making different choices, other communities are well advised to think about the consequences for child victims. The idea that St. Mary County illustrates one set of choices, but not by any means the only way, leads us to some final implications.

## IMPLICATIONS FOR OTHER COMMUNITIES AND PRACTITIONERS

Case studies offer highly contextual evaluations of particular phenomena. As such, findings from cases studies are not readily "generalizable" to other settings because making sense of them requires sensitivity to biographical, geographic, historical, and other contextual factors. That said, case-study findings ought to be able to provide a yardstick against which other communities can assess their practices. In this way, a particular case can serve as a standard against which others can both evaluate and interpret their own community practices. As with many qualitative research projects, the biggest contribution of the case study may not be its answers to the questions originally posed, but rather the newly framed questions generated from the investigation. We offer the following from our investigation of St. Mary:

- How are child victims treated from the beginning to the end of the legal process in your community (not just how are they treated at isolated junctures of the process such as accommodating them during courtroom testimony)?
- Are the professionals shouldering the burdens of these cases, or are they relying heavily on the child's ability to repeatedly tell a coherent and consistent account?
- Does the community take a holistic approach to investigations and prosecutions that keep the child the central focus?
- Is there clear community leadership?
- Who are the champions of issues in the community? Who has standing to pursue them?
- How high are public-service expectations set?
- Is the community using resources (human, technological, and the like) to maximum advantage?
- Is the community willing to take risks? Experiment? Learn from failures and build on successes?
- How well do law-enforcement agencies, CPS, and the prosecutor's office cooperate and communicate?
- Are formal procedures in place that institutionalize collaboration between CPS, police, and the prosecutor's office? What are informal working relationships like?
- How open are people in power to listening to frontline workers?
- What mechanisms are in place for ongoing reflection, evaluation, and adaptation of professional practice?
- Does the community learn through practice and formalize successful practice?
- Do workers understand both the needs and the standards of the other professionals in order to support them in their work? (Do CPS workers *really* know what is required for criminal prosecution? Do law enforcement officers *really* understand how to keep children safe?)
- Can teams of professionals each claim success in joint projects?
- Do community professionals respect the expertise of others? Are they willing to defer to that expertise?

• How fairly are suspects treated during the process? How often do they complain of unfairness?

• Does the system account for the complexity and full range of sexual offenses?

• Do offenders get treatment?

• Are sentences graduated in order to attempt to have severity of punishment fit the crime and to sort out the treatable from the untreatable offender?

• What primary system of values is the community operating from?

• Are formal procedures flexible enough to be adapted to changing personnel and political climate?

To some extent, then, we are suggesting that other communities start where we finish with St. Mary County. Its protocol was developed over time. The community made mistakes, learned, modified, experimented, and ultimately created a system that works for it. Other counties thinking about implementing some of these practices should be much more mindful at the outset of what its positions are on some of these basic features. For example, St. Mary County found a way in a single procedure to meet the practice needs of three separate institutions (CPS, law enforcement, and the prosecutor's office), whereas a community that is considering developing new policies might be best off starting with conversations about how to meet the different institutional needs of those at the table.

While this case study certainly blends what we know from the world of scholars and social scientists, it also attempts to understand and illuminate the wisdom and value-based choices that real-world practitioners make in communities throughout the United States. In the current discourse in professional practice areas, where evidence-based practice (EBP) rules the day, there are some real questions about the place of innovation, experimentation, and risk-taking. We hope that by taking a bottom-up approach to the practice world, we have also made a valuable contribution to understanding practice. Endeavors such as these seek to bridge the research, academic, and scientific communities with those of people out there actually doing the hands-on work. Finally, we believe that this courageous willingness of St. Mary County to engage in real-world problems by boldly moving forward with creativity and humility should be an inspiration to us all. Like Judge Richter, we hope that St. Mary will inspire you by example.

# Bibliography

Abrams, S., and Abrams, J. B. (1993). *Polygraph testing of the pedophile*. Portland, OR: Gwinner Press.

American Public Human Services Association. (2001). *Report of the child welfare workforce survey: State and county data and findings*. Retrieved October 30, 2006, from www.aphsa.org/Policy/Doc/cwwsurvey.pdf.

Amsterdam, A. G., and Hertz, R. (1992). An analysis of closing arguments to a jury. *New York Law School Law Review, 37*, 55–122.

Araji, S., and Finkelhor, D. (1985). Explanations of pedophilia: Review of empirical research. *Bulletin of the American Academy of Psychiatry & the Law, 13*(1), 17–37.

Association for the Treatment of Sexual Abusers (ATSA). (1993). *The ATSA practitioner's handbook*. Lake Oswego, OR: ATSA.

Association for the Treatment of Sexual Abusers (ATSA). (1997). *Ethical standards and principles for the management of sexual abusers*. Beaverton, OR: ATSA.

Association for the Treatment of Sexual Abusers (ATSA). (n.d.a.). Risk assessment policy statement. Retrieved February 23, 2008, from www.atsa.com/ppAssessment.html.

Association for the Treatment of Sexual Abusers (ATSA). (n.d.b.). Reducing sexual abuse through treatment and intervention with abusers. Retrieved February 23, 2008, from www.atsa.com/pptreatment.html.

Association for the Treatment of Sexual Abusers (ATSA). (n.d.c.). ATSA response to sex offender registration and notification act. Retrieved February 23, 2008, from www.atsa.com/html.

Avery, M. (1983). The child abuse witness: Potential for secondary victimization. *Criminal Justice Journal, 7* (1), 1–48.

Bagley, C., and Ramsey, R. (1986). Sexual abuse in childhood: Psychosocial outcomes and implications for social work practice. *Social Work and Human Sexuality, 4,* 33–47.

Barbaree, H., and Marshall, W. (1998). Treatment of the sexual offender. *Treatment of offenders with mental disorders* (pp. 265–328). New York: Guilford Press.

Barbaree, H., Marshall, W., and Hudson, S. (1993). *The juvenile sex offender.* New York: Guilford.

Becker, J., Abel, G., Mittelman, M., and Cunningham-Rathner, J. (1987). Self-reported sex crimes of nonincarcerated paraphiliacs. *Journal of Interpersonal Violence, 2*(1), 3–25.

Bennett, W. L., and Feldman, M. (1981). *Reconstructing reality in the courtroom.* New Brunswick, NJ: Rutgers University Press.

Ben-Shakar, G. (2002). A critical review of the control question test (CTQ). In M. Kleiner (Ed.), *Handbook of polygraph testing* (pp. 103–126). San Diego, CA: Academic Press.

Berliner, L. (2000). *Taping versus note-taking by forensic interviewers.* San Diego, CA: San Diego Conference on Child Maltreatment.

Berliner, L., and Elliott, D. M. (2002). Sexual abuse of children. In J. E. B. Myers, L. Berliner, J. Briere, C. T. Hendrix, C. Jenny, and T. A. Reid (Eds.), *The APSAC handbook on child maltreatment* (pp. 55–78). Thousand Oaks, CA: Sage Publications.

Berliner, L., and Lieb, R. (2001). *Child sexual abuse investigations: Testing documentation methods* (Document No. 01-01-4102). Olympia: Washington State Institute for Public Policy.

Bidrose, S., and Goodman, G. (2000). Testimony and evidence: A scientific case study of memory for child sexual abuse. *Applied Cognitive Psychology, 14,* 197–213.

Blumberg, A. S. (1967). The practice of law as confidence game: Organizational cooption of a profession. *Law and Society Review, 1*(1), 15–39.

Bolen, R., and Lamb, J. (2002). Guardian support of sexually abused children: A study of its predictors. *Child Maltreatment*, 7(3), 265–276.

Bolen, R., and Lamb, J. (2004). Ambivalence of nonoffending guardians after child sexual abuse disclosure. *Journal of Interpersonal Violence*, 19(2), 185–211.

Bolen, R., and Lamb, J. (2007a). Can nonoffending mothers of sexually abused children be both ambivalent and supportive? *Child Maltreatment*, 12(2), 191–197.

Bolen, R., and Lamb, J. (2007b). Parental support and outcome in sexually abused children. *Journal of Child Sexual Abuse*, 16(2), 33–54.

*Brady v. Maryland*, 373 U.S. 83 (1963).

*Brewer v. Williams*, 430 U.S. 387 (1977).

Brooks, P. (1996). The law as narrative and rhetoric. In P. Brooks and P. Gerwitz (Eds.), *Law's stories: Narrative and rhetoric in the law* (pp. 14–23). New Haven: Yale University Press.

Brooks, P. (2000). *Troubling confessions.* Chicago: University of Chicago Press.

*Brown v. Mississippi* (1936).

California Attorney General Office (1994). Child victim witness investigative pilot project: Research and evaluation final report.

Cares, R. (1986).Videotaped testimony of child victims. *Michigan Bar Journal*, 65(1), 46–50.

Carnes, C., and LeDuc, D. (1998). *Forensic evaluation of children.* Huntsville, AL: National Children's Advocacy Center.

Carnes, C., Wilson, C., and Nelson-Gardell, D. (2000). Addressing the challenges and controversies in child sexual abusing interviewing: The forensic evaluation protocol and research project. In K. C. Faller (Ed.), *Maltreatment in early childhood: Tools for research-based intervention* (pp. 83–104). New York: Haworth Press.

Carnes, P. (1990). Sexual addiction. In A. Horton, B. Johnson, L. Roundy, and D. Williams (Eds.), *The incest perpetrator: A family member no one wants to treat* (pp. 126–143). Thousand Oaks, CA: Sage Publications.

Cassell, P. G., and Hayman, B. (1996). Police interrogation in the 1990s: An empirical study of the effects of Miranda. *U.C.L.A. Law Review*, 43(3), 839–931.

Ceci, S., and Bruck, M. (1993). The suggestibility of the child witness: A historical review and synthesis. *Psychological Bulletin*, 113, 403–439.

Ceci, S., and Bruck, M. (1995). *Jeopardy in the courtroom: A scientific analysis of children's testimony.* Washington, DC: American Psychological Association.

Cheit, R. E., and Goldschmidt, E. B. (1997). Child molesters in the criminal justice system: A comprehensive case flow analysis of the Rhode Island docket (1985–1993). *Criminal and Civil Confinement, 23*, 267–310.

Cheit, R. E., and Mervis, D. (2007). Myths about the Country Walk case. *Journal of Child Sexual Abuse, 16*(3), 95–116.

Child Abuse Prevention and Treatment Act (CAPTA) of 1974, P. L. 93–247.

Child Welfare Information Gateway. (2008). Major federal legislation concerned with child protection, child welfare, and adoption factsheet. Retrieved September 23, 2008, from www.childwelfare.gov/pubs/otherpubs/major fedlegis.cfm.

Ciottone, R., and Madonna, J. (1996). *Play therapy with sexually abused children.* London: Jason Aronson.

Clark, S. J. (2003). An accuser-obligation approach to the confrontation clause. *University of Nebraska Law Review, 81*(3), 1258–1286.

Cohen, J., Berliner, L., and Mannarino, A. (2000). Treating traumatized children: A research review and synthesis. *Trauma, Violence, and Abuse, 1*, 29–46.

Cohen, J., and Mannarino, A. (1996). A treatment outcome study for sexually abused pre-school children: Initial findings. *Journal of the American Academy of Child and Adolescent Psychiatry, 35*, 42–50.

Cohen, J., Mannarino, A., Berliner, L., and Deblinger, E. (2000). Trauma-focused cognitive behavior therapy: An empirical update. *Journal of Interpersonal Violence, 15*, 1203–1223.

Cohen, J., Mannarino, A., and Deblinger, E. (2006). *Treating trauma and traumatic grief in children and adolescents.* New York: Guilford Press.

Corwin, D. (1995). Early diagnosis of child sexual abuse: Diminishing the lasting effects. In G. Wyatt and G. Powell (Eds.), *The lasting effects of child sexual abuse* (pp. 251–270). Newbury Park, CA: Sage Publications.

Cross, T., and Saxe, L. (1992). A critique of the validity of polygraph testing in child sexual abuse cases. *Journal of Child Sexual Abuse, 1*(4), 19–33.

Cross, T., and Saxe, L. (2002). Polygraph testing and child sexual abuse: The lure of the Magic Lasso. *Child Maltreatment, 6*(3), 195–206.

Cross, T. P., DeVos, E., and Whitcomb, D. (1994). Prosecution of child sexual abuse: Which cases are accepted? *Child Abuse & Neglect, 18*(8), 663–677.

Cross, T. P., Jones, L. M., Walsh, W. A., Simone, M., and Kolko, D. (2007). Child forensic interviewing in children's advocacy centers: Empirical data on a practice model. *Child Abuse & Neglect, 31*(10), 1031–1052.

Cross, T. P., Walsh, W. A., Simone, K., and Jones, L. A. (2002). Prosecution of child abuse: A meta-analysis of rates of criminal justice decisions. *Journal of Violence, Trauma & Abuse, 4*(4), 323–340.

Davies, D., and Faller, K. C. (2004). *Peer review and supervision of forensic interviews.* San Diego, CA: San Diego Conference on Child Maltreatment.

Deblinger, E., and Heflin, A. (1996). *Treatment for sexually abused children and their non-offending parents: A cognitive-behavioral approach.* Thousand Oaks, CA: Sage Publications.

Deblinger, E., Lippman, J., and Steer, R. (1996). Sexually abused children suffering posttraumatic stress symptoms: Initial treatment outcome findings. *Child Maltreatment, 1,* 310–321.

Deblinger, E., Mannarino, A., Cohen, J., and Steer, R. (2006). A follow-up study of a multi-site, randomized, controlled trial for children with sexual abuse related PTSD symptoms. *Journal of the American Academy of Child and Adolescent Psychiatry, 45*(12), 1474–1484.

Deblinger, E., Steer, R., and Lippman, J. (1999). Two-year follow-up study of cognitive behavioral therapy for sexually abused children suffering post-traumatic stress symptoms. *Child Abuse & Neglect, 23*(12), 1371–1378.

DeClue, G. (2002). Book review essay: Remaking relapse prevention for sex offenders and Practice standards and guidelines for members of the Association for the Treatment of Sexual Abusers. *Journal of Psychiatry and the Law, 30,* 285–292.

DeClue, G. (2003). The polygraph and lie detection. *Journal of Psychiatry & Law, 32*(30), 361–368.

Dershowitz, A. M. (1982). *The best defense.* New York: Vintage.

DeVoe, E., and Faller, K. C. (2002). Questioning strategies in interviews with children who may have been sexually abused. *Child Welfare, 81*(1), 5–32.

Drizin, S. A., and Colgan, B. A. (2004). Tales from the juvenile confession front: A guide to how standard police interrogation tactics can produce coerced and false confessions from juvenile suspects. In G. D. Lassiter (Ed.), *Interrogations, confessions and entrapment* (pp. 127–162). New York: Kluwer Academic.

Drizin, S. A., and Leo, R. A. (2004). The problem of false confessions in the post-DNA world. *North Carolina Law Review, 82*(3), 891–1007.

Dziech, B., and Schudson, C. (1989). *On trial: America's courts and their treatment of sexually abused children.* Boston: Beacon Press.

Everson, M., Hunter, W., Runyon, D., Edelsohn, G., and Coulter, M. (1991). Maternal support following disclosure of incest. *Annual progress in child psychiatry and child development, 1990* (pp. 292–306). Philadelphia: Brunner/ Mazel.

Faller, K. C. (1984). Is the child victim of sexual abuse telling the truth? *Child Abuse & Neglect, 8,* 473–481.

Faller, K. C. (1988a). *Child sexual abuse: An interdisciplinary manual for diagnosis, case management, and treatment.* New York: Columbia University Press.

Faller, K. C. (1988b). Criteria for judging the credibility of children's statements about their sexual abuse. *Child Welfare, 67*(5), 389–410.

Faller, K. C. (1990). Sexual abuse by paternal caretakers: A comparison of abusers who are biological fathers in intact families, stepfathers, and noncustodial fathers. In A. Horton, B. Johnson, L. Roundy, and D. Williams (Eds.), *The incest perpetrator: A family member no one wants to treat* (pp. 44–65). Newbury Park, CA: Sage Publications.

Faller, K. C. (1991). Polyincestuous families: An exploratory study. *Journal of Interpersonal Violence, 6*(3), 310–322.

Faller, K. C. (1994). Extrafamilial sexual abuse. In S. Kaplan and D. Pelcovitz (Eds.), *Child and adolescent clinics of North America* (pp. 713–727). New York: W. B. Saunders.

Faller, K. C. (1995). A clinical sample of women who have sexually abused children. *Journal of Child Sexual Abuse, 4*(3), 13–30.

Faller, K. C. (1996). *Evaluating children suspected of having been sexually abused.* Newbury Park, CA: Sage Publications.

Faller, K. C. (1997). The polygraph: Its use in decision-making about child sexual abuse. *Child Abuse & Neglect, 21*(10), 993–1008.

Faller, K. C. (2003). *Understanding and assessing child sexual maltreatment.* 2nd ed. Thousand Oaks, CA: Sage Publications.

Faller, K. C. (2005). Peer review of forensic interviews. San Diego, CA: San Diego Conference on Child Maltreatment.

Faller, K. C. (2007). *Interviewing for child sexual abuse: Controversies and best practice.* London: Oxford University Press.

Faller, K. C., Birdsall, W. C., Henry, J., Vandervort, F., Silverschanz, P. (2001). What makes sex offenders confess? An exploratory study. *Journal of Child Sexual Abuse, 10*(4), 31–49.

Faller, K. C., Birdsall, W., and Vandervort, F. (2006). Does successful criminal prosecution of child sexual abuse predict more severe sentences? *Child Abuse & Neglect, 30*(7), 815–828.

Faller, K. C., Birdsall, W. C., Vandervort, F., and Henry, J. (2006). Can the punishment fit the crime when suspects confess child sexual abuse? *Child Abuse & Neglect, 30*, 815–827.

Faller, K. C., and Henry, J. (2000). Child sexual abuse: A case study in community collaboration. *Child Abuse & Neglect, 24*, 1215–1225.

Fergusson, D. M., Horwood, L. J., and Lynskey, M. T. (1997). Child sexual abuse, adolescent sexual behaviors and sexual revictimization. *Child Abuse & Neglect, 21*, 789–803.

Fiedler, K., Schmidt, J., and Stahl, T. (2002). What is the current truth about polygraph lie detection? *Basic and Applied Social Psychology, 24*(4), 313–324.

Finkelhor, D. (1979). *Sexually victimized children*. New York: Free Press.

Finkelhor, D., Araji, S., Baron, L., Browne, A., Peters, S., and Wyatt, G. (1986). *A sourcebook on child sexual abuse*. Thousand Oaks, CA: Sage Publications.

Finkelhor, D., and Daro, D. (1997). Prevention of child sexual abuse. In M. E. Helfer, R. S. Kempe, and R. D. Krugman (Eds.), *The battered child* (pp. 615–626). Chicago: University of Chicago Press.

Finkelhor, D., Hotaling, G., Lewis, I., and Smith, C. (1990). Sexual abuse in a national survey of adult men and women. *Child Abuse & Neglect, 14*, 19–28.

Fowler, C., McDonald, J., and Sumski, M. (2005). Review of turnover in Milwaukee private agency child welfare ongoing case management staff. Retrieved April 22, 2007, from www.uky.edu/socialwork/cswe/documents/turnover-study.pdf.

*Frazier v. Cupp*, 394 U.S. 731 (1969).

Freeman, N., and Sandler, J. (2008). Female and male sex offenders: A comparison of patterns and risk factors. *Journal of Interpersonal Violence, 23*(10), 1394–1313.

Fulero, S. M., and Everington, C. (2004). Mental retardation, competency to waive Miranda rights, and false confessions. In G. D. Lassiter (Ed.), *Interrogations, confessions, and entrapment* (pp. 164–179). New York: Kluwer Academic.

Furby, L., Weinrott, M. R., and Blackshaw, L. (1989). Sex offender recidivism: A review. *Psychological Bulletin, 105*, 3–30.

*Fuster-Excolona v. Crosby*, 170 Fed. Appx. 627 (2006).

General Accounting Office. (2003). Child welfare: HHS could play a greater role in helping child welfare agencies recruit and retain staff (GAO Publication Number 03-357). Washington, DC: GAO.

*Gerstein v. Pugh*, 420 U.S. 103 (1975).

Gerwitz, P. (1996). Narrative and rhetoric in the law. In P. Brooks and P. Gerwitz (Eds.), *Law's stories: Narrative and rhetoric in the law* (pp. 2–13). New Haven: Yale University Press.

Giarretto, H. (1980). *Integrated treatment of child sexual abuse.* Washington, DC: National Center on Child Abuse and Neglect.

Gil, E. (1991). *The healing power of play.* New York: Guilford Press.

Gillham, B. (2000). *Case study research methods.* London: Continuum.

Ginkowski, R. (1986). The abused child: The prosecutor's terrifying nightmare. *Criminal Justice, 1*(1), 30–35.

Goffman, E. (1959). *Presentation of self in everyday life.* Garden City, NY: Doubleday.

Gray, E. (1993). *Unequal justice: The prosecution of child sexual abuse.* New York: Free Press.

Greene, R., and Nichols, D. (2000). *Minnesota Multiphasic Personality Inventory–II interpretive manual.* 2nd ed. Orlando, FL: Psychological Assessment Resources.

Grisso, T. (1980). Juveniles' capacity to waive Miranda rights: An empirical analysis. *California Law Review, 68*(6), 1134–1166.

Gross, S. R., Jacoby, K., Matheson, D. J., Montgomery, N., and Patil, S. (2005). Exoneration in the United States 1989 through 2003. *Journal of Criminal Law and Criminology, 95*(2), 523–555.

Groth, N., and Stevenson, T. (1990). *Anatomical drawings for use in the investigation and intervention of child sexual abuse.* Dunedin, FL: Forensic Mental Health Associates.

Hanson, K. (2003). Who is dangerous and when are they safe? Risk assessment with sexual offenders. In B. Winick and J. La Fond (Eds.), *Protecting society from sexually dangerous offenders: Law, justice, and therapy* (pp. 63–74). Washington, DC: American Psychiatric Association.

Hanson, R. K., Gordon, A., Harris, A. J. R., Marques, J. K., Murphy, W., Quinsey, V. L., et al. (2002). First report of the Collaborative Outcome Data Project on the effectiveness of treatment for sex offenders. *Sexual Abuse: A Journal of Research and Treatment, 14,* 169–194.

Haralambie, A. M. (1999). *Child sexual abuse in civil cases.* Washington, DC: American Bar Association.

Hare, R. (2005). *Psychopathy check list—revised.* 2nd ed. Toronto: Multi-Health Systems.

Henry, J. (1997). System intervention trauma to child sexual abuse victims following disclosure. *Journal of Interpersonal Violence, 12*(4), 499–512.

Henry, J. (1999). Videotaping child disclosure interviews: Exploratory study of children's experiences and perceptions. *Journal of Child Sexual Abuse*, 8(4), 35–49.

Hershkowitz, I., Lanes, O., and Lamb, M. E. (2007). Exploring the disclosure of sexual abuse with victims and their parents. *Child Abuse & Neglect*, 31(2), 111–132.

Hershkowitz, I., and Terner, A. (2006). The effects of repeated interviewing on children's forensic statements of sexual abuse. *Applied Cognitive Psychology*, 21,1131–1143.

Holmes, W. D. (1995). Interrogation. *Polygraph*, 24, 237–258.

Hunter, W., Coulter, M., Runyan, D., and Everson, M. (1990). Determinants of placement for sexually abused children. *Child Abuse & Neglect*, 14(3), 407–417.

Inbau, F., Reid, J., Buckley, J., and Jayne, B. (2001). *Essentials of the Reid technique: Criminal interrogation and confessions*. 4th ed. Gaithersburg, MD: Aspen.

Itzin, C. (Ed.) (2000). *Home truths about child sexual abuse: Influencing policy and practice*. New York: Routledge.

James, A. (2007). Giving voice to children's voices: Practices and problems, pitfalls and potentials. *American Anthropologist*, 109(2), 261–272.

Johnson, R., and Schrier, D. (1985). Sexual victimization of boys: Experience in an adolescent medicine clinic. *Journal of Adolescent Medicine*, 6, 92–105.

Jones, L., Cross, T., Walsh, W., and Simone, M. (2005). Criminal investigations of child abuse: The research behind "best practices." *Trauma, Violence, & Abuse*, 6(3), 254–268.

Jones, L., Cross, T., Walsh, W., and Simone, M. (2007). Do children's advocacy centers improve families' experiences of child sexual abuse investigations? *Child Abuse & Neglect*, 31, 1069–1085.

Jones, D., and McGraw, E. M. (1987). Reliable and fictitious accounts of sexual abuse to children. *Journal of Interpersonal Violence*, 2(1), 27–45.

Kamisar, Y. (1980). *Police interrogation and confessions*. Ann Arbor: University of Michigan Press.

Kamisar, Y., LeFave, W. R., Israel, J. H., and King, N. J. (2002). *Modern criminal procedure: Cases, comments, questions*. St. Paul, MN: West.

Kaplan, J. (1965). The prosecutorial discretion—A comment. *Northwestern University Law Review*, 60, 174–193.

Karp, C., and Butler, T. (1996). *Treatment strategies for abused children*. Thousand Oaks, CA: Sage Publications.

Kassin, S. M. (1997). The psychology of confession evidence. *American Psychologist, 52*(3), 221–233.

Kassin, S. M. (2006). A critical appraisal of modern police interrogations. In T. Williamson (Ed.), *Investigative interviewing: Rights, research, regulation* (pp. 207–227). London: Willan.

Kassin, S. M., Leo, R., Meissner, C., Richman, K., Colwell, L., Leach, A. M., and La Fon, D. (2007). Police interviewing and interrogation: A self-report survey of police practices and beliefs. *Law and Human Behavior, 31*, 380–400.

Kassin, S. M., Meissner, C., and Norwick, R. (2005). "I'd know a false confession if I saw one": A comparative study of college students and police investigators. *Law and Human Behavior, 29*, 211–227.

Keane, W. (1997). *Signs of recognition: Powers and hazards of representation in an Indonesian society.* Berkeley: University of California Press.

Keane, W. (1999). Voice. *Journal of Linguistic Anthropology, 9*(1), 271–273.

Kokish, R. (2003). The current role of post-conviction sex offender polygraph testing in sex offender treatment. *Journal of Child Sexual Abuse, 12*(3–4), 175–194.

Korobkin, L. H. (1998). *Criminal conversations: Sentimentality and nineteenth-century legal stories of adultery.* New York: Columbia University Press.

Labov, W. (2008). Oral narratives of personal experience. Retrieved September 28, 2008, from www.ling.upenn.edu/~wlabov/Papers/FebOralNarPE.pdf.

Lamb, M., Orbach, Y., Hershkowitz, I., Esplin, P., and Horowitz, D. (2007). A structured forensic interview protocol improves the quality and informativeness of investigative interviews with children: A review of research using the NICHD Investigative Interview Protocol. *Child Abuse & Neglect, 31*, 1201–1231.

Lamb, M., Orbach, Y., Sternberg, K., Hershkowitz, I., and Horowitz, D. (2000). Accuracy of investigators' verbatim notes of their forensic interviews with alleged child abuse victims. *Law and Human Behavior, 24*(6), 699–708.

Lamb, M., and Sternberg, K. (1999). Eliciting accurate investigative statements from children. Paper presented at the 15th National Symposium on Child Sexual Abuse.

Laws, R., Hudson, S., and Ward, T. (Eds.). (2000). *Remaking relapse prevention with sex offenders: A sourcebook.* Thousand Oaks, CA: Sage Publications.

Lawson, L., and Chaffin, M. (1992). False negatives in sexual abuse disclosure interviews. *Journal of Interpersonal Violence, 7*(4), 532–542.

Layton, J. (n.d.). How police interrogation works. Retrieved January 3, 2008, from http://people.howstuffworks.com/police-interrogation1.htm.

Leberg, E. (1997). *Understanding child molesters: Taking charge.* Thousand Oaks, CA: Sage Publications.

Lempert, R. (1991–92). Telling tales in court. *Cardozo Law Review, 13,* 559–573.

*Lem Woon v. Oregon,* 229 U.S. 586 (1913).

Leo, R. A. (1996). Miranda's revenge: Police interrogation as a confidence game. *Law & Society Review, 30*(2), 259–288.

Leo, R. A. (2004). The third degree and the origins of psychological interrogation in the United States. In G. D. Lassiter (Ed.), *Interrogations, confessions, and entrapment* (pp. 37–84). New York: Kluwer Academic.

Leo, R. A., and White, W. S. (1999). Adapting to Miranda: Modern interrogators' strategies for dealing with the obstacles posed by Miranda. *Minnesota Law Review, 84*(4), 397–472.

London, K., Bruck, M., Ceci, S. J., and Shuman, D. (2005). Disclosure of sexual abuse: What does the research tell us about how children tell? *Psychology, Public Policy and the Law, 11,* 194–226.

Lyon, T. D. (2001). Let's not exaggerate the suggestibility of children. *Court Review, 38*(3), 12–14.

Lyon, T. D. (2002a). Applying suggestibility research to the real world: The case of repeated questions. *Law & Contemporary Problems, 65*(1), 97–126.

Lyon, T. D. (2002b). Scientific support for expert testimony on child sexual abuse accommodation. In J. Conte (Ed.), *Critical issues in child sexual abuse* (pp. 107–138). Thousand Oaks, CA: Sage Publications.

Lyon, T. D. (2007). False denials: Overcoming methodological biases in abuse disclosure research. In M. E. Pipe, M. Lamb, Y. Orbach, and A. Cederborg (Eds.), *Disclosing abuse: Delays, denials, retractions and incomplete accounts* (pp. 41–62). Mahwah, NJ: Erlbaum.

Lyons, K. S., Zarit, S. H., Sayer, A. G., and Whitlatch, C. J. (2002). Caregiving as adyadic process: Perspectives from caregiver and receiver. *Journal of Gerontology: Psychological Sciences, 57B*(3), 195–204.

MacMurry, B. K. (1988). The nonprosecution of sexual abuse and informal justice. *Journal of Interpersonal Violence, 3*(2), 197–202.

Maletzky, B. M. (1991). *Treating the sexual offender.* Thousand Oaks, CA: Sage Publications.

Maletzky, B. M., and Steinhauser, C. (2002). A 25-year follow-up of cognitive/ behavioral therapy with 7,275 sexual offenders. *Behavior Modification, 26*(2), 123–147.

Malloy, L.C., Lyon, T. D., and Quas, J. A. (2007). Filial dependency and recantation of child sexual abuse allegations. *Journal of the American Academy of Child and Adolescent Psychiatry*, *46*(2), 162–170.

Marques, J. (1999). How to answer the question "Does sexual offender treatment work?" *Journal of Interpersonal Violence*, *14*(4), 437–451.

Marques, J., Wiederanders, M., Day, D., Nelson, C., and van Ommeren, A. (2005). Effects of a relapse prevention program on sexual recidivism: Final results from California's Sex Offender Treatment and Evaluation Project (SOTEP). *Sexual Abuse: Journal of Research and Treatment*, *17*(1), 79–107.

Marshall, W. (1989). Invited essay: Intimacy, loneliness, and sex offenders. *Behavior Research & Therapy*, *27*, 491–503.

Marshall, W., Laws, D. R., and Barbaree, H. (1990). *Handbook of sexual assault: Issues, theories, and treatment of the offender*. New York: Plenum.

Martone, M., Jaudes, P. K., and Cavins, M. K. (1996). Criminal prosecution of child sexual abuse cases. *Child Abuse & Neglect*, *20*(5), 457–464.

McGough, L. S. (1995). For the record: Videotaping investigative interviews. *Psychology, Public Policy, and Law*, *1*(2), 370–386.

McGough, L. S. (2002). Good enough for government work: The constitutional duty to preserve forensic interviews of child victims. *Law & Contemporary Problems*, *65*, 179–208.

McGough, L. S., and Warren, A. R. (1994). The all-important investigative interview. *Juvenile and Family Court Journal*, *45*, 13–29.

*McKune v. Lile*, 536 U.S. 24 (2002).

Mertz, E. (1994). Legal language: Pragmatics, poetics and social power. *Annual Review of Anthropology*, *23*, 435–455.

Mildred, J. (2003). Claims makers in the child sexual abuse "wars": Who are they and what do they want? *Social Work*, *48*(4), 492–503.

Millon Clinical Multiaxial Inventory (MCMI). (2005). Retrieved June 26, 2005, from www.pearsonassessments.com/tests/millon.htm.

Millon Clinical Multiaxial Inventory—II. (n.d.). Retrieved December 31, 2007, from www.cps.nova.edu/~cpphelp/MCMI-2.html.

*Minnesota v. Murphy*, 465 U.S. 420 (1984).

*Miranda v. Arizona*, 384 U.S. 436 (1966).

Montoya, J. (1993). Something not so funny happened on the way to conviction: The pretrial interrogation of child witnesses. *Arizona Law Review*, *35*, 927–987.

Morrison, W. (Ed). (2001). *Blackstone's commentaries on the laws of England*. London: Cavendish.

Muram, D. (1989). Child sexual abuse: Relationship between sexual acts and genital findings. *Child Abuse & Neglect, 13*(2), 211–216.

Murphy, C. A., and Murphy, J. K. (1997). Polygraph admissibility. *Update: National Center for Prosecution of Child Abuse, 10,* 1–2.

Myers, J. E. B. (1998). *Legal issues in child abuse and neglect practice.* 2nd ed. Newbury Park, CA: Sage Publications.

Myers, J. E. B. (2006). *Child protection in America: Past, present, and future.* New York: Oxford University Press.

National Center for the Prosecution of Child Abuse. (1997). *Child witnesses.* Washington, DC: NCCAN Clearinghouse.

National Child Abuse and Neglect Data System (NCANDS). (2003). Retrieved October 15, 2003, from http://nccanch.acf.hhs.gov/pubs/factsheets/canstats .cfm.

National Child Traumatic Stress Network (NCTSN). (2008). Empirically supported and promising practices for treatment of trauma. Retrieved September 21, 2008, from http://nctsn.org/nccts/nav.do?pid=ctr_top_trmnt_prom#q4.

National Children's Alliance. (n.d.). Standards for accredited members. Retrieved February 10, 2007, from www.nca-online.org/pages/page.asp?page_id=4032.

National Research Council, Committee to Review Scientific Evidence on the Polygraph. (2002). *The polygraph and lie detection.* Washington, DC: National Academies Press.

*Nix v. Williams,* 467 U.S. 431 (1984).

Oates, K., Jones, D. P. H., Denson, A., Sirotnak, A., Gary, N., and Krugman, R. (2000). Erroneous concerns about child sexual abuse. *Child Abuse & Neglect, 24*(1), 149–157.

Ochs, E., and Capps, L. (1996). Narrating the self. *Annual Review of Anthropology, 25,* 19–43.

Olafson, E. (2002). When paradigms collide: Roland Summit and the rediscovery of child sexual abuse. In J. Conte (Ed.), *Critical issues in child sexual abuse* (pp. 71–106). Thousand Oaks, CA: Sage Publications.

Olafson, E., Corwin, D. L., and Summit, R. C. (1993). Modern history of child sexual abuse awareness: Cycles of discovery and suppression. *Child Abuse and Neglect, 17*(1), 7–24.

Orbach, Y., and Lamb, M. (1999). Assessing the accuracy of a child's account of sexual abuse: A case study. *Child Abuse & Neglect, 23*(1), 91–98.

Palmer, S. E., Brown, R., Rae-Grant, N., and Loughlin, M. J. (1999). Responding to children's disclosures of familial abuse: What survivors tell us. *Child Welfare, 78*(2), 259–282.

Palusci, V. J., Cox, E. O., Cyrus, T. A., Heartwell, S. W., and Vandervort, F. E. (1999). Medical assessment and legal outcome in child sexual abuse. *Archives of Pediatric & Adolescent Medicine, 153*(4), 388–392.

Pearse, J., Gudjonsson, G. H., Clare, I. C. H., and Rutter, S. (1998). Police interviewing and psychological vulnerabilities: Predicting the likelihood of a confession. *Journal of Community and Applied Social Psychology, 8*, 1–21.

Pence, D., and Wilson, C. (1994). *Team investigation of child sexual abuse.* Thousand Oaks, CA: Sage Publications.

*Pennsylvania v. Ritchie*, 480 U.S. 39 (1987).

*People v. Johnson*, 119 Cal. App. 4th 976, 980 (2004).

Perlis Marx, S. (1999). Victim recantation in child sexual abuse cases: A team approach to prevention, investigation, and trial. In K. C. Faller (Ed.), *Maltreatment in early childhood: Tools for research-based intervention* (pp. 105–140). New York: Haworth Press.

Perry, N.W., and McAuliff, B. D. (1993). The use of videotaped child testimony: Public policy implications. *Notre Dame Journal of Law, Ethics, & Public Policy, 7*, 387–422.

Philips, S. (1984). The social organization of questions and answers in courtroom discourse. *Text, 4*, 25–48.

Philips, S. (1993). Evidentiary standards for American trials: Just the facts. In J. H. Hill and J. T. Irvine (Eds.), *Responsibility and evidence in oral discourse* (pp. 248–259). Cambridge: Cambridge University Press.

Poole, D., and Lamb, M. (1998). *Investigative interviews with children: A guide for helping professionals.* Washington, DC: American Psychological Association.

Povinelli, E. (2002). *The cunning of recognition.* Durham, NC: Duke University Press.

Raskin, D. (1989). *Psychological methods in criminal investigation and evidence.* New York: Springer.

Raskin, D., and Honts, C. (2002). The comparison question test. In M. Kleiner (Ed.), *Handbook of polygraph testing* (pp. 1–47). San Diego, CA: Academic Press.

Raskin, D., Kirschner, J., Honts, C., and Horowitz, S. (1988). Validity of control question polygraph tests in criminal investigation. *Psychophysiology, 25*, 474.

Reid, J. E., and Inbau, F. E. (1977). *Truth and deception, the polygraph technique.* Baltimore: Williams & Wilkins.

Russell, D. E. H. (1986). *Incest in the lives of girls and women.* New York: Basic Books.

Russell, D. E. H., and Bolen, R. (2000). *The epidemic of rape and child sexual abuse in the United States.* Thousand Oaks, CA: Sage Publications.

Salter, A. (2003). *Predators: Pedophiles, rapists, and other sex offenders—Who they are, how they operate, and how we can protect ourselves and our children.* New York: Basic Books.

Sas, L., and Cunningham, A. (1995). *Tipping the balance to tell the secret: The public discovery of child sexual abuse.* London: London Court Clinic.

Saunders, B. E., Berliner, L., and Hanson, R. F. (Eds.). (2004). *Child physical and sexual abuse: Guidelines for treatment.* Charleston, SC: National Crime Victims Research and Treatment Center.

Saxe, L., Dougherty, D., and Cross, T. (1987). The validity of polygraph testing: Scientific analysis and public controversy. *American Psychologist, 40*(3), 355–366.

Scheppele, K. L. (1989). Foreword: Telling stories. *Michigan Law Review, 87*(8), 2073–2098.

*Schmerber v. California,* 384 U.S. 757 (1966).

Scholz, R. W., and Tietje, O. (2002). *Embedded case study methods: Integrating quantitative and qualitative knowledge.* Thousand Oaks, CA: Sage Publications.

Scott-Hayward, C. S. (2007). Explaining juvenile false confessions: Adolescent development and police interrogation. *Law & Psychology Review, 31,* 53–76.

Sgroi, S. (1982). *Handbook of clinical intervention in child sexual abuse.* Lexington, MA: Lexington Books.

Simon, D. (1991). *Homicide: A year on the killing streets.* New York: Henry Holt.

Sjoberg, R., and Lindblad, F. (2002). Limited disclosure of sexual abuse in children whose experiences were documented by videotape. *American Journal of Psychiatry, 159*(2), 312–314.

Smith, D., Letourneau, E., Saunders, B., Kilpatrick, D., Resnick, H., and Best, C. (2000). Delay in disclosure of childhood rape: Results from a national survey. *Child Abuse and Neglect, 24*(2), 273–287.

Sorenson, T., and Snow, B. (1991). How children tell: The process of disclosure of sexual abuse. *Child Welfare, 70*(1), 3–15.

Spangenberg, R. L. (1986). Why we are not defending the poor properly. *Criminal Justice, 3,* 12.

Spangenberg, R. L. (1989). We are still not defending the poor properly. *Criminal Justice, 6*, 11.

Stake, R. E. (1991). *Custom and cherishing: The arts in elementary schools—Studies of U.S. elementary schools portraying ordinary problems of teachers teaching music, drama, dance, and the visual arts in 1987–1990*. Urbana: University of Illinois Press.

Stake, R. E. (1995). *The art of case study research*. Thousand Oaks, CA: Sage Publications.

Staller, K. M., and Nelson-Gardell, D. (2005). A burden in your heart: Lessons of disclosure from female preadolescent and adolescent survivors of sexual abuse. *Child Abuse & Neglect, 29*(12), 1415–1432.

*Standefer v. United States*, 447 U.S. 10 (1980).

State of Michigan, Governor's Task Force on Children's Justice and Department of Human Services. (2005). *Forensic interviewing protocol*. Rev. ed. Lansing: Department of Human Services.

*State v. Hodge*, 95 NJ 369; 471 A.2d 389 (1984).

*State v. Michaels*, 642 A. 2d 1372 (1994).

Stengel, Richard (1986). Sex busters: Meese commission and the Supreme Court echo a new moral militancy. *Time*, July 21.

Stephenson, C. (1992). Videotaping and how it works well in San Diego. *Journal of Interpersonal Violence, 7*(2), 284–288.

Stern, P. (1992). Videotaping child interviews: A detriment to an accurate determination of guilt. *Journal of Interpersonal Violence, 7*(2), 278–282.

Sternberg, K., Lamb, M., Orbach, Y., Esplin, P., and Mitchell, S. (2000). Use of a structured investigative protocol enhances young children's responses to free-recall prompts in the course of forensic interviews. *Journal of Applied Psychology, 86*(5), 997–1005.

Sullivan, T. P. (2004). *Police experiences with recording custodial interrogations*. Evanston, IL: Northwestern University School of Law, Center on Wrongful Convictions.

Summit, R. C. (1983). The child sexual abuse accommodation syndrome. *Child Abuse and Neglect, 7*, 177–193.

Terry, W. (1991). Perpetrator and victim accounts of sexual abuse. Paper presented at the Health Science Response to Child Maltreatment, Center for Child Protection.

Thatcher, D. (2006). The normative case study. *American Journal of Sociology, 111*(6), 1631–1676.

Thoennes, N., and Tjaden, P. (1990). The extent, nature, and validity of sexual abuse allegations in custody/visitation disputes. *Child Abuse & Neglect, 14*, 151–163.

Tiersma, P. M. (1999). *Legal language.* Chicago: University of Chicago Press.

Trocmé, N., and Bala, N. (2005). False allegations of abuse and neglect when parents separate. *Child Abuse & Neglect, 29*(12), 1316–1326.

Ullman, S. (2003). Social reactions to child sexual abuse disclosures: A critical review. *Journal of Child Sexual Abuse, 12*(10), 89–122.

*United States v. Armstrong,* 517 U.S. 116 (1996).

*United States v. Bass,* 404 U.S. 336 (1971).

*United States v. Bland,* 342 F. 2d 167 (1965).

*United States v. Rosa,* 17 F. 3d 1531 (1994).

Uphoff, R. J. (1999). The criminal defense lawyer: Zealous advocate, double agent, or beleaguered dealer? In L. Stolzenberg and S. J. D'Alessio (Eds.), *Criminal courts for the 21st century* (pp. 92–121). Upper Saddle River, NJ: Prentice-Hall.

U.S. Department of Justice Office of Victims of Crimes. (2004). State crime victim compensation and assistance grant programs. Retrieved December 24, 2007, from www.ojp.usdoj.gov/ovc/publications/factshts/compandassist/welcome.html.

Vandervort, F. (2004). Understanding child protection's past and its impact on current and future practice: An interview with Professor John E. B. Myers. *Michigan Child Welfare Law Journal, 8*(1), 11–18.

Vandervort, F. E. (2006). Videotaping investigative interviews of children in cases of child sexual abuse: One community's approach. *Journal of Criminal Law and Criminology, 96*(4), 1353–1416.

Vaughn, Diane. *The Challenger Launch Decision: Risky Technology, Culture, and Deviance at NASA.* Chicago: University of Chicago Press, 1996.

Veith, V. I. (1999). When the cameras roll: The danger of videotaping child abuse victims before the legal system is competent to assess children's statements. *Journal of Child Sexual Abuse, 7*(4), 113–121.

Walsh, W. A., Cross, T. P., Jones, L. M., Simone, M., and Kolko, D. J. (2007). Which sexual abuse victims receive a forensic medical examination? The impact of children's advocacy centers. *Child Abuse & Neglect, 31*(10), 1053–1068.

Walsh, W. A., Lippert, T., Cross, T. P., Maurice, D. M., and Davison, K. S. (2008). How long to prosecute child sexual abuse for a community using a children's advocacy center and two comparison communities. *Child Maltreatment, 13*(3), 3–13.

Webster, S., Bowers, L., Mann, R., and Marshall, W. (2005). Developing empathy in sexual offenders: The value of offence re-enactments. *Sexual Abuse: Journal of Research and Treatment, 17*(1), 63–77.

Williams, V. (1995). Response to Cross and Saxe's "A critique of the validity of polygraph testing in child sexual abuse cases." *Journal of Child Sexual Abuse, 4*(3), 55–72.

*W. M. v. State,* 585 So. 2nd 979, Fla. 4th Dist. Ct. App. (1991).

Wrightsman, L. S., and Kassin, S. M. (1993). *Confessions in the courtroom.* Newbury Park, CA: Sage Publications.

Yin, R. K. (2003a). *Applications of case study research.* Thousand Oaks, CA: Sage Publications.

Yin, R. K. (2003b). *Case study research: Design and methods.* 3rd ed. Thousand Oaks, CA: Sage Publications.

Yin, R. K. (2004). *The case study anthology.* Thousand Oaks, CA: Sage Publications.

# Contributors and Members of the
# Research Team

WILLIAM C. BIRDSALL was ordained as a Jesuit priest in 1966 after receiving his PhD in economics from the Johns Hopkins University. He left the priesthood in 1969 and became a policy analyst at the Social Security Administration. He taught economics at McMaster University, then taught research, statistics, and policy at the University of Michigan School of Social Work from 1973 until his retirement in 2002. He joined the sexual-abuse research group as the statistician in 2000, encouraging the initiation of the qualitative analysis of St. Mary's experience because the statistical analysis clearly could not reveal why it was so successful at prosecuting sexual abuse of children. He participated in a majority of the interviews and attended two trials.

ELANA D. BUCH is a doctoral candidate in Joint Doctoral Program in Social Work and Anthropology at the University of Michigan. She has published articles on ethnographic and feminist research methodologies and has taught classes on the history of anthropological theory. Her research focuses on the intersections of aging, low-wage work, kinship and social policy. Her dissertation is an ethnographic comparison of publicly and privately funded home care of older adults. Elana worked as a research assistant throughout the data-gathering phase of this project. In this role, she conducted several interviews (Studebaker, Jackson, Noeker, O'Dell, and Henry), most in conjunction with William Birdsall. She also helped facilitate the scheduling of other interviews, edited interview transcripts, managed data, and provided general organizational support during the first several years of the project. Elana acted as the resident anthropologist on the team, providing methodological advice about data collection and interpretation while pushing for greater attention to the ways that local cultural understandings about sex, gender, language, children, justice, and truth contributed to the development of the St. Mary County protocol.

KATHLEEN COULBORN FALLER, PHD, ACSW, is Marion Elizabeth Blue Endowed Professor of Children and Families, director of the Family Assessment Clinic, and principal investigator of the Recruitment and Retention of Child Welfare Employees Program and of the Early Assessment Project, all at the University of Michigan School of Social Work. She is the author of eight books and approximately seventy articles and book chapters. Six of the eight books are on child sexual abuse. She became fascinated with St. Mary County when she agreed to serve as research mentor for Jim Henry, then a new assistant professor, in 1998. Success in sexual-abuse case management is rare, and professional openness to sharing information about the process is even rarer. Faller, Henry, and other members of the research team published three articles using the St. Mary County court-file data. She has reviewed many videotapes of their child interviews and suspect polygraphs. She brings to the research team knowledge of the research and practice literature on child sexual abuse and thirty years of experience conducting child forensic interviews and family assessments when sexual abuse is suspected. She interviewed the two polygraph operators, the sex-offender assessment and treatment specialist, and three staff members from the Department of Human Services.

JIM HENRY has a professional history that includes more than eighteen years as a child welfare/protective services worker and more than ten years developing and providing trauma-informed instruction in the social work curriculum as a professor at Western Michigan University. He is the cofounder and director of the Southwest Michigan Children's Trauma Assessment Center through Western Michigan University. He has written several articles on child-welfare-system issues and trauma-informed assessment and interventions with maltreated children. He frequently presents talks on the impact of child trauma on development and behavior. He has been the primary liaison with St. Mary's County, supervising the collection and entry of court-file data and interviewing several professionals.

KAREN M. STALLER is associate professor at the University of Michigan School of Social Work. She holds a JD from the Cornell University Law School and a PhD from the Columbia University School of Social Work. She attended several meetings and listened to descriptions of the projects that the St. Mary study group was working on, suggesting a more qualitative approach to studying the community, from which humble beginnings this study was born. Staller participated in several interviews and attended one trial, and she took primary responsibility in designing the study and supervising its implementation. Often her role was to teach team members who were unfamiliar with qualitative methods how to think differently about asking and answering questions. Once the evidence was collected, she took the lead in team meetings in reading transcripts and analyzing the empirical evidence. Her role was to facilitate, coordinate, and synthesize the material from these analysis sessions, as well as to help prepare this book for publication.

FRANK E. VANDERVORT is clinical assistant professor of law at the University of Michigan Law School, where he teaches in the Child Advocacy Clinic and Juvenile Justice Clinic. He began his career as a deputy defender in the Juvenile Defender Office in Wayne County (Detroit), Michigan. For two years he was the executive director of the Children's Law Center in Grand Rapids, Michigan. In 1997, he became the program manager of the Michigan Child Welfare Law Resource Center at the University of Michigan Law School and joined the faculty in 2005. He writes and speaks frequently regarding the effect of the law on children. His contributions to this book include traveling to St. Mary County to observe one day of the Inman trial; participating in interviews with the three defense attorneys, the three prosecutors, a judge, and several community-based service providers; and conducting Jim Henry's interview. He read and provided feedback on each chapter and has made law-related contributions to a number of them.

# Index

*Page numbers in italics refer to illustrations.*